Day Hikes and Trail Rides In and Around Phoenix

Second Edition

by

Roger and Ethel Freeman

Gem Guides Book Co.

315 CLOVERLEAF DRIVE, SUITE F
BALDWIN PARK, CA 91706

Printing history:
1st edition 1988
Revised edition 1991
2nd edition 2000

ISBN 1-889786-10-1
Library of Congress Catalog Number 00-130062

Published in the United States of America by the Gem Guides Book Co., 315 Cloverleaf Drive, Suite F, Baldwin Park, California 91706

Cover design: Mark Webber
Cartography: Weller Cartographic Services Limited
Printed & bound in the United States of America

Photograph on page 16: "Tunnel" on Hidden Valley Trail, South Mountain

---

LIABILITY WAIVER

Due to the possibility of personal error, typographical error, misinterpretation of information, and the many changes both natural and man-made, the authors and publisher and all other persons or companies directly and indirectly associated with this publication assume no responsibility for accidents, injury, damage or any losses by individuals or groups using this publication. In rough terrain and hazardous areas we advise that all persons be aware of possible changes due to the elements or those hazards which may be man-made that can occur along any of the hiking or riding trails, and that these persons make all efforts possible to evaluate any hazard which may be present or anticipated.

Table of Contents

Dedication

The First and Revised Editions of this book were dedicated to Charles M. Christiansen, former Parks and Recreation Director for Phoenix in 1969-1978, then General Services Manager from 1978 to his tragic death in 1985.

During the years of preparation of this new edition we had frequent collaboration with civil servants in the many involved agencies. In many instances we found them to be dedicated to their work, far beyond the ordinary call of duty, and in ways that the public may not have reason to fully appreciate. We salute these fine people!

Special Dedication

During the preparation of this Second Edition we learned of the death of Dottie Gilbert on December 7, 1997. Dottie had been a tireless and persistent advocate for the Phoenix Mountains Preserve, a friend, and a supporter of our efforts from the start. The City of Phoenix has also recognized her work by establishing the Dottie Gilbert Sanctuary on the Squaw Peak Nature Trail. It is therefore very appropriate that we take this occasion to celebrate her contribution to Phoenix and to Arizona.

Preface to the Second Edition

It is now 16 years since we started coming from Vancouver twice a year to vacation in the Phoenix area, time enough to notice many changes: more people, many more housing developments. It has become a challenge to obtain clear pictures across the Valley comparable to those in the First Edition.

One thing that has not changed is the dedication of those with whom we have collaborated; we are indebted to them for their help.

The major changes in this edition are:

(1) New areas: Cave Creek Park (Maricopa County), trails in the Saguaro Lake, Bartlett Reservoir and Seven Springs areas of the Tonto National Forest, the Black Canyon Trail, extensive new trails in Usery Recreation Area and White Tank Mountains Park, and Scottsdale trails.
(2) The new trail ordinance making it a misdemeanor to be on a non-designated trail has led to the simplification of our descriptions and maps of the Phoenix Mountains Preserve and South Mountain.
(3) The elimination of overlapping trails in McDowell Mountain Regional Park has simplified their description. Some have been deleted.
(4) An extensive new trail system for Thunderbird Recreation Area.
(5) The construction of the Squaw Peak Parkway (SR 51) through Dreamy Draw has brought changes to tunnels and trail access, and a new bikeway.
(6) For the first time, Lookout Mountain has designated, signed trails and a circumferential trail.
(7) The southern access to South Mountain (Telegraph Pass) is finally available, along with new trails at the eastern end, new access points at 46th and 42nd Streets, a new western section of the National Trail, and the Desert Classic Trail around the southeastern end.
(8) In the Phoenix Mountains Preserve, there are new trailheads with extensive parking and facilities at Central Avenue and at 7th Street (North Mountain/Shaw Butte), 16th Street (Lookout Mountain), at 32nd Street & Lincoln Drive (Squaw Peak Area), at 40th Street, as well as from the Dreamy Draw Bikeway.
(9) The access to Camelback from the east has been obtained and a new trail connection built. Access through the Pointe Golf Course between Lookout and the central portion of the Preserve has been completed.

Areas still unsettled are a land dispute affecting a section of the Black Canyon Trail and the development of the regional park in the San Tan Mountains. The Sun Circle Trail is still not completed in several sections, and is not yet included here. Lake Pleasant trails, under development after raising the Waddell Dam, will likely be included in the next edition.

To reiterate what was said in the First Edition, the roughly 40-mile radius of downtown was chosen because it delineates an area generally within an hour's drive, convenient for day trips. (We have not included the western

Superstitions because it has coverage in another guidebook.) Each land management agency has a somewhat different set of policies, and we have adhered to these. They have checked each description before its finalization.

Many of the trails were developed for use by horses, or simply by horse usage. We address this guidebook to equestrians as well as hikers, joggers, and more recently, mountain-bikers. Generally we have not attempted to specify the appropriateness of a particular trail's usage except insofar as "hiker only" trails have been so designated by the managing authority, or indirectly by means of descriptions of steepness, loose rock, etc.

Heavily used desert trails are subject to braiding and new "trails" are often all-too-easily established by casual use. Many trails have unsigned, confusing junctions. We have dealt with this problem by giving a general description with major distances to the tenth of a mile, followed in most cases by a very detailed tabular description to the hundredth of a mile, meant only for actual use on the trail. Be aware that there have been many changes that we have not been able to personally check for this edition, so that new junctions may be there, and ones mentioned may have fallen into disuse or been blocked or obliterated. We are trying to gradually re-visit every one of them as time permits.

Because the format of the guide requires coordination of general (narrative) descriptions, tabular (detailed) descriptions, and maps, it is important to read the section *How to Use This Guide*. The *Suggestions for Hikers* and *On Horseback in the Phoenix Area* sections also have some essential pointers.

A few words must be said about responsibility. While we have taken every precaution of which we are aware to obtain and publish accurate information and to have it reviewed by agency staff, there are some limitations of which you should be aware:

(1) There is no guarantee of complete accuracy.
(2) Although each agency has reviewed the text, no official endorsement is implied or should be assumed. Boundaries shown may change, may not be entirely accurate, and are provided for general information only.
(3) Trails may change due to erosion, weather, usage patterns, and agency policy. Most are not regularly maintained or patrolled on the ground, and many are not signed or marked. Some are rough and steep. It is not difficult to become confused or lost, or to twist an ankle. The whole point of hiking or riding in the mountains is to get away from a city-like atmosphere. So enjoy your excursion, *but realize that you are accepting the risks entailed.*

You can help maintain the accuracy and usefulness of this guide. If you become aware of errors or changes, let us know at the address below. You may use the correction form in this book. The responsible agency should also be informed.

Roger & Ethel Freeman, Box 2033, Point Roberts, WA 98281
E-mail: roger_freeman@usa.net
Phone (604) 263-3900

Acknowledgements

So many people and organizations have contributed to this book that it is likely some will be missed in this extensive list. Such omissions are unintentional, and should be brought to our attention.

First we would like to thank our publisher, Al Mayerski of Gem Guides, his editor, Janet Francisco, and our cartographer, Angus Weller. Our special thanks go to our contributors, Margaret Bohannan, Jim Burke, Jim Colley, Jeff Hrycko, Denise Meridith, Bill Scalzo, Lee Waldron, "Pete" Weinel, and L.V. Yates, Jr.

As for the many others, it's easiest to list them according to their agency or group:

City of Phoenix

Main Office, Parks, Recreation & Library Department: In addition to Jim Colley (Director), Jim Coffman [now in Scottsdale] and later Jim Burke (Deputy Director) played major roles in our collaboration.

Northeast District: Sarah Hall (transferred), Jeff Spellman, Don Slater (retired), Ted Koester, Mark Wisehart, Paul Paonessa, Sue Arbogast, Winston Pierson, Glenn Ackley.

Central/East District: Don Gumeringer, Kathi Reichert, Frank Scherer, Sarah Hall (transferred), Rob Harman (transferred), Claire Miller (now in Scottsdale).

Northwest District: Bob Dionisio.

South District: Bob Burnett, Dan Gronseth, Randy Singh, Carlos Sotomayor, Don Gumeringer (transferred), Frank Scherer (transferred).

Maricopa County

Central Office: Bill Scalzo, Robert Hogg (who played a major coordinating role), Bob Skaggs (who was indefatigable in trail building and research), Bob Herring, Howard Gillmore (retired), and Dave Konopka.

Because of frequent moves of park personnel from one area to another over the past 10 years, we simply list those who have helped: Kent Bontrager, Leo Drumm, Shayne Hollandsworth, Bob Ingram, Charlie Johnson, Mark Lansing, Doug Prince, Jim Reichwein, Sally Skirball, Ken Taylor, Wally Vegors, Jerry Waehner, John De Young, and Jim Blackburn (volunteer).

We also had helpful collaboration with the Maricopa County Hiking and Equestrian Trails Committee.

Arizona State Parks & State Trails Coordinator

Larry Mutter hiked with us and gave counsel on many occasions before Ken Mahoney (now with BLM), Eric Smith (now in Prescott), Pam Gilmore (now Pam Gluck), and Jeff Hrycko arrived. Their support has been unflagging and is much appreciated.

Lost Dutchman State Park: Bob Sherman, Steve Jakubowski, and Diana Bishop. We also met with the Arizona State Committee on Trails [ASCOT].

City of Glendale

Lee Waldron provided us with much useful information.

City of Scottsdale

Don Meserve and Scott Hamilton helped us with our first forays into the McDowell Sonoran Preserve.

Tonto National Forest

W.G. ("Pete") Weinel has been our major contact, with additional help from Russ Orr, Greg Hanson, Don Van Driel, and Jeff Tillman, as well as Emily Garber, Vicki Collins, Kelly Jardine and Kathy Sheets in the Cave Creek Ranger District.

Bureau of Land Management

The lower section of the Black Canyon Trail is now included in this second edition. We had help from Rich Hanson, Carol Laver (transferred), Terry O'Sullivan, Ken Mahoney, Jack Ragsdale, John Reid, and Gretchen Ward (transferred).

Phoenix Mountains Preservation Council

Dottie and 'Gil' Gilbert, Dave Gironda, L.V. Yates, Jr., Chuck and Maxine Lakin, Charles (Chuck) Monroe, Anna Marsolo, and Paul Diefenderfer all showed interest in the project and were helpful in various ways.

Others

Michael Baker, Jr., Inc., Consulting Engineers: John Rorquist
Del Seppanen, formerly with the City of Phoenix Parks, Recreation & Library Department

How to Use This Book

General Advice

Since the tabular descriptions are very detailed, *it is very important to read the following section* to understand how these relate to the maps. Although we have provided maps and access diagrams, there is no substitute for full road maps; we advise that you obtain one or more if you are planning a trip near urbanized areas. Park or preserve boundaries may change with time; we have shown them for convenience only.

Trail Areas, Indicators, and Features

There is a special organization in this Guide of some of the trail areas in the Phoenix Mountains Preserve. Lookout and Shadow Mountains have their own sections because they are geographically isolated. In the extensive contiguous area from Shaw Butte to Squaw Peak, the arbitrary divisions are shown on the index map on the back cover. (For other areas, the situation is self-explanatory. The index map shows the geographic trail areas and therefore their corresponding book sections.) Note that summits of interest that are unnamed may be referred to by their elevation, thus **"Peak 1781."**

Each major trail has a text (and map) indicator. This is either the official number or letter and name (if any), or our own arbitrary letter or number, so that these are not confused with official numbers or letters of designated trails. All text numbers or letters are shown in brackets (such as [B]), and in boxes on the maps. (In Phoenix, the trail system is still undergoing change, with more "neighborhood access trails" to be designated in the future.)

We have been impressed with the many changes and improvements that have taken place. *But it has been impossible to check every trail again.* In Phoenix, especially, non-designated trails are being used less (because of legal discouragement and signing) or actively re-vegetated; many junctions we have indicated in the tabular, detailed descriptions were there recently, but will soon be obliterated. (We would appreciate hearing about these.)

Matching Book Descriptions and the Maps

Maps are in a separate section at the back of the book. Each has its number outside the map border in the upper right-hand corner.

Each trail section indicates the *map number* (which may be on more than one map). *NOTE*: if a trail is shown on the map in red but not numbered this is an indication that it has no independent description, but can be found under the numbered (or lettered) trail or road from which it diverges. There are many short trail segments to which this applies. In some cases where the trail is short and without many notable features, there is a short narrative description without tabular detail. *Trails indicated in black are either partly on private land* or for other reasons regarded as closed, undesignated, undesirable, or of no significance. They are shown only to eliminate confusion at trail junctions and for safety reasons; please do *not* regard their inclusion as a recommendation for use. In Phoenix, such use is a misdemeanor under the Trail Ordinance [see p. 20].

The direction of description chosen is usually from a lower elevation to a higher (if definitely an ascent), or from a road or trail access point to a point of interest. The Charles M. Christiansen Trail has its description divided into several segments; there is a separate summary tabulation for its entire length.

Abbreviations Used in Tabular Descriptions

L = left	N = north	NE = northeast	mi = mile
R = right	S = south	NW = northwest	4WD = 4 wheel drive
elev. = elevation		SE = southeast	NDT = non-designated trail
PC = Perl Charles Trail		SW = southwest	TH = trailhead
CMC = Charles M. Christiansen Trail			

Similarly, "sharp L," "half-L" and "W-bound" should be self-explanatory.

Using the Detailed Tabular Descriptions

The reverse or "Read Up" column on the right of the tabular descriptions serves as a useful source of information when traveling in the direction of the description: it indicates how far you still have to go. The descriptions themselves have to be reversed mentally for travel in the opposite direction.

For example:

Read Down ↓	Detailed Trail Description	Read Up ↑
0.00	From trailhead, head NW (1,480').	0.57
0.49	Keep L, approach canal.	0.08
0.55	**Junction:** join trail from R; parallel canal fence.	0.02
0.57	**Junction:** trail R descends to canal and can be followed to 1.49 mi and beyond. Near here a planned trail will head up the ridge-line.	0.00

Note that in reading up, "L" becomes "R" and vice versa, and "ascend" becomes "descend."

Distances in General versus Detailed Descriptions

For simplicity's sake, measured distances in the general descriptions have been shortened to the nearest tenth or quarter of a mile, e.g., 0.14 → 0.1, 0.23 → 0.25. In the detailed descriptions, distances are given to the nearest hundredth of a mile (0.01 mi = 52.8').

Suggestions for Hikers

With the Assistance of L. V. Yates, Jr.

The following hints are not meant to be exhaustive or definitive. (Detailed information is available in sources listed in the Bibliography, Appendix C). Everyone has different views on what is important in hiking. The season of the year, age, experience and size of party, elevation and length of trip all can create highly variable circumstances for which it is difficult to make general pronouncements. Seasoned hikers tend to be highly individualistic and therefore the ideas expressed here are mostly intended for the novice.

Safety

♦ Leave word about your start, destination, and estimated time of return with someone reliable. If rescue is required, contact the Maricopa County Sheriff's office, whose job it is to call out the rescue team.

♦ Large groups tend to separate into slow and fast hikers. Periodically check on your party, and have an experienced person bring up the rear. *Do not travel alone, especially in the back-country.*

♦ *Be prepared for changes in the weather.* The return route and familiar landmarks may become obscure or confusing when weather conditions change. Take extra clothing on moderate to long hikes.

♦ *Be prepared for injury* (bring first-aid material) *and for getting lost* (bring some food and ample water). Pack a flashlight and extra batteries.

♦ Don't roll rocks down steep slopes or cliffs. Someone may be below.

♦ In summer, flash floods may occur in normally dry washes. If thunderstorms are in the area, descend from elevated areas to avoid lightning.

♦ Prospect holes left by miners can be dangerous. Stay out of them!

♦ Poisonous reptiles and insects live in the desert. You are unlikely to have trouble if you only put your hands and feet in places you can see.

♦ The spines of some types of cactus, especially the "jumping" cholla, are very easy to collect in your skin, even through your shoes. Carry a comb and strong tweezers or long-nosed pliers to remove them.

Comfort

♦ *Rule #1 is: **bring sufficient water**. This cannot be overemphasized.*

♦ Wear comfortable clothing; use a hat, sunscreen and sunglasses.

- If you are not experienced and fit, take short hikes before long ones. This will give you a chance to assess your fitness and break in hiking boots. Bring an extra pair of socks. Treat potential blisters before they become major problems (carry moleskin, readjust socks when you rest).

- Insects are not generally a problem, but at certain times (especially near dusk) there may be mosquitoes, large and small flies, spiders, and even Africanized bees. Bring repellent, and of course your medicine if you are subject to severe reactions from specific stinging insects.

- Leave valuables at home. The next best place is in the trunk of your car.

- Take a spare car key and remember to turn off your headlights!

Mountain Ethics

Most of us enjoy hiking not only for exercise, but for the closer contact we feel with nature. *A respectful attitude to man and nature* makes many of these recommendations redundant: the ideas are then mostly "common sense."

- Flowers, rocks, and other "specimens" should be left in place. The best guide is "take nothing but pictures, leave nothing but footprints." An exception is garbage thoughtlessly left by others. This you *can* take out!

- Keep to the trails — *please do not cut across switchbacks* — it will contribute to the trail's eventual destruction through erosion.

- Do not remove markers, signs, or cairns — they are not souvenirs. Someone's safety or life could depend upon them.

- Please do not deface the desert with graffiti. It is especially important to respect Indian petroglyphs if you come across them.

- *"Pack it in — pack it out" applies to everything.* Orange peels, candy wrappers, pop bottles or cans are unsightly and non-biodegradable. Bury no refuse — animals will dig it up.

- If you smoke on the trail, be especially careful in disposing of cigarettes and matches. In Phoenix, a summer season smoking ban may be enforced under a 1996 smoking ordinance when there is fire danger.

- Respect private property.

- Other users of the mountains will be grateful if you avoid creating unnecessarily loud noises (for example, with "boom boxes").

- Use of trail-bikes or other motorized all-terrain vehicles off designated roads is prohibited in all park areas. Report problems to the responsible managing agency.

- Your dog deserves comfort and safety, too — at home!

On Horseback in the Phoenix Area

For me, there is no greater pleasure than riding in harmony with a good horse, enjoying the beauty and wildlife of the Arizona desert. To make the equestrian's trip more enjoyable and safe, here are a few tips that will be of help.

Water. For the rider, a canteen of water is a necessity. For the horse, there will be little or no water along the trails in this Guide. You may want to check with the appropriate managing agency. Be sure not to over-water a hot horse.

Clothing. Long, sturdy trousers, or chaps, are essential because of catclaw and cactus in some areas. Wear a hat with a brim for protection against the sun and a long-sleeved shirt. Shoes or boots with a heel are a must so that your foot will not hang up in the stirrup should you be thrown.

Equipment. A well-shod, good-conditioned, trail-savvy mount is advisable, because many of the trails are steep, narrow and rocky. The usual first-aid kit is good, plus a comb and pliers to extract cactus spines from you or your horse. Beware particularly of cholla. Horses encountering it for the first time can panic when, by brushing past it, it sticks to them.

Hikers and Bicyclists. A horse and rider can be intimidating to hikers, so act accordingly, with consideration and courtesy, when you meet them on the trail. Because of their unpredictability, horses do have the right-of-way over all other trail users. Upon seeing or hearing a horse approach, a hiker or bicyclist should step off on the downhill side of the trail, stand quietly without moving or making any fast movements, and speak in a calm and friendly voice. The horse may perceive a human, especially with a backpack, as some sort of monster coming down the trail and "spook," endangering both the rider and the hiker.

Similarly, the sight of a human astride a bicycle, silently moving towards them, or coming from behind, can frighten horses. The bicyclist should stop, announce his presence, and allow the horse to pass. Alternatively, when overtaking, give the rider time to move off the trail, then pass slowly with caution.

Rental Stables. Both the Phoenix and Maricopa County Parks and Recreation Departments have a list of reliable rental stables. You may also consult the Yellow Pages of the phone directory. Most stables can arrange guided rides.

Happy trails!

Margaret Bohannan, Former Chairman
Arizona Hiking and Equestrian Trails Committee

Weather

With an annual rainfall of only 7.5 inches, Phoenix is usually sunny, and especially so in the months of October through June. Snow in the valley is rare. During the summer months of July and August, however, the daily high temperature may be 105° or even as high as 120°. Afternoon and evening thundershowers are common between June and September, and moist air (a true monsoon) may be sucked up from the Gulfs of Mexico or California.

Below is a table of the average daily maximums for each month:

Month	Average Daily Maximum	Month	Average Daily Maximum
January	66°	July	105°
February	70°	August	103°
March	75°	September	98°
April	83°	October	88°
May	93°	November	75°
June	102°	December	67°

The best season is generally from late October through early May. But despite the high temperatures, one can usually hike and ride in the Valley's mountains during the summer if precautions are taken:

+ On days expected to be very hot, go very early in the morning, wear protective clothing (a hat, sunscreen, and light clothing), and bring *plenty* of water (at least a gallon if you will be out all day).

+ If you are new to the area or have any health problems, start out with very short trips and build up endurance slowly.

Because of the warmth, there is a temptation to hike or ride in shorts and a short-sleeved shirt and not to bring clothing to cover arms and legs — this is a dangerous mistake. Severe sunburn occurs easily during the summer months, but may occur at any time of the year, especially in those with light complexions. Heat exhaustion may be prevented by taking enough fluid and resting periodically in the shade.

Cool weather in combination with fatigue and wet, windy conditions may lead to hypothermia (dangerous lowering of the body's central core temperature). Due to impaired judgment, the impending hazard may not be accurately perceived.

Although you are not likely to see one, the area is subject to duststorms known as haboobs (miniature sandstorms), which are usually over quickly. Smaller disturbances known as dust devils can often be seen in the valleys.

Life in the Desert

No matter how arid the subtropical Sonoran desert may look, it abounds in beautiful and interesting animal and plant life. You will realize this if you enter the mountains after a rain and smell the creosote bush or see the blooming of the ocotillo. Did you know that the brittlebush can produce two different types of leaves, depending upon whether the season is moist or dry?

The easiest way to learn about plant life is to visit the Desert Botanical Garden adjacent to Papago Park at 1201 N. Galvin Parkway.[1] The Garden also offers guided Garden and wildflower tours, bird walks, classes and workshops (including special children's programs) and more. There is a Wildflower Hotline from March through the end of April with taped current reports.

There are many books on the subject. Most bookstores carry a few, but the Desert Botanical Garden's gift shop has an excellent selection. Our favorite is the *Deserts* book of the Audubon Society (McMahon, 1985), because it includes wildflowers, trees, shrubs, cacti, birds, reptiles, mammals, and insects. Others books are listed in Appendix C.

You are likely to see the following in the area covered by this book: *trees:* palo verde, mesquite, and ironwood; *shrubs:* creosote bush, white bursage, brittle-bush, ocotillo, fairy duster, jojoba, ratany, desert hackberry, desert broom, chuparosa; *cacti:* saguaro, cholla, barrel cactus, fishhook, prickly pear, hedge-hog; *desert agave* and *yuccas*; lizards, rattlesnakes, desert cottontails and black-tailed jackrabbits; coyotes; and groundsquirrels. Among the insects there are spiders, ants and bees.

Geology

The mountains in the Phoenix area reveal their structure much more readily than in other parts of the country where the rocks are covered with thick layers of soil, or with forest. Your enjoyment of the desert will be enhanced if you take the opportunity to learn about the land in the areas you visit.

This can be done through taking courses and on field trips with clubs or schools, but reading and observing are also sufficient to acquire more knowledge. We have supplied some information in certain sections of this guidebook, but not the complete explanation of all of the terms used. A geology book on Arizona will be very helpful. We recommend the books by Nations and Stump (1997) and Chronic (1986).

---

[1]There is an admission fee for non-members. Garden hours are 8:00 a.m. to 8:00 p.m. from October through April, and from 7:00 a.m. to 8:00 p.m. from May through September. Call 480-481-8134 for the Activities Hot-Line.

Easy, Attractive Hikes

If you're just starting out in the area, have little time, or you are hiking with small children, the following hikes may be worth considering.

When travelling with children, remember to carry a tweezers or small pliers to deal with any cactus they may encounter, and be careful near lake areas.

Area	Section, Name	Page	Map	Comments
Phoenix City - South	*South Mountain:* National Trail (west end), Javelina Canyon, Hidden Valley, Bajada (east)	94	9, 13	Wide variety of mountain and valley views, special rock features, sense of remoteness; first two can be taken part-way (involve ascents)
Phoenix City - North	*Squaw:* Circumference Trail, Squaw Peak Trail; Nature Trail, Quartz Trail	61	7, 8	Very popular, scenic, sometimes crowded trails (esp. Squaw Peak)
	North Mtn/Shaw Butte: Charles Christiansen Trail, Maxine Lakin Trail, Shaw Butte Road	43	5	Parts very easy; wide trails, some with moderate ascent
	Lookout: Circumference Trail	37	3	Short or complete (long) trips possible; some ascent
Valley West	*White Tank:* Waterfall Trail, Black Rock Trail; lower Ford Canyon Trail	190	22	First is very popular and easy, second is alternate
	Estrella: Rock Knob Trail, parts of Rainbow Valley Trail	152	18	Views of near-by Sierra Estrella range; some ascent
Northwest, Glendale	*Thunderbird:* Hedgpeth Trail [H-1], [H-2], [H-3], [H-4]	129	15	Variety of level or uphill walks, some with moderate ascents
East, near Mesa, Apache Junction	*Lost Dutchman*, especially Treasure Loop	203	24	Fine views of spectacular Superstition Mountains, easy walking
Northeast, Scottsdale, Mesa, Apache Junction	*McDowell:* North Trail, Wagner Long Loop, Scenic Trail, Hilltop Trail, Lousley Hill; *Scottsdale:* Taliesin-Lost Dog Wash.	164 / 138	23 / 16	Mostly level, lush desert vegetation (first-named); fire effects (second, third)
	Usery: Headquarters Hill, Cat Peaks, Wind Cave	178	21	Mountain and valley views, first two easy for children
	Tonto: Saguaro Vista, Butcher Jones; Lower Salt River Interpretive Trail; eastern section of Cave Creek Trail	218	25-29	Fine lake and mountain views, easy walking

Phoenix Parks

An Introduction

The City of Phoenix is surrounded by breath-taking scenery and contains within its borders some steep, rugged mountains — components of a casual and relaxed southwestern lifestyle. Efforts to protect these natural resources have been a partnership between Phoenix citizens and the Parks, Recreation and Library Department. Nothing makes this more evident than a recent election when our citizens voted for a modest sales tax increase to save thousands of acres of pristine desert adjacent to the city from development. So now we look forward to adding 15,000 more acres of wide-open spaces to the existing 27,000 aces of desert mountain and flatland parks.

As early as 1920 citizens organized a drive to preserve South Mountain Park, which anchors the southside of Phoenix. Through a continuing, concerted effort of city staff and citizens, this desert mountain park now boasts more than 16,500 acres and is considered the largest municipal park in the world.

In 1933 city voters, recognizing the importance of recreational spaces, approved the charter for the Parks, Playgrounds and Recreational Board, today the citizen-governed Phoenix Parks and Recreation Board.

During the 1960s continued growth threatened to develop over our most treasured desert assets. The City of Phoenix began to seek ways to protect our slopes and in 1972 instituted a master plan for the Phoenix Mountains Preserve.

As our desert holdings expand with more areas, new trails and facilities, so does the number of users. The Parks Department is called upon to meet these new demands with limited resources. On many of our park signs and in much of our literature you'll see the phrase "Don't Be A Trailblazer." It's a simple request for a simple action of staying on the trails. The Phoenix park rangers began this campaign as a way of educating park users about the concerns and needs of our fragile desert environment. We encourage each one of you who enjoys experiencing these unique urban parks to put them under your personal protection by following park rules and regulations.

I thank Roger and Ethel Freeman for being such willing trail guides in our desert parks and preserves. They have hiked and measured the trails, mapped the paths, and written the book which benefits both the casual and the frequent park user.

James A. Colley, CLP, Director
Parks, Recreation and Library Department

City of Phoenix Trail Ordinance

On June 30, 1993, the Phoenix City Council adopted a new ordinance providing the Parks and Recreation Board the authority to designate areas in the Mountain Preserves and Parks as either open or closed to public use. This ordinance is the result of more than two years' work by the Mountain Preserve Citizen Advisory Committee (MPCAC). The MPCAC became concerned with the condition of the trails in the mountain parks and the number of new trails being created by "trailblazers." Aerial photos showed clearly, during the past 20 years, that all areas of the mountain parks were being negatively impacted by new and unmanaged trails. The MPCAC recognized that the park rangers could only enforce City Ordinances and had no authority to control use on the fragile desert trail system in the 26,000-acre Mountain Preserves.

Working with the department staff and the community through volunteer organizations, and public workshops, the committee developed the ordinance during a two-year period. It provides the Parks and Recreation Board the authority to:

"...designate areas in each park and the Mountain Preserves as open or closed to public use. All designations shall be based on the protection of the natural, cultural, historical and other resources of the parks and Mountain Preserves. The Parks and Recreation Board may amend or revoke any designation made pursuant to this paragraph. Nothing in this paragraph shall prohibit an area designated by the Parks and Recreation Board as open to public use from being temporarily closed by the City Manager pursuant to Section 24-24 for emergency situations or by the Director of the Parks, Recreation and Library Department or his or her designee for administrative activities, including activities conducted for the purpose of safeguarding persons or property, implementing management plans and policies, or constructing, repairing, or maintaining recreational facilities or trails."

This ordinance, with its penalties (a minimum $50 fine and eight hours of community service), went into effect on August 1, 1994. The Parks, Recreation and Library Department has prepared a careful study of the trails system. The Department has recommended which primary trails are designated as open, which duplicate trails are closed, and started the process of evaluating secondary trail corridors for designation in 1995.

All hikers, horsemen, and bicyclists using the Phoenix Mountains Preserve should be aware of this new ordinance and make themselves familiar with the officially designated trails. Copies of the trail maps are available at all Phoenix Parks, Recreation and Library Department offices. Designated trails are clearly marked on the ground and closed areas will be signed.

James P. Burke, Deputy Director
Parks, Recreation and Library Department

City of Phoenix

Camelback/Echo Canyon Park

Camelback from Peak 2429 (Squaw area)

Introduction. At 2,704', Camelback Mountain is the highest peak in the Phoenix Mountains and a prominent landmark. In addition to the very popular summit trail, there are unusual rock formations, cliffs, caves, spires, and gendarmes like the Praying Monk. The Camel's Head and Bobby's Rock area are used for rock-climbing instruction and practice. The mountain is bounded by private property; please avoid trespassing.

History. The story of the preservation efforts is briefly outlined here:

The federal government reserved Camelback Mountain for an Indian reservation in 1879, then later changed its mind and issued deeds to private individuals from 1888-1900. Thus all of the mountain, except for State-owned portions reserved for schools, fell into private hands. During the 1920s to 1940s even these lands were sold.

Interest in preserving the mountain started in earnest with the Camelback Improvement Association in 1954 at a time when the mountain was not yet part of the City. Petitions were filed with Maricopa County against planned encroachments, though these had no legal status. The Maricopa County Planning and Zoning Commission decided on a maximum building elevation of 1,600' in approving subdivision or construction plans – but this had no legal force and people continued to build above that level.

Community groups that were formed in the late 1950s explored various possibilities, including the establishment of a state or county park, land trades, and purchases. Efforts to persuade landowners to deed land over to Maricopa County failed.

In November of 1960 the Arizona Conservation Council and Arizona Conservation Foundation were formed. The Council started a drive to protect land above 1,600' and started land acquisition proceedings. The federal government declined to declare Camelback a national monument. Congress also took no action on two bills introduced in 1962 (by John Rhodes) and in 1963 (by Barry Goldwater) to enable land exchanges.

In 1963-64 bills were introduced into the state legislature to enable state land exchanges, but these failed in spite of Governor Fannin's support. In 1965 the Preservation of Camelback Mountain Foundation, under the chairmanship of Barry Goldwater, was formed under the auspices of the Valley Beautiful Citizens Council. This represented a community-wide effort to acquire as much of the summit as possible, and culminated in success. In May of 1968 Mrs. Lyndon Johnson presided over a ceremony to conclude the acquisition process, along with Secretary of the Interior Stewart Udall, who presented a check for matching funds to Mayor Graham.

Saving of the mountain top, however, was not the end of the story. Access to the mountain was problematic and was contested by local landowners. The fence above the homes on the Camelback Mountain Trail represents an easement obtained only with great difficulty. The Park was finally opened in November of 1973.

Another more recent success is that the old trail to the summit from the east has been re-established on a partly new right-of-way.

Geology. Camelback is of unusual geological interest.[1] The Camel's Head consists of inclined, layered rock sediments (sandstones) of Tertiary age (70-100 million years ago), carved in places into alcoves and recesses by the wind. The Camel's hump, however, is composed of massive, ancient Precambrian granite (1.5 billion years old), originally formed from a cooling molten mass that was buried and later (60 million years ago) uplifted and weathered by wind and water. The expected sequence of Paleozoic and Mesozoic rocks between the Head and Back are missing (an "unconformity" in geological terms). The granite is about the same age as the lowest rocks in the Grand Canyon, whereas the sediments are younger than the Canyon's rim.

---

[1]Adapted from: JD Forrester (1959) *Geology of Camelback Mountain* (Dean, College of Mines, University of Arizona, Tucson), and H Chronic (1986) *Roadside Geology of Arizona*, Missoula, Montana: Mountain Press Publishing Co.

Maps. *Our Map 1.* The USGS 1:24,000 Paradise Valley quadrangle (1973) shows the area and part of the main trail, but detail is lacking.

Access. The park's entrance is off McDonald Drive just east of Tatum Boulevard, where Echo Canyon Parkway leads south 0.2 mile to the road end. There is also a new access point to the eastern end off Cholla Lane.

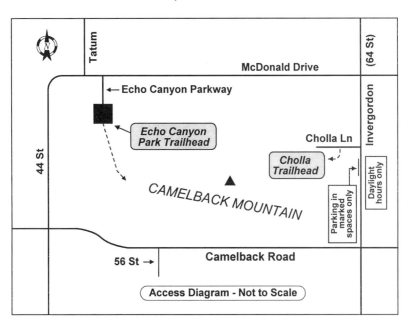

Facilities. This is a "totally natural" park with two ramadas, a parking lot, a drinking fountain at the trailhead at Echo Canyon, Port-a-Johns, but no other facilities. There are no facilities at the Cholla Lane Trailhead.

Recommended Hikes. The Camelback Mountain Trail (both segments) is steep and much more difficult than its length would indicate. The Echo Canyon Trail is much easier, but has few distant views.

Cautions. *Parking is difficult on weekends: come early, and try to car-pool! Parking is not allowed on area side-streets.* Respect private property. Please note that there have been many accidents on Camelback and the area is very exposed. Unless you are experienced and properly equipped, avoid the temptation to climb on the cliffs and rock formations. Stay on the trails!

[141] Camelback Mountain Trail WESTERN SEGMENT

General Description. This is an unusual and popular trail, with several spectacular sandstone rock formations along the way. Use great care: there are segments over steep, open rock or slippery dirt and gravel; part of the trail is braided and there are some steep drop-offs. From the trailhead cross a wash, then start a steady ascent past rock formations and trail junctions to a minor ridge-top at 0.3 mile. A fence is followed along the base of a huge cliff (part of which overhangs with sections requiring a hand-rail). At the top of a rise the railing ends and fine views start near the Camel's Neck. The trail crosses and recrosses the crest, then follows several gullies to the summit at 1.2 miles. Total ascent is 1,300'. For greatest enjoyment, allow at least a half-day for this trip.

At the summit there is a panoramic view, especially noteworthy toward Camelback's lower rock formations and across to Squaw Peak. The Eastern Segment continues down to Cholla Lane.

Access. From the road end (Echo Canyon Place) and ramada, go straight ahead, descending into a wash.

Read Down ↓	Detailed Trail Description	Read Up ↑
0.00	From parking lot (1,440'), pass ramada and descend.	1.16
0.01	**Junction:** trail R leads S for 0.11 mi, then ascends E to junction on [241] at 0.17 mi, just 100' S of ramada. Cross wash and ascend.	1.15
0.10	Pass huge rock on L (used for rock-climbing practice). On R is **junction** with [241], also leading 205' to ramada.	1.05
0.13	**Junction:** trail on R to ramada and [241], where this trail bears L.	1.04
0.15	Trail diverges and rejoins twice.	1.01
0.20	**Junction:** good view-point 75' to L.	0.96
0.25	**Junction:** NDT on R, then on L.	0.91
0.30	Top of rise (elevation 1,700'). Turn R. Fence line ahead. Trail levels briefly.	0.86
0.31	Parallel fence. Cliff above on R.	0.85
0.33	Ascend; start steep ascent in 150'.	0.82
0.38	Top of rise (elevation 1,740'). Descend; start steep ascent in 50'.	0.76
0.41	Hand-rail starts. Use caution.	0.74
0.43	Top of rise; drop briefly. Hand-rail ends.	0.72
0.45	Turn L, follow fence line at easier grade.	0.71
0.48	Hand-rail starts again.	0.68
0.50	Ascend steeply, with hand-rail.	0.66
0.52	Top of rise (1,940'), end of hand-rail. Excellent view-point off trail to L.	0.63
0.55	**Junction:** NDT sharp R.	0.60
0.57	Descend.	0.59
0.59	Ascend, then level off briefly.	0.57
0.61	Start steep rocky ascent up gully.	0.54
0.65	Top of rise (2,060'). Cross to S side of ridge.	0.50
0.67	Ascend to S of crest.	0.48
0.70	Top of rise (2,080'). Rocky knob on R.	0.45
0.72	Edge of crest line; trail meanders back and forth.	0.44
0.74	Go L, up over rocks at head of ravine, then cross it.	0.42
0.75	Cross over crest. Two routes diverge; take either. Canyon on L with rock formations. (Looking back, one can see a hole in the rock.)	0.41

0.81	Bear R, ascend up gully to SE. Above, there is a formation looking like a bird's head. Trail is braided; use care ascending up shallow valley.	0.35
1.04	Start ascent around S side of small ridge.	0.11
1.06	Turn L and up rocks.	0.10
1.11	Bear L (NE); bear L in 200'.	0.04
1.16	*Summit (2,704')*. Walk 225' to W along ridge for good view of Camel's Neck and Head area. Use care on NE side above steep cliffs. [The Cholla Trail (1998) continues down the ridge for 1.5 mi to reach Cholla Lane. From there, one must walk down 0.4 mi to the parking area. The first section down the ridge is very steep and rough.]	0.00

[141] Camelback Mountain (Cholla) Trail

General Description. This new trail, a relocation of an old trail, finally became available after 4 years of negotiations in 1998. The official opening was on National Trails Day, June 6th. The first section is new, leading through an easement around the Phoenician golf course, up the side of the ridge. After ¾ mile it joins the old pack trail, sidehilling the ridge, reaching it at two passes at 1 mile and then 275' further on. From here the trail is very narrow, rocky, and steep, with drop-offs on both sides. Extreme care must be used, and it is not recommended for children. It ascends to the summit at 1½ miles. Total ascent is 1,200'.

Access. From Cholla Lane. Limited parking (during day-time hours only) is available on the west side of Invergordon Road (64th St.), 0.1 mile south of Cholla Lane. You must walk up Cholla Lane for 0.3 mile to the trailhead. *Do not attempt to park on this road!* If you want to park at all, come early!

Read Down ↓	Detailed Trail Description	Read Up ↑
0.00	Leave Cholla Lane 0.29 mi from Invergordon at sign. Elevation 1,550'.	1.50
0.07	Top of rise above golf course.	1.43
0.15	Start steady ascent, bear R.	1.35
0.17	Switchback to R.	1.33
0.20	Steady ascent begins again. In 75', switchback up to L, then ease.	1.30
0.23	**Junction:** older trail angles L [to private property].	1.27
0.26	Excellent viewpoint over Superstitions, 4 Peaks.	1.24
0.33	Bear L (S), ascend steadily on narrower trail.	1.17
0.37	Turn R. Ascend SW across face of ridge,	1.13
0.41	Bear R.	1.09
0.42	Almost level trail.	1.09
0.47	Ascend steadily; head W.	1.04
0.48	Steep pitch.	1.03
0.50	Turn L, ease grade of ascent (briefly).	1.01
0.53	Top of rise. Viewpoint. Bear R, zigzag up (1,900').	0.97
0.57	Swing R, then ascend to N.	0.93
0.60	Excellent viewpoint on big rock (1,970').	0.90
0.63	**Junction:** at "Y", keep R.	0.87
0.66	Ascend steadily again.	0.84
0.67	Top of rise.	0.83
0.75	**Junction:** old trail descends sharp R.	0.75

0.76	Ascend steadily.	0.74
0.83	Steep pitch up rocks.	0.67
0.91	View of summit ahead.	0.59
0.97	Ascend again.	0.53
1.01	Top of rise. Ascend again.	0.49
1.03	Pass (2,210'). Head to R of crest.	0.47
1.09	**Pass.** In 75' ascend knife-edge with great care. Beyond this point extreme care is advisable, as there are steep drop-offs and the route is not always easy to follow.	0.41
1.18	Tricky spot; go up rocks to R.	0.32
1.24	Go very steeply up rocks.	0.26
1.27	Switchback right onto crest.	0.23
1.31	Go steeply up rocks, reach brief level area.	0.19
1.35	Come onto crest. Views of summit cliffs ahead.	0.15
1.44	Start final ascent (2,640'). Use care with cliff on R.	0.06
1.47	Turn R on crest, then L.	0.03
1.50	*Summit* (2,704'), fantastic views. Trail down to Echo Canyon TH continues.	0.00

[241] Echo Canyon Trail

General Description. This trail, less well known than the summit trail, leads into a rocky bowl at 0.5 mile, with unusual opportunities for exploration. The rock formations offer varied photographic possibilities under different light and weather conditions. The trail is less well defined than the summit trail, and there are many trails of use that may be confusing. Total ascent is about 75'.

Access. From Camelback Mountain Trail [141] at 0.12 mile.

Read Down ↓	Detailed Trail Description	Read Up ↑
0.00	Leave Camelback Mountain Trail [141] at 0.12 mi, heading S toward a ramada in view ahead (elevation 1,530').	0.48
0.03	**Junction:** [To R, side-trail leads W, to R of a sharp rock formation, reaching narrow gully in 385' and start of steep route in 435'. Gully leads to top of ridge with good views.] Turn L here and ascend.	0.44
0.04	Ramada atop minor ridge (1,535') and **junction:** to L, trail leads back to Camelback Mountain Trail [141] in 60'. Main trail descends gradually SW.	0.42
0.06	**Junction:** wide track. Turn L, up-hill here. (R is new trail descending 0.17 mi to Camelback Mountain Trail 65' from trailhead.)	0.40
0.08	**Junction:** turn R, drop over rock into minor wash on narrow trail, heading straight toward cliff face.	0.38
0.09	**Junction:** turn R at base of cliff (to L, trail of use heads back to ramada by different route in 290').	0.37
0.14	"Cave" in cliff on L (overhang) with fine view from it. Descend past it.	0.32
0.19	**Junction (4-way):** NDT crosses [descends on R; ascends L to hollow rock]. 25' further on, another branch of this trail of use crosses.	0.29
0.20	**Junction:** NDT ascends L into bowl beneath cliffs.	0.28
0.24	**Junction:** NDT descends R to private property.	0.24
0.30	Height-of-land (1,540'); good view-point just 50' to R. Descend 60' with Bobby's Rock on R, cliffs of Camel's Head on L. Pass ahead where trail ends is visible.	0.18
0.33	Switchback to R on descent. There are many confusing trails of use. Bear L.	0.15

0.36   Cross wash, then ascend. 0.12
0.38   **Junction:** cross NDT; contour along hillside. 0.10
0.43   Two small wind-carved alcoves in rocks on L. Pass one last NDT. 0.05
0.48   *Pass* (1,485'), end of official trail. (Ahead, poor NDT descends under and
       around huge boulders for 0.2 mile into private housing development — no
       trespassing.) On L at pass is spectacular cliff wall with overhang. On R is
       large rock, easily climbed for good views into rocky bowl that trail has crossed. ... 0.00

The start of Camelback Mountain Trail

City of Phoenix

Deem Hills

Deem Hills Trail

General Description. This is a new park area, opened in early 1994. At present there is only one trail, and that is incomplete. The ramada area and trail were developed with the assistance of Southwest Gas Employee Volunteers and the Eagle Scout Troop #222. Southwest Gas continues to maintain the trail. The almost-level trail leads toward the aqueduct. Total elevation gain is about 20-40'.

Maps. *Our Map 14.* The USGS 1;24,000 Hedgpeth Hills quadrangle (1957, photorevised 1981) covers the terrain but does not show the trail or road to the trailhead.

Access. From the trail-head parking lot, off 39th Avenue. From Interstate 17 (Black Canyon Freeway), take exit 218 (Happy Valley Road) and turn west. Be careful to take the first right turn (Frontage Road) immediately after the freeway exit on the west side (0.0 mile). Drive north 1.4 miles and turn left on Pinnacle Vista Road, passing 31st, 33rd, 35th, 37th, and finally 39th Avenue at 2.6 miles. At the latter the road turns north to the trailhead parking area at 2.7 miles.

Facilities. There is a ramada shelter (no tables) with drinking water, but no other amenities. Trails close at sunset, parks at 11:00 p.m.

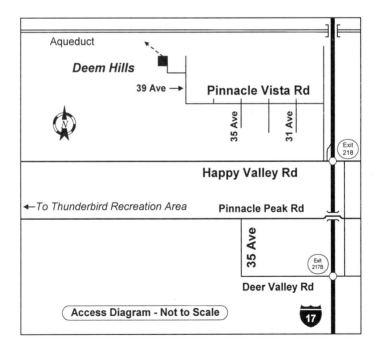

- 29 -

Read Down ↓	Detailed Trail Description	Read Up ↑
0.00	From trailhead, head NW (1,480').	0.57
0.49	Keep L, approach aqueduct.	0.08
0.55	**Junction:** join trail from R; parallel aqueduct fence.	0.02
0.57	**Junction:** trail R descends to aqueduct and can be followed L (W) to 1.49 mi and beyond. Near here a new trail will head up the ridge-line.	0.00

For further information, please contact the Northwest District, Phoenix Parks, Recreation and Library Department, 602-262-6575.

City of Phoenix

Papago Park

Introduction. Papago Park contains 888 acres and is literally in the midst of the city. In addition to its better-known facilities it has hiking, jogging, riding, orienteering and bicycling trails. Elevations range from 1,200' to almost 1,700'.

History.[1] Originally an Indian town site ("Papago" is a Pima name), it was a homesteading area (1889) and then was established as Papago Saguaro National Monument by Congress in 1914. This designation was abolished in 1930. The land was granted to the State of Arizona except for parcels transferred to the National Guard, sold to the City of Tempe, or purchased by the Salt River Valley Water Users Association. In 1932 some of the land was allotted to the Military District, Cactus Gardens, the Arizona Game and Fish Department, and the Salt River Agricultural Improvement and Power District. It finally became a City of Phoenix park (originally "Cactus Park") in 1959. In its early days it was too rugged for easy approaches because of the difficult desert brush and plants. The first road into the park area was built in 1916 with volunteer labor.

The pyramidal Hunt's Tomb (on top of one of the buttes just north of the Zoo) is that of George Wiley Paul Hunt (1859-1934), Arizona's seven-term governor, his wife, her parents, and three of her relatives. An Act of Congress was required to authorize the structure, a gift of school children and friends.

Geology. The Salt River Valley was formed some 29-30 million years ago, with extensive faulting events. More recent vulcanism (6-15 million years ago) helped form the up-thrown red rock (iron oxide-hematite) as part of what geologists call the "Basin and Range Province." Included within the park boundary are three buttes of a sedimentary formation that is directly related to Camelback Mountain's "Head" and therefore called the "Camel's Head Formation." The holes in the rocks are called *tafoni* and are characteristic of arid regions. They were not caused by wind, but by water that remained in holes and cracks, slowly soaking up and breaking down the minerals in the rocks. Overlying the bedrock landform known as a *pediment* is a thin veneer of sand and rock which has worn away in several spots to reveal bedrock outcrops. These made the land unsuitable for farming.

Maps. *Our map 2.* The 1:24,000 USGS Tempe quadrangle (1952, photo-revised 1982) shows the physical features but not the trails. Extensive reconstruction of Galvin Parkway, park access roads and parking areas in 1988 has made earlier maps obsolete. Further changes to the trail system are planned.

Access. The park's entrances are reached from Galvin Parkway between E. Van Buren and McDowell Road. (The access roads were rebuilt in 1988.)

Facilities. Open from 6:00 a.m. to 11 p.m., the park provides an 18-hole golf course and facilities for softball, archery, fishing in several small lakes, and picnicking in addition to the adjacent Phoenix Zoo and Desert Botanical Garden. There are picnic ramadas with drinking water and firepits, Hunt's Tomb and the Eliot Memorial. An orienteering course has been provided

---

[1]Information in this section and on Geology was adapted from RM Hochhaus (1983) *Papago Park: An Informational Background Report*, kindly provided by the Parks, Recreation & Library Department.

Lookout Mountain

[Previous page: The cliff on Camelback]   *Shaw Butte from North Mountain*

On the Christiansen Trail [Squaw Peak Area]

Typical scene in the Squaw Peak Area

National Trail at South Mountain

Fat Man's Pass (Hidden Valley Trail)

Bajada Trail in South Mountain

Looking into the Tonto from Thunderbird

Wind Cave [Usery, Tonto]

[Previous page: Camelback's "cave"]

Bradshaws from Cave Creek Park

Standing stone on Pemberton Trail (McDowell)

Scenic Trail after the Rio Fire (McDowell)

Equestrians on Rock Knob Trail [Estrella]

Sierra Estrellas from Pack Saddle Trail

Rugged terrain [White Tank]

Waterfall Trail [White Tank]

Northeast from Pass Mountain Trail [Usery]

[Previous page: City from South Mountain]

Lost Dutchman State Park

On the Black Canyon Trail

Lower Salt River area from Coon Bluff

Skull Mesa Trail below the summit

Cave Creek in autumn on Cave Creek Trail

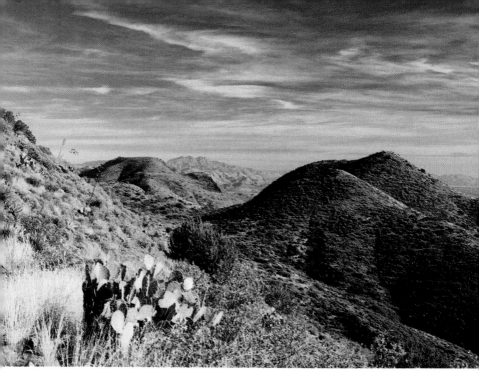

From the Bronco Trail looking east [Tonto]

Bartlett Reservoir [Tonto]

Sears-Kay Ruin in the Tonto

Saguaro Lake frrom the Vista Trail

through cooperation with Recreational Equipment, Inc [REI] in Tempe; a map is available from them or from the East District Office [see Appendix B].

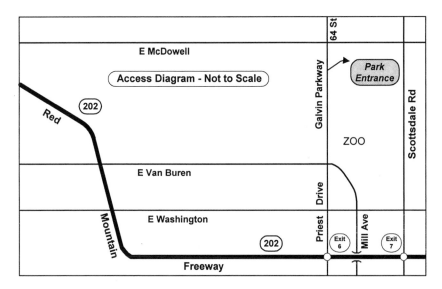

Recommended Hikes. There are a number of isolated rock outcrops. Hunt's Tomb is at the top of one of these in the southeastern section of the park, reached by a short trail from the parking area. A landmark known as the "Hole-in-the-Rock" adjacent to the Desert Botanical Garden is popular for scrambling. There is also good walking or jogging along the bikeway: along the Arizona Cross Cut Canal from McDowell Road on the north into the Desert Botanical Garden, then from the Hunt's Tomb area almost to the Alegre Drive crossing of the Canal where the bikeway leads into Canal Park (contiguous on the park's eastern side), to the College Avenue/McKellips Road area. (The map also shows several other outcrops that are off-limits to the general public, one adjacent to the Arizona National Guard Military Reservation, one on the Municipal Golf Course, and another between the Park and the Water Treatment Plant.) The trail indicators used here are our own arbitrary letters (e.g., [B]), since no trail has as yet been officially designated. *PLEASE NOTE* that a Master Planning process has started that will eventually lead to a system of designated trails. It is important not to travel off existing trails while this study is proceeding because of the fragile environment.

Cautions. Climbing on the steep sandstone rocks is for experts only and is not recommended for the ordinary hiker. Beware of road traffic through the park. Several areas have been heavily scarred by all-terrain vehicles and the maze of tracks can be confusing.

NOTE: The three short circuit trails described here are *hiker-only.* (There are separate riding trails along the golf course to the west.)

[A] (Park High Point)

General Description. A circuit trip of 0.8 mile provides variety, with a short climb to a saddle between the two parts of the butte at 0.2 mile and a steep descent to the amphitheater at ¼ mile. The trail then circles around the east side of the butte to return to its starting point. Ascent is 250'.

Access. From Galvin Parkway opposite the Zoo and Park entrance, walk the road on the opposite (west) side, then head north. Just after the road turns sharp left near a butte, you will see the Eliot Ramada on your left. Park there. Walk back east along the road for 250' or along a path just north of the road to the junction at the road.

Read Down ↓	Detailed Trail Description	Read Up ↑
0.00	From junction at road 250' E of Eliot Ramada parking lot, head N up track.	0.80
0.01	**Junction:** cross track and continue up toward gully.	0.78
0.08	Enter gully, continue ascent (avoid trail of use on L).	0.71
0.16	Top of rise (about 1,500'). VP to N. Descend to L. *Use care*, trail is steeper than on other side.	0.64
0.22	**Junction:** avoid trail to R; keep L, continue descent.	0.57
0.24	Top of amphitheater. Go to R along edge of it.	0.56
0.27	SE corner of amphitheater. Continue E.	0.52
0.32	**Junction:** where track crosses, go straight.	0.48
0.33	**Junction:** pass another track coming up from L.	0.46
0.37	With bluff ahead, keep to L of it where trail of use goes R and ascends.	0.43
0.39	Top of rise. Bear R away from track descending on L; descend gradually.	0.41
0.48	**Junction:** track descends L. Continue around flank of butte to S, then SW.	0.31
0.62	**Junction:** track descends on L.	0.18
0.68	**Junction:** tracks descend L & continue to R. Continue straight, descend slightly (upper route bearing R also leads back, paralleling road).	0.12
0.70	**Junction:** lower track. Go R, generally paralleling road.	0.09
0.80	**Junction:** *you are now back at start* (upper route enters here from R).	0.00

[B] Central Butte

General Description. There are two circuit trips here (0.6 mile and ¾ mile), as well as the short spur that leads to the high point on the butte at 0.2 mile. Ascent is about 150', depending upon which circuit trip is chosen.

Access. From Eliot Ramada; however, it is planned to move the trailhed to just west of Galvin Parkway, with parking on Galvin Parkway. (The Memorial, dedicated in 1964, is in recognition of William C. Eliot's contribution to the development of parks in the City of Phoenix, and Papago Park in particular.)

Read Down ↓	Detailed Trail Description	Read Up ↑
0.00	From Eliot Ramada parking lot's W end, take path heading SW.	0.27
0.01	Turnstile entrance into enclosure.	0.26
0.02	Eliot Memorial Ramada. Continue SW toward gate.	0.25

0.04 Leave enclosure thru gate, taking track SW toward butte. 0.23
0.14 **Junction:** to R is circuit trip returning. Go straight, ascending. 0.13
0.16 **Junction:** ahead trail ascends 130' (past another junction) to high point on butte (trail can then be followed 150' E to return to this circuit. Go L here to take either circuit. 0.11
0.19 **Junction (4-way):** trail sharp R ascends back toward top of butte trail (track also descends half-L). Continue. 0.08
0.27 **Junction:** wide track crosses. Here you can go R for the shorter circuit, or continue ahead for longer one. 0.00

Longer Circuit

0.00 Leave junction, continue around flank. Cross tracks in 60', 135', 225'. 0.32
0.07 **Junction:** 2 tracks descend to L in open area. Continue slightly R, around flank of butte. 0.25
0.10 **Junction:** track sharp L. 0.22
0.13 **Junction (4-way):** tracks L & R. Ascend. 0.29
0.16 **Junction (4-way):** tracks descend L & R. 0.16
0.21 **Junction (4-way):** eroded track ascends on R, descends on L. 0.11
0.25 **Junction:** *sharp R is shorter circuit.* Go slightly R. 0.07
0.28 **Junction:** cross track, continue around flank. 0.04
0.32 **Junction:** *you are now back at junction 0.14 mi from road,* 0.59 mi from start. ... 0.00

Shorter Circuit

0.00 Leave junction, ascend steadily up broad track. 0.22
0.02 **Junction:** trail of use enters from L. Continue ascent. 0.19
0.08 **Junction:** at top of rise, trail sharp L is eroded, ascends 135' toward side of subsidiary butte. Continue, descending. 0.13
0.11 **Junction:** where eroded track continues, descending, bear R on trail. 0.11
0.12 **Junction:** trail of use descends on L. Continue slightly R. 0.10
0.14 **Junction:** take wide track descending to L. 0.07
0.15 **Junction:** *longer circuit* enters from L. Track continues descending toward golf course. *Turn sharp R here* to return. 0.07
0.18 **Junction:** cross track, continue around flank of butte. 0.04
0.22 **Junction:** *you are now back at junction 0.14 mi from road,* 0.49 mi from start. 0.00

[C] Hole-in-the-Rock

General Description. This is a popular area for unusual views toward the south and southwest, and an easy short hike of only a little over 0.1 mile. The hike can be extended around the north side of the butte for a total of 0.2 mile. Ascent is about 120'. *Use care on rock!*

Access. Drive to the Zoo entrance off Galvin Parkway, but take a left turn. Pass a side-road and then a parking area on the right, then turn left, passing the ranger station on the right. At a 5-way junction, head straight across and into the parking area. Take the trail at the east side of the parking area.

Read Down ↓	Detailed Trail Description	Read Up ↑
0.00	From parking area, head E around the butte.	0.14
0.08	**Junction:** 125' to R is spur trail to another parking area and road loop. Turn L (N) and ascend steps, then turn L.	0.06
0.14	Reach Hole-in-the-Rock (just before final ascent, minor trail continues ahead, turning left around butte to return to road in 400', just N of where you started).	0.00

City of Phoenix

Lookout Mountain Area

Introduction. Lookout Mountain, the northernmost part of the Phoenix Mountains Preserve, is a visually striking feature lying between Bell Road on the north, 7th Street on the west, Cave Creek Road on the east, and Thunderbird Road on the south. It consists of a prominent summit butte (2,054') and a sharp knob that is 1,964' high, separated by a col at 1,883'. To the west of these summits (separated by a 1,690' pass) is a lower north-south ridge with three summits increasing in height from north to south: 1,704', 1,724', and 1,843'. This area is isolated from other parts of the Preserve.

Maps. *Our map 3.* USGS 1:24,000 quadrangles Union Hills (1964, photo-revised 1981) and Sunnyslope (1965, photorevised 1982).

Access. There are two major access points: (1) the best is to drive 0.9 mile south of Bell Road to the trailhead on 16th Street, just before a water tower. There is ample parking here. (2) The other is at Lookout Mountain Park off Acoma and 18th St. You can find the trail just beyond the far end of the parking lot, ascending to the northwestern corner to find the spur trail. Other access points are being developed as part of a master plan.

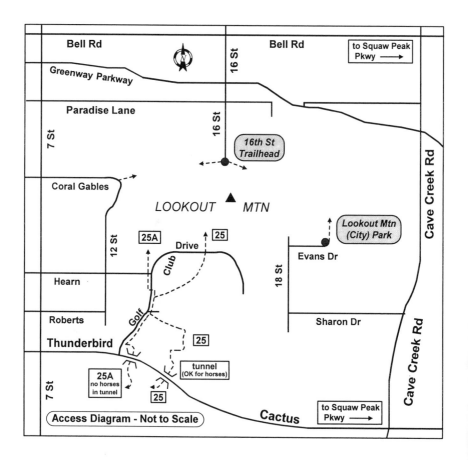

Facilities. At 16th Street there is only the trailhead at this time. There are facilities in Lookout Mountain (City) Park to the southeast, from which trail [25] ascends. Trails close at sunset, parks at 11:00 p.m.

Terminology. *The trail system described here will make little sense to the reader without looking at the map at the same time.*

Recommended Hikes and Trail Rides. There are now two major designated trails, replacing a formerly confusing network, as well as three access trails from the south [25], [25A], and Lookout Mountain City Park. The Summit Trail [150] has some quite steep sections, and is not suitable for horses or bicycles. The Circumference Trail [308] is quite varied, with much up and down but no very steep sections. Trail [25] gives access through the Pointe property to the main part of the Preserve south of Thunderbird Road; trail [25A] follows Golf Club Drive to pass under Thunderbird Road into the main portion of the Preserve.

Cautions. *Note that only four approaches are presently maintained and signed.* There are many other approaches from private land, now off limits. Access through those areas to Preserve land is illegal for non-residents; they are not described here except to identify junctions. Off-road vehicles used the area in the past and created several steep tracks that are being re-vegetated.

[25] Spur Trail

General Description. From the Circumference Trail it descends 1/3 mile to cross Golf Club Drive just east of 15th Place. It can be reached at this point along a paved path from the west end of Winchcomb Road, a short distance south of Lookout Mountain (City) Park. This is the most used section of the trail. The connection to the Preserve on the south is mostly used by equestrians. From Golf Club Drive it follows an easement a total of 1.4 miles through Pointe property and golf course to Thunderbird Road. *Details are:* it returns to Golf Club Drive and trail [25A] in 1/3 mile, follows them south for 0.2 mile, then leaves them, heading southeast along the golf course, up a hill, and descends to reach Captain Drefus Avenue in another 2/3 mile. The avenue is followed for another 0.2 mile to a tunnel under Thunderbird Road which can be used by horses. (See access diagram on first page of this chapter.) It is then in the Stony area for another ½ mile. Ascent is 120'.

Access. *From the north:* from the Circumference Trail [308] at 1.6 miles. *From the south:* from Captain Dreyfus Avenue at the tunnel, or see the Stony chapter.

[25A] Spur Trail

To go *north from Hearn Drive into the Lookout Mountain area,* find a narrow corridor just west of the intersection of Hearn and Golf Club Drive. Head north through it for ¼ mile, then ascend some 60' to the Circumference Trail [308] at 0.6 mile. (This point is at 1.64 miles on the Circumference Trail description.) The connection *south to Thunderbird* and the Stony area, mostly used by equestrians, is 0.9 mile, following Hearn a very short distance east, then south along Golf Club Drive almost to Thunderbird, where it heads briefly east, then south through a tunnel used by golf carts, hikers, and bikes *but not horses.* (See access diagram on first page of this chapter.) It is then in the Stoney area of this guidebook.

[150] Summit Trail

General Description. This is the most direct approach to the Summit. From the parking area just below the water tower, a combination of tracks ascends 200' with increasing steepness to become a trail. This heads into the col at 0.4 mile. The main trail continues east to the Summit at ½ mile. Total ascent to the Summit is 540'. It has fine views.

Access. Take 16th Street and park at the trailhead. This trail starts from the Circumference Trail [308] at 0.1 mile.

Read Down ↓	Detailed Trail Description	Read Up ↑
0.00	Leave Circumference Trail [308] (1,590') on good trail ascending S.	0.54
0.14	**Junction:** NDT on L; switchback to R, then to L in 120'. (Pass another NDT on R in 55').	0.40
0.19	Switchback to R (NDT on L, another on L in 60').	0.35
0.22	**Junction:** avoid NDT R; switchback to L (1,660'), then 5 more in next 300'.	0.32
0.29	Use care going up very steep pitch to S.	0.25
0.33	Switchback to L, then to R.	0.21
0.37	Go up rocks.	0.17
0.38	Reach pass (1,883'). There are very good views here. Remainder of ascent is steep, rocky, and braided, with some bad drop-offs. Turn L here (E), going to L of large rock. Use great care!	0.16
0.43	Reach crest. Main trail route by-passes hump on R.	0.11
0.51	Reach flat area on crest.	0.03
0.54	*SUMMIT* (2,054'). All-around views.	0.00

[308] Circumference Trail COUNTERCLOCKWISE

General Description. From the 16th Street trailhead this major trail encircles the mountain, giving access to the Summit Trail [150] and to Lookout Mountain Park and a spur trail [25A] to Hearn Road and one to Golf Club Drive [25].[*] Total mileage is 2.8 miles. Total ascent is 325' to the junction.

Access. On the south side of the parking area north of the water tower fence line a trail will be seen heading east and west.

---

[*]At around 2 miles, on the eastern side, marking was not clear in 1999 in a maze of other trails.

Read Down ↓	Detailed Trail Description	Read Up ↑
0.00	Leave 16th St. Trailhead, heading immediately SW and up (1,530').	2.79
0.10	**Important junction:** the Summit Trail [150] continues straight up the mountain; this trail turns sharp R here (1,590') and descends gradually to W. It is wide and rocky.	2.69
0.31	Cross deep wash.	2.48
0.33	**Junction:** keep L at trail post, ascending.	2.46
0.38	**Junction:** alternate rejoins. Start rocky, steep pitch for 200'.	2.41
0.47	Pass (2,130'). NDTs L & R. Descend.	2.32
0.50	**Junction:** go L where vehicleway descends ahead.	2.29
0.63	Cross wash.	2.16
0.64	Sag; ascend steadily.	2.15
0.73	Bottom of descent. Ascend briefly, then descend gradually.	2.06
0.81	**Junction:** NDT on R; keep L here, ascending.	1.98
0.94	**Junction:** NDT on R; ascend steadily to L on narrow trail.	1.85
0.98	Cross wash.	1.81
1.01	Trail braids, rejoins; keep L.	1.78
1.03	**Junction:** keep L, ascending steeply.	1.76
1.08	Top of rise (2,190'). Descend gradually to NE.	1.71
1.10	Bottom of descent.	1.69
1.17	Ascend rocky trail.	1.62
1.22	Reach crest; go L in confusing area. Use care here.	1.57
1.29	Cross wash.	1.50
1.34	Cross wash.	1.45
1.36	**Junction (4-way):** NDTs. Go R, descending.	1.43
1.40	**Important junction:** trail [25A] descends sharp R here toward homes and at 0.6 mi roadside connection on Golf Club Dr to Mountain Preserve in another 0.9 mi. Turn R, descend.	1.39
1.49	Cross wash. Start descent.	1.30
1.56	Bottom of descent.	1.23
1.64	**Important junction:** on R is trail [25] descending to Golf Club Dr in 0.4 mi, or to Winchcomb Dr, and continuing to main part of Preserve in 1.4 mi.	1.15
1.77	Turn sharp L.	1.02
1.83	**Junction:** R is spur to Lookout Mountain Park access [0.21 mi].	0.96
1.87	**Junction:** NDT on L. Ascend to N.	0.92
1.95	Switchback to L (SW).	0.84
1.97	Switchback to R at wash. Head N.	0.82
2.00	Turn L, ascend steeply (2,160'). In 80' turn R, along wash for 50'.	0.79
2.05	Switchback to L, ascend to SW.	0.74
2.09	Switchback to R at wash.	0.70
2.12	Top of rise (2,250'). Descend gradually to N.	0.67
2.18	**Junction (4-way):** avoid NDTs, continue descending, straight ahead.	0.61
2.21	Bottom of descent.	0.58
2.30	**Junction (4-way):** NDTs straight & L, in open area go R, descend steadily.	0.49
2.42	Turn sharp L (W).	0.37
2.45	Bottom of descent, cross small wash (2,060').	0.34
2.48	**Junction:** NDT sharp R. Head NNW to NW.	0.31
2.54	Near fence line. Bear L, ascending steadily on rocky trail to SW.	0.25
2.67	Water tower in view. Ascend steeply to top of rise in 45'. Drop to R (W).	0.12
2.74	Bottom of descent.	0.05
2.79	Back at start.	0.00

Lookout Mountain Park Access Trail

General Description. From Lookout Mountain Park, a trail ascends gradually out of that park to intersect the Circumference Trail [308] inside the Preserve in 1/5 mile. Ascent is 40'.

Access. Drive into Lookout Mountain Park by turning off Cave Creek Road onto Sharon Drive, then turning right onto 18th Street to Evans Drive, then right again to the large parking area. At the far end the trail will be found only a few feet away.

Read Down ↓	Detailed Trail Description	Read Up ↑
0.00	Leave parking area (1,520'). In 30' pass horse trough, then a hitching post.	0.21
0.03	Trail sign.	0.18
0.05	**Junction:** other trail from parking area enters on L.	0.16
0.09	Swing L.	0.12
0.12	Turn R.	0.09
0.13	Cross small wash.	0.08
0.17	Stone monument.	0.04
0.18	**Junction:** NDT on R; keep L.	0.03
0.20	Preserve sign.	0.01
0.21	**Junction:** this trail ends at Circumference Trail [308] (1,560') To R it is 0.96 mi, to L it is 1.83 mi, to 16th Street Trailhead.	0.00

City of Phoenix

North Mountain/Shaw Butte Area

Shaw Butte from North Mountain

Introduction. At 2,104' North Mountain is a major landmark. Although somewhat lower than Squaw Peak and Camelback, its summit provides a wide panorama. A paved road, gated near where it leaves 7th Street, rises almost to the fenced transmission towers at the summit. The area contains several subsidiary ridges and a section of the Charles M. Christiansen Trail. To the northwest, Shaw Butte (2,149') has two summits, reached by three approaches, two on service roads and one via trail. The tops of the two summits are private land (Arizona Public Service Company) but are open to the public at this time.

History. Around the turn of the century, the North Mountain area served as a campground for the Phoenix Indian School's pupils and their families. There are a number of closed mining shafts and pits, evidencing earlier interest in copper mining.

Maps. *Our map 5.* The USGS 1:24,000 Sunnyslope quadrangle (1965, photorevised 1982) shows a few trails, the North Mountain road and the roads up Shaw Butte (with a few inaccuracies).

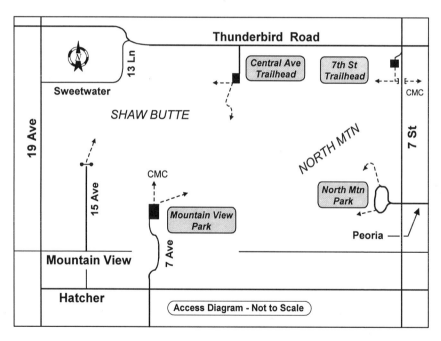

Access. North Mountain Recreation Area is served by a paved loop road reached from Peoria at 7th Street. The Charles M. Christiansen Trail is best reached from Mountain View Park. A new major trailhead on the west side of 7th Street was opened in 1994. Shaw Butte can be reached from the trailhead at the south end of Central Avenue or the north end of 15th Avenue north of Shangri-La Road. Changes are still taking place in marking and in obliterating non-designated trails. Therefore junctions shown in the following text may become obscure over the next few years.

Facilities. There are 12 ramadas (some with electricity) serving up to 350 people, and many uncovered picnic tables. Some areas are reserved, others first-come. Washrooms and drinking water are located at the large parking area at the park office near the Pima Ramada (Area 4). There are also washrooms at the Yavapai Ramada (Area 10). There is an orienteering course, with a master map available at the park office. As is true of other Phoenix Mountain Parks, facility hours are limited to 5:30 a.m. through 11:00 p.m. Trails close at sunset.

The Shaw Butte area has major facilities at Mountain View Park only. At Central Avenue Trailhead there is water, a bike rack, and a portable toilet.

Recommended Hikes and Trail Rides. The entire North Mountain area is honeycombed with trails, but many of them have no legal access points. We have described designated trails only. Others are indicated as "NDT" (non-designated trail). (The Shaw Butte area has fewer trails.) Numbers used are either official City of Phoenix numbers or (in two instances) our own letters for identification purposes. Officially numbered trails are listed first, and the North Mountain Area is covered before Shaw Butte. The easiest approach to North Mountain is the National Trail [44]; to Shaw Butte, the easiest approach is from Central Avenue [306]. The Christiansen Trail [100] is easy, but all in the valley. The Maxine Lakin Trail [60] also has some good views. There are many other viewpoints.

Cautions. Many of the trails are steep and rocky. As mentioned above, trail changes are still under way.

North Mountain Area

Lower North Mountain Road

General Description. The entire paved road is 0.9 mile long, with a short trail to the actual summit. Total ascent is 650'. The upper section is part of the National Trail [44] (see that description for the ascent of North Mountain). There are several junctions with trails. The ascent to the National Trail is 210' and the distance is 0.3 mile.

Access. *From the north:* the road leaves 7th Street 1.1 miles south of Thunderbird Road, just before the two sets of lanes rejoin. When approaching *from the south,* you will have to pass the area, then double back because of the dual roadway. There is very limited parking at the base of the road before the gate. *(Park authorities are not encouraging use of this parking area.)*

Read Down ↓	Detailed Trail Description	Read Up ↑
0.00	Leave 7th Street (elevation 1,450'). Pass gate in 100'	0.32
0.04	**Junction:** gravel road on L.	0.28
0.07	Road bends to L; narrow trail ascends draw on R.	0.25
0.10	Road bends to R (poor track ascends on L).	0.22
0.19	**Junction:** trail [100A] R at switchback to L (0.57 mi to CMC [100]).	0.13
0.21	Gate.	0.11
0.32	**Junction:** trail dropping L down steps is National Trail [44] to Maricopa Ramada in 0.17 mi. (Road continues ahead as National Trail [44], see below.) (Elevation 1,660' here.)	0.00

[40] Penny Howe Barrier-Free Nature Trail

In 1993 the Penny Howe Nature Trail was dedicated in the bowl of North Mountain Park.[1] It consists of two short loop trails connected by a stem that runs between The Yavapai and Maricopa ramadas. Interpretive signs are installed to increase appreciation of the history and other features of the area.

[44] National Trail NORTH MOUNTAIN FROM NORTH MTN PARK

General Description. From the Maricopa Ramada area, this trail ascends the side of a dry wash to a prominent trail junction and view at 0.1 mile, then up a short pitch to the North Mountain Road at 0.2 mile. It then follows the road and a short trail for almost 0.6 mile to the summit for a total distance of $^3/_4$ mile. (This is the easiest approach to North Mountain.) Total ascent is 170' to the road, 615' to North Mountain summit. The Trail then continues south to the Quechan Ramada (see reverse of next description).

Access. From Maricopa Ramada near the Recreation Area entrance.

Read Down ↓	Detailed Trail Description	Read Up ↑
0.00	Leave R side of Maricopa Ramada, elevation 1,490'. From signpost, ascend along side of wash.	0.74
0.14	**Junction (3-way):** trail L is alternate back to start (narrower). Go straight.	0.60
0.15	Pass (viewpoint to N). Switchback to L and up steps.	0.59
0.17	**Junction:** North Mountain Road (1,660'), trail [100A]. (To R, paved road descends 0.13 mi to where [100A] leads W 0.57 mile to 7th St.) From here, trail follows road up North Mountain.	0.57
0.25	Road turns sharp L; overlook.	0.49
0.44	**Junction:** wide trail to L quickly deteriorates.	0.30
0.67	Hairpin turn to L; good view of Shaw Butte.	0.07
0.71	**Junction:** where road turns sharp R and passes through fence ahead, ascend L (SW) on trail.	0.03
0.74	*Summit,* North Mountain, 2,104'. **Junction:** trail along crest to L is continuation of National Trail [44] from the south (see below). NDT straight ahead.	0.00

---

[1]A long-serving member of the Parks & Recreation Board, Penny Howe died in 1999.

[44] National Trail NORTH MOUNTAIN FROM THE SOUTH

General Description. This major trail ascends from the Quechan Ramada onto the ridge crest. It then takes a circuitous route along the east flank of North Mountain, finally ascending the crest to the summit at 0.6 mile where there are fine views in all directions. (It continues north to the Maricopa Ramada; see previous section.) Total ascent is 715'.

Access. Take the trail from the right side of the ramada which immediately crosses a wash.

Read Down ↓	Detailed Trail Description	Read Up ↑
0.00	From Quechan Ramada at 1,400', bear R and cross wash, ascending.	0.57
0.10	**Junction (5-way):** pass in ridge crest (1,523'). To L, trail leads onto summit of Peak 1700 or down to Ak-Chin Ramada. Even sharper L, poor NDT leads up crest toward Peak 1700. Ahead, NDT drops to a cul-de-sac in housing development (no public access). To continue, go N along sharp rocks, then bear L, to W of crest, up a draw.	0.47
0.18	Bear R.	0.39
0.19	Reach minor crest with NDTs. From here, ascend to E of crest, with ramadas and parking area in view below.	0.38
0.23	**Junction:** NDT on R.	0.34
0.26	Ascend more steeply; here there are 2 trails that rejoin ahead, beyond a tree.	0.32
0.28	**Junction:** just off main trail to R is knob with good view. Turn L here, ascend.	0.29
0.30	Views S to center of city. Turn R here.	0.26
0.34	With rocks ahead, switchback to R.	0.23
0.36	**Junction:** NDT on R (on descent, keep R here).	0.21
0.37	Reach main crest (1,910') and head N, climbing steep, braided trail.	0.20
0.41	Switchback to R.	0.16
0.46	**Junction:** NDT L (obscure here). Almost level trail ahead, marked with rocks on L. Towers in view ahead.	0.11
0.57	*Summit of North Mountain* (elevation 2,104'). Fence surrounds towers. **Junction:** National Trail [44] passes to E of tower fence, drops to road bend, continuing down to Maricopa Ramada. (See previous description.)	0.00

[44A] Peak 1700

General Description. This is the southernmost hump on North Mountain's ridge. There are two approaches via this loop: (1) From the Ak-Chin Ramada, the trail ascends to the ridge at 0.2 mile, joins the ridge route, and reaches the summit at 0.3 mile. (2) It is an easy ascent from the Quechan Ramada via the National Trail [44]: from the pass at 0.1 mile on that trail, this wide trail starts at an almost level grade, then switchbacks up at 0.1 mile. From there a steady ascent leads to the ridge crest in another 200', where the summit of Peak 1700 is just 0.1 mile ahead (0.4 mile total). Ascent is 230'.

Access. Start just west of the Ak-Chin Ramada, southernmost of the ramadas, or take National Trail [44] from the Quechan Ramada up to the pass in the ridge at 0.1 mile, then turn left, contouring along the western slope.

Read Down ↓	Detailed Trail Description	Read Up ↑
0.00	From Ak-Chin Ramada, ascend W, passing trails of use (elevation 1,370').	0.40
0.18	Switchback to L; ascend steadily up side of ridge..	0.22
0.21	**Junction:** on crest, narrow rough trail L leads to summit [pass first hump in 110', reach Peak 1700 with fine views at 0.28 mi]. To continue, turn R, along ridge	0.19
0.25	Top of hump is just to R.	0.15
0.26	**Junction:** straight ahead is poor trail generally following crest to pass in 420'. Turn L here for main trail, switchbacking down.	0.14
0.31	Level off, turn R (N).	0.09
0.40	**Junction (5-way), in pass** (1,523'): sharp R is poor NDT up crest of ridge to Peak 1700. Ahead is [44] up North Mountain. To L is NDT descending to private land. Go R to reach Quechan Ramada in 0.10 mi, and another 440' to R along park drive to Ak-Chin Ramada at start of this loop.	0.00

[60] Maxine Lakin Nature Trail FROM MOUNTAIN VIEW PARK

General Description. This trail, named for an activist in the Phoenix Mountains Preservation Council and avid equestrian, incorporates a new and some old segments. It leads from Mountain View Park to 0.5 mile, where it turns east to cross a wash and then meet a track heading south. At 0.9 mile it descends steadily to pass the north side of a retention dam and meets the previous trail at 1.1 miles. (The circuit back to Mountain View Park is 1.4 miles.) There are views across the valley toward Shaw Butte.

Access. From Mountain View Park near the Christiansen Monument, walk east on the paved path for 125', turning left for 35' to trail post #1.

Read Down ↓	Detailed Trail Description	Read Up ↑
0.00	Leave Mountain View Park from sidewalk just E of CMC Monument.	1.10
0.22	**Junction (4-way):** R is track 0.29 mi back to Mtn View Park; L goes uphill.	0.88
0.27	**Important junction:** on R is [60] returning; continue straight.	0.83
0.51	Turn R on new trail.	0.59
0.54	Cross small, rocky wash and another wash in 250'.	0.56
0.69	Trail becomes road.	0.41
0.85	**Junction:** on crest, narrow trail ahead leads 195' up hump with viewpoint. Turn R and descend steadily on rocky track.	0.25
0.97	Pass fence on L, level out, passing north of dam.	0.13
1.06	**Junction:** sharp L is trail along top of dam. Bear R.	0.04
1.10	**Junction:** you are now back at [60]. Mountain View Park is 0.27 mi to L.	0.00

[100] Charles M. Christiansen Trail EASTBOUND

MOUNTAIN VIEW PARK TO 7th STREET

General Description. The Christiansen Trail starts at Mountain View Park and leads through a flood works area, following an old road with an ascent of

160' through the wide valley separating North Mountain from Shaw Butte. It intersects many trails along the way, including trail [306] at 0.7 and 0.9 mile. It reaches a major junction with an old vehicleway east toward 7th Street [100A] at 1.4 miles, then at 1.7 miles turns east through a valley to 7th Street Trailhead at 2.1 miles, where this section ends. Total ascent is 160'.

Access. *Western end:* from the park at 7th Avenue. *Eastern end:* from the 7th St. Trailhead on the west side of 7th St.

Read Down ↓	Detailed Trail Description	Read Up ↑
0.00	Leave Mountain View Park (1,290'); head north. Start of trail [60] is E along sidewalk.	2.06
0.02	Monument to Charles M. Christiansen. Continue straight ahead.	2.04
0.15	**Junction:** minor trail to R.	1.91
0.17	**Junction:** wide track enters on L, from 7th Avenue. Bear R here.	1.89
0.30	Enter flood works, with fences on both sides. Old road crosses	1.76
0.63	**Junction:** trail sharp L leads back to Desert Cove Ave. and 7th Ave. in 0.17 mi. Ascend gradually.	1.43
0.70	**Important junction:** in open area, sharp L is the Shaw Butte Trail [306], which joins here (leads 0.51 mi onto road on Shaw Butte).	1.36
0.76	Old gate posts on either side. Ascend.	1.30
0.84	Junction: NDT L to 7th Ave.	1.22
0.92	**Important junction:** Shaw Butte Trail [306] on L (to Central Ave, 1.1 mi).	1.14
1.26	**Junction:** NDT trail on L ends on slopes of Shaw Butte.	0.81
1.36	**Junction:** wide trail [100A] leads R to North Mountain road in 0.57 mi, to 7th Street and to National Trail [44] in 0.7 mi.	0.70
1.43	**Junction:** NDT on R parallels previous trail. Cross wash.	0.63
1.46	**Junction:** road angles off to L.	0.61
1.59	**Junction:** sharp R is a short-cut trail.	0.47
1.61	**Junction:** NDT on L.	0.45
1.65	**Junction:** NDT on R parallels CMC and joins it in 0.17 mi.	0.41
1.67	**Major junction:** *CMC turns R here.* Connecting trail [C] ahead leads to flood works and Central Avenue trailhead via [306] in 0.53 mi.	0.39
1.77	**Junction:** road turns sharp L.	0.30
1.85	**Junction:** trail enters from R at acute angle.	0.21
1.89	**Junction:** wide track leads R and ascends. Descend here.	0.17
1.92	**Junction:** ignore road bearing L.	0.14
1.99	**Junction:** track goes R here. Pass signpost in 90'.	0.07
2.02	**Junction:** trail joins at acute angle on L. Pass trail map in 50'.	0.04
2.04	Gate. 30' beyond, turn L, descend into small wash; road continues ahead.	0.02
2.06	**Junction:** bear R; trail ahead leads 200' to W side of 7th St. & TH.	0.00

[100A] Connector

CHARLES M. CHRISTIANSEN TRAIL [100] to NATIONAL TRAIL [44]

General Description. A short link makes a loop trip possible around or over North Mountain. From the Christiansen Trail [100] an old vehicleway is followed up a valley to the north of North Mountain, reaching a pass at 0.4 mile and then new trail south to the North Mountain road at 0.6 mile, then up that road to meet the National Trail [44] at 0.7 mile. The road can then be followed to the summit or to North Mountain Park on [44].

Access. *From the west:* from the Christiansen Trail at 1.4 miles north of Mountain View Park. *From the east:* from the National Trail [44] 0.2 mile from Maricopa Ramada in North Mountain Park. Ascent is 150'.

Read Down ↓	Detailed Trail Description	Read Up ↑
0.00	Leave CMC [100] at 1.36 mi from Mountain View Park, heading SE.	0.70
0.19	**Junction:** old trail straight ahead closed; go L.	0.51
0.20	Cross wash.	0.50
0.26	Junction: NDT on R closed.	0.44
0.30	Junction: NDT on L closed.	0.40
0.40	Top of rise. Descend.	0.30
0.42	Junction: take new trail to R, away from old vehicleway.	0.28
0.47	Top of rise above cut on 7th St. road alignment.	0.23
0.57	**Junction:** North Mountain Road. Go R for National Trail [44] and North Mountain summit, total of 0.7 mi. To L, road leads down to 7th St. in 0.19 mi.	0.13
0.70	**Junction:** National Trail [44] descends L 0.17 mi to Maricopa Ramada, ascends on this road 0.57 mi to North Mountain's summit.	0.00

Shaw Butte Area

[306] Shaw Butte from Central Avenue

General Description. This circuit trip is the main approach, popular for joggers and local residents walking their dogs as well as for hikers. It is used frequently by service vehicles (move well off the road when they pass, to avoid being hit by flying rocks.) The views from the summit are excellent. First it ascends Shaw Butte to reach a spur road to the summit at $1^1/_4$ miles (total to summit, 1.4 miles). Just beyond, the road reaches the sag between the two summits and turns south, zigzagging down a ridge past the old Cloud 9 site to 1.9 miles, where trail drops into the valley to reach the Christiansen Trail at 2.4 miles. It turns north on that trail to 2.7 miles, where it leaves it to return to this trail (first around a retention dam) at 3.7 miles. Total ascent is about 800'.

Access. From Thunderbird Road drive 0.2 mile south on Central Avenue to its end, where there is an obvious parking area on the right (capacity limited).

Read Down ↓	Detailed Trail Description	Read Up ↑
0.00	Leave gate near end of Central Avenue (elevation 1,390').	3.72
0.03	**Junction (4-way):** on L is this trail returning (0.50 mi to CMC).	3.69
0.11	Road steepens.	3.61
0.25	**Junction:** trail R descends to private land.	3.47
0.27	Hairpin turn to L.	3.45
0.33	Bend to R; grade steepens, paving starts & ends again.	3.39
0.63	Paving ends.	3.09

0.65	**Junction:** track L 575' (100' ascent) to top of hump on ridge (1,890').	3.07
0.69	**Junction:** track L onto crest.	3.03
0.72	**Junction:** track L along crest to hump.	3.00
0.84	**Junction:** ignore old track ascending on L (peters out).	2.88
1.03	**Junction:** at crest (1,980), with views, is trail sharp L onto ridge in 175' and ending in 500'.	2.69
1.23	**Junction** (elev. 2,060'): to L is road spur to summit of highest peak *[details: in 160' rough track diverges to L; in 430' is a junction; a loop road returns on L, go straight 0.13 mi to top and relay towers. On R is black-top area for hanggliders on weekends and viewpoint. Continuing, loop road rejoins at 0.20 mi.]* Continue on main road (paved here), descending.	2.49
1.40	**Junction:** in sag, [A] goes straight, to western summit and Sweetwater.	2.32
1.43	Metal barriers on road.	2.29
1.61	**Junction of roads:** straight ahead, branch road descends to 15th Ave. Keep L.	2.11
1.64	**Junction:** on L is road up to old Cloud 9 Restaurant site; sharp L is steep track toward tower.	2.08
1.87	**Junction:** straight ahead road descends mountain; go sharp L, almost level, on branch of road.	1.85
1.93	**Junction:** where road [B] turns R to descend mountain (0.41 mi to 15th Ave.), go sharp L (E), descending on trail.	1.79
2.09	**Junction:** old road ascends valley to L; sharp R is road descending toward housing development; go half-R, descending.	1.63
2.18	Pass track on R, bear L to **junction:** track R descends to valley. Ascend.	1.54
2.20	**Junction:** NDT on L.	1.52
2.24	**Junction:** at top of rise, trail R leads 175' to viewpoint. Descend steeply.	1.48
2.37	**Junction (4-way):** track R to 7th Ave.; track L to CMC in 0.22 mi. Continue straight, cross major wash.	1.35
2.44	**Important junction:** CMC [100]. To R, Mountain View Park is 0.7 mi; turn L, joining CMC here.	1.28
2.50	Old gate posts on both sides. Ascend.	1.22
2.62	**Junction:** old road joins on L.	1.10
2.66	**Important junction:** where CMC continues, this trail bears L, descending.	1.06
2.70	Cross moderate wash.	1.02
2.75	Cross moderate wash.	0.97
2.92	Junction: closed NDT on R.	0.80
3.10	**Junction:** turn sharp and descend vehicleway.	0.62
3.13	Turn L, level out.	0.59
3.16	Junction: NDT (closed) on R.	0.56
3.51	**Important junction:** connector [C] to CMC [100] sharp R (0.32 mi).	0.21
3.56	Dam on R.	0.16
3.72	**Junction:** this segment meets [306], Shaw Butte Road, back at start. Central Ave. Trailhead is just to R.	0.00

[A] Shaw Butte from Sweetwater

General Description. This narrow, unmaintained trail is hard to see at either end. It can be used as part of a circuit trip by taking [306] up the Butte and walking the roads (Sweetwater to Thunderbird, then Central back to the start, about 1.7 miles). There are good views and the way is easy. Ascent is 660'.

Access. *From the bottom:* head south from Sweetwater, just east of the Fraternal Order of Police building, picking up the trail ahead. *From the top:* at the sag on the ridge, at 1.4 miles on [306]. Once reaching the western summit, be sure to head for the power poles descending the broad ridge to pick up the trail heading west.

Read Down ↓	Detailed Trail Description	Read Up ↑
0.00	From Sweetwater Rd. just E of Fraternal Order of Police building and its parking area (1,300') head S without defined trail, crossing track that parallels Sweetwater Sweetwater toward first power pole.	0.98
0.01	**Junction (4-way):** cross track parallelling Sweetwater (parking area to E).	0.97
0.17	**Junction:** trail on R leads to FOP building (private land). Ascend.	0.81
0.20	**Junction:** at crest, switchback to L. End of ridge is 250' to R.	0.78
0.23	Jog R & L, off of crest, descending gradually. Use care. Another trail is below.	0.75
0.26	**Junction:** to L is pass and 150' further N is top of bump on ridge. Turn R here.	0.72
0.31	**Junction:** trail of use enters on R (leads down draw, to private land). Ascend.	0.67
0.37	**Junction:** spur trail R 45' to hump on ridge. Turn L here, up crest, then keep L of crest in 65'.	0.63
0.43	Sag in ridge. Keep to R of rocks ahead.	0.55
0.44	Ascend twisting route up ridge, which broadens. *Use care finding trail.*	0.54
0.46	Steadier ascent begins.	0.52
0.72	Cross under power line; follow it generally SE to a track.	0.26
0.77	**Junction:** end of road loop on western summit of Shaw Butte (1,960'). From here it is 1.4 mi to Central Avenue, 0.78 mi to 15th Ave. via [306] & [B]. Keep L, pass windsocks, then pass tower on L.	0.21
0.80	**Junction:** on R is crossover to other side of road loop.	0.18
0.86	Tower on L.	0.12
0.89	**Junction:** on R is end of road loop. Descend.	0.09
0.98	**Junction:** in sag on ridge, [306] goes R to CMC in 1.04 mi; straight ahead to Central Ave. trailhead in 1.40 mi. (Elevation 1,900').	0.00

[B] Shaw Butte from 15th Avenue

General Description. Access from the south consists of an old way to the defunct Cloud 9 restaurant site (now on [306]). There are some good views. The rocky road ascends steeply for 0.2 mile to a junction. Here an alternate diverges west. Going right, there is soon another alternate. Taking the longer route, the road reaches a junction with [306] at 0.4 mile, where this segment ends. One can continue on [306] past the Cloud 9 site in another 0.3 mile (total of 0.6 mile), reaching the service road between the summits in a further ¼ mile, for a total of 0.8 mile. From that junction, either branch road can be taken to Shaw Butte's summits (0.3 mile to right to the highest, a total of 1.1 miles; or 0.2 mile to the left to the western summit on [A], a total of 1.1 miles).

Access. Drive east on Desert Cove Avenue from 19th Avenue for 0.4 mile to 15th Avenue, then left (north) on it, to its end at a barrier at 0.7 mile.

Read Down ↓	Detailed Trail Description	Read Up ↑
0.00	Leave 15th Avenue at barrier, ascending steeply (1,390').	0.41
0.18	**Junction of roads:** alternate (western) road ascends sharp L, 0.43 mi to [306] ahead. Go straight.	0.23

0.22	**Junction:** where short-cut goes sharp L (steeper, 0.13 mi shorter), bear slightly L for main route, ascending steadily.	0.19
0.41	**Junction:** at switchback, on R, trail [306] descends to CMC in 0.51 mi.	0.00

[C] Connector

CHARLES M. CHRISTIANSEN TRAIL [100] to SHAW BUTTE TRAIL [306]

The old route of the Shaw Butte Trail runs from the Christiansen Trail [100] where it turns east toward 7th St. across the valley, past the retention dam to join the new alignment of the Shaw Butte Trail [306] at 0.3 mile.

Read Down ↓	Detailed Trail Description	Read Up ↑
0.00	**Junction:** CMC turns R here (0.48 mi to 7th St.). Go straight (1,390').	0.32
0.04	**Junction:** trail R leads back to Central Avenue.	0.28
0.09	**Junction:** trail R is short-cut over dam (not much shorter). Keep L around flood works, then head E.	0.23
0.22	Bottom of descent in wash. Dam ahead.	0.10
0.30	**Junction:** track R to top of retention dam (short-cut). Turn L.	0.02
0.32	**Junction:** [306] enters from L. Ahead, junction with Shaw Butte road is 0.18 mi, Central Ave. Trailhead is 0.21 mi.	0.00

Shaw Butte from Mountain View Park

City of Phoenix

Shadow Mountain

Lookout Mtn from above reservoir on Shadow Mountain

Introduction. Shadow Mountain is an unofficial name applied to an isolated group of summits east of Lookout Mountain. The mountain has three parts. On the north is a rounded low summit 1,779' high, here designated "Peak 1779." The north peak is the highest and steepest, "Peak 1928." It has a steep-sided ridge trending south, leading to a 1,670' pass. Furthest to the south is the south summit, "Peak 1845." All offer good views of the valley and other nearby mountains. Ascents are 280' to 450', but some are quite steep for short distances. ("Peak 1928" on the topo map has been re-measured at 1926.5'.)

Maps. *Our map 4.* The USGS 1:24,000 Sunnyslope quadrangle (1965, photorevised in 1982) shows the topography, but none of the trails.

Access. There are several neighborhood access points: (1) from the reservoir access road east of Cave Creek Road; (2) three neighborhood trails off Avenue Joan d'Arc (north of 24th Street and Sweetwater) on the southeast; (3) a trail off 26th Place and Rue de l'Amour; (4) at the northwest corner of the area at Cave Creek Road; and a new legal access point at the corner of 25th Place and Acoma.

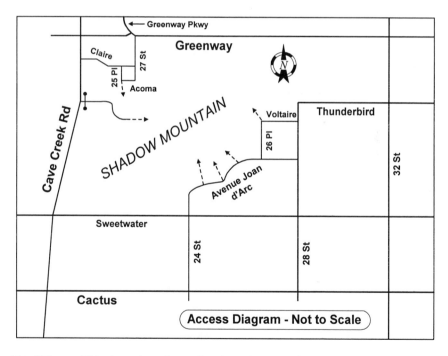

Facilities. This is a largely undeveloped area of the Phoenix Mountains Preserve: there are no ramadas, toilets, water fountains, or trail signs (there is one fountain on the north side as of November 1999). Trails close at sunset, parks at 11:00 p.m.

Recommended Hikes and Trail Rides. Indicator letters and names used are our own. No trail is presently designated or maintained, though a Master Plan is being developed, as it has been for other areas of the Preserve. A circumference trail [310] is planned, using some of the segments here, possibly with new trail construction. The area is so criss-crossed with trails and 4-wheel drive tracks that full description of all of them would only be confusing. We have therefore chosen a few logical sequences and destinations and indicated the short links from each of these to other trails. Most trails on the east slope of "Peak 1928" are in poor condition. Several trails receive frequent horse usage, especially parts of the Perimeter North [G] and Perimeter South [H] Trails.

Cautions. Preserve land often does not extend to the adjacent roads. This has resulted in trails that lead almost all the way around the recreation area, partly on private but still undeveloped land; access may be denied at any time by sign-posting or actual development. (Some of this land may be acquired subsequently for the Preserve.) Although our general policy is not to describe trails that cross private land, in this instance we have included some such trails where there is no current substitute. This has been indicated both on the map and in the text. *Be prepared to alter your plans if access is denied.* (Note: the Preserve boundary shown on the map is only approximate.)

In several locations trails have deteriorated and a double trail has resulted, with the lower of the two usually having less loose rock. The mountains in this area have steep slopes with tilted rock strata (shale) resulting in sharp-pointed rocks that can make a fall hazardous. The ridge of "Peak 1928" is especially steep, as is "Peak 1845" on the east side. Old four wheel drive tracks on the east-facing slopes are often steep and slippery on the descent.

[A] "Peak 1928" via Reservoir

General Description. A paved road ascends 0.4 mile to a covered reservoir and trail junction. From there a trail leads up to the ridge at 0.6 mile and a narrower trail then leads onto the summit at 0.7 mile. Ascent is 440'.

Access. On Cave Creek Road ¼ mile north of Sharon Drive, this gated, narrow paved road heads east. There is no parking along the shoulder of Cave Creek Road.

Read Down ↓	Detailed Trail Description	Read Up ↑
0.00	Leave Cave Creek Road at gate (elevation 1,490').	0.65
0.03	**Junction:** in open area on L, trail [G] leads N.	0.62
0.07	**Junction:** trail [G] on R; departure point is unclear in open area.	0.58
0.22	**Junction:** Shed on L. Poor old roads ascend slope on R.	0.43
0.30	Huge reservoir tank on L. Fence starts – keep to R (outside it).	0.35
0.36	**Junction:** trail ascends steeply on R (elev. 1,620'). (Fence ends on L in 310'; no trail beyond at that point.)	0.29
0.42	**Junction:** trail [B] on R (leads 0.10 mi to ridge, 0.24 mi to summit). Bear L, ascend.	0.23

0.45	**Junction:** narrow trail L [E] along ridge to "Peak 1779" in 0.10 mi. Continue on old road on a level grade.	0.20
0.53	Turn R, ascend.	0.12
0.57	**Junction (4-way):** at crest of ridge (1,620'), trail L and straight is Perimeter Trail North [G]. Go R, along crest.	0.08
0.63	**Junction:** [C] enters on L. Final ascent begins along crest to summit.	0.03
0.65	*Summit* (USGS bench mark here indicates 1926.5'). Trail ahead along ridge is [B]. Good views.	0.00

[B] "Peak 1928" via Reservoir (Alternate)

Follow [A] to 0.4 mile. At the junction (0.0 mile), ascend to the right on a good trail. Reach a junction at the crest at 0.1 mile (ahead 110' is another junction — a good horse trail descends to the south to join the Ridge Trail [F], and straight ahead a trail leads 480' along the crest, then descends 0.1 mile further to join the Perimeter North Trail [G]). From the junction, head east to 0.1 mile where [F] enters on the right, then to the summit at ¼ mile, where it meets [A] again. Ascent is the same as [A], or 440' from Cave Creek Road. Total distance from Cave Creek Road is 0.7 mile.

[C] "Peak 1928" from the East

General Description. Another (shorter) way to reach the summit ascends to a low pass, then attacks the summit ridge to 0.3 mile. Total ascent is 390'.

Access. From 26th Place where it bends east to become Rue de l'Amour. There is very limited parking along the road.

Read Down ↓	Detailed Trail Description	Read Up ↑
0.00	Leave bend where 26th Place becomes Rue de l'Amour, ascending between private homes.	0.29
0.05	**Junction:** trail R leads up, past a home, reaching another trail in 415'.	0.24
0.12	**Junction (4-way):** narrow trail to R [G] descends for 460' to a junction. On L, horse trail [G] ascends 550' to Ridge Trail [F]. Continue ascent.	0.17
0.21	**Junction:** in pass, a small hump is a 40' steep scramble to R, where a poor trail descends to E. Turn L here and ascend steadily.	0.08
0.25	Come out onto rocks, continuing steep ascent.	0.04
0.27	Ridge crest. In 30', reach **junction** with [A]. Go L on it to reach summit.	0.02
0.29	*Summit.* Ahead is [B] along crest (0.24 mi to [A], 0.66 mi to Cave Creek Rd).	0.00

[D] "Peak 1845" from the Southeast

General Description. "Peak 1845" can be reached by the Ridge Trail [F] from the north; this is an alternate. A climb of only 0.3 mile leads to fine views, but note that sections are quite steep. Total ascent is 350'.

Access. From Avenue Joan d'Arc 350' east of its start at 24th Street, take the trail north, uphill.

Read Down ↓	Detailed Trail Description	Read Up ↑
0.00	Leave Avenue Joan d'Arc (limited road-side parking); take trail N (1,500').	0.31
0.04	**Junction:** Perimeter Trail South [H]; go L on it. (To R, roundabout route to summit of "Peak 1845" takes 0.41 mi.)	0.27
0.09	**Junction (4-way):** go R (trail L to private land; trail straight ahead is Perimeter Trail South [H]). Ascend steeply with some loose rock.	0.22
0.17	**Junction:** trail on L descends to [H]; continue ascent.	0.14
0.25	**Junction:** ignore poor trail on R.	0.06
0.26	**Junction:** trail bearing L bypasses summit, leads to [F].	0.05
0.29	**Junction:** trail joins on L; go R, switchbacking up ridge. (L descends 50' to junction, then goes R 435' to connect with Ridge Trail [F].)	0.02
0.31	**Junction on crest at "Peak 1845":** R leads along bumps on ridge for 385', then ends. L (N) is Ridge Trail [F] to "Peak 1928" (0.57 mi away).	0.00

[E] "Peak 1779"

Follow [A] to ½ mile from Cave Creek Road, where this trail (much narrower) diverges to the left (northwest) on an easy grade. Ignore a poor trail to the right at 250'. Reach the crest of the connecting ridge at 410' and the summit at 0.1 mile. Ascent is 80'.

[F] Ridge Trail NORTH to SOUTH

General Description. "Peak 1928" is connected to "Peak 1845" (on its south) by a steep-sided ridge with several passes or sags. Use care – some sections are quite steep. Ascent is 200'.

Access. From the crest of "Peak 1928," 0.1 mile west of the summit.

Read Down ↓	Detailed Trail Description	Read Up ↑
0.00	Leave [B] on crest of "Peak 1928," 0.11 mi to W of summit. Descend to S. Short-cut trail from [B] soon enters on L.	0.43
0.05	**Junction:** poor trail on L ascends back up ridge crest.	0.38
0.08	**Junction:** horse trail enters R from ridge.	0.35
0.09	**Junction (4-way):** Perimeter North Trail [G] L & R in pass. Ascend to S.	0.34
0.13	**Junction:** trail splits; go either way.	0.30
0.16	**Junction:** branches rejoin.	0.27
0.18	**Junction:** in sag, wide, steep track descends L & R (both very poor). Ascend over hump.	0.25
0.23	**Junction:** poor track descends on L. Descend.	0.20
0.26	**Junction (4-way):** rocky track crosses (Perimeter South Trail [H] descends R for 0.17 mi to church; on L, [H] leads to Avenue Joan d'Arc in 0.15 mi).	0.17
0.29	**Junction:** trail S joins Perimeter South [H] in 385'.	0.13
0.34	**Junction:** poor track descends to R, then another within 40'.	0.09

0.36	**Junction:** trail ahead to [D] in 435' (0.08 mi).	0.07
0.38	Reach crest; continue SW on it.	0.04
0.43	**Junction at "Peak 1845":** straight ahead 385' leads over bumps on crest and ends; to R is [D], 0.31 mi to Avenue Joan d'Arc.	0.00

[G] Perimeter North Trail COUNTERCLOCKWISE

General Description. Around the northern section of the recreation area is a network of trails. This one encounters the least private land and connects with many others leading to ridges and makes possible several circuit trips around "Peak 1928" for a total of 1.9 miles. There are two ascents of about 200' each.

Access. On the east side of Cave Creek Road; park off the road shoulder, taking a spur trail heading southeast for 200' to the main trail. This trail can also be reached from the new trailhead at 25th Place & Acoma.

Read Down ↓	Detailed Trail Description	Read Up ↑
0.00	Leave spur trail junction 200' from Cave Creek Road, heading counter-clockwise (1,480'). Parallel Cave Creek Road (private land here).	1.86
0.34	**Junction:** turn L (E) on paved reservoir access road [A] just E of gate.	1.57
0.41	**Junction:** leave paved road to SW over E end of large cleared area with trail route not distinct at first (if you go too far, the cleared area ends — go back).	1.45
0.43	**Junction:** before open area ends, bear slightly L on narrower trail, crossing slopes to S.	1.43
0.67	**Junction:** join track that runs E-W. Parallel church parking area to S.	1.19
0.73	**Junction:** wide, steep, rocky track to L ascends past barrier to ridge in 0.13 mi, joins [B] there at 0.22 mi (0.38 mi total to "Peak 1928"). Turn R (S) here.	1.13
0.78	**Junction:** trail ahead is Perimeter South Trail [H]. Turn L, ascending (also Perimeter South Trail here).	1.08
0.84	**Junction:** turn L, ascend (Perimeter Trail South turns R). Parallel wash; take lower of two trails where it splits.	1.02
0.96	**Junction (4-way):** cross Ridge Trail [F]; descend with lower of two alternate routes the better one.	0.90
1.06	**Junction (4-way):** [C] crosses; R 0.12 mi to Avenue Joan d'Arc. Continue on narrower trail.	0.80
1.15	**Junction (4-way):** poor track ascends on L and descends on R (in 40' keep straight where steep track descends R to private land).	0.71
1.20	**Junction:** wide track on R descends 350' to valley and junction where trails lead E to private land.	0.67
1.22	**Junction:** narrow trail ascends L to ridge crest and [A].	0.65
1.26	**Junction:** trail R leads to private land. Continue straight.	0.60
1.29	**Junction:** trail R descends 435' to junction to private land.	0.57
1.31	**Junction:** trail R toward private land; bear L.	0.55
1.34	**Junction (4-way):** [A] ahead to Cave Creek Road in 0.57 mi; sharp L to "Peak 1928" in 0.52 mi. Turn sharp R here onto wide track on ridge.	0.52
1.38	**Junction:** trail sharp R to hump (1,693') in 460'; several trails to private land. Turn L here, descending.	0.48

1.62	**Junction:** main trail in open area; go L here (R to private land).	0.24
1.65	**Junction:** trail on R is new access to 25th Way & Acoma (0.1 mi).	0.21
1.86	**Junction:** spur trail R leads 200' to Cave Creek Road (back at start).	0.00

[H] Perimeter Trail South COUNTERCLOCKWISE

General Description. This description starts arbitrarily at the northernmost spur to Avenue Joan d'Arc, counterclockwise to lead near "Peak 1845." Ascent is about 250' around the flanks of "Peak 1845" for a total of 0.9 mile.

Access. Start from Avenue Joan d'Arc near where it bends to the east, ascending a steep, rocky trail. In 75' a short-cut leads southwest 315' to the Perimeter South Trail [H] southbound. Continue to 265' to intersect [H].

Read Down ↓	Detailed Trail Description	Read Up ↑
0.00	Leave 4-way **junction** heading N on narrower trail. Wider track (slightly L) leads 385' to Ridge Trail [F]. (This section is frequently used by horses.)	0.90
0.09	**Junction (4-way):** in sag, Ridge Trail [F] to R heads N, and to L to "Peak 1845" in 0.17 mi. Continue straight ahead, descending wide, rocky track.	0.81
0.14	**Junction:** poor track ascends R to ridge. Continue rocky descent.	0.76
0.20	**Junction:** sharp R is Perimeter North Trail [G]. Join it, bearing L.	0.70
0.26	**Junction:** at church parking area, Perimeter North Trail heads N. Turn sharp L here, paralleling parking area.	0.64
0.30	**Junction:** where poor track bears L, bear R across open area, then toward church itself on narrower trail, paralleling parking area.	0.60
0.42	**Junction:** where wide track continues ahead, turn L (S) onto narrower trail.	0.48
0.51	**Junction:** where trail continues R, toward area being developed, bear L on narrower trail, ascending.	0.39
0.55	**Junction:** trail joins from R.	0.35
0.56	**Junction (4-way):** trail to R goes up, then down to area being developed in 200'; to L, trail ascends 530' to [D] on ridge.	0.34
0.65	**Junction:** trail L is [D] up "Peak 1845" in 0.27 mi. Descend.	0.25
0.70	**Junction:** on R is [D] leading 195' down to Avenue Joan d'Arc.	0.20
0.79	**Junction:** spur trail R 220' to Avenue Joan d'Arc.	0.12
0.86	**Junction:** short-cut R 315' to 75' spur trail to Avenue Joan d'Arc. Ascend.	0.04
0.90	**Junction:** back at starting point: R leads down 340' to Avenue Joan d'Arc.	0.00

City of Phoenix

Squaw Peak Area

On the Quartz Ridge Trail

Introduction. Squaw Peak (2,608') is the highest point in the Phoenix Mountains Preserve[1]. Its views are superb. The Summit Trail is one of the nation's most popular hikes, but there are many other attractive options. Many subsidiary peaks, humps and valleys have good trails, so that much variety is available for the hiker and trail rider. The Charles M. Christiansen Trail passes through the northern section.

History. Squaw Peak's name was conferred by Dr. O. A. Turney in 1910. Originally the area was used for grazing and mining. The City of Phoenix obtained a long-term lease on it from the State in 1959.

Geology. Much of this area's rock is a metamorphic type of granite known as *schist*. The mountain tops are relatively young, poking up above the valley floors, covered with varying layers of material eroded from the summits. There is no gold in the area, but many old prospect holes and pits give evidence of past mining activity. Mercury (cinnabar) mines worked in the early 1900s are alleged to have resulted in the name "Dreamy" Draw from its mental effects. Kyenite (a combination of schist and quartz) was mined during World War II. You will find many examples of *desert varnish* on rocks.

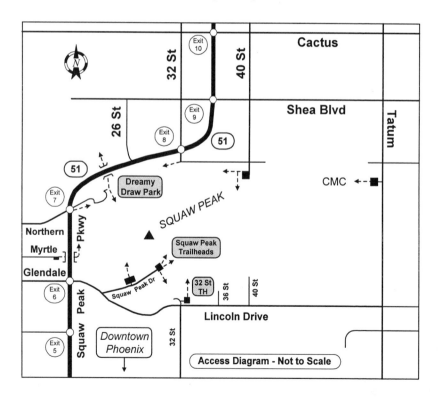

---

[1]Camelback is the highest peak in the Phoenix Mountains, but is not in the Preserve.

Maps. *Our maps 7-8.* The USGS 1:24,000 Sunnyslope quadrangle (1965, photorevised 1982) shows a few of the trails and old roads.

Access. There are 11 main access points *arranged clockwise* from (1) Squaw Peak Drive (6 separate points); (2) 22nd St., (3) the Arizona Canal at 16th St., and Myrtle Trailhead [Perl Charles Trail]; (4) from E. Pleasant Drive through the tunnel under Squaw Peak Parkway; (5) Dreamy Draw (5 separate points); (6) 32nd St. & Dunlap, (7) 38th St. & Dunlap; (8) 40th St.; (9) Tatum Boulevard; (10) 36th St. and Lincoln Drive; and (11) 32nd St. and Lincoln Drive. *Each of these access points is a separate section in this chapter.* See the **index** below to find trails. Remember: trails close at sunset.

In the detailed trail descriptions, "TH" = trailhead, "NDT" = non-designated trail, "PC" = Perl Charles Trail, "CMC" = Charles M. Christiansen Trail.

Index. The trail descriptions are organized around "access points," clockwise from Squaw Peak Drive. (Some trails deep in the area are included under the section on the Perl Charles [1A] *"PC,"* or Charles M. Christiansen Trails [100] *"CMC."*) *All trails are indexed below:*

Trail	Access Point	Page	Trail	Access Point	Page
[1A] PC Trail	AZ Canal/Myrtle	72	[300A] Alt	Squaw Peak Dr	68
[1A] PC Trail	E Pleasant Dr	73	[302]	Squaw Peak Dr	68
[8] Quartz	Squaw Peak Dr	64	[304] Nature	Squaw Peak Dr	69
[8A]	32 St & Lincoln	81	[A]	38 St	78
[8B] Ruth Hamilton Tr	Squaw Peak Dr	65	[B]	40 St	78
[100] (CMC)	Dreamy Draw; Tatum;	74, 80	[C]	36 St extension	81
[200]	Squaw Peak Dr	66	[D]	40th St	79
[200A]	Squaw Peak Dr	66	[E] Bikeway	(See Dreamy Draw)	77
[220]	Dreamy Draw	76	[F]	(See Dreamy Draw)	78
[220A]	Dreamy Draw	76	LV Yates Trail	40 St	79
[300] Summit	Squaw Peak Dr	67			

Facilities. Squaw Peak Drive is reached from Lincoln Drive between 16th and 24th Streets. It gives access to 17 ramadas, a ranger station, restrooms, and trails. Picnic ramadas serve up to 600, with electricity, drinking water, and firepits (8 ramadas first-come, 9 reserved). Facility hours are 5:30 a.m. through 11:00 p.m. (Dreamy Draw at 10:00 p.m.) Trails close at sunset.

Recommended Hikes. Trail indicators used here are either official numbers, or our own arbitrary letters for unnumbered but designated trails.

Despite the Trail Ordinance, heavy usage in some areas has led to a proliferation of undesignated trails. We have simplified this network, showing and describing all designated trails (some others are shown in BLACK) for location purposes only. Changes are still taking place.

The immensely popular Squaw Peak Summit Trail [300] is 1.2 miles long (ascent of 1,190'). It was extensively renovated in 1993. Good views can be obtained at points along the ridge without having to proceed all the way to the summit. The less crowded Circumference Trail [302] starts from the Summit Trail and leads all the way around the mountain over four passes (a long, strenuous trip). There is a Nature Trail [304] from the end of Squaw Peak Drive and one [220] from Dreamy Draw, with an associated shorter Children's Nature Loop [220A]. The Quartz Ridge Trail [8] leads from the Squaw Peak Nature Trail to the Charles M. Christiansen Trail and 40th Street through an attractive area. From the south side of the drive, short trails such as the Mohave [200] ascend the lower peaks which offer close-up views of Squaw Peak. These are linked up with various other segments. The Ruth Hamilton Trail [8A] links the trailhead at 32nd St. and Lincoln Drive with the Quartz Ridge Trail [8]. Trail [8B] descends to [304] near Squaw Peak Drive.

The easiest access to good views is from the end of 22nd Street north of Glendale. This is also a short-cut onto the Circumference Trail without climbing over Squaw Peak's ridge. From the north, there is good access from several points.

Important Note. The Squaw Peak Parkway (SR 51) has been completed through Dreamy Draw. Parking is not allowed on the road shoulder; only official access points can be used. The Myrtle Trailhead adjacent to the Perl Charles Trail [1A] provides another main access point, especially for equestrians. The three new trail tunnels under the Parkway are wider and have much better lighting than prior to the freeway completion.

Squaw Peak Drive Access Points

[8] Quartz Ridge Trail SOUTH to NORTH

General Description. From the pass north of the end of Squaw Peak Drive on the Nature Trail [304] at 0.4 mile, the Quartz Ridge Trail descends a valley, then crosses the divide between two major washes and heads east to a junction with [8A] at 1 mile. Here it turns north, ascending to a pass at 1.1 miles. It then makes a long descent past a quartz outcrop to reach the Charles M. Christiansen Trail at 2 miles, continuing ½ mile further to 40th St. Trailhead. Total ascent is 220'.

Access. *From the south:* take the Nature Trail [304] from the end of Squaw Peak Drive for 0.4 mile to the pass. This trail starts just 30' beyond, angling off to the right. *From the north:* at the northwest end of 40th St. Trailhead, 1 mile south of Shea Boulevard, descend to a wash; follow the wash to the left.

Read Down ↓	Detailed Trail Description	Read Up ↑
0.00	Leave Nature Trail [304] just 30' N of pass.	2.51
0.43	**Junction:** half-L is spur 100' to old vehicleway.	2.08
0.53	**Junction:** join old road on L, head E.	1.98
0.65	**Junction:** old road sharp L. Follow it to R.	1.86
0.74	**Junction:** sharp L is crossover across wash 250' to another road.	1.77

0.75	Turn R in wash, following it.	1.76
0.77	**Junction:** trail R is [8A] heading S to [8B] in 0.6 mi. Continue in wash, then ascend R, out of it.	1.74
0.95	**Junction:** old track sharp L.	1.56
1.01	**Junction:** vehicleway [C] on R (leads S to 36th St. in 0.62 mi). Turn sharp L.	1.50
1.06	Road ends; descend on trail briefly.	1.45
1.08	Ascend, level off briefly in 100'.	1.43
1.19	Pass (1,860'). Good views, especially off trail to E.	1.32
1.24	**Junction:** trail splits, alternate on R.	1.27
1.29	Cross wash.	1.22
1.30	**Junction:** alternate rejoins on R. Pass field of cactus.	1.21
1.50	Cross small wash.	1.01
1.54	Approach wash; reach level area along it on L in 150'.	0.97
1.65	**Junction:** NDT half-L.	0.86
1.68	Flat area.	0.83
1.69	**Junction:** NDT on R leads to LV Yates Trail.	0.82
2.01	**Junction:** CMC L & R. To R it is only 390' to the junction with LV Yates Trail and main trail to Tatum Blvd.	0.50
2.25	Turn L (W), then R (N) in 220'.	0.26
0.36	Cross wash.	0.15
0.41	**Junction:** trail of use to L.	0.10
0.44	Follow wash to L.	0.07
2.47	**Junction:** join trail [B] from L; go R, uphill.	0.04
2.51	**Junction:** NW corner of 40th St. Trailhead.	0.00

[8B] Ruth Hamilton Trail   WEST to EAST

General Description. This trail was rebuilt in 1996 and was named after Ruth Hamilton, one of the dedicated volunteers of the Phoenix Mountains Preservation Council whose efforts to sustain the Preserve have been tireless. There is a monument to her at the eastern end of the trail. From the Nature Trail [304] it climbs steadily 380' in 0.4 mile to a pass with good views, then descends steeply to a junction with trail [8A] at ½ mile and to 36th St. at 0.9 mile. (Total ascent is 200' going from east to west.)

Access. *From the west,* at 0.1 mile on the Nature Trail [304] just north of the end of Squaw Peak Drive. *From the east,* from the gate on the extension of 36th St.

Read Down ↓	Detailed Trail Description	Read Up ↑
0.00	From [304] 0.13 mi N of Squaw Peak Drive, at post, head SE, ascending.	0.88
0.04	Switchback to R.	0.84
0.06	**Junction:** NDT on L.	0.82
0.08	Sag in ridge, top of rise. Ascend.	0.80
0.12	Ascend steadily over rocks to L of crest.	0.76
0.15	Ease grade of ascent.	0.73
0.27	Top of rise. Descend briefly.	0.61
0.29	Cross small wash; ascend steadily.	0.59
0.39	Very steep pitch up rocks. Use care.	0.49
0.41	Ease grade.	0.47

0.44   Top of rise, pass. Just before pass, avoid NDT sharp L. Descend. 0.44
0.53   **Junction:** trail [8A] R 1.17 mi to Lincoln Drive, L to Quartz Trail [8]. Ascend. 0.35
0.88   **Junction:** paved road L & R (1,750'). 0.00

[200] Mohave Trail

General Description. Access to several scenic areas is possible from this short trail leading up the ridge south of Squaw Peak. The views of Squaw Peak are very fine. Ascent is 270'.

Access. Leave Mohave Ramada (off Squaw Peak Drive at 0.8 mile) near its eastern end. Use care because of several alternate routes and steep slopes.

Read Down ↓	Detailed Trail Description	Read Up ↑
0.00	Leave Mohave Ramada (paved loop off Squaw Peak Drive, elevation 1,500'), ascending S from upper ramada.	0.38
0.08	**Junction:** on R is NDT back to Mohave Ramada in 0.08 mi. From this point ascent eases as trail contours around minor 1,700' summit.	0.30
0.09	**Junction:** spur on L leads in 200' to trail [200A]. Above are very sharp rock formations. Side-hill the mountain with very good views of Squaw Peak.	0.29
0.21	**Junction (4-way):** in pass (1,610'), NDTs L & R. To continue up Peak 1788, cross pass, bear slightly L (W) and up, keeping to L of crest.	0.17
0.24	**Junction:** alternate trail rejoins.	0.14
0.29	Switchback to R (*use care*, trail appears to continue ahead, but ends).	0.09
0.32	Switchback to L at crest. (NDT on R descends.)	0.06
0.37	**Junction:** this trail turns R. (Wide trail ahead here leads onto flat area.)	0.01
0.38	**Junction:** narrow trail ahead leads toward actual summit (can be scrambled up); trail to L on flat leads 40' to hitching post.	0.00

[200A]

General Description. From the Mohave Ramada there is a brief, steep ascent southeast for 0.1 mile to a pass, then a descent into a valley and a sidehilling around the mountain's base to 0.4 mile, where the trail starts an ascent to reach another pass at 0.8 mile. A brief, steady drop then terminates at [8A] at almost 1 mile.

Access. *From the west,* at Mohave Ramada, Squaw Peak Drive. *From the east,* from [8A] ¼ mile north of the trailhead at 32nd Street and Lincoln Drive. Total ascent is 250'

Read Down ↓	Detailed Trail Description	Read Up ↑
0.00	Leave Mohave Ramada (paved loop off Squaw Peak Drive, elevation 1,500'), ascending S from upper ramada.	0.95
0.09	**Junction:** in pass (1,630'), NDT L, spur 200' R to trail [200]. Descend 100' into valley ahead.	0.86
0.15	**Junction:** NDT on R. Keep L going S along base of mountain.	0.80

0.37	**Junction:** NDT ascends on L.	0.58
0.72	**Junction:** NDT R to private land. Go sharp L here, rising 100'	0.23
0.82	**Junction:** in pass (1,600'), NDT ascends L. Start steady 160' descent to E.	0.13
0.95	**Junction:** this trail ends at [8A] (1,420'). To R, it is 0.23 mi to 32nd St. TH at Lincoln Drive.	0.00

[300] Squaw Peak Summit Trail

General Description. The popularity of this trail is legendary. Hundreds of hikers and runners use it every day, thousands on weekends. (Trail rehabilitation was completed in 1993, with some sections paved and others with retaining walls.) The trail starts from either end of the parking area, or from the first parking area nearer to the Alternate Summit Trail; a sign indicates the park rules. Switchbacks are numerous. At ¼ mile the crest of the first ridge is reached and a junction with side-trails (one to a hump on the ridge, the other [300A] returns to Squaw Peak Drive). From here the trail swings from one to the other side of the ridge, reaching a major junction at 0.6 mile where the Circumference Trail [302] descends north. The crest becomes rougher, with frequent steep rock bluffs so that the trail only occasionally crosses it. Steepness increases after 0.9 mile, with occasional handrails. At 1.1 miles the grade steepens and finally a notch is reached. To the left is the peak usually climbed; to the right, a scramble leads to the true summit, both at 1.2 miles from the start. Views are fantastic! Ascent is 1,210'.

Access. After entering the Recreation Area on Squaw Peak Drive, take the first major left turn (spur road) to the parking area. The prominent trail leaves either end.

Read Down ↓	Detailed Trail Description	Read Up ↑
0.00	Leave parking area at sign (1,400').	1.20
0.04	**Junction:** trail from E end of parking area joins from R.	1.16
0.13	Switchback to R, then to L.	1.07
0.18	Viewpoint (1,500'). Turn R (N).	1.02
0.24	**Junction:** trail L [300A] descends side-valley to return to Squaw Peak Drive and main TH 0.51 mi (it also intersects previous trail to hump on ridge).	0.96
0.27	Switchback to L.	0.94
0.29	Turn R, onto ridge, then R again.	0.92
0.32	First of 4 switchbacks in next 250'.	0.89
0.41	Switchback to L (SW). Elevation 1,700'.	0.80
0.43	**Junction:** reach subsidiary ridge crest; short trail to L leads to rocky outcrop. Turn R here, then bear L.	0.77
0.48	Level area on crest; in 150' switchback to R (N).	0.73
0.57	**Junction (4-way):** Circumference Trail [302] drops to L. Sharp L is old trail down to Circumference Trail (avoid it). Elevation 1,890'.	0.63
0.60	First of 6 switchbacks in next 0.11 mi.	0.60
0.72	Reach crest just N of outcrop, then drop over side, following ridge to W of it.	0.49
0.86	Switchback to R over to crest, then zigzag up.	0.34
0.90	Brief level area on crest (2,190'), with tree providing some shade.	0.30
0.92	Switchback to R (SE), then L, then R. Continuous steep switchbacks beyond. ...	0.28

0.98	Reach crest (2,270').	0.22
1.02	Switchback to L, between rocks.	0.18
1.04	Railing on R. Good views.	0.17
1.07	Switchback to R (E), then to L, with railing.	0.13
1.09	On crest, switchback to R. Grade eases.	0.11
1.10	Switchback to L.	0.11
1.11	Reach crest again, head N. Grade eases.	0.09
1.14	Final ascent begins over very steep rocks. *Use care*.	0.06
1.19	Notch between two summits. Turn L for one usually ascended.	0.01
1.20	*North Summit, Squaw Peak* (2,580'). For highest (S) summit (2,608'), head SE from notch, descending on E side of crest, then cautiously work your way up to the peak over sharp rocks.	0.00

[300A] Alternate Summit Trail

If you want some variety and relative solitude for the lower part of the Squaw Peak Summit Trail [300], or just a quick circuit trip with views, try this trail. From the south end of the Squaw Peak Summit Trail parking area, head south at a sign, passing a parking area in 825'. (There is also an access point from that area.) The trail then swings around to the north and starts to parallel the wash and ascend at 0.3 mile, then more steadily at 0.4 mile. It is then steady all the way to a junction at ½ mile where a spur trail leads right to a hump on the ridge in 200'. Continue on for another 40' to the Squaw Peak Summit Trail [300]. From here the summit is 1 mile further. Ascent is 230'.

[302] Circumference Trail CLOCKWISE

General Description. This is one of the finest trails in this guidebook. It starts on Squaw Peak's ridge and makes a long (0.4 mile) switchbacking descent to the valley from Squaw Peak's ridge. You then head north, crossing several washes, to a minor ridge crest and then a pass where the Perl Charles Trail joins at 0.9 mile. From there it starts a long 500' ascent to the highest pass at 1.7 miles. The Perl Charles Trail and Nature Trail [304] then diverge at 2.1 miles. The route winds southward through the valley to the end of Squaw Peak Drive (which is reached via the Nature Trail at 2.6 miles from the start) and continues along the west side of the parkway to return to the Summit Trail parking area at 3.2 miles (3¾ miles total if the first part of the Summit Trail is included).

Access. From 0.6 mile on the Squaw Peak Summit Trail, or from junctions on the Perl Charles Trail [1A] at 1 mile and 2.2 miles and on the Nature Trail [304] at 0.1 mile and 0.6 mile. It can also be reached from the Hopi and Navajo ramadas on the north side of Squaw Peak Drive.

Read Down ↓	Detailed Trail Description	Read Up ↑
0.00	From 0.57 mile on Squaw Peak Summit Trail [300] (1,890'), descend to N. Switchbacks start in 80'.	3.17
0.12	Switchback #7, to L, makes a long traverse, followed by 10 switchbacks.	3.05

0.36 Bear R (W). 2.81
0.39 **Junction:** trail L leads to private land (no sign here). Turn R, ascending
      gradually to N. 2.78
0.44 Cross a wash. 2.73
0.53 Shade tree on R. Ascend steadily. 2.64
0.56 Cross a wash, then another in 200'. 2.61
0.65 Turn R, into a wash, then L out of it. 2.52
0.66 Switchback R, ascend steadily, then L. 2.51
0.71 Reach ridge crest (1,660') with good views. 2.46
0.75 Trail zigzags L and R, descending, then levels out. 2.42
0.83 Cross a wash, bear L, then descend gradually. 2.34
0.91 **Important junction in pass** (1,610'): trail descending ahead is Perl Charles
      Trail [1A] (junction in valley is ¼ mi away; leads W to 22nd St. access point).
      Bear R here (with Perl Charles coinciding), ascending away from pass. 2.26
0.98 Top of rise (1,630') in level, pleasant area. 2.29
1.06 Cross wide wash, then climb N out of it. 2.21
1.17 Switchback to R, ascending steadily. 2.10
1.19 Level area, cairn. Head into valley (not the one trail finally climbs). 2.18
1.22 Turn L, ascending steadily to N, then turn R. 2.15
1.29 Top of rise (1,840'); descend. 2.08
1.30 Cross a wash and ascend, then another wash in 0.16 mi. 2.07
1.49 **Junction:** NDT L ascends to pass. Final pass is now in view ahead (1,920'). ... 1.68
1.54 Switchback to L, then to R in 150',then ignore NDT crossing. 1.63
1.59 Switchback to L (viewpoint just off trail to R). Start final ascent over loose
      rock; use care. 1.58
1.68 **Junction in pass:** here, at elevation 2,120', wide NDT to W ascends.
      Descend 200' in elevation from pass on loose, rocky trail with 9 switchbacks. 1.49
1.89 Turn L (N), then bear R. 1.28
1.90 **Junction:** NDT diverges L (1,900'). 1.27
1.97 Cross wash. 1.20
2.07 **Important junction:** at Dottie Gilbert Sanctuary (plaque) PC [1A] and
      Nature Trail [304] go R; Nature Trail coincides from here. 1.10
2.15 **Junction:** sharp L is crossover to Nature Trail in 480'. Ascend gradually to S. .. 1.02
2.20 **Junction** on L with crossover trail, 0.23 mi to Nature Trail. 0.97
2.26 Trail diverges, then rejoins in 125'; take either branch. 0.91
2.32 Cross wash. 0.85
2.40 Descend S-curve. NDT and steep-walled canyon on L. 0.77
2.58 **Junction:** trail post for [302]. [Straight ahead, Nature Trail descends into
      wash at 200', bears L and ascends up a concrete, walled path, reaching
      signboard at NW corner of parking area at end of Squaw Peak Drive in 350',
      for total of 2.64 mi (3.21 mi from start of Squaw Peak Summit Trail).] 0.59
2.64 Cross wash, bear L and level out. 0.53
2.75 **Junction:** trail straight ahead leads to Hopi Ramada in 110'. Bear R here,
      ascend gradually. 0.42
2.77 Pass large rock on R. 0.40
2.78 **Junction:** trail on L descends to parking area. Bear R, ascend more steadily. .. 0.39
2.79 Sign-post (NDT descends here). 0.38
2.80 **Junction:** cross wide NDT, then level out. 0.37
2.92 Bear R, ascend; then cross a wash, descend again, crossing 2 small washes. ... 0.25
3.07 **Junction:** cross NDT. 0.10
3.12 **Junction:** at E end of parking lot, a spur trail ascends to join Summit Trail. 0.05
3.17 W end of parking lot, Summit Trail start (1,440'). 0.00

Peak 2429 from Dottie Gilbert Sanctuary

Squaw Peak from Trail [300]

[304] Squaw Peak Nature Trail CLOCKWISE

General Description. This is a 1½ mile long loop trail with several short-cuts. It provides access to the Perl Charles Trail [1A] from Squaw Peak Drive.

Access. Head north from the end of Squaw Peak Drive down a paved path (or from the Apache Ramada, descend 100' to wash, joining trail in 100').

Read Down ↓	Detailed Trail Description	Read Up ↑
0.00	Leave end of Squaw Peak Drive at signboard; steps lead down into wash.	1.44
0.03	Cross major wash, ascend steeply.	1.41
0.07	**Junction:** Circumference Trail [302] L to base of Squaw Peak and other ramadas (joins here). Go straight, ascending steadily beside steep wash.	1.37
0.33	Cross wash.	1.11
0.45	**Junction:** in pass, unmarked crossover on R to other side of Nature Trail in 0.23 mi. Keep L, with Circumference Trail. There are fine views here in an unspoiled area.	0.99
0.51	**Junction:** NDT straight ahead; turn L here, with Circumference Trail.	0.93
0.53	Cross small wash.	0.91
0.59	**Important junction:** go sharp R (descending) on PC [1A] where Circumference Trail and PC go L (uphill). On opposite side is the Dottie Gilbert Sanctuary plaque in appreciation of her many years of effort, through the Phoenix Mountains Preservation Council, to defend the Mountain Preserve.	0.85
0.60	**Junction:** faint NDT on R.	0.84
0.68	**Junction:** turn L, descending. Note, trail of use on R, no trail post here.	0.76
0.69	Cross major wash, bear R.	0.75
0.70	**Junction:** NDT sharp L up valley.	0.74
0.75	**Junction:** PC leaves this trail, ascending L. Keep straight, paralleling wash.	0.69
0.83	**Junction:** NDT on R;	0.61
0.87	Cross moderate wash.	0.57
0.97	**Junction:** NDT on L to Quartz Trail [8] in 75'.	0.47
0.98	**Junction:** just 25' past last junction, crossover trail sharp R back to this trail in 0.23 mi.	0.46
1.06	**Important junction:** Quartz Ridge Trail [8] sharp L, to 40th St. TH.	0.38
1.08	Pass (1,790'). NDT angles to L here. Begin steep, rocky descent.	0.36
1.24	Descend steps to cross major wash, then ascend out of it.	0.20
1.25	Cross major wash.	0.19
1.27	Top of rise.	0.17
1.31	**Junction:** on L is trail [8B], the Ruth Hamilton Trail, leading up to pass and beyond (360' ascent, good views).	0.13
1.42	Cross wash.	0.02
1.43	**Junction:** trail splits; take either branch.	0.01
1.44	Squaw Peak Drive (1,610'). Original start of this trip is just to R.	0.00

22nd Street Access Point

This is an easy access point for the Perl Charles Trail [1A] and to get views from passes in the ridge or from the tops of minor peaks. Drive north from

Glendale Avenue on 22nd Street to its end (there is limited on-street parking). The trail leads 270' to the Perl Charles junction, where it is 0.4 mile left, over a ridge, to the "Split" on that trail, and only 0.2 mile right to a pass (views). The Circumference Trail is 0.6 mile to the right.

Arizona Canal/16th St./Myrtle Access Points

A trail along the northeast bank of the Arizona Canal connects with the Phoenix Mountains Preserve via the Perl Charles Trail [1A] from 16th Street *[see description below]*. (For more information about the Perl Charles Trail, and its main loop from the "Split," see the E. Pleasant Drive Access Point.)

[1A] Perl Charles Trail

FROM ARIZONA CANAL to "SPLIT"

General Description. This section leads north along a right-of-way constructed next to the sidewalk on the east side of 16th Street to Myrtle, then east along the north side of Myrtle until it enters Myrtle Wash. It passes the end of Myrtle Road where there is a trailhead parking area on the south side (this is where most equestrians will access the trail), and enters a long tunnel under the Squaw Peak Parkway. It then heads north, paralleling the Parkway along a sound wall. Private property with houses is rounded at 1.1 miles and the "Split" where the loop starts is reached just 150' beyond. This is 2/3 mile from the Myrtle Trailhead. *For the continuation of this trail, see the E. Pleasant Drive Access Point.*

Access. *From the south:* from the point where 16th Street crosses the Arizona Canal, and from Myrtle Trailhead. *From the north:* just east of the tunnel under the Squaw Peak Parkway from E. Pleasant Drive, a total of 0.2 mile, then south 300' to the junction.

Read Down ↓	Detailed Trail Description	Read Up ↑
0.00	Leave Arizona Canal at 16th St. (N-side paved bike route), paralleling 16th St, heading N on its E side (Perl Charles Monument here).	1.11
0.13	Cross Myrtle to N side, turn R along it.	0.98
0.25	Cross Dreamy Draw Drive, then enter Myrtle Wash.	0.86
0.50	**Junction:** Myrtle Trailhead parking area is 185' above (to S) at end of Myrtle. Enter tunnel.	0.71
0.60	Turn L (N) on E side of tunnel, ascending for 340', paralleling Parkway.	0.61
0.74	State Avenue & 20th St. on R.	0.51
0.84	Orangewood St. on R. Gate 75' beyond.	0.27
1.08	Round corner of housing development on R, ascend.	0.03
1.11	**Important junction:** in open area where wide trail (PC clockwise) continues N (past E. Pleasant Drive access), PC counterclockwise *(as described here)* ascends steadily to R (NE).	0.00

E. Pleasant Drive Access Point

There is a tunnel under the Squaw Peak Parkway at E. Pleasant Drive (there is very limited on-street parking). Here horses from local stables enter the Preserve. This approach follows the service road south from the east end of the tunnel to the Perl Charles Trail for a total of 0.2 mile. The Perl Charles Trail clockwise (northbound) is to the left; to reach the trail counterclockwise (as described in this guidebook), head south for ¼ mile to the "Split" on the Perl Charles Trail [1A] (½ mile total).

> The plaque on the Perl Charles Trail monument on the east side of the Squaw Peak Parkway 135' south of the E. Pleasant Drive Access has this inscription: "Dedicated to one who worked endlessly for the preservation of the mountains he loved." It was erected on April 10, 1982, by the Phoenix Mountains Preservation Council, Park Foundation of Phoenix, and the City of Phoenix Parks, Recreation and Library Department.

[1A] Perl Charles Trail CLOCKWISE

General Description. From the "Split" the trail ascends briefly but steadily to a pass, drops to the 22nd Street Access, then climbs, drops into a hidden valley, and ascends to join the Circumference Trail [302] at 1 mile. The trails lead over a high scenic pass at 1.8 miles on the flank of Squaw Peak, then descend steeply to reach the Dottie Gilbert Sanctuary and the Nature Trail [304] at 2.2 miles Shortly the Perl Charles Trail leaves the Nature Trail and swings north and then west around the mountain, crosses many non-designated trails to join the Charles M. Christiansen Trail at 3.6 miles. It coincides briefly with that trail, then heads west, following an old mine road to a junction with a trail to the Dreamy Draw Bikeway [D] at 4.3 miles. It then side-hills southwest, passing the E. Pleasant Drive Access at 4.9 miles to rejoin itself at the "split" at 5.2 miles. *[Add 1.1 miles to distances below for travel to or from the Arizona Canal at 16th St., or 0.6 mile for travel to or from Myrtle Trailhead.]*

Access. From the "Split" 0.3 mile east and south of the end of E. Pleasant Drive, via the tunnel under the Squaw Peak Parkway.

Read Down ↓	Detailed Trail Description	Read Up ↑
0.00	Leave the "Split," heading NE and ascending steadily.	5.15
0.04	**Junction:** NDT half-L leads to N. Continue ascent.	5.11
0.07	**Junction:** NDT on R; bear L, still ascending steadily.	5.08
0.19	Top of rise, views. Switchback to R (E) on almost level trail.	4.96
0.22	**Junction:** join old PC sharp L, keep R and up.	4.93
0.28	**Junction:** at pass, 2 NDTs on L, and on R. Descend steadily.	4.87
0.40	**Important junction:** 22nd St. Access on R (370').	4.75
0.98	**Important junction:** join Circumference Trail [302] (R to 40th St TH.	4.17
1.78	Pass (2,120'). Descend.	3.37

2.17	**Junction:** on R, [304] and [302].	2.98
2.32	**Important junction:** [304] straight on; bear L. NDT on R.	2.83
3.58	**Important junction:** join CMC (R to 40th St & Tatum Blvd).	1.57
3.82	**Important junction:** leave CMC on L.	1.33
3.92	**Junction:** NDT straight; go sharp R.	1.23
4.00	**Junction:** NDT on L. Bear R.	1.15
4.17	Bend to R (N).	0.98
4.30	**Junction:** sharp R descends to TH on Dreamy Draw Bikeway [D] in 300'.	0.85
4.64	Ravine.	0.51
4.65	"Cookout area" on R.	0.50
4.91	**Junction:** E. Pleasant Drive Access on R.	0.24
5.15	"Split" again.	0.00

Dreamy Draw Access Point

[100] Charles M. Christiansen Trail   WEST to EAST

DREAMY DRAW to [E] NEAR 40th ST. TRAILHEAD

General Description. This is a long and varied section of the Trail. It leaves the junction 100' north of the Dreamy Draw parking area, runs in a tunnel under the Dreamy Draw Bikeway [E], and then heads west and south. Crossing a major wash, it then heads generally east to its junction with the Perl Charles Trail at 0.8 mile. (This is a complex route, with dozens of junctions). It then follows the valley north and east to a junction with the Quartz Ridge Trail [8] at 2.8 miles and reaches a junction at 2.9 miles. The 40th St. Trailhead is ½ mile north. The trail continues east to Tatum Boulevard at 4 miles. Ascent is 340', descent is 220'.

Access. *At the western end:* from the junction 100' north of the Dreamy Draw parking area (reached off Northern Avenue). *At the eastern end:* 0.4 mile south of 40th Street, or 1.1 miles west of Tatum Boulevard.

Read Down ↓	Detailed Trail Description	Read Up ↑
0.00	**Junction** 100' N of parking area (1,380'). Head R here, following wash, entering tunnel at 0.10 mi.	2.92
0.15	**Junction:** Nature Trail [220] on R, across wash. Ascend to L.	2.77
0.16	**Junction:** sharp L is NDT.	2.76
0.20	**Junction:** on R is short-cut to Nature Trail [220] in 80'. Go straight, uphill.	2.72
0.22	**Junction:** [220] goes straight; sharp R to other side of [220]; go half-R (SE).	2.70
0.29	Top of rise (1,497').	2.63
0.42	**Junction:** on L is [220A]. Descend.	2.50
0.44	**Junction:** NDT on L.	2.48
0.46	Mine tailings in flat area on R. Ascend.	2.46
0.54	Cross wash, then pass NDT on R in 45' and switchback to L thru pass.	2.38
0.57	**Junction:** NDT on L. Bear R.	2.35
0.61	**Important junction:** Nature Trail [220] straight ahead (back to Dreamy Draw in 0.52 mi). Turn L here; in 35' cross wash.	2.31

0.62   **Junction:** NDT on R. 2.30
0.66   **Important junction:** sharp L is [220], just 30' before top of rise. 2.26
0.68   **Cross deep wash.** 2.24
0.69   **Junction:** on R is NDT Switchback to L here, ascend rocky trail. 2.23
0.72   **Junction:** on R is NDT. Keep L. 2.20
0.74   **Junction:** sharp R is NDT. Keep L. 2.18
0.75   **Important junction:** on R is PC joining. Bear L. 2.17
0.76   **Junction:** sharp R is [F] to Dreamy Draw. Continue straight. 2.16
0.82   **Junction:** NDT on L. 35' past previous junction NDT leaves this trail sharp R. .. 2.10
0.86   **Junction:** NDT on L. Trail improves past 0.91 mi. 2.06
0.96   **Junction:** on R is NDT. Pass another in 50' on R. 1.96
0.99   **Important junction:** PC on R, uphill. Continue on easy trail. 1.93
1.09   **Junction:** on R is poor NDT. 1.83
1.12   **Junction:** NDT on L; 30' further there is a 4-way junction of NDTs L & R. 1.80
1.13   **Junction (4-way):** NDTs on L & R. 1.79
1.17   **Junction:** NDT on L. Pass cut-off trail on L. 1.75
1.18   **Junction:** NDT on L. Bear R. 1.74
1.19   **Junction:** NDT on R; bear L here. 1.73
1.21   **Junction:** NDT sharp R uphill. 1.71
1.31   **Junction:** NDT on L is old CMC; go R here (8 MI marker in 15'). 1.61
1.32   **Junction:** NDT on R. Bear L, cross wash. 1.60
1.35   **Junction:** NDT on L. Turn R. 1.57
1.38   **Junction:** NDT on L. 1.54
1.41   **Junction:** NDT on R. 1.51
1.49   **Junction:** NDT on L, uphill. Descend into wash. 1.43
1.52   **Junction:** NDT on L; leave wash, go R up bank, pass NDT on L, turn sharp R. .. 1.40
1.57   **Important junction:** [B] sharp L to 32 St & 40th St TH. 1.35
1.67   **Junction:** NDT uphill on R. 1.25
1.73   **Junction:** wide NDT on R. 1.19
1.76   **Junction:** NDT on L. 1.16
1.78   **Junction (4-way):** NDTs L & R. 1.14
1.88   **Junction:** NDT on R. 1.04
1.93   **Junction:** NDT on L. 0.99
1.98   **Junction:** NDT on R; bear L. 0.94
2.02   **Junction:** NDT sharp L. 0.90
2.03   **Junction:** NDT on R. Cross wash. 0.89
2.07   **Important junction:** R is trail to Quartz Ridge Trail [8] in 0.55 mi. (This
        may become a designated trail in the future.) 0.85
2.23   **Junction:** NDT sharp R. Cross wash. 0.69
2.26   **Junction:** old vehicleway sharp R to Quartz Ridge Trail [8] in 0.68 mi. (This
        may become a designated trail in the future.).................................... 0.66
2.40   **Junction:** NDT L crosses wash. 0.52
2.41   **Junction:** NDT on L crosses wash. 0.51
2.57   **Junction:** L is crossover 410' to trail on N side of main wash. 0.35
2.61   **Important junction:** sharp L is [A] to 38 St. 0.31
2.85   **Junction (4-way):** on R is Quartz Ridge Trail [8] toward Squaw Peak Drive
        or via [8A] to 32nd & Lincoln TH; on L [8] leads N to 40th St. TH in 0.5 mi.
        Continue straight, passing NDT on R in 65'. 0.07
2.92   **Important Junction (4-way):** *here there is a choice.* Spur [D] goes N
        0.37 mi *[see 40th St. Access]* for a total of 3.29 mi from Dreamy Draw. For
        Tatum Boulevard, go straight ahead *[see that access for details]*, 1.08 mi,
        for a total of 4.0 mi. To the R, LV Yates Trail heads S to Peak 2429 (1,543'). 0.00

[220] Dreamy Draw Nature Trail

General Description. From the Dreamy Draw access point, go through the tunnel and then head south, ascending a ridge. At $1/2$ mile there is a junction with the Charles M. Christiansen Trail, from which it diverges shortly to climb a pass and a crest with fine views at 0.9 mile. It then descends north and west back to its beginning. Ascent is 380'; descent is the same. There are signs for points of interest, and a brochure has been published.

Access. One hundred feet north of the Dreamy Draw parking area this trail starts at the signboard and coincides with the Charles M. Christiansen Trail heading east through the horse tunnel. It then immediately diverges right.

Read Down ↓	Detailed Trail Description	Read Up ↑
0.00	Leave signboard (1,380'), heading E through tunnel.	1.64
0.15	**Junction:** where CMC ascends L, this trail crosses minor wash.	1.49
0.17	**Junction:** NDT sharp R to highway.	1.47
0.20	**Junction:** NDT on L. Turn R, ascend.	1.44
0.24	**Junction:** NDT on R. [7 more junctions on R, ahead, along ridge.]	1.40
0.50	**Junction:** Last NDT on R.	1.14
0.52	**Important junction:** CMC and Children's Loop [220A] go straight. Turn sharp R, cross wash.	1.12
0.55	**Important junction:** turn sharp L (narrow trail); CMC goes straight.	1.09
0.61	**Junction:** NDT on L. Turn R, ascend.	1.03
0.70	**Junction:** NDT on R. Turn L, ascend eroded trail.	0.94
0.72	**Junction:** keep R where abandoned route diverges L.	0.92
0.77	**Junction:** on L is eroded abandoned route.	0.87
0.85	**Junction:** at pass, 40' to R is NDT, descending. Turn L up crest.	0.79
0.92	Top of rise on crest with fine views. Descend.	0.72
1.02	**Junction:** NDT on R.	0.62
1.05	**Junction:** NDT on L. Turn R here.	0.59
1.18	**Junction (4-way):** straight ahead leads around to loop; NDT on R. Go L.	0.46
1.43	**Junction:** on L is [220A], Children's Nature Loop. Go straight.	0.21
1.45	**Junction:** NDT ascends on R, rejoins ahead.	0.19
1.52	**Junction:** NDT ascends on R.	0.12
1.57	**Junction (4-way):** sharp L is CMC; half-L is short-cut. Join CMC, straight ahead.	0.07
1.59	**Junction:** new trail on R, 0.11 mi up to loop [see map].	0.05
1.64	**Junction:** on L is start of [220] – end of this Nature loop.	0.00

[220A] Children's Nature Loop

General Description. A short series of trail segments reduces the length and ascent of the main Dreamy Draw Nature Trail [220]. Total distance is $1 1/4$ miles from Dreamy Draw and back to it. Ascent is 200'; descent is 140'.

Access. Description starts from $1/2$ mile on [220], but access can be considered to also be at Dreamy Draw.

Read Down ↓	Detailed Trail Description	Read Up ↑
0.00	Leave Nature Trail [220], 0.52 mi from Dreamy Draw. Head E, following CMC. ..	0.58
0.03	Junction: on R is trail to [220] in 190'. Ascend over low pass.	0.55
0.06	Junction: poor NDT straight ahead. Turn sharp R, cross wash, ascend to L.	0.52
0.14	Mine tailings on L.	0.44
0.19	Junction: on R is NDT.	0.39
0.21	Important junction: CMC is straight ahead. Go R.	0.37
0.22	Junction: NDT on R. Turn L.	0.36
0.36	Junction: [220] L & R. Go L.	0.22
0.39	Junction: NDT on R (rejoins ahead).	0.19
0.46	Junction: NDT on R (rejoining).	0.12
0.51	Junction: CMC sharp L. Continue straight.	0.07
0.53	Junction (4-way): NDT on R; short-cut on L.	0.05
0.58	Junction: [220] on L. Dreamy Draw is 0.15 mi ahead.	0.00

[E] Dreamy Draw Bikeway

NORTHERN AVE. to 32nd ST.

General Description. The popular Bikeway (paved) generally follows the location of the northbound lanes of the old Dreamy Draw highway. Where it approaches close to the freeway, a sound wall has been installed. There is some small ascent and descent as it parallels the freeway for 2.2 miles.

Access. *From the southwest:* the bikeway starts at a ramp at the northern end of Royal Palm Drive where it turns south to become Dreamy Draw Drive; the ramp crosses over a freeway ramp, and then joins the Northern Avenue underpass, then paralleling Northern on the south side. *From the northeast:* from 32nd Street just south of Squaw Peak Parkway exit 8, near Mountain View Road. It can also be reached from trailheads at Dreamy Draw parking area, and at Malapai Drive. For the latter, take 32nd Street south from the freeway to Mission Lane, turn right (west), then north on 29th Street to Malapai.

Read Down ↓	Detailed Trail Description	Read Up ↑
0.00	Leave Royal Palm Drive, cross over on-ramp.	2.18
0.15	Follow Dreamy Draw Drive on S side, from E side of freeway interchange.	2.03
0.63	Junction: access point R 300' to Perl Charles Trail [1A].	1.55
0.75	Junction: trail [F] ascends on R for 0.22 mi to end at CMC & PC Trails.	1.43
0.82	Junction: paved trail L leads down to ramadas, rest rooms, and parking area for Dreamy Draw Park.	1.36
1.06	Junction: on R, trail leads down to tunnel under bikeway and CMC.	1.12
1.58	Bottom of descent.	0.60
1.75	Bike/pedestrian overpass of freeway on L.	0.43
1.77	Malapai Drive 110' to R.	0.41
2.18	Junction: bikeway ends at 32nd St.	0.00

[F]

An old vehicleway ascends for 0.2 mile from the Dreamy Draw Bikeway [E] at
¾ mile to reach the Charles M. Christiansen Trail.

32nd Street (North) Access Point

From the gate at the south end of 32nd Street, a short, easy trail heads south,
ascending gradually, and meets trail [B] in 0.2 mile. Combined with trail [B], it
is 1.1 miles to the Christiansen Trail. Ascent is only 60'.

38th Street Access Point

[A]

General Description. From 38th Street a wide track (used by service
vehicles) leads south along a major wash to a flat, open area at 0.3 mile, then
continues, crossing the major wash to the Charles M. Christiansen Trail.

Access. From the south end (gated) of 38th Street.

Read Down ↓	Detailed Trail Description	Read Up ↑
0.00	Leave 38th Street (1,500'). Cross over stile next to gate. Just beyond is [B] to L & R (L leads to 40th St in 0.28 mi).	0.47
0.05	**Junction:** NDT enters on R (to private land).	0.42
0.31	**Junction:** NDT sharp L.	0.16
0.32	**Junction:** NDT on L.	0.15
0.34	**Junction:** NDT sharp R.	0.13
0.42	**Junction:** NDT half-L descends to cross wash, joins CMC in 490'.	0.05
0.47	**Junction:** leave vehicleway, crossing wash to CMC in 320'.	0.00

40th Street Access Point

[B] To Charles M. Christiansen Trail

General Description. The trail leaves the trailhead, crosses a deep wash,
and runs along the north boundary of the Preserve, passing trail [A], then
heading further away from the developed area at about 0.6 mile. A side-trail
to 32nd Street is passed at 1 mile, then a gradual ascent leads to the
Christiansen Trail at 1.4 miles. Ascent is less than 100'. There are many
cross trails, since this is a very heavily used area.

Access. *From 40th Street* and Shea Boulevard head south on 40th Street for 1 mile to the trailhead. The trail departs from the northwest corner. *From the Christiansen Trail*, 1.6 miles from Dreamy Draw.

Read Down ⬇	Detailed Trail Description	Read Up ⬆
0.00	Leave TH at NW corner (1,490'). Descend to a wash, where at a **junction** the Quartz Trail [8] heads S. Ascend W here.	1.17
0.28	**Junction (4-way):** trail [A] R almost immediately to 38th St., L to CMC in 0.47 mi.	0.89
0.38	**Junction:** trail splits; keep L.	0.79
0.45	**Junction:** alternate re-enters on R. Head away from homes.	0.72
0.60	**Junction:** NDT on L.	0.57
0.78	**Junction:** trail on R to 32nd St.	0.39
0.94	**Junction:** NDT on R to 32nd St.	0.23
1.07	**Junction:** NDT on L.	0.10
1.15	**Junction:** NDT near CMC.	0.02
1.17	**Junction:** CMC, L 1.4 miles to Tatum Blvd, R 1.6 miles to Dreamy Draw.	0.00

[D] Spur to [100] (Charles M. Christiansen Trail)

General Description. The trail enters a broad valley on an old mining road, then joins the main trail from the east (Tatum Boulevard) at 0.37 mile. *Note that this is the shorter of the two entrances to the Christiansen Trail heading west.* Ascent is 90'. There are many trails of use.

Access. *From 40th Street* and Shea Boulevard head south on 40th Street for 1 mile. The trail (an old mine road) heads south on the same alignment as 40th St., at a gate on the east side of the trailhead.

Read Down ⬇	Detailed Trail Description	Read Up ⬆
0.00	Head S on road at gate (1,450'). Ascend gradually.	0.37
0.15	Top of rise. Descend very gradually with open valley on R.	0.22
0.17	Cross small wash.	0.20
0.24	**Junction:** NDT trail angles to L.	0.13
0.26	Cross moderate wash.	0.11
0.37	**Junction:** CMC to Tatum Blvd. on L (1.08 mi), and to R here. Ahead, LV Yates Trail continues to Peak 2429 in 1.1 mi (elevation here is 1,543').	0.00

L. V. Yates Trail to Peak 2429

General Description. L. V. Yates, Jr., is another dedicated member of the Phoenix Mountains Preservation Council. The road that starts as the spur to the Charles M. Christiansen Trail south of 40th Street continues south of where the main trail turns west. Gradually, then steadily, the old mining road ascends the slope west of Peak 2429, making a switchback to the north at $1/2$ mile where the way diverges and becomes a foot and horse trail, ascending a draw. This is constructed trail, with many switchbacks, but has eroded sections. Switchbacks continue all the way to 0.9 mile just below the ridge crest. The main trail heads north around the peak on an easy grade to 1 mile, where the trail turns south again and ascends to the summit at 1.1 miles. Views are excellent. Ascent is 890'.

Access. The trail leaves the Charles M. Christiansen Trail junction 0.4 mile south of the 40th Street Trailhead, or 1.1 miles west of Tatum Boulevard. Head south on the old mining road. For better walking, you can also take the Quartz Ridge Trail [8] south to the Christiansen Trail (½ mile), then head a short distance east to the starting point.

Read Down ↓	Detailed Trail Description	Read Up ↑
0.00	Leave CMC Trail junction heading S (1,543').	1.08
0.23	**Junction:** NDT ascends steeply on L.	0.85
0.33	**Junction:** NDT on R descends to valley.	0.74
0.35	On L is cairn with old cross in it.	0.73
0.50	**Important junction:** where road steepens and makes hairpin bend to L (N), take trail R; there is another faint trail on R from road ahead (road ends at boulder field in 380'). Elevation 1,840'. Trail starts out level, crosses a minor wash, then ascends, paralleling wash.	0.57
0.56	Use care to avoid side route on R that ends; keep on top of rocks, then bear R.	0.52
0.59	Switchbacks (21 of them!) begin.	0.49
0.88	**Junction:** main trail heads N, contouring along side of Peak 2429. Ahead 35' is crest (2,320') with views of Camelback, South Mountain, Squaw Peak.	0.20
0.99	**Junction:** at crest N of Peak 2429, poor trail leads 350' toward next summit; from there a 250' scramble leads to its top. Turn sharp R here, ascending on good trail.	0.09
1.01	Switchback to L, then to R.	0.06
1.03	**Junction:** at white cairn, continue straight ahead; NDT trail sharp L crosses over ridge and in 410' descends side ridge to private land.	0.05
1.08	*Summit, Peak 2429.* Fine views.	0.00

Tatum Boulevard Access Point

[100] Charles M. Christiansen Trail

General Description. This link follows a strip of land in a wash between developed areas for a little over half a mile, then gradually ascends 130' on the north side of the wash to a low pass at 0.9 mile. Finally a gradual descent leads to the LV Yates Trail and spur to 40th Street Trailhead at 1.1 miles.

Access. On Tatum Boulevard there is a small parking area opposite Tomahawk Trail on the east; this is 1.3 miles south of Shea Boulevard and 2¼ miles north of Lincoln Drive.

Read Down ↓	Detailed Trail Description	Read Up ↑
0.00	Limited parking at Tatum Blvd.; Preserve sign. Elevation 1,380'.	1.08
0.08	Flood control channel on R.	1.00

0.18	Flood control channel on R.	0.90
0.25	Bear R where NDT continues ahead.	0.83
0.29	**Junction:** NDT crosses (L leads to private road). Go straight.	0.79
0.36	Cross wash and ascend.	0.72
0.37	Bear L on bank of wash, paralleling wash.	0.71
0.61	**Junction:** NDT descends on L. Bear R, ascend.	0.47
0.64	Cross small wash.	0.44
0.80	"10 MI" sign.	0.36
0.86	Two large saguaros on R. Continue ascent.	0.28
0.89	Cross wash.	0.19
0.93	Pass (1,550') and **junction:** NDT angling R is short-cut to 40th Street spur in 0.19 mi. On L, in open area, is another NDT. Continue on CMC at arrow, descending gradually.	0.15
1.08	**Junction:** 40th St. spur [D] on R (to TH in 0.37 mi). Vehicleway on L (LV Yates Trail). *CMC westbound continues straight ahead (1,543').*	0.00

36th Street/Lincoln Drive Access Point

Drive north on 36th Street to a locked gate (1,740'). *There is no legal parking here.* 375' north of the gate is a junction: the old road to the right leads to private property. There is a choice of two routes:

[C]

Straight ahead is a paved section past a prominent white house (an in-holding in the Preserve), then a gravel road (partly deteriorated and by-passed by trail at 200' for 195') to the junction with the Quartz Ridge Trail [8] at 0.6 mile. There is a 120' ascent and some drop at the end.

[8B] Ruth Hamilton Trail

(See Squaw Peak Drive section for full description.) A rough road ascends west for 1/4 mile to trail [8A] (north 0.6 mile to [8], south to 32nd St. & Lincoln Drive Trailhead) and then continues steep and rough over a pass at 0.4 mile and drops to the Nature Trail [304] at 0.9 mile.

32nd Street/Lincoln Drive Access Point

[8A] SOUTH to NORTH

General Description. An important new public access point was opened in early 1996 with completion of the Ruth Hamilton Trail. From the 32nd Street Trailhead at Lincoln Drive, head up a valley to a junction with trail [200A] at

0.25 mile. The main wash is crossed at 0.4 mile, then a rise is topped shortly after. A steep ascent begins at 0.5 mile, and switchbacks start across the steep slope at 0.8 mile. The top and the Ruth Hamilton Trail [8B] are reached at 1.1 miles. From here the trail descends a wash to the Quartz Ridge Trail [8] at 1.8 miles. Total ascent is 520'.

Access. *From the south,* at the trailhead parking lot on the north side of Lincoln Drive head east to its end, where there is a trailhead sign. *From the north,* on the Quartz Ridge Trail 1³/₄ miles from 40th St. Trailhead or from [8] at 1.2 miles east of the end of Squaw Peak Drive.

Read Down ↓	Detailed Trail Description	Read Up ↑
0.00	Leave Trailhead parking lot (1,832').	1.77
0.22	Cross wash.	1.55
0.23	**Junction:** [200A] ascends L.	1.54
0.33	Top of rise.	1.44
0.36	Cross main wash.	1.41
0.41	Swing R & L, around side-wash.	1.36
0.45	Top of rise. Descend rocky trail.	1.32
0.48	Bottom of descent. Swing R, ascend.	1.29
0.50	Landmark: very large white boulder on L.	1.27
0.51	Steep ascent begins.	1.26
0.52	Small sag; ascend steadily on rocky trail.	1.25
0.57	Top of rise (1,660'). Descend to L on rocky trail.	1.20
0.66	Start steady ascent.	1.11
0.70	As trail approaches edge of wash, it turns R.	1.07
0.78	First switchback, to R (S) at wash.	0.99
0.81	Switchback to L (N); long traverse, nice walking.	0.96
0.91	Switchback to R, ascend steeply.	0.86
0.96	Switchback to L (W), ease grade of ascent.	0.81
1.05	Switchback to R (E).	0.72
1.07	Switchback to L.	0.70
1.09	Bear R.	0.68
1.11	Turn L (W) around head of wash.	0.66
1.13	Switchback to R.	0.64
1.14	**Junction:** NDT 75' L to top of hump. Top of rise. Bench on R. Descend.	0.63
1.17	**Junction:** Ruth Hamilton Trail [8B] L & R (1,840'); descend valley along wash.	0.60
1.30	**Junction:** NDT short-cut R crosses wash, returns to this trail in 410'.	0.47
1.46	**Junction:** NDT R returns; keep L.	0.31
1.51	**Junction:** NDT returns; level trail from here.	0.26
1.77	**Junction:** Quartz Ridge Trail [8] in wash (1,630'); this trail ends.	0.00

City of Phoenix

Stoney/Echo Mountain Area

Squaw Peak & Peak 2429 from Stoney

Introduction. Stoney Mountain is an unofficial name for a long, steep-sided ridge west of Squaw Peak. For the purposes of this guidebook we have defined the "Stoney Area" as bounded by 7th Street on the west, 24th St. and Dreamy Draw on the east, Thunderbird and Cactus on the north, and Northern Avenue on the south. (There is no significant named feature in the pie-shaped area between Cave Creek and 7th Street.) The highest peak is 2,020'. Peaks rise 400-500' above the surrounding valley. On the south there is a section locally known as "Echo Mountain" (highest summit 1,845').

The section west of Cave Creek Road has one north-south trending steep-sided summit at 1,833'. On its north, paralleling Thunderbird, are a series of ridges and bumps from 1,500' to almost 1,700' in elevation.

Maps. Our Map 6. The USGS 1:24,000 Sunnyslope quadrangle (1965, photorevised 1982) shows a few old roads but almost none of the trails.

Access. There are several access points. Some additional neighborhood access trails may eventually be designated. Changes are still taking place, and all junctions indicated may not be visible as non-designated trails are obliterated. As is true of other Phoenix Mountain Parks, facility hours are limited to 5:30 a.m. through 11:00 p.m. (Dreamy Draw at 10:00 p.m.) Trails close at sunset.

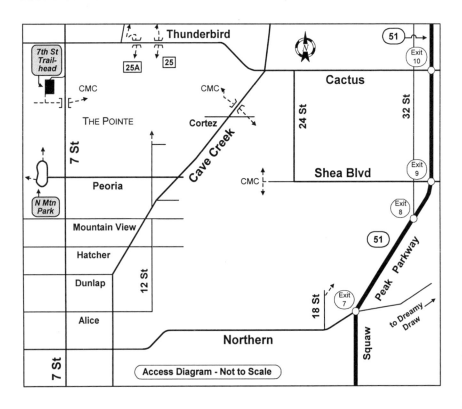

Recommended Hikes and Trail Rides. Letters used for designation are our own, so as not to confuse designated (numbered) trails with these. The Charles M. Christiansen Trail is abbreviated "CMC" in tabular detailed text. This is the best trail hikers and trail riders *and is described in two sections.* (Because there are some confusing junctions, considerable detail is provided.)

Cautions. The tilted rock strata have resulted in a very steep spine to this range. Trails tend to have quite sharp, up-thrust rocks on which it could be quite painful to fall.

[25] NORTHBOUND

CHARLES M. CHRISTIANSEN TRAIL to THUNDERBIRD ROAD

General Description. From the CMC at $^1/_2$ mile east of 7th St. Trailhead, this trail ascends (60') north for $^1/_4$ mile to a low pass. (At that point there is a loop to the west around the low summit, back to this trail's start in $^1/_2$ mile.) Trail [25] then turns east briefly, leaves a junction with the Ridge Trail [B] at 0.3 mile, and heads north on a circuitous route to a junction with [25A] at 0.4 mile. Another 600' east leads to the tunnel (horses, hikers, bicyclists) under Thunderbird at a total of $^1/_2$ mile. On the north side of the tunnel, the trail turns northwest along Captain Dreyfus Avenue, then over a low pass in the Pointe Golf Course, and is described in the Lookout Mountain chapter. The entire length to the Circumference Trail on Lookout Mountain [308] is 1.9 miles. Ascent to the tunnel is 80'.

[25A] NORTHBOUND

FROM [25] to THUNDERBIRD ROAD

General Description. From the junction on [25] north of the Christiansen Trail, head north 0.1 mile to the golf course. A paved path leads under Thunderbird Road (no horses) and then heads around to the west to Golf Club Drive, where this trail follows the road 0.9 mile to Hearn Road and ascends up a narrow right-of-way to meet the Circumference Trail [308] around Lookout Mountain at 1.6 miles. (See Lookout Mountain chapter.) Ascent is 80', descent 80'.

[100] Charles M. Christiansen Trail EASTBOUND

7th STREET to CAVE CREEK ROAD

General Description. From 7th Street Trailhead the tunnel is followed under 7th Street to a public corridor around the north side of The Pointe at Tapatio Cliffs, then a low hill is ascended. A wide track is then followed up a valley before climbing over a pass at 0.7 mile and following a complex route over the hills and down to — and under — Cave Creek Road at 1.9 miles. Ascent is 200', descent 240'.

Access. *From the east:* leave Cortez Road just east of Cave Creek Road, heading north. There is limited parking here. *From the west:* from the 7th Street Trailhead.

Read Down ↓	Detailed Trail Description	Read Up ↑
0.00	**Junction:** 7th St. TH spur and CMC.	2.01
0.03	Enter tunnel under 7th Street.	1.98
0.09	**Junction:** trail R leads a few feet to Pointe's public parking area (1,440').	1.92
0.15	**Junction:** private road on L; Pointe parking on R. Head uphill on narrow trail.	1.86
0.22	**Junction (4-way):** cross NDTs (viewpoint).	1.79
0.26	**Junction:** cross private road.	1.75
0.45	**Junction (4-way):** join 2 tracks from L; keep R on wide track.	1.56
0.53	**Junction:** on L is [25] to tunnel under Thunderbird, trail [B], and access to Lookout Mtn.	1.48
0.59	**Junction:** bear R from track on ascending trail.	1.42
0.62	**Junction:** sharp L is closed trail. Ascend, avoiding trail on L.	1.38
0.73	Turn sharp L here.	1.27
0.78	Pass (1,550'). Descend, then ascend.	1.23
0.82	Former junction with NDTs. Bear L, ascend.	1.19
0.88	**Junction:** poor tracks (NDTs) join from L. Keep R, uphill.	1.13
0.91	**Junction:** on R is access [D] from Cholla & 12th St. Continue ahead on easy, wide track, narrowing to trail.	1.09
0.97	**Junction (4-way):** NDT crosses diagonally.	1.04
1.01	**Junction (4-way):** NDT on L & R. Continue on trail.	1.00
1.07	**Junction:** sharp R is closed NDT. Turn L here onto track.	0.93
1.09	**Junction:** NDT sharp L descends. Turn R here.	0.92
1.15	**Junction:** bear L where NDT enters on R.	0.86
1.21	**Junction:** sharp R is Sunnyside Access [H]. Continue straight ahead on wide, level track.	0.80
1.30	**Junction:** where local stable trail (to [B]) continues onto ridge, turn R, descending parallel to wash on L, passing several NDTs.	0.71
1.72	**Junction:** trail on L joins Loop Trail [A] used by stables in 80'.	0.29
1.81	**Junction:** road on R.	0.20
1.82	**Junction:** NDT on R; descend.	0.19
1.86	Turn R, paralleling Cave Creek Road, which is above.	0.15
1.91	W end of tunnel.	0.10
1.93	Turn R on E side of tunnel.	0.08
2.01	**Junction:** Cortez Road (1,400'). Cave Creek Road is just to R here. Go across road, diagonally L, to continue.	0.00

[100] Charles M. Christiansen Trail   EASTBOUND

CAVE CREEK ROAD to DREAMY DRAW

General Description. An old vehicleway is followed along the west side of some hills to 0.4 mile, where the trail ascends over a shoulder and reaches Shea Access. A circuitous route around the developed land to the east leads past private homes before climbing over a pass at 2 miles and rounding the flank of a minor summit to reach Dreamy Draw at 3 miles. Ascent is 450', descent is also 450'.

Access. *From the west:* leave Cortez Road just east of Cave Creek Road, heading southeast at the junction. *From the east:* leave the Dreamy Draw parking area heading north 100' to a junction, then left (west) through the tunnel under the Squaw Peak Parkway.

Read Down ↓	Detailed Trail Description	Read Up ↑
0.00	Leave Cortez Road E of Cave Creek Road (1,400'). Climb bank onto trail heading SE.	2.97
0.04	**Junction (4-way):** NDTs cross. Go half-L along old road paralleling Cortez.	2.93
0.07	**Junction:** turn R off vehicleway, past barrier, on wide, easy trail (ahead [100B] leads 0.63 mi to Cholla Access and returns to this trail at 0.55 mi).	2.90
0.39	**Important Junction:** track ahead is to Sahuaro Access [G] in 0.48 mi. Turn sharp L here, onto ascending trail.	2.57
0.41	**Junction:** in open area, keep L where track continues, ascending trail.	2.56
0.55	**Junction:** trail sharp L is Cholla Access [100B]. Bear R and descend.	2.42
0.58	**Junction (4-way):** track crosses diagonally.	2.39
0.66	**Junction (5-way):** NDTs sharp-R, R, & L. Bear half-L on level track.	2.31
0.69	**Junction:** sharp L is NDT. Pass fence line and other tracks.	2.28
0.77	**Junction:** NDT on L.	2.20
0.84	**Junction (4-way):** NDT crosses diagonally.	2.13
0.93	**Junction:** Shea Access is 335' to L. Continue level, above homes.	2.04
1.33	**Junction:** NDT on L. Ascend over low pass.	1.64
1.36	**Junction:** on L is NDT (1,580').	1.61
1.45	**Junction:** NDT ahead to private land; go uphill to R on trail, circling around private homes, then descend.	1.52
1.78	**Junction (4-way):** NDTs cross.	1.19
1.82	**Junction:** bear R where NDT diverges L.	1.15
1.90	**Junction:** bear R, joining ascending track.	1.07
1.96	**Junction:** alternate trail on R rejoins here.	1.01
2.00	Pass (1,600). Descend steeply, passing loop track on L.	0.97
2.23	**Junction:** NDT ascends on L.	0.74
2.26	**Junction:** on R is Hatcher Access [E] (0.27 mi). Bear L on trail.	0.71
2.29	**Junction:** on R 135' is junction in open area with Hatcher Access [E]. Orchid Lane Access [F] to S is 0.6 mi. 18th St. Access [J] is 0.9 mi. Soon pass mine shaft on R.	0.68
2.41	**Junction:** turn L from track onto trail.	0.56
2.53	**Junction:** NDT descends on R. Ascend, then descend.	0.44
2.67	**Junction:** at top of rise, turn L and descend.	0.30
2.72	**Junction:** turn L from track onto trail.	0.25
2.74	**Junction:** join track at barrier; bear R, downhill.	0.23
2.76	**Junction:** wide track (NDT) joins on L. Bear R onto track.	0.21
2.82	**Junction:** NDT on L. Descend steadily.	0.15
2.85	W end of tunnel.	0.12
2.87	Emerge from E end of tunnel under Squaw Peak Parkway.	0.10
2.90	**Junction:** cross track, keep R.	0.07
2.97	**Junction:** spur trail R to Dreamy Draw parking area in 100' (elev. 1,400'). CMC continues E by turning L here.	0.00

[100B] and Cholla (East) Access   WEST to EAST

General Description.[1] This is a loop trail. From the Christiansen Trail just south of Cortez, this trail heads east, first as an old vehicleway, ascends a low ridge, then parallels a wash, descending gradually to Cholla Trailhead (23rd St.) at 0.6 mile. It returns westward, then south almost to the end of Desert Cove, then takes a circuitous route west, over a ridge, dropping to meet the Christiansen Trail again at about 0.8 mile, a total of 1.4 miles. Ascent is 100'; descent is 100'.

Access. *At the northwestern end:* at the Christiansen Trail 2.9 miles west of Dreamy Draw (0.1 mile east of Cave Creek Road). *At the eastern end:* at the western end of Cholla St. at 23rd St. *At the southwestern end:* at the Christiansen Trail at 0.6 mile on that trail east of Cave Creek Road, 2.4 miles west of Dreamy Draw.

[A] Loop Trail   CLOCKWISE

General Description. From near the Christiansen Trail, this trail used by local stables runs north, then east above Thunderbird Road, south along Cave Creek Road to a viewpoint at 0.6 mile, then back west again to its start at 0.8 mile. Ascent is 160'.

Access. From the Christiansen Trail 0.3 mile west of Cave Creek Road, take a spur trail across the wash for 80' to the junction.

Read Down ↓	Detailed Trail Description	Read Up ↑
0.00	Leave junction, head N, ascending gradually (1,420').	0.83
0.01	**Junction:** this trail returns on R.	0.82
0.06	**Junction:** alternate narrow trail on L, 15' shorter. Keep R.	0.77
0.12	**Junction:** join alternate from L.	0.71
0.15	**Junction:** on L is start of trail [B] to hills to NW. Go R on good trail.	0.68
0.22	**Junction:** with ruined building ahead, turn R, cross wash, descend.	0.61
0.31	**Junction:** poor NDT to L to ruin. Keep straight on.	0.52
0.36	**Junction:** bear R where spur trail descends on L to [B]. Reach top of rise and descend.	0.47
0.41	**Junction:** NDT descends L to Thunderbird.	0.42
0.43	**Junction:** NDT slightly L ahead to private property. Turn R on wide vehicleway, almost level, with views over Cave Creek Road.	0.40
0.58	**Junction:** NDT descends to private property on L. Swing around to L.	0.25
0.62	**Junction:** in pass (1,510'), side trail L leads to viewpoint on bump in 155'. Descend steep, rocky trail.	0.21
0.73	Turn R, parallel wash on L, on easy trail.	0.10
0.83	**Junction:** this trail ends at its start; CMC is 80' to L.	0.00

---

[1]The final segments of designated trail [100B] between 23rd St., Cholla, and the Christiansen Trail [100] had not been established at time of publishing. There are several entrance points from 23rd St., and many trails to the west. Some trail posts are in place, not necessarily on the final trail location. There is no point in our describing all of these. Since distances are short, heading west will soon lead you to the Christiansen Trail.

[B] Ridge Trail EAST to WEST

TRAIL [A] to TRAIL [25]

General Description. A hiker/horse trail gives good views from the northern ridge. Ascent is 260', descent the same.

Access. *From the east:* at Loop Trail [A] 0.2 mile north of the Christiansen Trail, 0.7 mile west of Cave Creek Road. *From the west:* from trail [25] 0.2 mile north of the Christiansen Trail 0.4 mile from 7th St.

Read Down ↓	Detailed Trail Description	Read Up ↑
0.00	Leave [A] to NW, ascend.	0.96
0.18	**Junction:** spur trail R connects to Loop Trail ([A] in 0.22 mi. Turn sharp L (W), ascending broad crest.	0.78
0.41	**Junction:** spur trail L descends 60' (0.16 mi) to CMC.	0.55
0.47	Summit (1,690'). Descend W with good footway.	0.49
0.54	Second summit (1,680'). Descend good trail along crest.	0.42
0.65	Trail loops, rejoins in 55'.	0.31
0.85	Open area. Descend rocky trail.	0.11
0.95	**Junction:** NDT on R trail heads N to valley.	0.01
0.96	**Junction:** R [25] leads to valley and crossing under Thunderbird Rd to Lookout Mountain, and trail [25A]. Straight ascends to pass in 235', then [25] descends S 0.25 mi to the CMC.	0.00

[C] Valley Trail EAST to WEST

General Description. From the Christiansen Trail and back to it — the distance is shorter, but it is much less scenic. Descent is 60'.

Access. *From the east:* at the Christiansen Trail, 0.8 mile from Cave Creek Road. *From the west:* at the Christiansen Trail, ½ mile from 7th Street.

Read Down ↓	Detailed Trail Description	Read Up ↑
0.00	Leave CMC where it ascends L, 0.8 mi W of Cave Creek. Descend gradually.	0.47
0.01	**Junction:** NDT on L, uphill to CMC in 75'.	0.46
0.11	**Junction (4-way):** NDT on R; sharp L is rocky NDT.	0.36
0.15	**Junction (4-way):** uphill on L is rocky NDT; NDT descends on R.	0.32
0.24	**Junction:** rough NDT on L into wash.	0.23
0.29	In open area, bear R (NE).	0.19
0.32	Open area narrows, this track heads W. Picnic area on L.	0.15
0.35	**Junction:** NDT on L; continue; in 30' pass crossover on R to other picnic area.	0.12
0.39	**Junction:** NDT on R. Pass near picnic area.	0.08
0.45	**Junction (4-way):** NDTs sharp L to CMC in 170'.	0.02
0.47	**Junction:** CMC E-bound sharp L, uphill, and W-bound straight ahead. This trail ends.	0.00

[D] Cholla (West) and 12th St. Access

From end of Cholla at 12th St. it is $^1/_2$ mile to the Charles M. Christiansen Trail 0.9 mile east of 7th St Trailhead and 1.1 mile west of Cave Creek Road. The way is all old vehicleway, often rocky, and the ascent is about 160'.

[E] Hatcher Access WEST to EAST

HATCHER DRIVE to CHARLES M. CHRISTIANSEN TRAIL

General Description. An old vehicleway descends into the center of the Preserve area and reaches the Charles M. Christiansen Trail in 0.3 mile.

Access. *From the west:* at Hatcher Road at 16th St., Hatcher Drive bears south. Take it to its end, an unpaved parking area. *From the east:* at 0.7 mile from Dreamy Draw on the Charles M. Christiansen Trail.

Read Down ↓	Detailed Trail Description	Read Up ↑
0.00	Leave Hatcher Drive (1,495'), descending.	0.27
0.03	**Junction:** steep NDT uphill on L.	0.24
0.05	**Junction:** NDT descends on R.	0.22
0.07	**Junction:** in wide open area, NDT descends R.	0.20
0.13	**Junction:** in messy area, NDT descends R.	0.14
0.16	Bear R.	0.11
0.21	**Important 4-way junction:** straight ahead is track crossing over to CMC in 380'; to R is Orchid Lane Access [F] (0.63 mi). On L is NDT.	0.06
0.27	**Junction:** Charles M. Christiansen Trail [100].	0.00

[F] Orchid Lane Access to Charles M. Christiansen Trail

SOUTH to NORTH

General Description. There is some up-and-down on this neighborhood access trail, which has many possibly confusing junctions along its 0.7 mile length. Total ascent is about 120'; descent is 70'.

Access. *From the south:* from Orchid Lane and 17th Place. *From the north:* from the Charles M. Christiansen Trail 0.7 mile from Dreamy Draw, 2.3 miles east of Cave Creek Road.

Read Down ↓	Detailed Trail Description	Read Up ↑
0.00	At Orchid Lane and 17th Place, head N (1,360'), ascending.	0.69
0.18	Pass (1,505') and **junction (4-way):** sharp R is NDT descending along wash; to R is 290' NDT to top of bump on ridge (1,576') with views. Descend.	0.51
0.21	**Junction:** bear R.	0.48
0.23	**Junction:** NDT to R descends to cross wash, joining parallel trail.	0.46
0.26	**Junction (4-way):** NDT on R descends into valley, on L ascends but does not lead anywhere of significance.	0.43

0.31	Cross wash.	0.38
0.34	**Junction:** where trail rejoins track from fenced-in area, turn R (N).	0.35
0.38	Follow fence line on L.	0.31
0.40	**Junction:** turn R (sharp L is NDT thru fence)	0.29
0.46	Cross wash.	0.23
0.48	**Junction:**	0.21
0.63	**Junction:** Hatcher Access [E] on L. Turn R, cross wash.	0.06
0.69	**Junction:** CMC is to L and R (elevation 1,580').	0.00

[G] Sahuaro Access to Charles M. Christiansen Trail

WEST to EAST

General Description. Access via Sahuaro is an old vehicleway ascending to cross many other trails and tracks. There is one high point, otherwise it is an ascent all the way (100' total).

Access. *From the west:* take Sahuaro off of Cave Creek Road just north of Peoria, and drive to the very end of the road where Preserve signs will be seen. *From the east:* on the Christiansen Trail 0.4 mile from Cortez near Cave Creek Road, 2.6 miles from Dreamy Draw.

Read Down ↓	Detailed Trail Description	Read Up ↑
0.00	Leave E end of Sahuaro, near maintenance office of NE District Parks (1,360').	0.48
0.02	**Junction:** trail on R is being revegetated — ignore it. Go straight.	0.46
0.08	**Junction (4-way):** sharp R is trail to Peoria access in 945', S to Cheryl Access; half-L is NDT in open area. Go straight.	0.40
0.11	**Junction:** NDT joins on L. This trail narrows, descends gradually.	0.37
0.13	**Junction (4-way):** trail R leads S to Peoria/Cheryl Accesses, NDT half-R is poor. Bear L here, ascending gradually.	0.35
0.31	**Junction:** at top of rise, NDT on R. Descend, then level out on wide trail.	0.18
0.38	**Junction:** R is NDT (old vehicleway) to CMC in 0.29 mi.	0.10
0.40	**Junction:** in open area, NDT to R; L is poor NDT to flood control area. Go straight, descending. Pass NDT on L in 130' descending to W.	0.09
0.44	**Junction (4-way):** in open area, NDT to R peters out, on L poor NDT descends toward flood works.	0.04
0.48	**Junction:** CMC W-bound to Cave Creek Rd ahead 0.39 mi, CMC E-bound goes sharp R (elevation 1,460') for 2.57 mi to Dreamy Draw.	0.00

[H] Sunnyside Access to Charles M. Christiansen Trail

SOUTH to NORTH

This short trail gives access to the middle of the CMC between Cave Creek Road and 7th Street. From the dead end of Sunnyside west of 16th Street, go around a home, over a berm, and turn right, steadily uphill on a rocky old vehicleway. The footway is rough. At 0.16 mile there is a 4-way junction. The Christiansen Trail goes left and right here; a nondesignated trail continues. (This point is 1.2 mile east of 7th St Trailhead, or 0.8 mile west of Cave Creek Road.) Ascent is 60'.

[J] 18th Street Access SOUTH to NORTH

From 18th St. 1/5 mile north of Northern Avenue, a neighborhood access trail on the east side leads east onto a diversion dam, leaves it at 0.2 mile, crosses the main wash at 0.4 mile and then parallels it, reaching Orchid Lane [F] and Hatcher Access [E] at 0.85 mile. The Charles M. Christiansen Trail [100] is reached in 0.9 mile. Ascent is gradual.

Shea Access to Charles M. Christiansen Trail

EAST to WEST

From the end of Shea Boulevard west of 21st Place this very short spur trail gives access to the Charles M. Christiansen Trail 0.9 mile east of Cave Creek Road and 2 miles west of Dreamy Draw. It reaches the Trail in 355'. There is no significant ascent.

Trails off Cave Creek Road (Sahuaro to Gold Dust)

There are neighborhood trails from the ends of Sahuaro at 15th Way, Peoria, Cheryl, and Gold Dust (off of Cinnabar at 17th St. The map shows these. There are two more or less parallel north-south trails, the western one lower, the eastern one higher up the slope. The western one starts north from Cheryl, running to Peoria, and the longer eastern one runs from Gold Dust to Sahuaro Access. Short spurs connect the two. Both are about 1/3 mile long.

Charles M. Christiansen Trail [100] Summary

Eastbound

Read Down ↓	Description of Major Points
0.00	Mountain View Park. Trail heads north, past monument.
0.70	**Junction:** [306] sharp left.
0.92	**Junction:** [306] half-left to Shaw Butte and Central Avenue Trailhead.
1.36	**Junction:** [100A] right to North Mountain Road in 0.6 mile.
1.67	**Junction:** [C] straight ahead to Central Avenue Trailhead. Turn right.
2.06	**Junction:** spur left 300' to 7th Street Trailhead; enter tunnel under 7th Street.
2.59	**Junction:** Trail [25] on L to Thunderbird, on to Lookout Mountain area.
4.07	Cortez just east of Cave Creek Road.
4.46	**Junction:** Sahuaro Access [G] straight ahead; turn left.
5.00	**Junction:** Shea Access 335' to east.
6.36	**Junction:** Hatcher Access [E] on right (west); ahead on left Orchid Lane [F], 18th St [J]
7.04	**Junction:** Dreamy Draw 100' to right; keep left here. Go through tunnel.
7.65	**Junction:** Nature Trail [220] straight ahead; go left.
7.79	**Junction:** Perl Charles Trail [1A] joins on right.
8.03	**Junction:** Perl Charles Trail [1A] leaves on right.
9.89	**Junction:** Quartz Ridge Trail [8] on right and left.
9.96	**Junction:** LV Yates Trail on right; spur [E] left 0.4 mile to 40th Street Trailhead.
11.04	This trail ends at Tatum Boulevard.

Westbound

Read Down ↓	Description of Major Points
0.00	Leave Tatum Boulevard, heading west.
1.08	**Junction:** LV Yates Trail on left; spur [E] right 0.4 mile to 40th Street Trailhead.
1.15	**Junction:** Quartz Trail left and right.
3.01	**Junction:** Perl Charles Trail [1A] joins from left.
3.25	**Junction:** Perl Charles Trail [1A] leaves on left.
3.39	**Junction:** Nature Trail [220] on right.
4.00	**Junction:** Dreamy Draw 100' to left.
4.68	**Junction:** Hatcher Access [E], Orchid Lane Access [F] & 18th St. [J] on right.
6.04	**Junction:** Shea Access 335' to east.
6.58	**Junction:** Sahuaro Access L; turn R.
6.97	Cross Cortez Road just before tunnel under Cave Creek Road.
8.45	**Junction:** trail [25] north to Thunderbird tunnel and Lookout Mountain.
8.98	**Junction:** spur 300' right to 7th Street Trailhead.
9.37	**Junction:** spur [C] on right to Central Avenue Trailhead.
9.68	**Junction:** [100A] on left to North Mountain Road in 0.6 mile.
10.12	**Junction:** [306] sharp right.
10.34	**Junction:** [306] right to 7th Avenue and Shaw Butte.
11.04	Mountain View Park.

City of Phoenix

South Mountain

Sierra Estrellas from the Bajada Trail

Introduction. South Mountain is reputed to be the world's largest municipal park. There is no doubt that it is an impressive and popular area, with much variety for the recreationist. A Master Plan for the park is being implemented over the next few years, and has already led to some significant changes in the area.

History. The park area is alleged to have been claimed for Spain by Father Marcos de Niza, traveling through the area in 1539. (His inscription[1] is to be seen on the short trail south of the ramadas off the Pima Canyon Road.) The area to the east was the Yaqui Indian village of Guadalupe. In 1694 Father Kino passed through the area, but the first Americans did not arrive until about 1838. Charles Holbert became first custodian of the new park in 1929 and dedicated himself to the development of a largely inaccessible area. Starting in 1933, this task was eased by the efforts of the Civilian Conservation Corps.

Geology. The South Mountain area actually consists of three parallel ranges trending northeast-southwest like the White Tank Mountains. They represent a "metamorphic core complex" of intrusive and metamorphic rock that welled up and extended in the northeast-southwest direction. Rocks to be seen today in the western part of the park are mostly granitic *gneiss* (coarse-grained rock with alternating light and dark minerals) and *schist* (better-defined planes of minerals result in easy cleavage), both of Precambrian age. In the eastern part of the park the rocks are intrusive granite, much younger than those in the western end. In some places *petroglyphs* have been carved or pecked into the rock surfaces; these are usually 500-1500 years old.

Maps. *Our maps 9-13, "South Mountain A" through "South Mountain E."* The USGS 1:24,000 quadrangles Laveen (1952, photorevised 1973), Lone Butte (1952, photorevised 1973) and Guadalupe (1952, photorevised 1982) show the topography and some of the trails, but there have been many changes since these were published.

Access. There are several main access points within the park itself, which is entered either from the south end of Central Avenue or the Pima Canyon Road leading to the Marcos de Niza Ramadas and the eastern end of the National Trail [162]. From the north there are separate access points for the Mormon, Kiwanis, Ranger, Holbert, Javelina, Ma-Ha-Tauk, and Beverly Canyon Trails, as well as from the "T Bone Steak House" on 19th Avenue (crosses private land). From the south there is a new main access point off the end of Desert Foothills Parkway and at Desert Broom in Ahwatukee, as well as a walk-in access at San Gabriel Drive .

Facilities. Picnic ramadas serve up to 3,100, with electricity, drinking water, toilets and fire-pits (250 first-come, the remainder reservable). Trails close at sunset; parks close at 11:00 p.m.

Recommended Hikes and Trail Rides. Numbers used are official City of Phoenix numbers for designated trails. Other trails have names, but no numbers. Non-designated trails are now off-limits, so are not included,

[1]There is some doubt as to its authenticity.

though where they are visible they may be mentioned (indicated as "NDT"). All trails are multi-use, though in some cases they may not be suitable for most equestrians or mountain-bikers. Almost all of the trails are highly recommended. The western and eastern sections of the National Trail are especially scenic and provide almost continuous distant views. The Telegraph Pass Trail is an easy 1.2 miles. The Javelina Canyon Trail (2 miles) offers variety and views without much climbing.

Cautions. The closing and re-vegetating of non-designated trails and old four-wheel drive tracks has been under way for some time. These areas are usually signed "closed," or deliberately blocked with rocks or brush. *Please avoid using these routes.* In some areas there are many undesignated trails that can be confusing, especially in bad weather. Significant junctions with these trails are noted in the detailed tabular descriptions, though some of them may disappear soon; trail changes are still being made. Keep in mind, also, that some trails are very long and traverse rugged terrain. Don't be fooled by South Mountain being inside the city limits!

The number and length of trails has necessitated a very large chapter. Below is a table of contents for this chapter.

[62] Kiwanis Trail

General Description. Built by members of the Kiwanis Club, opened in 1926, and improved by the Phoenix chain gang, this trail was confusing because of many side-trails and minor trails of use; marking has now been improved. From the Kiwanis Trailhead parking lot it ascends a valley past several rock dams (built for water storage and erosion control but unsuccessful for these purposes) and then runs between the bends of the highway to reach it at about 1 mile near the National Trail. Ascent is 400'.

Access. From the Kiwanis Trailhead parking lot, at the bend in the road. *(Map 11 — South Mountain C)*

Read Down ↓	Detailed Trail Description	Read Up ↑
0.00	Leave trailhead, ascending (1,590'). On other side of road bend is Las Lomitas Loop.	1.04
0.04	Pass picnic tables, go up wide trail at end of open area.	1.00
0.07	**Junction:** trail of use on L (alternate route).	0.97
0.10	**Junction:** alternate rejoins.	0.94
0.18	**Junction:** 50' to R is rock wall and grassy area. Go straight.	0.86
0.23	Start steady, rocky ascent.	0.81
0.30	Level area, stone dam.	0.74
0.36	Dam. Start steady ascent in 150'.	0.68
0.40	**Junction:** alternate trail on L; go straight.	0.64
0.42	Cross under power line. Trail goes up and down.	0.62
0.53	Trail runs alongside wash.	0.51
0.54	Ascend in wash for 45', leave it to R.	0.50
0.56	Switchback to R, then 3 more.	0.48
0.58	**Junction:** trail of use on R; big dam on L.	0.46
0.75	Ascend rocky trail between bends of Summit Road.	0.29
0.88	Ascend to R, then switchback to L.	0.16
1.02	Cross wash, ascend steadily, then steeply.	0.02
1.04	**Junction:** highway, signpost (1,990') in Telegraph Pass. National Trail W-bound is 30' S, E-bound is 530' N of here.	0.00

[64] Holbert Trail

General Description. The trail first leads from the (usually) locked Activity Complex gate to the trailhead at 0.4 mile, then over rolling terrain near the base of the mountain to briefly join a road past a water tank and ascends by a scenic route up the side of a major valley past unusual rock formations to a junction with the 0.2-mile side-trail to Dobbins Lookout (and road) at 2.3 miles. Beyond, it continues up for another ¼ mile to the Summit Road at 2.6 miles, and then another 0.4 mile to the TV Tower Road and the National Trail. Ascent is 1,050'.

Access. *From the Activity Complex gate*, follow the road for 0.4 mile to the actual trailhead on the south side; *from the top*, from Summit Road *(see Map 11 — South Mountain C).*

Read Down ↓	Detailed Trail Description	Read Up ↑
0.00	Leave Activity Complex gate (1,350').	2.98
0.44	Leave parking area at sign-post.	2.54
0.51	**Junction:** bear L, go over hill.	2.47
0.55	**Junction:** with cookout area on R, cross road, head E, following posts near base of mountain slopes.	2.43
0.67	Pass petroglyphs on rock on L.	2.31
0.86	Bottom of deep wash; ascend.	2.12
0.96	**Junction:** join paved road, go R on it.	2.02

1.02	**Junction:** leave road on R, at angle; in 200' pass along fence for 80'.	1.96
1.13	Bear R.	1.85
1.20	Top of rise. Side-hill, ascend valley side. Apparently dry waterfall on R.	1.78
1.57	Turn L.	1.41
1.64	Switchback to R.	1.34
1.74	Cross wash.	1.24
1.79	Turn L, then to R in 250'.	1.19
1.85	**Junction:** 90' to R is fine viewpoint. Pass rock cave on L in 0.18 mi.	1.13
2.12	Switchback to L.	0.86
2.16	Switchback to R, then to L in 55', just above wash.	0.82
2.22	Switchback to R at unusual rock formation, then switchback to L in 95'.	0.76
2.29	**Junction:** to R, side trail ascends 300' to Dobbins Lookout (2,350'). *[details: at 90' go straight, switchback to L at 265', R at 0.13 mi, where spur trail R leads 60' to viewpoint; Dobbins Lookout is at 0.21 mi, 2.5 mi from start.]*	0.69
2.31	Switchback to L, then pass trail of use.	0.67
2.37	Enter moderate wash, leave it in 60'.	0.61
2.43	**Junction:** switchback to L, then to R.	0.55
2.55	Summit Road (2,255'). Go L on road for 75'.	0.43
2.56	Leave Summit Road on steps, bear R.	0.42
2.57	Turn L, ascending steadily up scenic ridge crest.	0.41
2.84	Ease grade of ascent, crest broadens.	0.14
2.92	**Junction:** TV Road, go R on it.	0.06
2.94	**Junction:** National Trail E.	0.04
2.98	**Junction:** National Trail W (this trail ends).	0.00

[162] National Trail EAST to WEST

> This trail is described in 5 sections, a total of 14.6 miles

PIMA CANYON to BUENA VISTA LOOKOUT

General Description. A popular trail segment leads from the Pima Canyon road along a very scenic section, past the Hidden Valley loop trail at 1.4 and 1.9 miles, then on to Buena Vista Lookout on Summit Road, a distance of 3.6 miles. Ascent is 890'.

Access. *At the eastern end,* the trail leaves on a dirt road at 1.1 miles from the gate at the end of paving at the Marcos de Niza ramadas, 0.6 mile west of the park entrance at 48th Street. **Note: the road must be walked.** *At the western end* it departs from Buena Vista Lookout. *(Maps 12, 13 — South Mountain D, E)*

Read Down ↓	Detailed Trail Description	Read Up ↑
0.00	Leave Pima Canyon road loop (1,580') after 1.1 mile road walk. Head *NW*.	3.59
0.03	Cross major wash and ascend.	3.56
0.06	**Junction:** slightly R is the Mormon Loop Trail (1.34 mi), also leading in 0.17 mi to the Javelina Canyon Trail. To continue, turn L here. Turn R in 60', then L in 40' more and ascend.	3.53

0.09	Ascend more steadily, then turn L.	3.50
0.12	Switchback to R.	3.47
0.16	Switchback to L where trail ahead has been closed.	3.43
0.20	Turn R along hillside.	3.39
0.23	Switchback to R.	3.36
0.25	Top of rise (closed trail on R). Bear L, ease grade of ascent.	3.34
0.34	Reach crest of ridge.	3.25
0.43	Bear R and side-hill to E.	3.16
0.47	Switchback to L.	3.12
0.52	Trail post. Old trail on L is closed.	3.07
0.53	**Junction:** on crest is viewpoint to R.	3.06

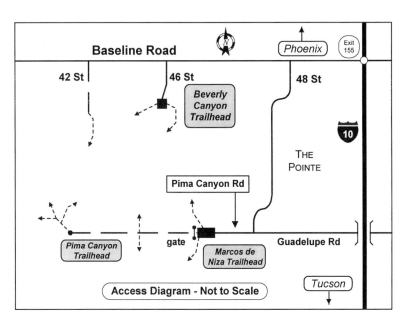

0.58	**Junction:** ignore NDT (track) on L.	3.01
0.64	Go steeply up to L.	2.95
0.65	Cross over crest of ridge, then take narrow trail to L of hump.	2.94
0.68	**Junction:** on crest, 50' to R is viewpoint.	2.91
0.72	Pass through area of huge rocks.	2.87
0.83	Turn sharp R.	2.76
0.85	Go L.	2.74
0.88	Switchback to R.	2.71
1.00	Go through area of huge rocks.	2.59
1.05	Jog L, then sharp R. Ahead, there are several rocky areas that provide natural shelters.	2.54
1.29	Old metal sign on L (ignore).	2.30
1.35	**Junction:** Hidden Valley Trail on L. Keep R for main trail.	2.24
1.48	**Important junction:** sharp R is Mormon Trail [264].	2.11
1.53	**Junction:** NDT on L. Leave wash, bear R.	2.06
1.56	**Junction:** NDT on L.	2.03

1.58	Switchback to L.	2.01
1.68	Go L, ascending, then to R.	1.91
1.69	Top of rise (viewpoint). Turn L.	1.90
1.76	Switchback to R, up to top of rise. In 200', turn R, then L.	1.83
1.87	Top of rise.	1.72
1.90	**Junction:** trail of use on L by-passes Fat Man's Pass on Hidden Valley Trail.	1.69
1.92	**Important junction:** Hidden Valley Trail on L.	1.68
1.95	Enter wash, then stay in it for 325'.	1.64
2.13	Turn R, then L.	1.46
2.19	Jog R, then to L.	1.40
2.29	Cross wash and ascend through rocky area.	1.30
2.39	**Junction:** NDT on L.	1.20
2.45	**Junction:** NDT sharp L.	1.14
2.50	Cross 3 washes in next 0.13 mi, the last near rock shelter on R.	1.09
2.67	Cross wash, then another in 300'.	0.92
2.83	Cross wash.	0.76
2.88	**Junction:** NDT on L.	0.71
3.01	Shelter in rocks on L.	0.58
3.02	National Trail sign on L.	0.57
3.03	**Junction:** NDT on R.	0.56
3.06	**Junction:** NDT on R rejoining.	0.53
3.20	**Junction:** NDT on R.	0.39
3.22	**Junction (4-way):** NDT R & L.	0.35
3.59	Buena Vista Lookout (2,360'). To N, Geronimo Trail [262] descends toward valley.	0.00

[162] National Trail   EAST to WEST

BUENA VISTA LOOKOUT to TELEGRAPH PASS

General Description. This trail segment leads from Buena Vista Lookout to a long descent of the ridge north of South Mountain's highest peak (Mt. Suppoa, 2,690'), closed to the public because of the presence of dozens of transmission towers. After passing the summit, the trail takes a very scenic route to Telegraph Pass at 3 miles. Ascent is 320', descent is 440'.

Access. *Eastern end:* the trail leaves Buena Vista Lookout. *Western end:* it departs from the Summit Road in Telegraph Pass. *(Maps 11, 12 — South Mountain C, D.)*

Read Down ↓	Detailed Trail Description	Read Up ↑
0.00	Leave Buena Vista Lookout (2,360'). Follow road W.	3.01
0.08	Leave road just past small parking area on L.	2.93
0.09	**Junction:** trail L to hump. Ascend gradually, paralleling road.	2.92
0.16	**Junction:** cross dirt road, continue on level trail. "Chinese Wall" of rocks can be seen ahead.	2.86
0.27	Top of rise. Bear L and descend.	2.74
0.32	Level out, then reach top of rise in 0.12 mi.	2.69
0.59	Bend of road below.	2.41
0.63	Top of rise.	2.38

0.72	**Important junction:** reach TV Tower Road (across road, just to R of road, is the Holbert Trail [64]. Cross road, follow it to L.	2.29
0.77	**Junction:** leave road on R (sign).	2.24
0.95	Pass to R of rocky hump.	2.06
1.06	Top of rise.	1.95
1.10	Start descending past towers on summit.	1.90
1.11	Turn sharp L.	1.89
1.16	**Junction:** NDT L to highway in 235'; another in 40'.	1.85
1.27	Turn L. Route goes up and down, bypassing summit.	1.73
1.68	Cross moderate wash.	1.32
1.92	Go onto side-ridge. In 45', start descent.	1.09
2.11	**Junction:** cross dirt road (R to highway).	0.90
2.25	Bear L on scenic route with good views. In 45' pass under phone line.	0.76
2.51	Cross wash.	0.50
2.63	**Junction:** old trail descends R to highway in 50'. New trail continues along hillside.	0.38
2.76	Switchback to R, then to L.	0.25
2.79	Turn R onto crest (shortly thereafter there is a 100' spur to hump on L).	0.22
2.86	Turn sharp L, off crest. Turn sharp L in 150'.	0.15
2.90	Switchback to R and down.	0.11
2.91	**Important junction:** Telegraph Pass Trail descends on L to Desert Foothills TH, 1.18 mi. Keep R.	0.10
2.92	Join road (viewpoint to N 230' to R along road); go L.	0.09
3.01	**Telegraph Pass** (1,990').	0.00

[162] National Trail EAST to WEST

TELEGRAPH PASS to SAN JUAN ROAD

General Description. This trail segment leads from Telegraph Pass past Eagles Nest Lookout up a high ridge and generally keeps on or near the crest for 1.4 miles where it passes the Ranger Trail. There is then a long, partly new section that descends 1,000' thru a beautiful valley to the San Juan Road at 5.8 miles. Ascent is 850', descent is 1,630'.

Access. *At the eastern end,* the trail leaves Telegraph Pass at a signpost. *At the western end* from the San Juan Road trailhead parking area. *(Maps 9-11 — South Mountain A-C).*

Read Down ↓	*Detailed Trail Description*	*Read Up* ↑
0.00	Leave Telegraph Pass (1,990'), ascending W at signpost.	5.84
0.04	Turn R, then switchback to L in 195'.	5.80
0.13	**Junction:** switchback to R (spur trail ahead leads 65' and then a further 135' to a viewpoint).	4.51
0.16	Viewpoint on L. Bear R, ease grade of ascent.	5.68
0.21	Reach crest again; turn R, avoiding poor trails of use.	5.63
0.25	Ascend into side-valley.	5.59
0.28	**Junction:** NDT on L. Go straight.	5.56
0.30	Switchback to L, then in 200' switchback to R (old stone ramada on L).	5.54
0.37	**Junction:** NDT ascends straight ahead. Bear R here.	5.47

0.38	**Junction:** NDT on L. Ascend rocky area.	5.46
0.39	**Junction:** NDT rejoins on L.	5.45
0.54	Reach crest, bear slightly R with easy walking.	5.30
0.63	**Junction:** NDT sharp L.	5.21
0.65	Reach top of rise; descend from hump.	5.19
0.77	Switchback to L, then turn R in 50'.	5.07
0.84	Start steady ascent.	5.00
0.88	Top of rise. Return to crest in 110'.	4.96
0.97	Top of small summit. Pass another hump on crest.	4.87
1.10	Top of major summit with excellent views. Descend.	4.74
1.16	Bottom; ascend gradually.	4.68
1.21	Top of rise on crest.	4.63
1.26	Hump on R, just off trail.	4.58
1.28	**Junction:** trail R to top of hump.	4.56
1.35	**Junction:** NDT on R. Descend to R.	4.49
1.38	**Important junction:** Ranger Trail descends on R to 5 Tables in 0.74 mi.	4.46
1.43	**Junction:** trail on L returns from 1.35 mi. Continue up crest.	4.41
1.50	Cross wash, bear slightly L with easy ascent.	4.34
1.67	**Junction:** poor NDT sharp R.	4.17
1.89	Ridge broadens.	3.95
2.00	Flat area on L; ascend.	3.84
2.06	Turn L; reach top of rise in 150', then descend.	3.78
2.31	Switchback to R, ascend.	3.53
2.33	Top of rise. Bear L and descend gradually.	3.51
2.40	**Junction:** NDT on L.	3.44
2.45	**Junction:** NDT sharp L (overgrown) leads S to private land. Continue side-hilling.	3.39
2.55	Reach crest. Descend in 200'.	3.29
2.63	Bottom. Ascend to L of peak ahead.	3.21
2.71	Top of rise (excellent viewpoint in attractive area).	3.13
2.83	Reach crest; descend, reaching bottom in 65', another sag in 200'.	3.01
2.94	**Junction:** 100' R to hump. Descend easily to bottom in 400'.	2.90
3.07	Reach crest, descend to L.	2.77
3.17	Reach crest again, ascend to top of rise (cairn) in 250', descend.	2.67
3.32	Turn R, level off.	2.52
3.33	Switchback down to L.	2.51
3.39	Bottom. Ascend gradually.	2.45
3.42	Pass white rocks.	2.42
3.47	Reach crest again (minor top).	2.37
3.52	Last hump on ridge (it is almost all downhill from here).	2.32
3.70	Switchback to R, then to L in 65'.	2.14
3.84	Descend loose rock, switchback to R, then to L .	2.00
3.89	At location of old junction, keep L, swinging around end of crest.	1.95
4.03	Crest (1,960'). Start steep drop SSW with excellent views.	1.81
4.11	Switchback to L, then to R in 45'.	1.73
4.31	Top of rise	1.53
4.50	Cross small wash at bottom of subsidiary valley. Descend to W.	1.34
4.63	Bottom of descent.	1.21
4.65	Top of rise in beautiful, hidden valley, high above main wash.	1.19
4.75	Bottom of descent.	1.09
4.76	Top of rise.	1.08
5.07	Cross wash in valley bottom; ascend briefly.	0.77
5.16	Pass (1,350'), views. Descend to W.	0.68

5.19	Switchback to R, continue descent.	0.65
5.37	**Junction:** avoid old vehicleway on L; in 50' cross small wash.	0.47
5.47	Cross small wash.	0.37
5.55	Cross small wash.	0.29
5.68	Cross major wash.	0.16
5.75	**Junction:** keep R.	0.09
5.82	**Important junction:** Keep L (Bajada Trail on R).	0.02
5.84	San Juan Road (1,300').	0.00

[162] National Trail EAST to WEST

SAN JUAN ROAD to SAN JUAN RAMADA

General Description. This trail segment leads from the San Juan Road to the pass, ramada and trailhead at the road end. It leads over a mostly flat slope toward the pass in the range. Crossing several washes, it heads northwest to 0.8 mile, then north to parallel the road, ascending to the Alta Trail next to the road end at 1½ miles. Ascent is 50'.

Access. *At the eastern end,* the trail leaves the road at 4.3 miles from the entrance gate at a trailhead parking area. This is 1.9 miles west of the Alta Trailhead. *At the western end* it departs from the Alta Trail just a few feet east of the stone wall at the ramada and trailhead. *(Map 9 — South Mountain A.)*

Read Down ↓	Detailed Trail Description	Read Up ↑
0.00	Leave San Juan Road, heading NW at signpost (1,310'), 260' W of trailhead.	1.50
0.10	Head slightly R, cross small wash onto flat plain.	1.40
0.12	Cross old road, turn L (W).	1.38
0.16	Cross major wash.	1.34
0.36	Cross major wash; head toward mountain slopes.	1.14
0.42	Cross major wash, head W.	1.08
0.83	Cross small wash, then swing around to N, descending gradually.	0.67
0.96	Road parallels trail below on L. Ascend gradually.	0.64
1.50	**Important junction:** Alta Trail R, in pass. San Juan Ramada on L at road end (1,320'). National Trail continues W along the ridge.	0.00

[162] Extension of National Trail — Peak 1600

FROM SAN JUAN RAMADA

General Description. For a relatively short trip with fine views of South Mountain and the Sierra Estrella as well as Phoenix, this trail is perfect. It leaves the San Juan road end, and ascends steadily up the crest, past several bumps, to one of the last peaks on the ridge at 0.6 mile. Ascent is 300'.

Access. From the end of the San Juan Ramada parking lot, head northwest. *(Map 9 — South Mountain A.)*

Read Down ↓	Detailed Trail Description	Read Up ↑
0.00	Leave parking area at N end (1,320'), heading NW up ridge, passing several trails of use on R.	0.63
0.12	**Junction:** NDT on R. Ascend.	0.51
0.14	**Junction:** poor NDT on R.	0.48
0.22	**Junction:** on crest, NDT rejoins on R.	0.40
0.30	Leave crest; follow ridge along its N side, ascending gradually.	0.32
0.37	Cross over crest to S side.	0.26
0.40	Crest again: stay on it or close to it from here. Start final ascent in 400'.	0.22
0.53	Switchback to R, then to L in only 15'.	0.09
0.54	**Junction:** at L switchback, NDT on R leads onto crest in 125'.	0.09
0.55	Top of rise, almost on crest. Descend, reach bottom in 100'.	0.07
0.58	**Junction:** NDT on R, onto crest.	0.04
0.63	Top of Peak 1600. Fine views.	0.00

[262] Geronimo Trail

This formerly popular trail from the Boy Scout Heard Pueblo to National Trail at Buena Vista Lookout is due to be reopened when a trailhead parking area is established east of Heard Pueblo. (It may be included in the next edition.)

[264] Mormon Trail

General Description. This trail ascends by a circuitous route and switchbacks to a pass at 1.2 miles, then descends briefly to the National Trail at 1.4 miles. Ascent is 730'. It was rehabilitated in 1995 by REI volunteers.

Access. From Euclid at 24th Street. *(Map 12 — South Mountain D.)*

Read Down ↓	Detailed Trail Description	Read Up ↑
0.00	Leave road at dirt barrier on rocky, wide trail (1,290'). In 200', bear L on rocks.	1.39
0.06	**Junction:** trail R ascends for 210' to poor viewpoint.	1.33
0.10	**Junction:** trail on L rejoins. Bear R, up rocks for 100', then level off.	1.29
0.14	Overhanging rock on R.	1.25
0.31	**Junction:** trail to R descends, ends at poor viewpoint.	1.08
0.34	**Junction:** trail L to hump in 135'.	1.05
0.36	Bottom of descent. Ascend; turn L in 150' and ascend again.	1.03
0.41	**Junction:** cut-off on L.	0.98
0.44	**Junction:** NDT on L (blocked); switchback to L.	0.95
0.51	Switchback to L, then again in 0.06 mi.	0.88
0.63	Switchback to R, then to L in 130'.	0.76
0.71	Switchback to R.	0.68
0.75	**Junction:** 40' L is viewpoint near hump.	0.64
0.93	Cross wash.	0.46
0.98	Reach bottom of descent. Turn L in 200'.	0.41

1.16   **Important junction:** in pass, trail L (Mormon Loop) leads to National Trail [162] in Pima Canyon in 1.34 mi. Only 40' up this side-trail is spur leading 285' up to small summit. 0.23

1.25   **Junction:** NDT on L. 0.14

1.33   **Junction:** this trail splits, reaching National Trail either way (L is 340'; go R). 0.06

1.39   **Junction:** National Trail (1,960'). 1.48 mi L to Pima Canyon; 2.11 mi R to Buena Vista Lookout. 0.00

[362] Alta Trail   WEST to EAST

General Description. Traveling east, the trail (built by the CCC) starts from the San Juan Ramada at the road end in a pass, at the junction with the National Trail [162]. This section is moderately strenuous on a well-built trail with very good views, but there are sections that have slumped. It ascends steadily up a valley to 1.1 miles, then circles around the valley's head to a pass at 1½ miles where short side-trails lead to fine views. From there it switchbacks down and contours around Maricopa Peak, reaching the ridge crest at 2.7 miles and passing or going over several peaks with the last summit at 3.1 miles. The trail then makes a long, switchbacking descent to reach the Alta Trail parking lot at San Juan Road at 4.6 miles and a junction with a spur to the Bajada Trail. *It is not recommended for equestrian or mountain-bike use.* Total ascent is 1,300', descent is 1,100'.

Access. *At the western end,* from San Juan ramada; *at the eastern end* from the Alta Trailhead parking lot at 2.4 miles west of the park entrance. *(Maps 9, 10 — South Mountain A, B.)*

Read Down ↓	Detailed Trail Description	Read Up ↑

0.00   Leave ramada at sign-post, heading E. There is a junction (to the R) at the start (National Trail heading SE), as well as to the W at the parking area (National Trail W). Elevation here is 1,320'. 4.57

0.41   Switchback to R, then to L, ignoring short-cut trail. 4.16

0.44   End of ridge and viewpoint. View of peak ahead. Continue ascent. 4.53

0.70   Cross wash, bear L around end of valley, ascending; in 100' switchbacks start. .. 3.87

0.80   Go around end of subsidiary ridge. Ascent continues. 3.76

0.98   Switchback to R, up open rock. Use care. 3.59

1.09   Top of rise, viewpoint. Ease grade. 3.48

1.13   **Junction:** spur trail R 45' to viewpoint. Ascend. 3.44

1.17   Switchback to R, level off along ridge. 110' beyond switchback is viewpoint just off trail to R. Contour around N side of head of valley. 3.40

1.38   Trail switchbacks again, on ascent. 3.19

1.43   Cross ridge crest; switchbacks follow. 3.14

1.52   Pass; turn L and follow ridge just N of crest. 3.05

1.54   **Junction:** spur trail to L leads 190' onto hump with good viewpoint of main ridge and Maricopa Peak; spur trail R, up minor crest, leads onto main ridge in 0.10 mi. (There, at junction, spur R leads 190' to hump; spur L leads 110' to another rise and route [no trail] to Maricopa Peak.) Descend switchbacks. 3.03

1.72   Ridge crest (2,325'). Head into larger valley. Trail soon ascends again. 2.85

1.82   Base of cliffs on R. Ascend gradually. 2.75

2.01	End of ridge; switchback to R, around it.	2.56
2.13	Top of rise; switchback down to R, then turn R in 250'.	2.44
2.20	Landmark: big rock on R.	2.37
2.41	Bear R into valley, up and down, gradually ascending.	2.16
2.50	Trail passes just below ridge crest on R. Continue just below crest.	2.06
2.71	Cross over crest to S side of ridge.	1.86
2.77	Reach crest again; follow it, then contour along N side of next summit on ridge. .	1.80
2.87	Crest again. Follow S side, ascending gradually.	1.70
2.92	Ascend. Subsidiary ridge on R.	1.65
3.00	Crest again. Ascend, heading toward last summit.	1.57
3.07	Last summit of ridge.	1.50
3.09	Switchback to L, then trail levels off.	1.49
3.12	Turn L into valley, then follow circuitous route.	1.45
3.37	Switchback to R, off crest, then to L.	1.20
3.48	Top of rise. Descend gradually.	1.09
3.53	Switchback to L; other turns and switchbacks follow.	1.02
3.66	Turn to R; trail makes long traverse.	0.91
3.71	Cross ridge crest, descending steadily.	0.86
3.78	Landmark: pass stone bench on L.	0.79
4.15	Cross wash, switchback to L, and descend steadily over loose rock. Beyond, trail is almost level and not well defined.	0.42
4.38	**Junction:** where the old trail continued straight, new trail turns R, descending to cross a moderate wash in 25'.	0.19
4.44	Turn L, then to R in 150'.	0.13
4.57	**Junction:** road (1,540'). *For National Trail, and return to start, turn R on road for 1.8 mi, then take trail for 1.5 mi: total to return is 3.3 mi.* Or take the Bajada Trail via the spur across the road, for 2.4 mi to San Juan Rd, then 1½ mi to San Juan Road end, a total of 3.9 mi.	0.00

Bajada Trail, Western Segment   EAST to WEST

ALTA TRAILHEAD to NATIONAL TRAIL

General Description. The Christown YMCA was instrumental in the creation of this attractive 3½-mile-long trail. The best hiking portion is the western segment, described first. From the Alta Trailhead, a spur climbs briefly to the main trail, then ascends and gradually side-hills the valley, running along the brink of the main wash, with fine views of Maricopa Peak above and the Sierra Estrella range to the west. It crosses many steep washes that drop from the ridge just to the south, and has much up and down travel. From 1½ miles it gradually descends toward the flat area where it ends at the National Trail [162] at 2.8 miles, only 100' from San Juan Road. There is a 320' descent, but the actual elevation change is closer to 600', with 150' of ascent in and out of washes.

Access. *At the eastern end of this segment,* at 3.2 miles from the gate and park administration office on San Juan Road. *At the western end,* 4.3 miles from the entrance gate, from 100' on the National Trail [162]. *(Maps 9, 10 — South Mountain A, B.)*

Read Down ↓	Detailed Trail Description	Read Up ↑
0.00	Leave Alta Trailhead (1,540') (across road is start of Alta Trail [362]), cross wash in 100', ascend to reach main trail. .	2.30
0.05	**Important junction:** main trail (marked by post #2) L & R. Turn R (SW), ascend steadily above wash.	2.25
0.14	Level off.	2.16
0.25	Turn L (E), ascend.	2.05
0.27	Turn R, ease ascent.	2.03
0.28	Cross rocky small wash. Side-hill, then descend gradually.	2.02
0.43	Cross small wash.	1.87
0.46	Switchback down to R.	1.84
0.47	Cross small wash; ascend briefly.	1.83
0.51	Good viewpoint in fine area (1,650'). Descend gradually.	1.79
0.59	Top of rise. Switchback to R, downhill.	1.71
0.60	Cross major wash. Go up and down on side-hill.	1.70
0.70	Descend steadily to N, along wash.	1.60
0.72	Cross wash.	1.58
0.76	Top of rise.	1.54
0.87	Start across wash area (several tracks).	1.43
0.94	Switchback to L and down.	1.36
0.97	Cross moderate wash. On opposite side, descend gradually toward flat area.	1.33
1.37	Cross moderate wash (1,480').	0.93
1.89	Cross moderate wash.	0.41
2.06	Old trail joins.	0.24
2.23	Switchback to R & down.	0.07
2.25	Cross major wash.	0.06
2.30	**Junction:** National Trail to L & R. This trail ends. Turn R to San Juan Rd in 100'. Across road, in 25' there is a **junction** to R, to trailhead parking in 285'.	0.00

Bajada Trail, Eastern Segment WEST to EAST

ALTA TRAILHEAD to RANGER TRAIL

General Description. The eastern segment of the Bajada Trail runs east, paralleling San Juan Road, then at 0.6 mile crosses Summit Road. It passes several washes and rises to a few viewpoints, but it is always close to the road. This section ends at the Ranger Trail at 1.3 miles. There is 70' of ascent, but the actual elevation change is closer to 110'.

Access. *At the western end,* at 3.2 miles from the gate and park administration office on San Juan Road. *At the eastern end,* from 0.4 mile on the Ranger Trail. *(Maps 9, 10 — South Mountain A, B.)*

Read Down ↓	Detailed Trail Description	Read Up ↑
0.00	Leave Alta TH (1,540'), cross wash in 100'.	1.31
0.05	**Junction:** main trail; go L (E).	1.26
0.11	**Junction:** spur trail L down to San Juan Road in 85' (1,560').	1.20
0.26	Cross small wash.	1.05
0.33	Cross wash.	0.98

0.57	Cross Summit Road near its junction with San Juan Road (1,610'), head E on level trail at first, then descend gradually.	0.74
0.59	Cross moderate wash. In 75' cross another wash, then others are crossed at 100' and at 350'.	0.72
0.70	Top of rise, trail post #3. Cross several small washes.	0.61
1.05	Descend steadily to R	0.26
1.06	Trail post #2, close to Summit Road.	0.25
1.19	Cross moderate wash.	0.12
1.21	Top of rise at post #1. Descend to N.	0.10
1.29	Level out.	0.02
1.31	**Junction:** Ranger Trail L & R (post #5). This trail ends. It is 0.2 mi down to Derby Loop, 0.43 mi to Five Tables TH.	0.00

Beverly Canyon Trail NORTH to SOUTH

General Description. From Beverly Canyon and Marcos de Niza Trailheads several new easy trails have been developed. They have no major ascents, but provide access to a pleasant area now being re-vegetated. This trail links the two trailheads and is 1.8 miles long. There are only a few small ascents amounting to a total of 350'.

Access. *At the northern end:* from the 46th St./Beverly Canyon Trailhead off Baseline Road. *At the southern end:* at the Desert Classic Trail 0.6 mile east of San Gabriel Walk-in. *(Map 13 — South Mountain E.)*

Read Down ↓	Detailed Trail Description	Read Up ↑
0.00	Leave Beverly Canyon (46th St.) Trailhead at E side (sign-board), ascending gradually E, then S. Elevation 1,230'	1.76
0.11	Top of rise, pass (1,280').	1.65
0.13	Bear R at post, alongside homes on level trail.	1.63
0.25	**Junction:** sharp L is NDT to private land.	1.51
0.28	**Junction:** leave vehicleway, descending L at post.	1.48
0.30	Cross wash.	1.46
0.45	**Junction:** bear R (L ascends steeply to power line).	1.31
0.49	**Junction:** keep R on level.	1.27
0.58	**Junction:** go L, ascending steadily (NDT on R descends to wash).	1.18
0.60	**Junction (4-way):** NDT L & R.	1.16
0.61	Start steady ascent, followed by steeper section.	1.15
0.62	**Important junction:** Beverly Canyon Trail straight ahead; side-trail to Loop One sharp L here, ascending vehicleway to reach Marcos de Niza Ramadas in ½ mi. Descend and cross main wash twice.	1.14
0.86	**Important junction:** Loop One sharp L. It joins here for the next 500'.	0.90
0.96	**Important junction:** Loop One departs, on L, ½ mile to Marcos de Niza Trailhead at Pima Canyon Road.	0.80
1.14	**Important junction:** on R is Ridgeline Trail ascending.	0.62
1.27	**Junction:** Pima Canyon Road (no vehicles). Ascend steadily on old 4WD track, avoiding side-trails.	0.49
1.51	Pass. Descend steeply.	0.25
1.76	**Junction:** Desert Classic Trail (1,370'). Pearce access is 0.16 mi ahead.	0.00

Box Canyon Loop EAST to WEST

HOLBERT TRAIL to LAS LOMITAS LOOP

General Description. This trail segment is complex. From the Holbert Trail it parallels the Activity Complex road, intersects the Center Trail at 0.4 mile near the Interpretive Center, then continues on to end on the Las Lomitas Loop at 0.8 mile. Ascent is 50'.

Access. *At the eastern end,* the trail leaves the Holbert Trail at its trailhead at the Activity Center parking lot. *At the western end* it leaves the Las Lomitas Loop at 0.3 miles. *(Map 9 — South Mountain A.)*

Read Down ↓	Detailed Trail Description	Read Up ↑
0.00	Leave Holbert Trail at trailhead, heading W (1,350'),	0.79
0.06	Trail post #1 alongside parking area.	0.73
0.17	**Junction:** spur sharp R down to parking area; continue straight.	0.62
0.19	Trail post #3. Head along hillside, paralleling parking area.	0.60
0.29	Leave parking area; head toward small hill.	0.50
0.35	**Junction:** at trail post #4, in small pass, Center Loop is just a few feet to R.	0.44
0.39	**Junction:** Center Loop crosses (trail posts #3 & #14).	0.40
0.44	Trail post #5. Head W.	0.35
0.49	Trail post #6. In 45' reach top of rise.	0.30
0.51	**Junction:** NDT to L; on R, short-cut leads 160' to spur on this trail. In 30' reach trail post #7.	0.28
0.58	Trail post #8. Ascend to S.	0.21
0.77	**Junction:** NDT sharp R. Trail post #10, top of rise.	0.02
0.79	**Junction:** In wash, Las Lomitas Loop L & R at trail post #16.	0.00

Center Loop EAST to WEST

General Description. This trail is an easy loop that circles a draw near the Environmental Education Center. Ascent is about 50'.

Access. *From the Interpretive Center,* on the Activities Complex road, the trail leaves the paved walkway at a kiosk. *(Map 11 — South Mountain C.)*

Read Down ↓	Detailed Trail Description	Read Up ↑
0.00	Leave the trail kiosk 185' from the Center, heading E. (1,350').	0.38
0.02	Top of rise. Descend, swing R.	0.36
0.05	**Junction:** At trail post #1, spur trail leads 100' R to top of hill with view.	0.33
0.07	Trail post #2. Head S.	0.31
0.10	**Junction:** Cross Box Canyon Loop at trail post #3/14.	0.28
0.12	Trail post #4/13. Ascend.	0.26
0.15	Trail post #5.	0.23
0.17	**Junction:** trail of use to R at trail post #6. Turn L, ascend SSE.	0.21
0.20	Turn R at trail post #7. In 25' is **junction:** go sharp L at trail post #8, ignoring trail of use on R.	0.18
0.22	**Junction:** bear L, trail of use ahead at trail post #9.	0.16

0.23	Cross small wash; head N.	0.15
0.28	Trail post #10. Trail goes up and down.	0.10
0.32	Top of rise.	0.06
0.34	**Junction:** trail of use on R; turn L and down. Trail post #11.	0.04
0.36	Trail post #12 on flat. Head W.	0.02
0.38	**Junction:** Rejoins original route at #13/4.	0.00

Crosscut Trail   EAST to WEST

LAS LOMITAS LOOP to MA-HA-TAUK TRAIL

General Description. From Las Lomitas Loop, cross the bajada, meet the Hideout Loop, cross the road to the Equestrian Area (passes between Round Pen and the Arena), the bottom of the Ranger Trail, San Juan Road to reach the Max Delta Loop at $^1/_2$ mile. Join that trail briefly, then start climbing up a ridge to reach the Ma-Ha-Tauk Trail (good views) at just over 1 mile. Ascent is about 300'.

Access. *At the eastern end,* the trail leaves the Las Lomitas Loop at 0.7 mile. *At the western end* it leaves the Ma-Ha-Tauk Trail 0.8 mile south of 19th Ave. Trailhead. *(Map 9 _ South Mountain A.)*

Read Down ↓	Detailed Trail Description	Read Up ↑
0.00	Leave Las Lomitas Loop trail post #14, heading W (1,550'),	1.03
0.08	**Junction:** Hideout Loop (trail post #1) diverges L, uphill.	0.95
0.10	**Junction:** Cross Las Lomitas Road.	0.93
0.30	**Junction:** Ranger Trail L in Equestrian Area. Continue straight ahead.	0.73
0.37	**Junction:** Cross San Juan Road.	0.66
0.47	**Junction:** Max Delta Loop (1,450'). Join it, going L (W) at post #14.	0.56
0.51	**Junction:** Leave Max Delta Loop on R at post #16, 0.12 mi W of Big & Little Ramadas Road. Ascend gradually W, then steadily.	0.52
0.71	Cross small, deep wash.	0.32
0.76	Just after post 10, go R, cross wash, ascend S along eroded, rocky trail.	0.27
0.81	**Junction:** go L and ascend. Straight ahead is trail to ramada in 325'.	0.22
0.92	Turn R, ascend steeply up rocks.	0.11
0.93	Post #12. Trail is steep and eroded, use care.	0.10
1.00	**Junction:** ignore NDT on R. Go L on crest.	0.03
1.01	Trail post #14, on crest.	0.02
1.03	**Junction:** this trail ends at Ma-Ha-Tauk Trail at a crest with good views. R, 0.79 mi to 19th Ave TH; to L, it is 0.45 mi down to Max Delta Loop.	0.00

"Chinese Wall" on the National Trail

On the Alta Trail

Derby Loop WEST to EAST

MAX DELTA LOOP to RANGER TRAIL

General Description. This is a short crossover trail. Descent is 40'.

Access. *At the western end,* the trail leaves the Max Delta Loop ½ mile from the junction of Summit & San Juan Roads. *At the eastern end* it departs from the Ranger Trail 0.2 mile south of the Five Tables Trailhead. *(Map 9 — South Mountain A.)*

Read Down ↓	Detailed Trail Description	Read Up ↑
0.00	From Max Delta Loop at trail post #26, turn S.	0.93
0.06	**Junction:** cross San Juan Road (1,560').	0.87
0.08	Descend gradually to L (SE).	0.85
0.14	Ascend to E.	0.79
0.23	Turn L, enter wash, go in and out of it.	0.70
0.29	Ascend steadily out of wash, then head S.	0.64
0.34	Cross wash, ascending to L.	0.59
0.41	Cross small wash.	0.52
0.54	**Important junction:** Ranger Trail L & R (L to ramadas and gravel road in 0.21 mi; elevation 1,550'). Continue.	0.39
0.58	Cross moderate wash.	0.35
0.61	Cross moderate wash, ascend steadily to E.	0.32
0.70	**Junction:** cross old vehicleway.	0.23
0.84	Cross small wash.	0.09
0.88	**Junction:** NDT on L. Road visible ahead.	0.05
0.93	**Junction:** Las Lomitas Road (elevation 1,580').	0.00

Desert Classic Trail EAST to WEST

MARCOS de NIZA RAMADAS to SAN GABRIEL WALK-IN

General Description. This trail segment is heavily used by mountain bikes, but moderate numbers of hikers make use of it as well. Ascent is about 100'.

Access. *At the eastern end,* the trail leaves the Marcos de Niza Ramadas at the western end of Pima Canyon Road on the southwest side of the parking area. *At the western end* it departs from the San Gabriel Walk-in at the end of San Gabriel Avenue and 40th Place. *(Map 13 — South Mountain E.)*

Read Down ↓	Detailed Trail Description	Read Up ↑
0.00	Leave ramadas, heading S (1,390').	1.53
0.02	**Junction:** trail from R (gate area, posts #1 & 2, same distance).	1.51
0.03	**Junction:** trail R up to Marcos de Niza Inscription.	1.50
0.11	Bear R, ascend.	1.42
0.15	Top of rise, with top of rock hump 40' to L. Descend.	1.38
0.28	Post #5. Turn R, ascending.	1.25
0.31	Bear L.	1.22

0.32	Post #6, top of rise, descend.	1.21
0.64	Post #9. **Junction:** sharp L is NDT.	0.89
0.70	Beside wall of housing development on L.	0.83
0.74	Post #10.	0.79
0.82	**Junction:** trail spur sharp L to Pearce access. Turn R, ascend. [7610/960]	0.73
0.92	**Junction:** NDT sharp L.	0.63
0.95	Top of rise above wash.	0.60
0.96	Cross moderate wash.	0.59
0.97	Post #11. **Junction:** Beverly Canyon Trail ascends R.	0.58
1.02	Start ascent.	0.53
1.07	Post #11. Top of rise.	0.48
1.11	Cross moderate wash.	0.44
1.37	Post #14. **Junction:** NDT on L, then branch of it in 55'.	0.18
1.43	Post #15, top of rise. **Junction:** NDT on R, closed trail on L.	0.12
1.53	**Junction:** San Gabriel Walk-in access spur on L (500'). Only 45' to Western Star Blvd at 40th Place, but no parking there (elevation 1,355'). Ahead, Desert Classic Trail leads to Desert Foothills Parkway trailhead in 7.57 mi.	0.00

Desert Classic Trail   EAST to WEST

SAN GABRIEL WALK-IN to TELEGRAPH PASS TRAILHEAD

General Description. This long trail segment is heavily used by mountain bikes, but moderate numbers of hikers make use of it as well. It follows a complex route up and down, crossing innumerable washes, along the base of the mountain. Ascent is about 900'.

Access. *At the eastern end,* the trail leaves the San Gabriel Walk-in at the west end of San Gabriel Avenue. *At the western end* it departs from the Telegraph Pass Trailhead on Desert Foothills Parkway, and coincides with that trail for 0.4 mile. *(Maps 11-13 — South Mountain C,D,E.).* Numbered trail posts make location easy.

Read Down ↓	Detailed Trail Description	Read Up ↑
0.00	Leave trail junction at post #16, 0.11 mi N of San Gabriel parking (1,355').	7.57
0.03	**Junction:** from L.	7.54
0.09	Top of rise.	7.48
0.10	Descend steeply to L.	7.47
0.11	Cross moderate wash.	7.46
0.12	Post #18; switchback to R.	7.45
0.32	Post #19, at top of rise, head L, descending gradually to S.	7.25
0.48	Post #20. Turn R, descend.	7.09
0.49	Cross large wash.	7.08
0.51	Post #21 [pulled out!]. **Junction:** NDT L, and sharp R.	7.06
0.54	Cross small wash.	7.03
0.57	Top of rise. Descend, cross valley.	7.00
0.67	Post #22; top of rise, **junction:** NDTs on L.	6.90
0.71	Cross small wash and ascend steadily.	6.86
0.78	Brink of wash; descend.	6.79
0.80	Cross moderate wash.	6.77

0.82	Post #23. Descend gradually along hogback.	6.75
0.85	Bottom of descent.	6.72
0.91	Cross wash, ascend.	6.66
0.99	Post #24. With bank of wash ahead, turn sharp L, descend paralleling wash.	
	Trail makes big loop.	6.58
1.17	Post #25. Turn R, descend steeply to wash.	6.40
1.19	Cross large wash, ascend for 125', turn R along wash.	6.38
1.34	Top of rise. Bear L, descend gradually to SW.	6.23
1.45	**Junction:** NDT on L. Post #26. Top of rise. Descend steeply to R.	6.12
1.48	Cross major wash, ascend steeply out of it.	6.09
1.51	Top of rise.	6.06
1.58	Cross small wash.	5.99
1.66	**Junction:** NDT on R; keep L.	5.91
1.68	Top of rise; turn L.	5.89
1.97	Trail runs parallel to property line for 200'.	5.60
2.04	Cross small wash, ascend steeply.	5.53
2.06	Post #31, next to water tank ("Horse Tank"). **Junction:** side-trail L 500' to boundary and tank service road, junction E Kachina Drive & S Equestrian Dr. ..	5.51
2.14	**Junction:** at top of rise, on L is spur trail back to other side-trail.	5.43
2.23	Cross small wash, ascend.	5.34
2.27	Cross wash, ascend out of it.	5.30
2.29	**Junction:** Ignore NDT on R. Post #33.	5.28
2.30	Post #34. Bottom of descent. Head up major wash, then out of it in 130'.	5.27
2.64	Post #37. Bear R at **junction:** NDT L to private land.	4.93
2.72	Post #38. **Junction:** NDT on L, back to previous side-trail.	4.85
2.86	Post #39. Turn L with rocks ahead.	4.71
2.98	Post #41. Ascend to W.	4.59
3.22	Cross very large wash.	4.35
3.32	**Junction:** at post #45, NDT on L.	4.25
3.37	**Junction:** NDT on R.	4.20
3.42	**Junction:** at post #46, old trail on R; go L (S).	4.15
3.54	**Junction:** keep R. Post #47.	4.03
3.59	Cross moderate wash. Enter wild area away from houses.	3.98
3.73	Cross small wash, swing W, ascend gradually, paralleling wash.	3.84
3.85	Cross wash.	3.72
3.96	**Junction:** at post #49, old vehicleway sharp R is closed.	3.61
4.00	Post #50. Swing L, then R.	3.57
4.15	**Junction:** at post #51, NDT is on L (closed). Ascend to SW.	3.42
4.44	Post #52. Descend to L.	3.13
4.74	Cross moderate wash, ascend steep pitch, in 250' cross major wash.	2.83
4.94	**Junction:** NDT on L; keep R. Post #54.	2.63
5.08	Swing L, descending and paralleling canyon.	2.49
5.18	Cross major wash.	2.39
5.42	Cross wash.	2.15
5.45	Post #57. Descend, join wash for 50', then leave it on R.	2.12
5.58	In and out of wash.	2.01
5.62	Cross wash.	1.97
5.75	**Junction:** at pass, NDT ascends on L. Post #59.	1.84
5.83	Switchback to L.	1.76
6.28	Above big wash.	1.31
6.34	**Junction:** Go R, descend.	1.25
6.39	Post #63. Parallel floodway.	1.20
6.44	Post #64. Top of rise, level.	1.15

6.49	Post #65. Parallel property line.	1.10
6.51	Bottom of descent, cross wash.	1.08
6.61	Floodway on L.	0.98
6.78	Cross wash. Floodway on L.	0.78
7.14	**Junction:** Telegraph Pass Trail L & R (signs). Trail to L is paved. Take it to reach Desert Foothills Trailhead (0.43 mi).	0.43
7.36	Swing L, then R.	0.22
7.41	Pass thru open barbed-wire fence.	0.16
7.57	**Junction:** Trailhead at Desert Foothills Parkway *[TOTAL 9.1 mi]*. (1,480').	0.00

Hidden Valley WEST to EAST

General Description. One of the most spectacular and varied trips in the park, this half mile trail is also an alternate to the main National Trail route. It includes the very narrow Fat Man's Pass [shown in color picture #13], petroglyphs, and a tunnel through the huge rocks. Allow much more time than the distance of only a bit over one half mile indicates. (There is a bypass of Fat Man's Pass from the National Trail just east of the junction.)

Access. On the National Trail, the *western end* is 1.4 miles, and the *eastern end* 1.9 miles, from Pima Canyon Road. *(Map 12 — South Mountain D.)*

Read Down ↓	Detailed Trail Description	Read Up ↑
0.00	Leave National Trail. In 85' turn L through Fat Man's Pass (or one can bypass it by going over the rocks). Use care.	0.53
0.03	Emerge from rocks, then follow wash.	0.50
0.06	Leave wash on L.	0.47
0.10	Cross wash.	0.43
0.14	Descend rocks, go under low rock (caution), then over and under rocks.	0.39
0.24	Cross brushy wash. Trail of use to L, to cave. Turn R.	0.33
0.25	**Junction:** keep L (trail braids). In 60' turn L.	0.32
0.32	Join wash.	0.21
0.38	Valley turns L. Petroglyphs on R. Descend rocks.	0.15
0.43	**Junction:** NDT on R, past shelter rock.	0.10
0.46	Go through rocks, then through spectacular tunnel in 50'.	0.07
0.51	**Junction:** NDT on R.	0.02
0.53	**Junction:** National Trail (0.13 mi to L is Mormon Trail junction).	0.00

Hideout Loop EAST to WEST

LAS LOMITAS LOOP to CROSSCUT TRAIL

This short trail segment leads from the Las Lomitas Loop near the ramadas, runs southwest skirting the base of two hills, then turns north to parallel Las Lomitas Road and end at the Crosscut Trail at 0.64 mile. Ascent is minimal. *(Map 9 — South Mountain A.)*

Javelina Canyon Trail EAST to WEST

BEVERLY CANYON to PIMA CANYON

General Description. A new trail was built up the canyon in 1994-5. In the spring there are beautiful slopes covered with poppies. From 46th St. (Beverly Canyon) entrance, the trail leads to a junction with a spur to 42nd St. and then turns up a wash, side-hilling up with increasing views to a pass above Pima Canyon Trailhead at 1¾ miles. It then descends ¼ mile to the Mormon Loop and National Trails near Pima Canyon Trailhead. Ascent is 520'.

Maps. *Our Map 13.* The USGS 1:24,000 quadrangles Guadelupe (1952, photorevised 1982) and Lone Butte (1952, photorevised 1967 and 1973) cover the approaches but do not show most of the trail.

Access. *Eastern end:* from 46th Street or 42nd Street, south of Baseline Road. *Western end:* from Pima Canyon Trailhead.

Read Down ↓	Detailed Trail Description	Read Up ↑
0.00	From the large parking lot at 46th Street, a trail heads W (1,100').	2.08
0.20	**Junction (4-way):** ignore trails L & R.	1.88
0.37	**Junction:** turn R at trail post.	1.71
0.38	Cross wash, switchback to R and up.	1.70
0.39	**Junction:** join old trail, go R.	1.69
0.46	**Junction:** several trails in area; ascend to R, L, R again, then descend from top of spur.	1.62
0.52	**Junction:** bottom of descent, by fence, with covered reservoir on other side (1,160'). [To R, trail leads past a junction on the R at 0.11 mi, ending at a dirt parking lot at 0.14 mi (trailhead sign), at 42nd St., 0.21 mi S of Baseline.] Continue to L here, along reservoir fence.	1.56
0.58	End of reservoir; turn L, ascending gradually.	1.50
0.66	Top of rise (1,200').	1.42
0.75	Bottom of descent, cross small wash, ascend.	1.33
0.77	**Junction:** old trail sharp R; swing around to L.	1.31
0.80	**Junction:** NDT on L; another branch of it in 60'.	1.28
0.87	**Junction:** NDT on L.	1.21
1.00	**Junction:** NDT on L.	1.08
1.08	Top of rise; rock pinnacle on R.	1.00
1.17	Cross side-wash. Ascend steadily.	0.91
1.21	Top of rise (1,320'). Climb higher on side-hill.	0.87
1.39	Cross side-wash.	0.69
1.47	Top of rise.	0.61
1.56	**Junction:** NDT on R.	0.52
1.58	Cross side-wash.	0.50
1.63	Ascend steadily.	0.45
1.74	Pass (1,520'). Pima Canyon Trailhead in view below. **Junction:** keep R where Ridgeline Trail heads L.	0.34
1.82	Cross main deep wash.	0.26
1.84	**Junction:** NDT on L. Ascend to trail post in 25'. This trail ENDS at Mormon Loop Trail. Go L 0.17 mi to National Trail and 0.24 mi to Pima Canyon Trailhead at end of old, now gated road.	0.24

2.01   **Junction:** National Trail. Go L on it. 0.07
2.08   Pima Canyon Trailhead (1,580'). End of paved road is 1.1 mi E, at closed gate. .. 0.00

Las Lomitas Loop   EAST to WEST

PONDEROSA STABLE to RANGER TRAIL

General Description. This trail segment is 2 miles long. Ascent is 100'.

Access. *Eastern end,* the trail leaves the entrance road just west of Ponderosa Stable near "Scorpion Gulch." A trail post is visible where it leaves the road. *Western end* it departs from the Ranger Trail at 0.2 mile from Five Tables Trailhead. *(Map 9 — South Mountain A.)*

Read Down ↓	Detailed Trail Description	Read Up ↑
0.00	Leave road (1,340'), descending toward wash.	1.99
0.03	Reach main wash at post #1, head up wash.	1.96
0.12	**Junction:** NDT enters sharp L (post #2).	1.87
0.13	Cross under Activity Complex road bridge.	1.86
0.24	**Junction:** NDT on R; keep L. Post #5.	1.75
0.31	**Junction:** Box Canyon Loop on L.	1.68
0.56	Parks Dept fence on R.	1.43
0.60	Post #11. **Important:** turn L, ascending out of wash.	1.39
0.69	**Important junction:** on R is Crosscut Trail. Go L.	1.30
0.78	**Junction:** NDT on R. Ascend. Post #16.	1.21
0.85	Turn R. Post #17.	1.14
0.89	Ascend to R, out of wash. In 45' is post #19. Switchback to R.	1.10
0.90	**Junction:** trail straight ahead is Hideout Loop. Turn L here, cross road.	1.09
1.05	Cross road.	0.94
1.18	Cross Kiwanis Road near Kiwanis Trail parking area.	0.91
1.60	Cross Las Lomitas Road.	0.39
1.99	**Junction:** Ranger Trail L & R (1,520'). R 0.22 mi to Five Tables TH.	0.00

Loop One   COUNTERCLOCKWISE

General Description. The route of this loop is much more complex than that of the Loop Two. It is a pleasant 1.3 mile walk (including the stem of the loop), with several short ascents.

Access. *At the southern end:* from the Marcos de Niza Ramadas on Pima Canyon Road. *At the western end:* from the Beverly Canyon Trail at 1 mile from Beverly Canyon Trailhead. *(Map 13 — South Mountain E.)*

Read Down ↓	Detailed Trail Description	Read Up ↑
0.00	Leave western side of ramada above Pima Wash, just before gate. Descend, head N. Elevation 1,390'	1.32
0.04	**Junction (5-way):** Pima Wash Trail crosses. Alternate trail from E end of ramadas joins. Ascend steadily.	1.28

0.22   **Junction:** trail L to Pima Canyon Road [this trail, returning]. Go R. 1.10
0.36   **Junction:** Loop Two on R (1.43 mi long). Go L, ascending. 0.96
0.41   **Junction (4-way):** at crest of ridge, NDT trail ahead is connector to Beverly
       Canyon Trail. NDT R is trail along a ridge toward Loop Two. Go L, uphill here,
       with some good views. 0.91
0.68   **Junction:** Beverly Canyon Trail sharp R & L. Go L here and join it. 0.64
0.78   **Junction:** turn L where Beverly Canyon Trail continues to SW. 0.54
0.88   **Junction:** turn L where trail R continues to Pima Canyon Road in 0.24 mi. 0.44
1.10   **Important junction:** back at start of Loop. To R, road is 0.22 mi away. 0.22
1.32   Pima Canyon Road at Marcos de Niza ramadas [back at start]. 0.00

Loop Two   COUNTERCLOCKWISE

General Description.   This is a pleasant 1.4-mile stroll around two minor summits with occasional views to the south and east, then enclosed in a valley. The entire loop can be easily done in an hour.

Access. *At the western end:* from Loop One, 0.2 mile from the Beverly Canyon Trail or 1/3 mile from Marcos de Niza Trailhead. *(Map 13 — South Mountain E.)*

Read Down ↓	Detailed Trail Description	Read Up ↑
0.00	Leave junction with Loop One at 0.36 mi. Elevation 1,400'.	1.56
0.13	**Junction:** Actual loop starts: Loop Two returns on L; keep R, descend.	1.43
0.19	**Junction:** NDT on R leads back to Marcos De Niza TH in 0.27 mi. Trail is mostly level along base of ridge.	1.37
0.33	**Important junction:** At post #9, half-R, descending, is connection to Pima Wash Trail. In 235' there is an NDT on the R, then again in another 420'.	1.23
0.36	**Junction:** NDT angling R.	1.20
0.41	**Junction:** NDT on R.	1.15
0.49	Cross wash.	1.07
0.61	**Junction:** NDT on R at post #7.	0.95
0.64	**Junction:** NDT on R at top of rise; post #	0.92
0.68	**Junction:** NDT on R at post #6. Start turning L (N).	0.88
0.78	Turn end of ridge, head N past golf course.	0.78
0.88	**Junction:** road R to golf course (private); post #5. Keep L here (NW).	0.68
1.06	**Junction:** Pointe cookout area on R (private) (post #4).	0.50
1.20	**Junction:** NDT on R; bottom of descent, post #3.	0.36
1.31	Top of rise. Descend.	0.25
1.43	**Junction:** back at start of stem of Loop.	0.13
1.56	**Junction:** back at start of Loop. Pass (1,440').	0.00

Mah-Ha-Tauk Trail   NORTH to SOUTH

General Description.   This is a mostly steep equestrian trail between 19th Avenue on the north and the Max Delta Loop. A ridge top is reached at 0.6 mile and the junction with the Cross Cut Trail at 0.8 mile. The last ¼ mile is a very steady descent to the valley floor at 1¼ miles. There are good views.

Ascent is 630'.

Access. *At the northern end:* from the 19th Avenue Trailhead, 0.8 mile south of Dobbins Road. *At the southern end:* at Max Delta Loop post #22. *(Map 10 — South Mountain B.)*

Read Down ↓	Detailed Trail Description	Read Up ↑
0.00	Leave end of 19th Ave. (1,320'). Immediately start ascent.	1.24
0.03	**Junction:** NDT on L.	1.21
0.04	Enter Preserve.	1.20
0.05	Trail post #1. Ascend up wide vehicleway.	1.19
0.12	Jog L & R; faint NDT joins L.	1.12
0.14	**Junction:** NDT sharp L. Park sign.	1.10
0.20	Vehicleway continues; take trail L.	1.04
0.23	**Junction:** NDT on R; turn L, start steep ascent.	1.01
0.35	Beside big wash on R.	0.89
0.43	Cross shallow wash. Trail bears L, along base of mountain.	0.81
0.45	Trail steepens, with loose rock.	0.79
0.48	Top of rise. Level briefly.	0.76
0.52	Switchback to L (trenched).	0.72
0.54	Top of rise. Attack ridge itself from here.	0.70
0.64	Top of rise. Trail post #4. Viewpoint (1,700'). Descend to R.	0.60
0.74	Swing R, descend.	0.50
0.77	Round end of small wash.	0.47
0.79	**Junction:** Crosscut Loop L at trail post #5. (0.52 mi to Max Delta Loop.)	0.45
0.84	**Junction:** NDT ascends on R. Keep level.	0.40
0.88	Trail post #6. Excellent views of main mountain. Swing R (avoid steeper NDT on L).	0.36
0.93	Cross small wash.	0.31
0.99	Start steady descent.	0.25
1.07	**Junction:** NDT descends on L. Go R, rising.	0.17
1.08	Trail post #8; descend steeply.	0.16
1.10	**Junction:** NDT on R; keep L.	0.14
1.11	Bottom of descent. Cross small wash.	0.13
1.13	**Junction:** NDT sharp R ascends. Go L at trail post #9, descending E, then NE.	0.11
1.24	**Junction:** Max Delta Loop at post #22 (1,550'). Crosscut Loop Trail is 0.43 mi to L here.	0.00

Marcos de Niza Loop Trail

From the Marcos de Niza ramadas at the west end of Pima Canyon Road, this short loop trail leads to the inscription rock, now behind a protective barrier. The trail starts at 170' past the beginning of the Desert Classic Trail and a ramada, at the southwest corner of the area. At 365' it turns sharp R, ascending steps. It goes sharp left at 440'. Reaching the inscription at 560', 0.1 mile from the road. The trail continues back down, with one switchback at 640', and reaches the beginning at 770'. Ascent is 50'.

Max Delta Loop   EAST to WEST

ALL WESTERN STABLES to BAJADA TRAIL

General Description. This trail parallels the San Juan Road. It has many branches and connections, and is mostly used by equestrians. From just west of the bend in the entrance road near All Western Stables it parallels the road, then ascends the ridge above the administrative headquarters, dropping to cross the "T"-Bone Trail and the road to Big and Little Ramadas at 0.9 mile. It then meets the Crosscut Trail and soon the Ma-Ha-Tauk Trail, continues up and down, rising to a few viewpoints, crossing numerous washes, generally parallel to the road, to reach the junction of Summit Road and San Juan Roads, where it joins the Bajada Trail across the way at a total of 2.2 miles. Ascent is 90'.

Access. *Eastern end:* the trail leaves the All Western Stables near the park entrance. *Western end:* it departs from the Bajada Trail at the junction of Summit and San Juan Roads. *(Map 9 — South Mountain A.)*

Read Down ↓	Detailed Trail Description	Read Up ↑

Segment 1. All Western Stable to Big/Little Ramadas Road

0.00	Leave All Western Stable area at trail post, 265' from road (1,350').	0.93
0.16	Monument on L to South Mtn Park (1973), near gatehouse on road. In 40' pass post #2.	0.77
0.19	**Junction:** NDT crosses, with several branches. Road is close on L. Soon start ascent up hillside.	0.74
0.34	**Junction (4-way):** NDT L & R. Post #4.	0.59
0.36	Top of rise; descend.	0.57
0.45	Bottom of descent, close to road.	0.48
0.60	Top of rise, views, post #7.	0.33
0.67	Pass under telephone line. Ascend steadily past Administrative Headquarters, passing post #8.	0.26
0.77	**Junction:** NDT sharp R toward water tank, on crest. Post #9. Go L along crest (warning sign that this is above Police Academy Shooting Range).	0.16
0.83	Top of rise, views.	0.10
0.89	**Junction:** on R is "T" Bone Trail to Platform and 19th Avenue in 0.96 mi.	0.04
0.93	**Junction:** Big & Little Ramadas Road; cross it to continue. (1430').	0.00

Segment 2. Big/Little Ramadas Road to Bajada Trail

0.00	Leave road at post.	1.25
0.06	**Junction:** NDT L is short-cut to Crosscut Trail.	1.19
0.08	**Important junction:** trail L is Crosscut Trail (joins). Post #14.	1.17
0.12	**Junction:** Post #16, Crosscut Trail on R (joins Ma-HaTauk in 0.56 mi).	1.13
0.55	**Important junction:** Ma-Ha-Tauk on R. Post #22.	0.70
0.71	**Important junction:** Post #26, Derby Loop L.	0.54
0.86	Cross old vehicleway.	0.39
1.04	Cross deep wash.	0.21
1.07	Top of rise.	0.18
1.25	**Junction:** San Juan Road (1,610'). Bajada Trail L & R across it.	0.00

Mormon Loop   WEST to EAST

General Description. This is a pleasant 1.3-mile alternate for the National Trail out of Pima Canyon, and can be combined with the Mormon Trail. **Access.** *At the western end:* from the Mormon Trail at 1.2 miles or $\frac{1}{4}$ mile from the National Trail. *At the eastern end:* at Pima Canyon Road. *(Maps 12, 13 – South Mountain D, E.)*

Read Down ↓	Detailed Trail Description	Read Up ↑
0.00	Leave junction with Mormon Trail, heading E. In 40' at **junction** head around S side of hump (side-trail straight ahead leads up hump in 285').	1.34
0.56	Top of minor summit; descend.	0.78
0.68	**Junction:** sharp L is horse trail to private property.	0.66
0.70	**Junction:** in pass, trail ahead to hump in 445'; descend to S, then turn E.	0.64
0.90	Cross moderate wash, then side-hill above it.	0.44
1.17	**Important junction:** Javelina Trail to L (1.84 mi to Beverly Canyon TH at 46th St); cross another NDT in 70'.	0.17
1.27	**Junction:** NDT descends on L. Continue straight.	0.07
1.28	**Junction:** cross NDT, then in 25' turn L, descend. Cross wash, then in 35' go L on trail where NDT ascends on R.	0.06
1.34	**Junction:** at triangle is National Trail [162]. To L on it, Pima Canyon Road is 330' away.	0.00

Pima Wash Trail

General Description. The Pima Canyon Wash is used largely as an equestrian access to avoid use of the old Pima Canyon Road. It leaves the Pointe Golf Course near Loop Two, passing a 0.1-mile connecting trail from the Pima Canyon Road 0.2 mile before its end at the Marcos de Niza Ramadas. Continuing, it exits the wash at 0.4 mile onto the north bank and follows it with views south, intersecting the Ridgeline Trail at $\frac{3}{4}$ mile. It then re-enters the wash except for brief detours out of it, to 1.4 miles where it leaves the south side of the wash to ascend the bank and cross an old parking turn-out, following the bank, re-entering the wash, and finally ending at the National Trail at 1.6 miles.

Access. *From the Pima Canyon Road,* at 0.2 mile before the end, a trail post indicates the connector, which steadily descends 125' to the wash, crossing it, and reaching the main trail in 325'. *From Loop Two,* at $\frac{1}{3}$ mile, there is a trail post where this trail starts, visible from the Loop. *(Map 10 – South Mountain B.)*

Read Down ↓	Detailed Trail Description	Read Up ↑
0.00	Leave white post in Golf Course area (1,340'), heading W.	1.64
0.11	**Junction (4-way):** Connector crosses, L to Pima Canyon Road 0.15 mi before its end; R to Loop Two.	1.53
0.14	**Junction (4-way):** Loop One crosses, to Marcos de Niza Ramadas on L in 205'. Post #9.	1.50

0.25	**Junction (4-way):** NDT crosses.	1.39
0.41	Ascend	1.23
0.58	Post #13, level. Go up & down.	1.06
0.67	**Junction:** NDT sharp L. Post #14.	0.97
0.75	**Junction:** NDT sharp R.	0.89
0.80	**Junction:** NDT L; keep R.	0.84
0.84	**Junction:** NDT on R.	0.80
0.87	**Important junction (4-way):** Ridgeline Trail L & R. Post #15.	0.77
0.89	**Junction (4-way):** NDT L & R.	0.75
0.91	Leave wash on L. Post #17.	0.73
0.95	Back in wash.	0.69
0.96	Leave wash on L.	0.68
0.98	Rejoin wash, which is narrow and rocky here.	0.66
1.02	Rock overhang on R.	0.62
1.08	Leave wash briefly on L. Post #20. Return to wash.	0.56
1.11	**Junction (4-way):** NDT L & R (partly obliterated).	0.53
1.17	Leave wash on L. Post #21.	0.47
1.21	Rejoin wash.	0.43
1.30	Leave wash on R.. Post #22.	0.34
1.31	Go over rocks.	0.33
1.39	Go L, ascend steadily. Post #23.	0.25
1.43	Cross former parking area.	0.21
1.44	Leave parking area on R.	0.20
1.45	Post #25. Bear R.	0.19
1.47	Bench on R just above wash.	0.17
1.52	Back in wash. Post #26.	0.12
1.57	**Junction (4-way):** steep NDTs L & R.	0.07
1.59	**Junction:** NDT sharp L. Post #27.	0.05
1.64	**Junction:** National Trail L to trailhead (start), and sharp R, west-bound.	0.00

Ranger Trail

General Description. This old trail leads from Five Tables Trailhead parking lot up to the Summit Road at 0.7 mile and then ascends to the National Trail at 1.4 miles, an ascent of 300' to the road and 800' to the National Trail. On the way it crosses Las Lomitas Loop and Derby Loop, and then the Bajada Trail.

Access. 0.5 mile from the second gate and park administration office, turn left on a paved road. Take the first right turn to the Five Tables Trailhead parking lot next to the major wash (there is a drinking fountain here). The trail post can barely be seen looking west along the wash. *(Map 10 – South Mountain B.)*

Read Down ↓	Detailed Trail Description	Read Up ↑
0.00	Leave ramada area (1,460'), heading W on track. [Trail actually starts 0.19 mi farther N but is not very clearly marked.]	0.68
0.06	**Junction:** where NDT continues ahead, turn L and descend to wash.	0.62
0.09	Cross major wash, ascend out of it for 50' .	0.59

0.20	**Junction:** NDT on L.	0.48
0.22	**Important junction (4-way):** Las Lomitas Loop on L (to Las Lomitas, Kiwanis Trailhead); Derby Loop on R to San juan Road.	0.46
0.42	**Important junction:** Bajada Trail on R, to Summit & San Juan Roads.	0.26
0.63	Switchback to L, then to R in 165'.	0.05
0.68	Summit Road (1,760').	0.00

0.00	Leave road 180' below small parking area on S side.	0.74
0.09	Switchback to L.	0.65
0.27	**Junction:** on L is closed trail. In 15' reach switchback to R, where NDT into ravine ahead.	0.48
0.65	Switchback L, above valley.	0.10
0.74	**Junction:** National Trail L & R (2,260'). (180' L, 240' R to crest.).	0.00

Ridgeline Trail   WEST to EAST

JAVELINA CANYON TRAIL to BEVERLY CANYON TRAIL

General Description. This is a rugged trail traversing a ridge for almost its entire length, with good views, but much up and down and no shade on a hot day. It leaves the Javelina Canyon Trail, reaching peaks at 0.15, 0.3, 0.5, 0.6, and 0.7 miles. It then makes a long, steady descent to the Beverly Canyon Trail at 0.9 mile. The Pima Canyon Road is 0.1 mile further on.

Access. *Western end:* from the Javelina Trail at 1.7 miles, at the pass 0.3 mile above Pima Canyon Trailhead. *Western end:* at the Pima Canyon Road, 0.8 mile west of the gate, at a trail post. *(Maps 12, 13 — South Mountain D, E.)*

Read Down ↓	Detailed Trail Description	Read Up ↑
0.00	Leave junction with Javelina Canyon Trail in pass. Heading E, level along ridge.	1.01
0.06	Start ascent.	0.95
0.17	Peak at post #8.	0.84
0.20	End of crest; descend.	0.81
0.28	Bottom of descent.	0.73
0.33	Top of rise with peak just above. Go L, N of top.	0.68
0.35	Descend off top.	0.66
0.38	Bottom of descent.	0.63
0.41	Small hump.	0.60
0.43	Bottom of descent.	0.58
0.45	Top of hump on ridge, post #7.	0.56
0.50	Top of peak. Descend steadily.	0.51
0.55	Bottom of descent.	0.46
0.60	**Junction:** NDT angles to L.	0.41
0.62	**Junction:** NDT L at summit of peak. Descend steadily to R.	0.39
0.66	Bottom of descent, ascend easily.	0.35
0.70	Top of rise.	0.31
0.83	Ease, then switchback L & R.	0.18
0.89	**Important junction:** Beverly Canyon Trail L & R. Go R, coinciding with it.	0.12

0.90	Top of rise, descend.	0.11
0.96	**Junction:** NDT half-L. Post #2.	0.05
0.97	Wash; ascend.	0.04
1.00	**Junction:** NDT half-L.	0.01
1.01	**Junction:** Pima Canyon Road. Straight ahead is continuation of Beverly Canyon Trail. On road L, Marcos de Niza Ramadas and gate at road end is 0.79 mi away.	0.00

"T" Bone Trail   NORTH to SOUTH

General Description. From the restaurant area there is a somewhat confusing area with about 0.2 mile of ascent to reach public land. A valley is side-hilled on a wide trail to $^2/_3$ mile, where the Platform is reached and then there is a gradual descent to the Max Delta Loop at 1 mile. Ascent is 200'.

Access. *At the northern end,* the trail leaves 19th Avenue near the restaurant at W Lodge Drive, at the southeast corner of the open area. Note that the first area is private property, so access can change or be denied, and there is no signage. *At the southern end* it departs from the Max Delta Loop 225' east of Big & Little Ramadas Road. *(Map 9 _ South Mountain A.)*

Read Down ↓	Detailed Trail Description	Read Up ↑
0.00	Leave SE corner of open area around T Bone Steak House, heading SSE (1,280'). (This first section is across private land.)	0.96
0.06	**Junction:** trail sharp L.	0.90
0.10	Top of rise. Turn L, join track from R.	0.86
0.21	**Junction:** trail of use on L (to private land). Continue R, trail narrows.	0.75
0.29	Cross small wash, then another in 50'.	0.67
0.39	**Junction (4-way):** cross NDT track. Descend into wash.	0.57
0.42	**Junction:** avoid trail on R in wash; keep L.	0.54
0.43	**Junction:** avoid trail sharp L. Ascend. Post #4.	0.53
0.49	Top of rise.	0.47
0.52	**Junction:** NDT on L. Bottom of descent. Side-hill up mountainside.	0.44
0.60	Turn L, ascend steadily.	0.36
0.65	**Junction:** NDT on R.	0.31
0.66	Level traverse around Platform. Views N.	0.30
0.75	Short-cut R, up steps to Platform, and beyond to parking area in 285'.	0.21
0.82	Near Little Ramadas on R.	0.14
0.88	**Junction:** NDT sharp R.	0.08
0.96	**Junction:** Max Delta Loop (1,430') L & R. Big & Little Ramadas Road is just 225' to R here.	0.00

Petroglyphs near the Holbert Trail

Rock dam on the Kiwanis Trail

Telegraph Pass Trail

DESERT FOOTHILLS PARKWAY to SUMMIT ROAD and National Trail

General Description. From the trailhead, a paved trail ascends for 0.4 mile; there it joins the old trail which is wide and well-worn, passing the junction with the Desert Classic Trail. The valley becomes more narrow and the trail switchbacks up, with some good views, to a junction with the National Trail and the Summit Road just beyond (1.2 miles). There is a very fine viewpoint from the Summit Road.

Access. From the Maricopa Freeway (I-10), take the Chandler Boulevard exit, then head west. After 5 miles, turn right at a major intersection at Desert Foothills. Take it almost as far as you can go (2.8 further miles), near a sign "road ends," where there is a large trailhead parking lot on the right. This was established by the Del Webb Corporation on June 2, 1995. *(Map 11 — South Mountain C.)*

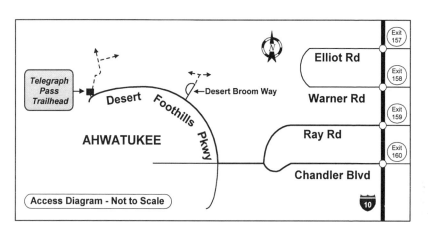

Read Down ↓	Detailed Trail Description	Read Up ↑
0.00	From trailhead parking, head NE toward water fountain and start of paved trail. Elevation 1,480'.	1.18
0.16	Pass thru open barbed-wire fence.	1.02
0.21	Cross wash, swing R, then L, uphill, passing a hump on the R.	0.97
0.38	Top of rise.	0.80
0.43	End of paving. In 55' at post & sign is **junction:** on R is Desert Classic bicycle path leading to Pima Canyon. Continue on wide, good trail (original location).	0.75
0.58	Post, no marker.	0.60
0.75	Post, no marker.	0.43
0.76	Brink of wash; go up alongside it.	0.42
0.81	Up rocks.	0.37
0.84	Switchback to L, then to R, at unmarked post. Trail rises steeply.	0.34

0.88	Post, unmarked.	0.30
0.89	Cross side-wash from R, ascend rocky trail [use CAUTION on way down.]	0.29
0.91	Eroded, trenched, steep.	0.27
0.94	Post, unmarked.	0.24
1.00	Post, unmarked.	0.18
1.06	Turn sharp R, cross wash, ascend far bank.	0.12
1.09	Switchback to L.	0.09
1.17	Junction: National Trail on R heads E.	0.01
1.18	This trail ends at Summit Road. To R 230' is viewpoint over Phoenix. To L along road is Kiwanis Trail on R in 530' and, on the L, National Trail West in 560'. Elevation 1,990'.	0.00

Maricopa Peak

Glendale Parks

An Introduction

Glendale's Thunderbird Park is a prime example of Sonoran Desert environment surrounded by — and within easy reach of — city dwellers. Categorized as a conservation park, it is protected from residential and commercial development and has as one of its mandates the retention of natural areas.

The 1,180-acre park has varied desert terrain, which includes a low mountain range, interesting geological formations, water features that offer natural habitats for local wildlife, as well as outdoor recreational opportunities for those who desire a break from the city hubbub.

Studies reveal that there are more than 41 varieties of trees, shrubs and cacti. There are also over 85 species of animals that inhabit the park.

Multi-use trails, summit views, picnic areas and a small lake for bird watching are features that make the area attractive to outdoor enthusiasts.

Lee Waldron, Parks & Recreation Superintendent
Parks & Recreation Department, City of Glendale

City of Glendale

Thunderbird Recreation Area

Introduction. Thunderbird Recreation Area consists of 1,082 acres located in the Hedgpeth Hills north of Glendale. Hiking trails climb to the tops of three summits. Many new trails were built in 1998-99, partly with volunteer and Boy Scout effort. The Recreation Area has been receiving much more usage in the past few years as housing developments in the vicinity expand.

History. The Hedgpeth Hills are named after a family that homesteaded in the region and pioneered the northwest part of the Salt River Valley in the later years of the last century. The park name derives from the air force's large primary training facility south of the park (Thunderbird Field No. 1) in World War II. Use of the area for picnicking by Glendale residents predated the park's establishment and the area was also used for hunting cottontails and quail. Lack of water in the area and rugged terrain made the land unsuitable for homesteading and at best marginal as rangeland. Significant mineralization is absent. In 1951-52 the City of Glendale acquired the land from the federal government.

Geology. The Hedgpeth Hills jut upward from the alluvial plain of Deer Valley, a northward extension of the Salt River Valley. They consist largely of igneous and metamorphic rocks, with the eastern part a tilted fault block consisting of basaltic lavas. Rock units in the western part contain some rocks of Precambrian Age (1-1.5 billion years old). Schist and quartzite are the oldest rocks, originally shale and sandstone that were later subjected to intense heat and pressure. Lava flows occurred during Tertiary and Quaternary time. Current topography is probably less than 1 million years old. The dominant wash trending southeasterly through the area past the amphitheater and picnic area is along a concealed fault.

Maps. *Our map 15.* The USGS 1:24,000 Hedgpeth Hills quadrangle (1971) shows the Recreation Area but no trails. There is a small map put out by the Glendale Recreation Department showing facilities and trails.

Access. SR 101 (Agua Fria Freeway) is open from I-17 to 51st, 59th, and 67th Avenue exits. There are 3 main trailheads ["TH"] used in maps and text:
(1) From the Black Canyon Freeway (I-17) take the Deer Valley/Pinnacle Peak exit (#217) and continue past Deer Valley on Frontage Road to Pinnacle Peak Road. Drive west for 2.6 miles to the large parking lot on the left, just before the road turns left at 55th Avenue (this is referred to in the text as *"55th Ave. TH"*).
(2) Continuing on Pinnacle Peak Road, the main picnic area trailhead (*"59th Ave. TH"*) is on the right 1.4 miles further. This is 3.6 miles north of Bell Rd. on 59th Avenue and 1.6 miles north of the Freeway.
(3) Where 51st Avenue ends (turning west), north of Bell Road and the Agua Fria Freeway, there is limited parking at the bend, just before trail [H-1] heads up the hillside (*"51st Ave. TH"*).
(4) There are other entrances at many places in the Recreation Area, specifically near the reservoir, and from 67th Avenue. There is also limited on-street parking on West Pinnacle Peak Drive, just north of 55th Ave. and Pinnacle Peak Road; a short unofficial trail leads back to [H-1] and [H-3].

Facilities. There are several picnic ramadas with covered tables, cooking grills and fire-pits, and there is drinking water and a comfort station. The horse staging area (ramadas 2 & 3) at 59th Avenue Trailhead also has hitching posts and troughs. The gate is closed from sunset to 7 a.m. There is no camping and the area is closed to off-road travel and unlicensed vehicles. Ground fires and amplified music are prohibited, as is horseback riding in the picnic loop. There is no electricity available.

Recommended Hikes. Numbers used are those of the City of Glendale. The best are the circuit loop [H-2] up Peak 1862 on Hedgpeth Ridge, the long loop [H-1], the loop of [H-3] up the summits to the north, and the short [H-4] to Peak 1682.

Cautions. *These are arid hills with rough terrain. Carry enough water.* Rattlesnakes are said to frequent the area. The ramadas and trailhead at the pass on Pinnacle Peak Road are to be closed, due to the hazards of the highway at the top of the pass.

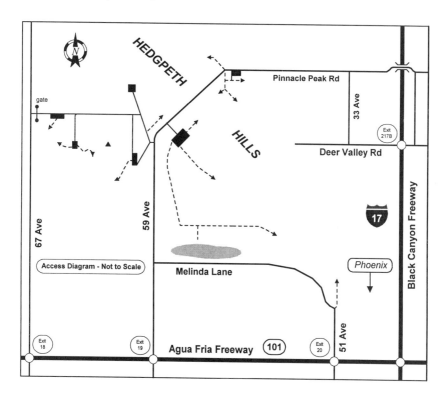

[H-1]

This long trail (4.9 miles) is described in 3 segments. Access is described on the previous page.

Read Down ↓	Detailed Trail Description	Read Up ↑

55th Avenue Trailhead to 59th Avenue

0.00	From 55th Ave. and Pinnacle Peak Road, at kiosk, head SW, ascending gradually. Elevation 1,390'. Parallel road, which is just below on L (S).	0.94
0.48	Top of rise, across from ramadas on opposite side of Pinnacle Peak Road.	0.46
0.70	**Junction:** trail [H-3] on R (N).	0.24
0.78	Cross road, go thru picnic area (comfort stations, ramadas, parking).	0.16
0.94	**Junction:** *59th Ave. TH* (1,320'). Next segment leaves SW from just S of road up to Amphitheater. Trail [H-4] departs from top of Amphitheater road.	0.00

59th Avenue Trailhead to 67th Avenue

0.00	Leave TH, heading W (1,320').	1.28
0.02	Cross wash, then an open area. In 65', turn R, start ascending.	1.26
0.05	**Junction:** trail on R is closed.	1.23
0.17	Top of rise; descend; sidehill.	1.11
0.22	Top of rise.	1.06
0.41	Viewpoint above valley ahead.	0.87
0.45	Descend from first of 4 switchbacks in 400'.	0.83
0.53	Bottom of descent. Cross wash.	0.75
0.59	Top of rise.	0.69
0.72	**Junction:** on R is trail [H-4B] ascending toward trail [H-4] and reservoir TH (1,320'). Continue, descending.	0.56
0.84	Fence at SW corner of Recreation Area. Turn R (N) here, on flat.	0.44
0.90	**Junction:** NDT on L here. Keep R.	0.38
0.98	Cross small wash. Parallel 67th Ave on L, cross open area.	0.30
1.19	**Junction:** NDT R toward reservoir.	0.09
1.28	**Junction:** ahead 200' is 67th Ave. entrance gate. [H-5] goes R (E) here.	0.00

55th Avenue Trailhead to 51st Avenue

0.00	Leave 55th Ave. TH on south side of Pinnacle Peak Road, heading S (1,390').	2.70
0.16	**Junction:** [H-1A] on E, and to parking area. Ascend S & SE.	2.54
0.27	**Junction:** trail [H-2] on L (E). Head R (W), ascending gradually.	2.43
0.61	Top of rise; ramadas (1,450'). Continue through area.	2.09
0.63	**Junction:** trail L back to ramadas.	2.07
0.68	Bottom of descent.	2.02
0.72	Switchback to L.	1.98
0.73	Cross small wash; ascend.	1.97
0.74	Top of rise. Level, then go up & down, to S.	1.96
0.80	Cross small wash.	1.90
0.81	Ascend.	1.89
0.84	Top of rise (1,450').	1.86
0.90	Switchback to R and to L, descending.	1.80
0.93	Switchback to R.	1.77

0.94	Switchback to L.	1.76
0.98	Cross small wash.	1.72
0.99	Level, bottom of descent.	1.71
1.00	Switchback to R.	1.70
1.02	Switchback to L and descend.	1.68
1.07	Turn L (S). Make steady descent toward lake.	1.63
1.14	.Trail of use on R; keep L, heading E on level.	1.56
1.30	**Junction:** side-trail 225' R to lake.	1.40
1.50	Start side-hilling ascent of mountain-side.	1.20
1.59	Level way on rocky side-hill.	1.11
2.05	**Junction:** paved road crosses, gate on L; on R leads down 0.19 mi to Melinda Lane in housing development (can be followed back to Melinda Lane and 59th Ave.). Elevation 1,340'. Continue along mountain-side.	0.65
2.70	End at 51st Ave. TH (1,310'; limited parking) at bend in road at 51st Ave.	0.00

[H-1A]

From [H-1] just south of 55th Avenue and Pinnacle Peak Road, west of the parking area, the level trail leads east, passing the large parking area. At ½ mile start swinging south toward the base of the mountain, then at 0.6 mile swing west, paralleling the base of the mountain. The junction with [H-1] is reached at 1.1 miles.

[H-2]

General Description. This trail leads from 55th Avenue Trailhead on the south side of Pinnacle Peak Road up the ridge. The crest is reached at ¾ mile and the highest summit (Peak 1862 with fine views), at 1 mile. From there the trail leads down the crest and switchbacks down a valley to the ramadas at the top of the pass at 1.7 miles. Ascent is 500'.

Access. From 55th Ave. Trailhead on Pinnacle Peak Road, take [H-1] south for ¼ mile to the junction.

Read Down ↓	Detailed Trail Description	Read Up ↑
0.00	From junction with [H-1] (1,390'), head E initially.	1.70
0.05	Switchback to L.	1.65
0.07	Switchback to R.	1.63
0.14	Start steady ascent.	1.56
0.16	Switchback to R.	1.54
0.18	Switchback to L, ascending steeply.	1.52
0.21	Top of rise.	1.49
0.33	Switchbacks (10 of them) start again. At 0.58 come onto end of crest.	1.37
0.66	**Junction:** trail of use on L. Keep R.	1.04
0.77	Hump on ridge on R (no trail). Reach edge of crest; views open.	0.93
0.95	Viewpoint at edge of crest.	0.75
1.02	**Junction:** Summit, Peak 1862, with fine views. Trail heading E is [H-2A]. [It continues to another summit and beyond to reach its end at 0.11 mi.] Descend crest.	0.68

1.23 Summit on crest (1,820'). Turn R, descend into valley, using switchbacks. 0.47
1.70 Trail terminates at ramadas on [H-1] at top of pass. (1,450'). 0.00

[H-3] North Hedgpeth Mountain Circumference Trail

CLOCKWISE DIRECTION

General Description. From the junction ¼ mile from 59th Ave. Trailhead on [H-1], this trail heads north. There is a long, gradual ascent of the mountainside for about ¾ mile, where it rounds the end of the ridge and heads north into a shallow valley. At about 0.8 mile it starts switchbacking up to reach the crest (1 mile) where fine views begin. It leads up and down to the highest summit at 1.6 miles. The descent is gradual and to the northeast for about 100' in elevation, to a junction with a side-trail [H-3A] to a viewpoint. It then switchbacks down, swinging east to 2.7 miles, where a side-trail leads to W. Pinnacle Hill Drive. Just beyond there is a junction with [H-1] near Pinnacle Peak Road. Ascent is about 500'.

Access. *For the western end:* leave trail [H-1] ¼ mile east of the picnic area (59th Ave. Trailhead). *For the eastern end:* at 55th Ave. Trailhead.

Read Down ↓	Detailed Trail Description	Read Up ↑
0.00	**Junction:** from [H-1], go L (NW), ascending gradually.	2.66
0.36	Top of rise (1,450').	2.30
0.52	Top of rise.	2.14
0.54	Bottom of descent.	2.12
0.60	Brief steep pitch up.	2.06
0.69	Round end of ridge, head N across shallow valley.	1.97
0.71	Ascend steadily to R (E).	1.95
0.81	Switchback to R, rising steadily toward ridge ahead (1,430').	1.85
0.91	Instead of climbing to top of ridge, switchback to L (1,520').	1.75
1.03	Bear R up crest, with fine views (1,580').	1.63
1.14	Top of rise.	1.52
1.17	Top of rise.	1.49
1.22	Bottom of descent.	1.44
1.25	Top of rise. Pass rocky hump on R (1,620').	1.41
1.31	Bottom of descent. Ascend just on N side of crest.	1.35
1.40	Turn R, ascend steadily, the L onto crest.	1.26
1.44	Pass just L of rocky hump.	1.22
1.54	Start long ascent.	1.12
1.57	Switchback to R, then to L in 60'.	1.09
1.62	Switchback to L.	1.04
1.65	Summit of highest point on ridge (1,760'). Head sharp L (NE) to continue.	1.01
1.69	Turn L.	0.97
1.70	Switchback to L, then to R in 55'.	0.96
1.92	**Junction:** side-trail [H-3A] straight ahead leads down to viewpoint in 360'.	0.74
1.97	Switchbacking descent starts, to L (W).	0.69
2.10	Cross crest, bear L (NW). Start more switchbacks in 115'.	0.56
2.33	Turn R (E).	0.33

2.38	More switchbacks.	0.28
2.63	**Junction:** main trail continues straight ahead. To L, trail leads 390' past a flood basin to W. Pinnacle Hill Drive (limited on-street parking available).	0.03
2.66	**Junction:** at trail kiosk, [H-1] goes R. To L, across road, is continuation of [H-1]. It is 125' L to 55th Ave. at Pinnacle Peak Road.	0.00

[H-4] EAST to WEST

General Description. From the top of the dirt road above the amphitheater the wide, well-defined trail leads northwest at a sign, gradually ascending along the base of the mountain to a major junction at 0.3 mile. Here the trail turns left (south), ascending by switchbacks to the summit at 0.7 mile. Ascent is 325'.

Access. For the east end, walk up the Amphitheater Road, northern branch.

Read Down ↓	Detailed Trail Description	Read Up ↑
0.00	Leave road near amphitheater, at a sign (elevation 1,370'). Head NW.	0.71
0.21	Cross wash.	0.50
0.27	**Junction:** steep track [closed] ascends L onto crest of ridge in 170'.	0.44
0.30	**Junction:** a short distance R is "Lookout Point" and trail [H-4A] L 450' down to reservoir parking area. This trail continues sharp L (1,475' here).	0.41
0.45	**Junction:** [H-4B] on R, to trail [H-1]. Switchback to L, ascend to N.	0.26
0.51	**Junction:** avoid cut-off trail on R. Go slightly L, on level grade.	0.20
0.52	Switchback to R, avoiding trail of use on L. .	0.19
0.53	**Junction:** avoid cut-off on R. Head SW, ascending.	0.18
0.58	Viewpoint on crest (1,620'). Ascend N slope, passing trails of use on R (circle around summit).	0.13
0.69	Turn R (N) onto crest.	0.02
0.71	Summit of Peak 1682. Excellent views.	0.00

[H-4A]

From the covered reservoir (heads south from parking area) this well-kept trail ascends the side of the ridge for 450' to a flat area with viewpoint and junction with trail [H-4]. It gives easy access to Peak 1682. Ascent is 75'.

[H-4B] SOUTHWEST to NORTHEAST

General Description. From trail [H-1] near the southwest corner of the Recreation Area, a brief but steep ascent of 220' leads to two summits with good views in less than ¼ mile, and a junction at 1/3 mile with trail [H-4].

Access. *From the south:* from trail [H-1], 0.7 mile west of 59th Avenue Trailhead. *From the north:* from trail [H-4] at ¼ mile above the reservoir parking area.

Read Down ↓	Detailed Trail Description	Read Up ↑
0.00	From **junction** with [H-1] near S boundary, ascend steadily to N, switchbacking (elevation 1,320').	0.31
0.04	Bear L (NW).	0.27
0.15	Top of rise (1,540'); views.	0.16
0.20	Bottom of descent.	0.11
0.22	Summit (1,520'). Descend.	0.09
0.28	Bottom of descent (1,460'). Ascend.	0.03
0.31	**Junction:** this trail ends at trail [H-4] R & L (1,490'). On R it is 0.26 mi up to Peak 1682. On L, it is 0.24 mi down to the road and reservoir parking area.	0.00

[H-5] WEST to EAST

General Description. From near the 67th Avenue gate this trail ascends a hillside, meets trail [H-5A] and gradually descends past picnic ramadas to cross a road at 0.3 mile. It continues over a hillside and down to a ramada at 0.6 mile, with a branch to another ramada. Ascent is 50'.

Access. *From the west:* 200' east of 67th Avenue gate, on trail [H-1]. *From the east:* at area 'B' on the lower spur road, or area 'G' on the upper road north of 59th Avenue Trailhead. See map.

Read Down ↓	Detailed Trail Description	Read Up ↑
0.00	Leave [H-1] E of 67th Ave. gate, ascend hillside to E.	0.64
0.04	Top of rise. Pass cemented-in post, heading E.	0.60
0.05	**Junction:** to R, trail [H-5A] ascends to top of ridge and to reservoir TH. Continue to E, descending gradually.	0.59
0.10	**Junction:** trail angling L leads to ramada. Pass it.	0.54
0.14	**Junction:** sharp R is trail of use.	0.50
0.15	**Junction:** trail from ramada joins on L. Pass large parking and picnic area.	0.49
0.31	**Junction:** Recreation Area road (paved). Cross it, find trail continuing.	0.33
0.46	Top of rise, hill on R. Descend.	0.18
0.50	Descend rocky trail.	0.14
0.57	**Junction (4-way):** go straight.	0.07
0.58	**Junction:** on R is spur 1/8 mi to parking area 'G' at connecting road between upper and lower roads (see map).	0.06
0.59	**Junction:** turn R where trail of use parallels fence line on L.	0.05
0.64	Picnic tables, ramada at end of lower road (Area 'B').	0.00

[H-5A] EAST to WEST

General Description. From the reservoir parking area, a short popular section of this trail climbs to a bump on the ridge with good views in only about 0.1 mile. The trail continues west along the crest, but then becomes confused with old vehicle-ways and trails of use. It descends to [H-5] near the 67th Ave. entrance gate at 0.3 mile. Ascent is 70'.

Access. From reservoir parking area on the east, and 450' east of 67th Avenue gate on trail [H-5] on the west.

Read Down ↓	Detailed Trail Description	Read Up ↑
0.00	Leave reservoir parking area (1,390'), heading uphill to NW.	0.31
0.02	Turn L.	0.29
0.03	Switchback to L, steadily up.	0.28
0.06	Top, viewpoint (1,450'). Continue on crest, to WSW.	0.25
0.13	Western summit 30' off trail on L (1,430'). Descend to R of it.	0.18
0.16	**Junction:** closed vehicleway sharp R. Stay on crest.	0.15
0.19	**Junction:** trail of use on R. Continue straight.	0.12
0.21	Ascend last hump on ridge.	0.10
0.24	Peak, views; trail of use descends to L. Go sharp R, descending.	0.07
0.25	Turn R, then make 4 switchbacks.	0.06
0.28	**Junction:** trail of use sharp R ascends back onto crest. Go L.	0.03
0.31	**Junction (4-way):** on L is steep trail of use descending from summit. Half-L is trail [H-5] descending toward 67th Ave. Cross it, descending to N.	0.00

City of Scottsdale

McDowell Sonoran Preserve

Introduction. It is exciting that Scottsdale has been developing trails (mountain and flat-land) as part of a long-range plan. This description covers the first substantial trail to be opened in the 8,300+ acre McDowell Sonoran Preserve. Future trails will connect various developments and road-ends, as well as flat-land developments and washes.

Maps. *Our map 16.* The USGS 1:24,000 quadrangles McDowell Peak (1962, photorevised 1982) and Sawik Mountain (1964, photorevised 1982) show some of the trail location.

Facilities. There are no facilities other than a parking lot at 104th & 102nd Streets.

Cautions. *This trip has more up-and-down than might be estimated from the topographic maps. Allow enough time, and carry enough water.*

Taliesin-Lost Dog Wash Trail EASTERN SECTION

General Description. From the north end of 128th Street, the trail ascends an old jeep trail or via a parallel trail to the Preserve boundary at $^1/_3$ mile. It continues to climb steadily to 0.7 mile (240' of elevation) then turns west and crosses a deep wash. At 0.9 mile a new trail diverges left, climbing onto a ridge outcrop with good views to the Lost Dog Overlook at 1.1 miles. This is a good lunch spot. A drop of 140' southwest into Lost Dog Wash at 1.6 miles is followed by a long traverse up the hillside above the wash with good views. Finally at 2.7 miles the jeep road is reached again and followed northwest to the pass at 3.2 miles. Here the Taliesin Saddle Overlook is on a short spur trail. (The trail continues from here as the western section to McDowell Mountain Ranch at 104th and 102nd Streets.) Net ascent is 500'. Revegetation is in process in a number of areas by the McDowell Sonoran Land Trust; please observe signs.

Access. Off the end of 128th Street, 1.6 miles north of Shea Boulevard. Take 124th Street north for one-half mile, then turn right on Via Linda for one-half mile, then left on 128th Street for 0.6 mile. Park on the left near the road end.

Read Down ↓	Detailed Trail Description	Read Up ↑
0.00	Leave road end, start steady ascent up old jeep road. Elevation 1,730'.	3.15
0.09	**Junction:** alternate trail on R parallels the road.	3.06
0.32	**Junction:** alternate trail rejoins on R.	2.83
0.33	Gate. In 45' cross into McDowell Sonoran Preserve (sign). The way steepens from here.	2.82
0.55	**Junction:** vehicleway enters on L (1,938').. Grade eases.	2.60
0.71	**Junction:** in open area on R, trail heads into valley, ascends ridge. Top of rise; descend steadily L.	2.44
0.77	Cross main wash, ascend steadily.	2.38
0.78	Top of rise; head W, almost level.	2.37
0.89	Cross wash. Ascend steeply out of it.	2.26
0.91	Turn R, ascend (sign).	2.24

0.93	**Junction:** where road continues steeply uphill, turn L on trail (cairn & sign).	
	Side-hill.	2.22
0.98	**Junction:** keep R ascending on old vehicleway, views.	2.17
1.04	Top of rise. Head SSE, level.	2.11
1.07	Start descent.	2.08
1.10	**Junction:** Lost Dog Wash Overlook 80' to L (1,980'). Turn W, descend.	2.05
1.15	Bottom of descent. Head W.	2.00
1.21	Start descent.	1.94
1.29	Bottom of descent.	1.86
1.35	**Junction:** keep R. Trail L leads toward 124th St (1,880'). Keep R.	1.80
1.48	**Junction:** closed vehicleway descends steeply to R.	1.67
1.49	Swing L, then to R, descending to S.	1.66
1.57	**Junction:** at bottom of descent, go R (NW), up and down.	1.58
1.62	Cross major wash.	1.53
1.67	Cross wash.	1.48
1.71	Switchback to L.	1.44
1.73	Top of rise. Descend gradually.	1.42
1.86	Cross small wash, ascend steadily up hill-side to NW onto scenic ridge.	1.29
2.12	Top of rise.	1.03
2.23	Top of rise. Descend steadily to W, then NW.	0.92
2.30	Cross small wash.	0.85
2.32	Top of rise.	0.83
2.33	Cross moderate wash.	0.82
2.34	Switchback to R and up.	0.81
2.41	Cross large wash.	0.74
2.42	Cross moderate wash.	0.73
2.43	Switchback to L. Ascend to N.	0.72
2.59	Top of rise.	0.56
2.66	Cross small wash.	0.49
2.68	**Junction:** take vehicleway to L.	0.47
2.85	Cross wash.	0.30
3.15	**Junction:** Taliesin Saddle Overlook is 265' on L. Elevation 2,120'.	
	Western section continues ahead 2.77 mi to trailhead at McDowell	
	Mountain Ranch (104th & 102nd Sts.)	0.00

Taliesin-Lost Dog Wash Trail WESTERN SECTION

General Description. This trail ascends a wash through the McDowell Mountain Ranch development, circling around it to the north, then ascending on an old road to meet the eastern section at the junction to Taliesin Saddle Overlook at 2¾ miles. Net ascent is 540'.

Access. From Shea Boulevard, 92nd Street runs north, becoming 94th Street north of Cactus, then Thompson Peak Parkway beyond Thunderbird. From where it crosses Frank Lloyd Wright Boulevard it is 0.8 mile (past the new bridge over the Central Arizona Project Canal) to 104th Street. Turn right here (south) then take the first right onto 102nd Street, then immediately right into the parking lot. The trailhead is across 104th Street.

Read Down ↓	Detailed Trail Description	Read Up ↑

0.00   Start at parking lot. Elevation 1,580' Cross 104th St. 2.77

0.04   Mule Deer Trailhead sign (paved trail). Do not take it. Continue S along
104th St. 2.73

0.08   Descend to L, away from road. 2.69

0.09   Turn sharp L (E) at bottom (sign). 2.68

0.22   Enter wash. 2.55

0.24   Leave wash. 2.53

0.28   Pass under bridge (105th St.). 2.49

0.32   Private tennis courts on R. Bear L. 2.45

0.37   **Junction:** private trail on R. 2.40

0.40   Enter wash. 2.37

0.66   Ascend hillside on R. 2.11

0.71   Descend to wash, cross it in 45', then parallel it. 2.06

0.87   Turn R. 1.90

0.88   Cross wash. 1.89

0.97   Enter wash, follow it. 1.80

1.00   Turn R out of wash, then in 110' head N from side-wash. 1.77

1.13   Descend back to side-wash. 1.64

1.19   Leave side-wash on R. 1.58

1.22   Landmark: eroding cliffs above on R. 1.55

1.28   Turn R out of wash. 1.49

1.31   Cross small wash. 1.46

1.62   Cross wash. Then parallel it. 1.15

1.83   Cross small wash. Ascend out of valley. *[This is a new section around a new
housing subdvision (1999) since our field work was completed.]* 0.94

2.27   **Junction:** non-designated trail on R. 0.50

2.31   Cross wash. 0.46

2.35   **Junction:** road ascends to L. Continue straight. 0.42

2.50   Cross Taliesin Wash, start steady, rocky ascent. 0.27

2.77   Pass. **Junction:** Taliesin Saddle Overlook is 265' to R (2,120'). Trail
continues as the eastern section for 3.15 mi to the end of 128th St.. .... 0.00

Maricopa County

An Introduction

The Maricopa County Park System was created over 45 years ago, based on the foresight of community leaders. Today this park system is the largest county parks operation in the United States, with over 115,300 acres of open space. These areas have been planned and developed to provide regional outdoor recreation opportunities for the fastest-growing county in the nation, with a population approaching 2.4 million people. Our County regional parks provide open space, beautiful deserts, mountain venues, and a 10,000 acre lake.

Our park system is only as valuable as the services and opportunities we can provide to the public. Critical to the provision of these services has been the creation of an extensive trail system. This trail system was developed in part through master plans in the 1960s, 70s, and 80s, and includes hiking, biking, riding, barrier-free and interpretive trails, and competitive tracks.

Today we are taking new strides to improve and enhance this trail system. Two trails planners are now part of our staff, along with a part-time assistant. A volunteer trail program helps us maintain and improve these facilities. Also, we continue to expand our working relationships with federal agencies, such as the Department of Interior's Bureau of Land Management and the Department of Agriculture's Forest Service. This includes sharing management of adjacent areas, exchanging personnel, and interconnecting our trails, thereby creating even better opportunities for the public.

As we move into the 21st Century, it becomes even more important to maintain open spaces and recreational opportunities for our ever-expanding population. We are committed to providing outstanding regional parks and a high quality system of multi-purpose trails for public enjoyment.

William Scalzo, Director
Maricopa County Parks and Recreation Department

Maricopa County

Cave Creek Regional Park

Introduction. Cave Creek Recreation Area was opened in October of 1992. It has 2,922 acres and forms an important addition to the Maricopa County Parks System. There are interesting geologic formations and scenic views into the Tonto National Forest, 4 miles to the north. Elevations range from 1,880' to 3,060'. None of the park's peaks is presently named, although local names are applied. In the past these foothills were extensively prospected for gold, silver, copper, mercury, talc, and chrysocolla. Over 40 claims were filed, but nothing of continuing value was produced.

Old horse, jeep, and mining trails penetrate the area. Further trail and facility development will take place over the next few years. Fortunately, there is already an excellent network of trails available which enable hikers, mountain-bikers and equestrians to spend an hour or a day exploring. (Note that the names and locations of these trails have already undergone changes and will continue to do so.)

Maps. *Our Map 17.* The USGS Cave Creek (1965) and New River SE quadrangles (1964), both photorevised in 1981, cover the topography.

Access. From 32nd Street off Carefree Highway. From the junction with Cave Creek Road south of the town of Cave Creek, turn left onto Carefree Highway for 2.8 miles to the 32nd Street turn-off on the right. The park entrance and gate is 1.5 miles further.

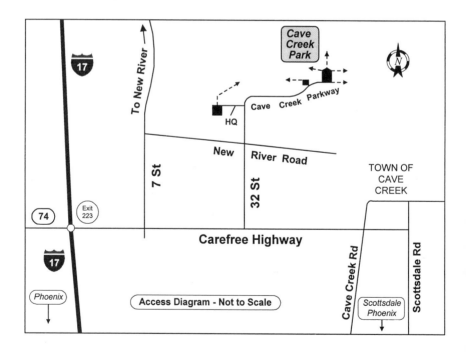

Cautions. Abandoned mine diggings can be extremely hazardous; a few are over 50' deep. Some of the trails are rocky and narrow. Mountain-bikers should be prepared to walk their bikes and ride with caution. All users should stay on trails, and vehicles must remain on roads.

Facilities. Park hours are 6 a.m. to 6 p.m. Like other County Parks, there is a $3.00 daily vehicle fee ($50 for an annual pass). There are 43 individual (first come, first served) picnic sites in the main loop area with grilles, tables, fresh water, electrical outlets and nearby restrooms. Ramadas may be reserved. The Horse Staging Area is located at the end of Cave Creek Parkway, just south of the Day Use Picnic Area. In the southwest corner of the park is a group campground and children's playground, with restrooms, fire pits, and ramadas. Cloud Road within the Recreation Area is closed and to be renovated to trail in the near future.

[A] Go John Trail CLOCKWISE

General Description. One of the best circuits in the park, the Go John Trail is varied in its scenery and type of footway. It consists of old vehicleways and new trail construction, with good views. From the trailhead, the vehicleway ascends steadily for over 300' in elevation, with gradually expanding views to the south. At the pass at 0.8 mile, the views open to the north (Tonto National Forest). For a quarter mile there is a sometimes steep descent to a junction with the Overton Trail [B] at 1.1 miles. Follow a wash valley to 1.5 miles, where new trail heads east across country for almost a mile, then swings up to Gunsight Pass at just under 3 miles. Heading east again, it swings around into a broad valley to commence climbing westerly over a ridge which has good views. At 4.2 miles a jeep road starts on the final descent, the road being reached at 4.9 miles. Total ascent is 800'.

Access. Both ends are at the Trailhead Parking Lot at the north end of the Day Use Picnic Loop off Tonalite Drive, 0.9 mile east of the junction of Cave Creek Parkway and Olivine Avenue (past the Park entrance). This description starts at the north end (Trailhead #2). The trail here is an old vehicleway that can be seen ascending ahead.

Read Down ↓	Detailed Road & Trail Description	Read Up ↑
0.00	From Trailhead Parking Lot at Picnic Loop N end, ascend N at sign (2,120').	4.88
0.17	**Junction:** avoid vehicleway on R (dead-ends).	4.71
0.20	Cross major wash.	4.68
0.23	**Junction:** where eroded, steep vehicleway continues ahead for 450', turn R on better alignment.	4.65
0.39	Switchback to L.	4.49
0.56	**Junction:** rejoin vehicleway, turn R, ascend steadily on vehicleway.	4.32
0.57	Cross wash. Good views open. Ascend.	4.31
0.66	Ascend steeply over rocks.	4.22
0.76	**Junction:** old track on L, barbed-wire fence on R.	4.12
0.78	Pass (2,470'), views extend (spur trail 215' L to viewpoint). Descend steadily to N.	4.10

0.80	Fenced-off mine shaft on L. Descend loose, rocky trail with care.	4.08
0.89	Cross wash, ease grade of descent.	3.99
0.94	Descend steadily again on rocky trail.	3.94
0.95	Cross small wash, turn L, level.	3.93
1.01	Top of rise. bear L, descend.	3.87
1.05	**Junction:** ignore obscure trail on L.	3.83
1.11	**Junction:** Overton Trail [B] enters sharp L. Continue ahead.	3.77
1.12	Cross wash.	3.76
1.22	Top of rise. Descend hogback between two wash valleys.	3.66
1.28	Descend steeply to E.	3.60
1.30	Cross wash.	3.58
1.32	Cross wash; follow it.	3.56
1.35	Cross main wash.	3.53
1.41	Cross side-wash from L.	3.47
1.44	Leave wash.	3.44
1.45	**Junction:** leave vehicleway (leads to Park boundary and into State land (permit required). Ascend steadily R on trail. (From here, trail winds along to the E, above a large valley to the N.)	3.43
1.60	Top of rise.	3.28
1.66	Top of rise, then ascend again.	3.22
1.74	Descend steadily.	3.14
1.77	Bottom of descent.	3.11
1.88	Cross wash.	3.00
1.97	Top of rise.	2.91
2.02	Top of rise	2.86
2.19	Turn L.	2.69
2.33	Cross small wash.	2.55
2.37	Cross small wash.	2.51
2.39	**Junction:** on L is trail to State land (permit required); go R here, ascending easily. In 300' trail climbs and becomes eroded for 700'.	2.49
2.61	False pass.	2.27
2.64	Top of rise, views.	2.24
2.66	Top of rise (viewpoint 75' to L).	2.22
2.72	Barbed-wire fence. Descend steadily with good views.	2.16
2.88	**Junction:** keep L (less trenched alternative on R; trails rejoin in 65').	2.00
2.89	Cross wash.	1.99
2.91	Cross wash, then go thru wash for 160'.	1.97
2.95	Cross wash, ascend.	1.93
2.98	Gunsight Pass (2,530'). Good views.	1.90
3.23	**Junction:** where old trail continued ahead, turn sharp R (S) on new trail. Ascend easily up broad valley.	1.65
3.51	Old and new trails join. Maintain SW direction.	1.37
3.87	Top of rise.	1.01
3.93	Field of quartz.	0.95
4.01	Excellent viewpoint.	0.87
4.05	Top of rise, views. Cross scenic side-hill.	0.83
4.08	Descend steadily.	0.80
4.12	Bottom of descent.	0.76
4.14	Top of rise (2,390'), views, side-hill steep slopes again.	0.74
4.18	Come onto crest.	0.70
4.21	End of ridge.	0.67
4.23	Jeep road starts, with Picnic Loop in view below.	0.65
4.25	Turn R.	0.63

4.32	Bottom of descent.	0.56
4.51	Top of rise (2,290').	0.37
4.57	**Important junction:** where vehicleway bends L in level area (Jasper Trail [F], and continues S, take trail R, crossing major wash.	0.31
4.61	Cross deep wash. Ascend out of it to W.	0.27
4.88	**Junction:** Trailhead Parking Lot N of Picnic Loop, back at start.	0.00

[B] Overton Trail SOUTH to NORTH

General Description. A somewhat shorter loop can be made with this trail and the first part of the Go John Trail [A] for 3½ miles, giving a good idea of the variety of terrain and history of the area.

From the trailhead, the trail heads west just above the ramadas, paralleling Cave Creek Parkway, passing a wash, mine tailings, a side-trail to Trailhead #2, climbs the ridge and meets the Clay Mine Trail [C] at ½ mile. Mostly level old vehicleway is followed northwest (passing briefly out of the Park) to new trail at just over 1 mile. This drops into a wide valley, picks up an old vehicleway at 1.2 miles, and ascends northeast. At 1.4 miles a scenic trail section begins, climbing over a high pass at 2,450'. Here there are very good views. A steep descent ends this trail at the Go John Trail at 2.4 miles. A 1.1-mile return over another pass on the latter trail makes a good loop trip. Total ascent is about 125'.

Access. *For the southern end,* leave from the southwest corner of Trailhead #2, or the parking area for Trailhead #1, cutting off 0.3 mile but adding 395' of ascending trail. *For the northern end,* from 1.1 miles on the Go John Trail [A].

Read Down ↓	*Detailed Trail Description*	Read Up ↑
0.00	From TH #1 (Go John Trail parking), head S (2,080').	2.66
0.03	Turn R at end of parking area.	2.63
0.17	Leave road on R. Descend gradually, passing playground.	2.49
0.29	With ramada on L, turn R, descend steadily.	2.37
0.31	Cross major wash.	2.35
0.33	Cross moderate wash. Ascend to W.	2.33
0.36	Top of rise.	2.30
0.39	Cross small wash.	2.27
0.48	Swing to L, ascend.	2.18
0.52	**Junction:** side-trail L to Trailhead #2 in 475'.	2.14
0.72	**Junction (4-way):** Clay Mine Trail [C] on L (2,150'). On R is a closed old mining road. Continue straight ahead, descending very gradually on another mining vehicleway.	1.94
0.87	Cross wash.	1.79
0.97	Boundary; pass out of Park briefly.	1.69
1.16	Re-enter Park. Ascend gradually.	1.50
1.27	**Junction:** where mining road continues ahead (ends in arroyo in 0.12 mi), turn L, descend N into valley.	1.39
1.37	Cross wash., head N.	1.29
1.41	**Junction:** vehicleway joins from L (private land). Turn R and ascend broad valley toward pass ahead.	1.25

1.67	Vehicleway ends, trail begins.	0.99
1.74	Turn R (S), ascend steeply (mine workings below on R).	0.92
1.79	Level.	0.87
1.83	Ascend steeply (zigzag).	0.83
1.89	Top of rise (2,340').	0.77
1.91	Ascend into defile on beautiful trail.	0.75
1.93	Top of rise (2,360').	0.73
2.08	Highest pass (2,450'), views.	0.58
2.17	Descend steadily.	0.49
2.22	Turn L, then R. Descend steeply.	0.44
2.26	Cross small wash, level near hump, then drop.	0.40
2.66	**Junction:** Go John Trail [A] (jeep road) on R. It is 1.11 mi back to the Picnic Loop over the pass from here. This trail ends.	0.00

[C] Clay Mine Trail EAST to WEST

General Description. A connection between the Family Campground and the Overton Trail is provided by this interesting trail. It passes an old clay mine[1] with a horizontal adit and a shaft (it is hazardous — do not enter!). Because of no parking at the Family Campground for those not camped there, and no horse usage through that Campground, the trail description is from east to west.

From the Overton Trail, the trail leads along a ridge crest with good views, then descends down the side to the mine at 0.6 mile, continuing on new trail to the Campground at 0.8 mile. Total descent is 220'.

Access. *For the eastern end,* leave the Overton Trail [B] at 0.7 mile. *For the western end,* from the Family Campground, *for those camped there only.*

Read Down ↓	Detailed Trail Description	Read Up ↑
0.00	From Overton Trail [B] (2,130').	0.79
0.03	Top of rise.	0.76
0.05	Bottom of descent. Ascend, to L (S) of summit.	0.74
0.13	Top of rise.	0.66
0.19	**Junction:** trail R closed.	0.60
0.22	Turn R.	0.57
0.31	Turn L, descend briefly.	0.48
0.33	Start steady ascent.	0.46
0.36	Top of rise.	0.43
0.41	Bottom of descent.	0.38
0.43	Descend gradually to R, side-hill.	0.36
0.59	Junction: trail of use ascends L to top of mine shaft [do not use].	0.20
0.62	Mine on L. Use care here. No horses beyond this point.	0.17
0.68	Cross obliterated vehicleway.	0.11
0.69	Pass historic foundation on L. Turn R. Cross moderate wash.	0.10
0.79	This trail ends at the Family Campground (1,930'), between sites 6 & 8 on Jasper Way East. Olivine Ave. is 450' to L, Cave Creek Parkway 0.4 mi L.	0.00

---

[1]The clay was mined to make a mineral powder claimed to have health benefits when added to water.

Clay Mine

Looking into the Tonto from the Go John Trail

[D] Slate Trail WEST to EAST

General Description. Several valleys are followed by this trail, with old mine workings visible. There are no distant views. The official trail ends at the Recreation Area boundary, so one must return the same way. Beyond is State land (a permit is required from the State Land Department to cross it). From the Picnic Loop, follow the vehicleway east, passing the Jasper Trail [F] at 0.3 mile and a junction with the Flume Trail [E] at 0.9 mile. The route then ascends a valley for a quarter of a mile, descending to the boundary at 1.5 miles. Total elevation gain is 40'; descent is 90'.

Access. For the *western end,* leave the Day Use Picnic Loop at its southeast corner.

Read Down ↓	Detailed Trail Description	Read Up ↑
0.00	From Day Use Picnic Loop, SE corner, head E on vehicleway.	1.52
0.31	**Junction:** Jasper Trail [F] ascends to L. Keep straight.	1.21
0.37	**Junction:** non-system mine road ascends on R. Continue on level vehicleway.	1.15
0.86	Cross main wash.	0.66
0.92	**Junction:** Flume Trail [E] goes R here (2,140'). Keep L, turn gradually to N, ascending easily.	0.60
1.04	Top of rise.	0.48
1.13	Cross small wash.	0.39
1.20	**Junction:** vehicleway on R. Descend gradually to E.	0.32
1.40	Top of rise, descend.	0.12
1.50	Bottom of descent.	0.02
1.52	Park boundary (sign may be down or missing); official trail ends, State Land ahead (permit required). Elevation 2,030'. Return the same way.	0.00

[E] Flume Trail WEST to EAST

General Description. An old vehicleway leads along a major wash where there is evidence of mine explorations and then an old wood and earthen flume, used for farming irrigation. Part of the trail leads briefly out of the Park, where access could be denied. [There are plans to re-route that section.] From the Slate Trail [D], the trail leads up a valley, crossing and re-crossing a wash. There is some ascent, with a steep pitch, to a half mile. Then it descends, again making wash crossings, to pass the old flume at 0.9 mile. The Park boundary is at 1.2 miles, leading past large Cave Creek Wash to re-enter the Park and reach old roadway at 1.5 miles (one can continue 500' to the Recreation Area boundary). Total ascent is about 125'.

Access. *For the western end,* from 0.92 mile on the Slate Trail [D]. *For the eastern end,* from Cloud Road (closed, to be obliterated), but the start is confusing.

Read Down ↓	Detailed Trail Description	Read Up ↑
0.00	From Slate Trail [D], 1,990', head S & E up a valley.	1.50
0.01	Cross main wash. Trail is rough here.	1.49
0.08	Join wash; leave it on L in 60'.	1.42
0.12	Join wash, go L in it for 160'.	1.38
0.19	Start steady ascent on R.	1.31
0.20	Top of rise, descend.	1.30
0.21	Cross side-wash, ascend steadily.	1.29
0.43	In wide area, level off, then descend gradually.	1.07
0.50	Start ascending rocky hillside.	1.00
0.54	**Junction:** old mine road ascends steeply on R.	0.96
0.57	**Junction:** avoid revegetated trail above on R.	0.93
0.62	**Junction:** avoid trail R.	0.88
0.69	**Junction:** avoid trail R.	0.81
0.75	Descend steadily.	
0.76	Cross wash.	0.74
0.78	Cross wash.	0.72
0.81	**Junction:** on L is wide trail. Keep R.	0.69
0.89	**Junction:** trail sharp L.	0.61
0.90	Remains of old flume. Ascend steadily S.	0.60
0.92	Top of rise, level, above wash.	0.58
1.09	Boundary cairn (no sign). Leave Park (access may be denied).	0.41
1.14	Bear R. Cave Creek Wash visible ahead.	0.36
1.15	**Junction:** trail of use descends L.	0.35
1.29	Re-enter park by gate. Beyond is **junction:** trail of use descends steeply to L.	0.21
1.46	**Junction:** trail of use on R. Go L here in confusing area.	0.04
1.50	**Junction:** Old "New River Road," now abandoned and slated for renovation to trail (1,960'). This has been a confusing area with many trails and vehicleways of use. [The trail continues for 500' across the road to Recreation Area boundary, where it enters Bureau of Land Management land, but private land is also in the area.]	0.00

[F] Jasper Trail   NORTH to SOUTH

General Description. A short connector, this segment is useful for those heading back to the bottom of the Day Use Picnic Loop, rather than the northern end. It drops gently 70' down to the level valley in 0.2 mile.

Access. *For the northern end,* leave the Go John Trail at 0.3 mile from its end. *For the southern end,* from the Slate Trail, 0.3 mile from its start at the southeast corner of the Day Use Picnic Loop.

Read Down ↓	Detailed Trail Description	Read Up ↑
0.00	From Go John Trail [A] (2,150'), descend.	0.16
0.01	Top of rise. Descend gradually.	0.15
0.16	**Junction:** Slate Trail [D] L & R. Elevation 2,080'.	0.00

Maricopa County

Estrella Mountain Regional Park

Introduction. The Sierra Estrellas ("star mountains") are a prominent range when viewed from Phoenix (to the southwest, beyond South Mountain). They extend from the northwest tip of Pinal County northwesterly to the Gila River near its junction with the Salt. On the southwest they are bordered by Rainbow Valley (Waterman Wash), an area now the site of a large residential development.

The park occupies about one-third of the Estrellas (18,592 acres) in the foothills of the higher ranges. The highest elevation in the park is 3,650'. (No trail presently ascends from the park to the high peaks.)

Extensive residential development of the area west of the park (Estrella Ranch) is continuing.

History. The Park area had religious significance for the Pima Indians who lived nearby along the fertile Gila River lowlands. Twelve archeological sites are located within the park, mostly representing temporary camps (one was permanent). Nine of the sites were occupied by the Hohokam peoples who were in the area between A.D. 500 and 1450. During the historic period the area was controlled by the Pima and Maricopa Indians and was used as a hunting and gathering range.

The park area was also along the route of the California-bound trappers and drovers, perhaps including Kit Carson. To the south of the range was the Gila Route of Kearny's Army of the West, the Mormon Battalion, and thousands of Argonauts.

Geology. Geologically the Sierra Estrellas are similar to the White Tank Mountains, although there are no "tanks" or tinajas.

Maps. *Our map 18.* The USGS 1:24,000 Avondale SE and Avondale SW quadrangles (both 1957, photorevised 1978) show the general topography and some of the old roads, but no trails.

Access. From Phoenix, take Interstate 10 west to Exit 126, Estrella Parkway, at sign "Estrella Park." (This is 2 miles west of Litchfield Road Exit 128.) Head south, crossing SR 85 at 3.7 miles, continuing on to West Vineyard Avenue at 5.1 miles; turn left to the park entrance at 5.7 miles. Turn right on Casey Abbott Drive South (one way) for 1.6 miles to 143rd Drive and Arena Drive, at which point the 143rd Drive parking area is straight ahead (and new trailhead 1 mile further[1]), the Rodeo Arena another 0.3 mile to the right, and the new trailhead on the alignment of the old Rock Knob Trail 1 mile from 143rd Drive parking area. (Alternatively, you can go south from Exit 128 on Litchfield Road through Goodyear. After 2.3 miles take SR 85 to the right for 1.2 miles, then turn left on Bullard, 5.7 miles total to the park entrance.) [See access diagram.]

Facilities. The entrance fee is $3 for vehicle and passengers ($50 annual pass), $1 for hikers, bicyclists and equestrians without vehicles. The park has 56 acres of grass, 8 ramadas (with electricity and lights), comfort stations and picnic tables. There is a golf course, but no camping. Back-country camping is by free permit. *Phone: 623-932-3811; Box 252, Goodyear 85338.*

---

[1]See page 163 for details.

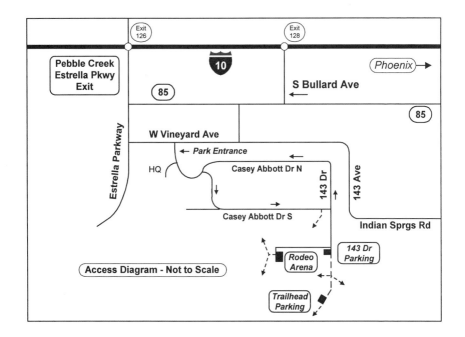

Recommended Hikes and Trail Rides. The trail designations used are official Maricopa County letters. There are 5 designated trails and their branches; one is quite long (Rainbow Valley [A]). Most trails have few markings or signs, and there are numerous trails of use that can be confusing. The best for a one-day hike are: the northern and western sections of the Rainbow Valley Trail [A] using a number of alternatives on the return; the Spur [D], Rock Knob Trail [E], or eastern section of the Rainbow Valley Trail with any of these for the return from the Pack Saddle Trail [B]. Any combination is good on horseback. The northeastern section east of the Pack Saddle Trail is being developed for competitive bike racing.

Cautions. *Note that this park's terrain is very arid, with broken, sharp rock dissected by washes. Cross-country travel can be arduous if you are lost. Use care, and always carry plenty of water and sun protection.*

[A] Rainbow Valley Trail COUNTERCLOCKWISE

General Description. A long, 19.4-mile trail loop leads over scenic hills, mountain-sides, through passes, deep washes, and over flat desert. There are excellent views. *Since not many will take the full loop, the detailed description that follows is divided into 7 segments. At the end of each segment the total distance from the start is indicated.*

Access. From the trailhead sign at the west side of the Rodeo Arena (traveling counter-clockwise); or 0.2 mile south of the 143rd Drive parking area (traveling clockwise); or via trail [A-2] that leaves Casey Abbott Drive South, just east of Amphitheater Drive East, before the road turns south to 143rd Drive parking area. There are many other points at which this trail can be intersected by other trails.

Read Down ↓	Detailed Trail Description	Read Up ↑

SEGMENT 1
Rodeo Arena to Rainbow Valley Connector [A-1]

0.00	Leave Rodeo Arena (1,015'), heading straight W at sign.	1.75
0.03	**Junction (4-way):** join [A] running N-S here; Spur Trail [D] goes straight (connects with Rainbow Valley Trail via Spur Trail North Connector [D-1] in 1.94 mi). Go R, uphill.	1.72
0.07	**Junction:** where trail of use continues straight (up ridge), keep R, ascend.	1.68
0.08	Top of rise; view of valley and downtown Phoenix. Cross several washes.	1.67
0.27	**Junction:** Connector Trail [A-1] leads sharp L for 0.23 mi to rejoin Rainbow Valley Trail at 1.75 mi on out-bound loop. Continue up and down.	1.48
0.52	Top of rise.	1.23
0.59	Pass (1,040'). Descend on very rocky trail.	1.16
0.67	**Important junction:** [A-2] ahead to Casey Abbott Dr S in 0.29 mi. *[Details from N: leave Casey Abbott Dr S at 185' E of Amphitheater Drive E. Cross wash in 35', head S briefly, paralleling road, cross wash at 310', ascend steadily to junction at 0.29 mi.]* Turn L here, descend steadily.	1.08
0.68	**Junction:** on R spur trail descends 170' to reach Amphitheater Drive, heads down it to reach Casey Abbott Drive S at 0.23 mi.	1.07
0.70	Cross 3 small washes, ascend; level out in 250'.	1.05
0.79	**Junction:** steep, rocky track descends R for 165' to Amphitheater Drive. Continue level.	0.96
0.86	**Junction:** another steep, rocky track descends R for 190' to Amphitheater Drive, thence down Amphitheater Drive to Casey Abbott Drive S in 0.16 mi.	0.89
0.97	Cross small wash, ascend, switchback to R in 100', then level out in 80'.	0.78
1.02	Ignore trail of use descending on R. Go L, ascending.	0.73
1.16	Pass old mine site on L, ease ascent, then pass another.	0.59
1.23	**Junction:** NDTs L & R.	0.52
1.31	Turn around end of ridge.	0.44
1.33	**Junction:** NDT on L & R. Descend steadily on rocky trail, then ease in 150'.	0.42
1.40	Pass, views. Avoid trails of use on R and up crest on L.	0.35
1.54	Cross small wash; reach top of rise in 150' and descend.	0.21
1.64	Cross small wash.	0.09
1.66	Cross very small but deep wash, ascending steadily on opposite side.	0.11
1.68	**Junction:** trail of use to R peters out; go L.	0.07
1.75	**Junction:** Connector Trail [A-1] straight ahead leads L 0.23 mi back to Rainbow Valley Trail (0.50 mi total to Rodeo Arena trailhead) *[saves 1.25 mi]*. (elevation 1,070')	0.00

SEGMENT 2
West end of connector [A-1] to Spur Trail North Connector [D-1]

0.00	Leave Connector [A-1], ascend to R.	2.16
0.08	**Junction:** at top of rise on ridge (views), trail of use leads L (short-cut to Rodeo Arena). Keep R. In 350' descend more steadily and bear R.	2.08
0.29	Top of ridge. Side-hill on R (W) side of it.	1.87

0.37   Ascend to R of crest. 1.79
0.47   Turn R and descend, crossing small wash in 110'. 1.68
0.52   Descend. In 250' reach top of rise with fence on R. 1.64
0.66˙   Pass (1,160') with fence on R. Descend. 1.50
0.96   Cross moderate wash, then turn sharp L, paralleling wash. 1.20
1.00   Start ascending at very small wash. 1.16
1.11   Switchback up to R, then to L in 100', then to R in 35'. 1.05
1.20   Reach crest of subsidiary ridge; level out (1,280'). 0.96
1.25   Top of high point with good views (1,380'). Descend steadily. 0.91
1.28   Turn R, descend off crest. 0.88
1.52   Edge of major wash, trail forks: take either branch. 0.64
1.54   Enter wash, turn L in it, then take minor branch to R. 0.62
1.67   Turn sharp R, uphill (use care here). 0.49
1.76   Cross moderate wash. 0.40
2.07   Turn R, then L in 100', descending toward W. 0.09
2.16   **Junction:** sharp L is Spur Trail North Connector [D-1] (leads to Spur Trail [D]
        to Rodeo Arena in 1.10 mi). (1,075'). *[3.91 mi from start at Rodeo Arena.]* 0.00

SEGMENT 3
Spur Trail North Connector [D-1] to Spur Trail [D]

0.00   Leave junction with Spur Trail North Connector [D-1], ascending steadily up
        valley. 1.03
0.40   Pass (1,290'). Descend gradually. 0.63
0.64   Top of rise with rock hump on L; reach pass (1,330') in 100'. 0.39
0.73   Pass (1,370'). Descend steeply on eroded trail. 0.30
1.03   **Junction:** To L is Spur Trail [D] back to Rodeo Arena in 1.97 mi (1,160').
        [4.94 mi from start at Rodeo Arena.]... 0.00

SEGMENT 4
Spur Trail [D] to Pack Saddle Trail [B]

0.00   Leave junction with Spur Trail [D] (1,160'); cross large wash in 100'. 1.64
0.23   Cross very small wash; ascend high above major wash with views. 1.42
0.43   Level out beside deep wash. 1.21
0.61   Pass (1,370'). Descend gradually. 1.03
0.68   Begin steady descent. 0.96
0.79   Swing around to N, then to R (SE). 0.85
0.84   Parallel major wash on R. 0.80
0.88   Cross moderate wash. 0.76
1.00   Follow along ridge and almost reach its summit; then side-hill gradually down. 0.64
1.14   Bear R, descend more steadily. 0.50
1.22   Cross moderate wash. Head S. 0.42
1.29   **Junction:** [see inset map] spur trail [B-1] leads R 0.38 mi to [B]. Just beyond,
        on L is [E-1], connector to Rock Knob Trail [E] in 0.62 mi. (Elevation 1,260').
        Descend gradually. 0.35
1.64   **Junction:** Pack Saddle Trail [B] (1,225'); go R on it. *[6.58 mi from start at
        Rodeo Arena.]*.. 0.00

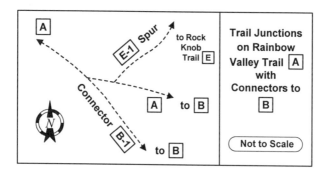

Trail Junctions
on Rainbow
Valley Trail [A]
with
Connectors to
[B]

Not to Scale

A

Spur [E-1]
to Rock Knob Trail [E]

Connector

[A] to [B]

[B-1]

to [B]

SEGMENT 5
Pack Saddle Trail [B] back to Pack Saddle Trail

0.00	**Junction:** Pack Saddle Trail [B], go R on it (1,225').	8.97
0.01	Enter wash; keep R up it.	8.96
0.07	Keep L where wash splits.	8.90
0.08	Leave wash on R; rejoin it in 200'.	8.89
0.16	**Junction:** Connector [B-1] on R, to Rainbow Valley Trail in 0.40 mi (at 1.29 mi in previous section). *Pack Saddle Trail ends here.* Continue on vehicleway, passing toe of ridge. Way becomes rockier.	8.81
0.34	Top of rise.	8.63
0.45	Track enters on L, then another in 70'.	8.52
0.53	**Junction:** 4WD road ascends on R.	8.44
.46	Road corner. Road turns L on sandy flats.	7.51
1.50	**Junction:** in very broad Corgett Wash, jeep road goes L. Continue.	7.47
1.80	**Junction:** ignore vehicleway on R (old Pack Saddle Trail).	7.17
2.10	Ruins on R (W).	6.87
2.70	**Junction:** ignore vehicleway to R.	6.27
3.65	**Junction (4-way):** vehicleways on R & L.	5.32
4.10	Vehicleway bends to R, then to L, becomes a bit steeper, rockier.	4.87
4.50	**Junction:** vehicleway on L.	4.47
4.85	**Junction:** vehicleway splits. *Go sharp L*, descending gradually, parallel to major wash on R.	4.12
5.25	**Junction:** where vehicleway continues ahead, take trail to R.	3.72
5.32	**Junction:** go R, descending toward wash.	3.65
5.44	**Junction:** trail R ascends steeply back to jeep road. Continue.	3.53
5.56	Take trail R, ascending out of wash, at arrow.	3.41
5.58	Bear L on trail.	3.39
5.61	Top of rise. Descend gradually.	3.36
5.84	Cross moderate wash.	3.13
6.00	Top of rise.	2.97
6.15	Top of rise.	2.82
6.42	Moderate wash. Follow it up for 90', leave it on L, head N.	2.65
6.46	Bear R (NE), paralleling wash.	2.51
6.52	Bear L, ascending away from wash.	2.45
6.74	Descend into major wash.	2.23
6.77	Ascend to L out of wash, then switchback up.	2.20
6.79	Top of rise. Turn R, parallel wash.	2.18

6.96	Top of rise.	2.01
7.52	Descend into wash, follow it to R.	1.45
7.54	Switchback L out of wash. *USE CARE*, this turn is obscure.	1.43
7.59	Descend L into deep wash.	1.38
7.61	Bottom. Follow it down. In 50', ascend steeply to R, out of wash.	1.24
7.73	Cross moderate wash.	1.24
7.90	Descend into major wash; head L down it, then in 90' ascend R out of it.	1.07
7.94	Brink of wash. Descend.	1.03
8.36	Cross moderate wash.	0.71
8.34	Cross moderate wash.	0.63
8.97	**Junction (4-way:** Pack Saddle Trail [B] L & R. Rainbow Valley Trail turns R on it (1,245'.) *[15.55 mi from start at Rodeo Arena.]* Note that there is an old trail continuing straight across this junction; this is now an undesignated trail.	0.00

SEGMENT 6
Pack Saddle Trail [B] to Gadsden Trail [C]

0.00	Follow Pack Saddle Trail [B] (old jeep road) to R (N) (1,245').	2.76
0.24	Turn R.	2.52
0.26	Cross small wash.	2.50
0.31	**Junction:** trail on L short-cuts jeep road on R.	2.45
0.36	**Junction:** rejoins. Parallel wash.	2.40
0.53	Turn R.	2.23
0.63	Top of rise.	2.13
0.68	Bottom of descent, in wash (4WD scars on hillsides here.) Turn L.	2.08
0.71	**Important junction:** where Pack Saddle Trail [B] continues ahead, *this trail turns L, out of wash.*	2.05
0.95	Cross small wash, ascend, then go up and down.	1.81
1.02	**Junction:** trail of use heads S at cairn. Go straight, ascending.	1.74
1.14	Top of rise at minor pass (1,360').	1.62
1.32	Cross small wash, turn R (E).	1.44
1.39	Swing L (N). Ascend, crossing several small washes.	1.37
1.79	Major pass (1,480'). Descend steadily N (over very loose rock at first).	0.97
2.18	Level out (1,230').	0.58
2.25	Parallel wash on L, then ascend gradually.	0.52
2.35	Top of rise.	0.41
2.38	**Junction:** trail of use. Bear R. Trail improves.	0.38
2.51	Cross moderate wash.	0.24
2.65	Top of rise.	0.11
2.76	**Junction:** On R is Gadsden Trail [C]. (Elevation 1,100'.) To continue, descend. *[18.31 mi from start at Rodeo Arena.]*	0.00

SEGMENT 7
Gadsden Trail [C] to Rodeo Arena

0.00	Leave Gadsden Trail [C] junction, descending.	1.11
0.02	Cross moderate, deep wash; ascend.	1.09
0.05	Top of rise; others at 0.10 and 0.13 mi.	1.06
0.20	Cross two washes close together. Then side-hill, ascending.	0.91
0.74	**Junction:** spur trail L toward [E].	0.37
0.77	**Junction:** trailhead road; go R, down it (leads to 143 Dr parking area).	0.34
0.82	Cross wash, heading W, climb out of it (use care with route).	0.29
0.84	**Junction (4-way):** ignore trails of use L & R.	0.27

0.87	Keep L at hitching post, avoiding trail of use to R.	0.24
0.98	Cross wash.	0.13
1.00	**Junction:** trail of use sharp L, then another in 30'.	0.11
1.02	Cross large wash.	0.09
1.04	**Junction:** trail of use on R; keep L.	0.07
1.08	**Junction (4-way):** straight ahead, Rainbow Valley Trail [A] continues; Spur Trail [D] goes L here. Go R.	0.03
1.11	This trail ends at Rodeo Arena parking lot (1,015'). *[19.42 mi total from start.]*	0.00

[A-1] Rainbow Valley Connector

A short (0.23-mile) segment connects the two sides of the Rainbow Valley Trail, avoiding the trip around the ridge just south of the entrance area. The trail makes an easy descent from west to east, crossing a small wash at 0.10 mile. Where it meets [A], there is a short-cut 190' short of the main junction.

[B] Pack Saddle Trail   NORTH to SOUTH

History. According to Ben Humphreys[2], this was part of the first road from Yuma to Fort Whipple via Gila Bend and what was later Phoenix. At first it was a horse trail, later probably a buck-board route.

General Description. At present this 3 mile-long trail consists of a jeep trail that leads in and out of washes. Parts of it are slow and sometimes very hot going for those on their own feet. It provides connections with the Gadsden [C], Rock Knob [E] and Rainbow Valley [A] trails and therefore makes possible several short or moderate loop trips. It partly overlaps sections of the Rainbow Valley Trail. Total ascent is about 330', descent about 140'.

Access. Reach the northern end by way of the Gadsden Trail [C] at 2.9 miles from 143rd Drive Trailhead. Reach the southwestern end via the Rainbow Valley Trail [A] and Connector [B-1] at 6.6 miles from the Rodeo Arena.

Read Down ↓	**Detailed Trail Description**	**Read Up ↑**
0.00	**Junction:** Gadsden Trail [C] on W. Head S (1,075'). (This area is currently being developed as a new entrance.)	3.02
0.54	4WD track up opposite bank.	2.48
0.76	Switchback to R.	2.26
0.77	Bend in road ahead to R; instead, short-cut to L across & over bend in road.	2.25
0.78	Rejoin road in wash. Follow wash.	2.24
0.92	Where wash turns L, ascend to R, out of wash.	2.10
1.07	**Junction:** 4WD track ascends very steeply to R where wash heads L.	1.95
1.13	Go into wash again, follow it.	1.89
1.33	Leave wash on R, uphill, where it bends to L.	1.69
1.36	Cross level area, then 3 very small washes.	1.66
1.61	Ignore old tracks off to R. Bear L, descend.	1.41

---

[2]Cited in a quotation from Ida Smith in John Annerino's *Adventuring in Arizona*, 1991, p. 196, San Francisco: Sierra Club Travel Guides. Others have cast doubt on this story.

1.64 On bench, steep scar of 4WD track leads up knob on R & another on L. 1.38
1.67 **Junction:** 4WD tracks L & R. 1.35
1.73 **Junction:** Rainbow Valley Trail [A] on R (N to 143 Drive in 2.48 mi). Where
      wash splits, ascend between two branches. .... 1.__
2.04 **Junction:** 4WD track on R. Top of rise. Keep L. 0.98
2.09 **Junction:** turn L. 0.93
2.22 Top of rise (USGS Bench Mark on L, 1,256'). 0.80
2.42 **Junction:** Rainbow Valley Trail [A] goes L here (1,240'). ['On R, 20' before
      this, trail to R is <u>not</u> Rainbow Valley Trail [A], but is original trail]. 0.60
2.64 **Junction:** Rock Knob Trail [E] ascends on R (1,220'). Bear L,
      back into wash. Pass several washes, entering main wash. 0.38
2.86 **Junction:** uphill on R is Rainbow Valley Trail [A]. 0.16
2.87 Enter wash; keep R up it. 0.15
2.93 Bear L where wash splits. 0.09
2.94 Leave wash on R. 0.08
2.98 Rejoin wash. 0.04
3.02 **Junction:** on R is Connector [B-1] to Rainbow Valley Trail in 0.40 mi. This
      trail ends here. (Continuing, Rainbow Valley Trail passes toe of ridge on way
      to SW corner of the Park.) 0.00

[C] Gadsden Trail   WEST to EAST

General Description. For a moderate (2.4 mile), varied trip not too far from
civilization, the Gadsden Trail is ideal. It leaves the Rainbow Valley Trail [A],
ascends to a pass, crosses several washes, then descends to the Pack
Saddle Trail [B].

Access. From 143rd Drive parking area, take the road south for 0.2 mile to
the Rainbow Valley Trail [A], and follow it for ¾ mile.

Read Down ↓	Detailed Trail Description	Read Up ↑
0.00	**Junction:** leave Rainbow Valley Trail [A].	2.40
0.08	Cross moderate wash.	2.32
0.14	Go thru little pass.	2.26
0.16	**Junction:** trail of use on L, another in 150'.	2.24
0.31	**Junction:** trail of use on R.	2.09
0.41	Bend in wash.	1.99
0.55	Turn R, cross moderate wash.	1.85
0.64	Cross major wash, ascend out of it for 100'.	1.76
0.83	Cross 4WD vehicleway.	1.57
0.86	Cross moderate wash, then switchback out of it.	1.54
1.19	Cross small, deep wash.	1.21
1.71	Pass (1,120').	0.59
1.96	Enter wash, follow it to L, then over into smaller branch wash.	0.44
2.09	Go L in large wash, then climb out of it.	0.31
2.14	**Junction:** at vehicleway, go L.	0.26
2.23	**Junction:** leave vehicleway on trail on R.	0.17
2.40	**Junction:** start of Pack Saddle Trail [B] on R (jeep road). This trail ends.	0.00

[D] Spur Trail

General Description. From the trailhead several washes are crossed on the way to a junction at 1.1 miles where the Spur Trail North Connector [D-1] leads west to the Rainbow Valley Trail. The trail then ascends somewhat more steadily to end at the Rainbow Valley Trail at 2 miles. As a way into the center of the Park, it is somewhat more difficult (and more scenic) than the Rock Knob Trail [E]. Total ascent is about 210'.

Access. From the Rodeo Arena trailhead, head west for 90' to intersect the trail (also the Rainbow Valley Trail). Go straight.

Read Down ↓	Detailed Trail Description	Read Up ↑
0.00	The trail leaves the Rodeo Arena Trailhead (1,015').	1.97
0.03	**Junction (4-way):** Spur Trail goes straight where Rainbow Valley Trail [A] goes R & L. Cross moderate wash.	1.94
0.11	Top of rise. Head S toward Rock Knob.	1.86
0.26	Cross moderate wash, ascend out of it.	1.71
0.32	**Junction:** obscure vehicleway angles to R.	1.65
0.38	Ascend.	1.59
0.42	Top of rise.	1.55
0.47	**Junction:** vehicleway re-enters on R.	1.50
0.51	Top of rise.	1.46
0.63	Cross small rocky wash. (In next 0.24 mi cross 5 more washes.)	1.34
0.93	Top of rise (1,100').	1.04
0.98	Top of rise.	0.99
1.01	Cross toe of ridge on R.	0.96
1.08	**Junction:** ignore short-cut angling L.	0.89
1.10	**Junction:** Spur Trail North Connector [D-1] on R to Rainbow Valley Trail [A]) in 0.84 mile. (Elevation 1,100'.)	0.87
1.17	Descend. In 50', switchback to L.	0.81
1.20	Cross major wash.	0.79
1.21	Level out, parallel wash (4WD vehicleways on side of wash).	0.78
1.68	Cross moderate wash (branch of main wash).	0.30
1.97	**Junction:** Rainbow Valley Trail [A] on R on sandy flat (1,210'), back to Rodeo Arena. Trail ahead is Rainbow Valley Trail to S. This trail ends.	0.00

[D-1] Spur Trail North Connector   EAST to WEST

General Description. The connection between this trail and the Rainbow Valley Trail was re-worked in late 1987 and colored tapes were placed on it. Ascent is insignificant except for washes. (It is planned to connect it on the east to the new trailhead.)

Access. From Rodeo Arena Trailhead take the Spur Trail [D] for 1.1 miles.

Read Down ↓	Detailed Trail Description	Read Up ↑
0.00	Leave main Spur Trail 1.10 mi from Rodeo Arena by angling to R (1,100').	0.84
0.09	Turn R, descend into wash.	0.75

0.11	Turn L into moderate wash and follow it. In 35' ascend out of it to R.	0.73
0.14	Reach brink of wash, level out.	0.70
0.17	Turn L into moderate wash.	0.67
0.18	Leave wash on R.	0.66
0.27	Cross moderate, deep wash.	0.57
0.84	**Junction:** at Rainbow Valley Trail [A] this trail ends. [To R (N) it is 2.66 mi back to Rodeo Arena via shortest route, or 3.91 mi via full route. To L (S), Rainbow Valley Trail meets Spur Trail [D] in 1.03 mi and Pack Saddle Trail [B] in 3.48 mi.]	0.00

[E] Rock Knob Trail   NORTH to SOUTH

General Description. The Rock Knob Trail is the easiest and shortest way into the center of the park (it is an old vehicleway, and the first 1 mile is now (2000) driveable to the trailhead). Leaving the end of 143rd Drive, the new dirt road follows the old location of this trail for 1 mile to the trailhead, where it starts, runs past a junction at a wash, then gradually ascends and leads into the pass between Rock Knob (1,801') on the east and the unnamed peak (1,781') to its west. It then crosses a major washout on the road and descends gradually to the Pack Saddle Trail [B] at 1.8 miles. Ascent is 230'.

Access. *At the northern end*, from the southeastern corner of the trailhead. *At the southern end*, from the Pack Saddle Trail [B].

Read Down ↓	Detailed Road Description	Read Up ↑
0.00	The trail leaves the 143rd Drive parking area at a gate (990').	2.86
0.20	**Junction:** in wash, rainbow Valley Trail [A] leads R to Rodeo Arena (may be unmarked).	2.66
0.21	**Junction:** on ascent out of major wash, trail to L is Rainbow Valley Trail [A]. Ascend gradually on wide road.	2.65
0.82	Cross moderate wash, then turn L in 100'.	2.04
1.00	**Junction:** trail of use on L.	1.86
1.02	New trailhead.	0.00

Read Down ↓	Detailed Trail Description	Read Up ↑
0.00	Leave trailhead, ascending S.	1.84
0.18	**Junction:** trail of use on L.	1.66
0.40	Bear R.	1.44
0.42	Cross small wash.	1.42
0.44	Bear L.	1.24
0.62	Trail narrows, ascend steadily.	1.06
0.70	Cross small wash; parallel large wash on R.	0.98
0.97	**Junction:** trail of use on L [leads up around small knob for 360', then peters out]; keep R, descend steeply.	0.71
0.99	Cross major deep wash, ascend steeply, reaching top in 75'.	0.85
1.12	Pass, views.	0.72
1.16	**Junction:** on R, Rock Knob Spur [E-1] leads 0.62 mi to Connector [B-1] just below its junction with Rainbow Valley Trail [A] (1,320'). Beyond, this trail descends gradually.	0.68

1.22	Top of highest rise.	0.62
1.55	Cross small wash.	0.29
1.59	Top of rise (1,310').	0.25
1.84	**Junction:** Pack Saddle Trail [B] L & R (1,210') 60' before wash and is not obvious. On L (N), it leads 0.91 mi to Rainbow Valley Trail [A]. On R (S), [B] leaves, Rainbow Valley Trail [A] W- & S-bound is 0.22 mi away.	0.00

[E-1] Rock Knob Spur Trail

A narrow trail leads from 1.2 miles on the Rock Knob Trail [E] southwest across several washes for 0.6 mile to connect with the Rainbow Valley Trail [A] just 70' east of Pack Saddle Connector [B-1].

Maricopa County

McDowell Mountain Regional Park

Introduction. The 21,099-acre McDowell Mountain Regional Park is located 15 miles northeast of Scottsdale on the eastern slope of the McDowells, an impressive group of mountains rising to 4,002'. They separate Paradise Valley from the Verde Valley and are prominently visible from Phoenix. The park area itself slopes between the high ranges on the west and the Verde River to the east from elevations of 3,100' to 1,550'. It is known for its abundant Sonoran desert vegetation and has several excellent trails. *Note:* On July 8, 1995 a lightning storm ignited a major fire, damaging much of the park area (14,100 acres), which was temporarily closed for 4 months. Due to the sparing of root systems and revegetation of selected areas, vegetation is now returning, but for the present much of the lush vegetation is considerably reduced. The map shows the approximate boundary of the fire. You can compare affected and unaffected areas in this manner. (The photographs in this section were taken before the fire.) (Areas of unburned vegetation are in the northeast corner (North [E], Scout [H], and Eagle [I] Trails) and on most of the Goldfield Trail [C] and parts of the Pemberton Trail [B].)

History. Five archeological sites within the park area include sherd areas and small villages along arroyos, probably representing temporary camps. During the historic period the area was within the range of the Southeastern Yavapai Indians.

Mining has never been of importance though prospectors swarmed over the area after the discovery of gold in the Prescott area in 1853. There are only traces of minerals and consequently no mining towns sprang up.

The main historic significance of the area is centered on nearby Fort McDowell, established by five companies of California volunteers in 1865. The fort's location was determined by King Woolsey's expedition against the Tonto Apaches in 1864. In 1890 the troops were withdrawn and the military reservation was transferred to the Bureau of Indian Affairs. The fort provided several services to settlers (mail, constable, and marriage) before such officials were available in Phoenix. The remains of the fort are on what is now the Fort McDowell Mohave-Apache Indian Reservation southeast of the park boundary near the Verde River.

The park area itself was desert cattle range. There is no available water except in cattle tanks. The rainfall supports attractive desert vegetation but is insufficient for crops. There was one stock raising homestead (Whitehead, 1919-1926) and the Pemberton Ranch. Stock grazing was continuous until 1993, when leases expired.

Geology. The west side of the park contains some rocky hills of Precambrian igneous and metamorphic rocks. From the east the area slopes gently toward the Verde River due to the common level of surfaces between arroyos. There is, however, a steep escarpment along the eastern side of the park, of which Lousley Hill and the Asher Hills (just to the north of the boundary) are one part. Washes and arroyos are steep-sided with a depth of 20-100 feet.

After a lake was formed in the area in Tertiary time, vulcanism started in the late Tertiary period: volcanic ash covered especially the northern and eastern parts of the park, falling on top of lacustrine clay deposits and forming beds of tuff. The Asher and Lousley Hills are remnants of the erosion of Tertiary lacustrine and alluvial deposits in the Pleistocene Epoch.

Predominant rock types are granite and schist, with some gneiss and quartzite in the western part. The best granite exposure (massive and coarse-grained with large talus blocks) is at Rock Knob, which is probably a disintegrated fault block. Huge granite erosion remnants and outcrops (some looking like druid stones) are present [see picture]. Deposits of sand, gravel, and boulders have resulted from erosion from the McDowell Mountains to the west, transport through the canyons formed by block faulting, and spreading out in fan shape. In the eastern section the land appears to be a largely featureless plain dissected by washes trending southeast.

Maps. *Our maps 19-20.* The USGS 1:24,000 McDowell Mountain and Fort McDowell quadrangles (1974) show the area and a few of the roads, but not the trails. A small park map is available at the park, showing the new trails and the area affected by the 1995 fire.

Access. See diagram below. The park's main entrance is reached from Phoenix via Shea Boulevard to the Fountain Hills Boulevard turn-off, thence north 4.2 miles through Fountain Hills to the park entrance on the left. An alternate approach from the north is via Pinnacle Peak Road to Rio Verde Drive, 10.3 miles to Forest Road, where you turn right for 4.5 miles to the entrance on the right. *Note that there is a $3.00 park entrance fee.*

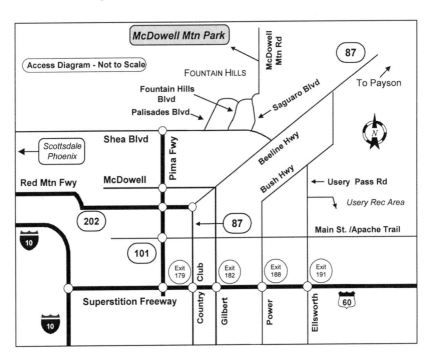

Facilities. The park has two large family picnic areas with 88 picnic tables, grills, and comfort stations; 80 family campsites and a Group Campground with ramada and sani-station (advance reservations required), large Trailhead Group Area and Scout Field Camp. *Phone: 480-471-0173.*

Recommended Hikes and Trail Rides. The trail letters used are those of Maricopa County. Please note that several trails are *hiker only:* [A], [F], [G], [I]. Trail [D], [E] and [H] may be used for biking. Trails [B] and [D] are multi-use trails Of the short trails, probably the most scenic is the Lousley Hill Trail [A]. The Hilltop Trail [C] is short, with fine views. The Scout Trail [H] is an easy short loop through typical desert, and the Eagle Trail [I] leads up a rocky knob with a good view. The Wagner [F] Short Loop Trail provides an easy walk near the Family and Group Campgrounds. The North Trail Loop [E] is moderately long, but has unspoiled vegetation and fine distant views. The new Scenic Trail [D] gives excellent views for little effort, but is 3.4 miles long. Best for a full day's hike or a trail ride is the Pemberton Trail [B].

Cautions. The distances on the Pemberton Trail [B] are quite long and the terrain broken and confusing if the trail is lost. The results of the fire may lead to more trail damage after a storm than would usually be encountered. Otherwise, general cautions apply.

[A] Lousley Hill Trail

General Description. For a short climb, this 1¼-mile trail offers wide views of the Verde Valley, the Superstitions, and the Four Peaks. There are extensive fields of teddy bear ("jumping") cholla. Use care; pieces may be lying on or near the trail and can easily penetrate shoes and clothing. This is a *hiker-only* trail.

From the picnic area, the trail heads across country, then crosses a wide wash at 0.1 mile, reaching a junction at 0.2 mile. Here take the right fork, ascending the hillside by switchbacks to the summit at 0.5 mile. Heading along the crest, the trail then descends to a cliff-top at 0.8 mile where it switchbacks down the crest and then into a valley at 0.9 mile and the previous junction at 1.0 mile. Ascent is 270'.

Access. Take McDowell Mountain Park Drive 5 miles to Lousley Drive South and find the trailhead 0.4 mile further along it, in the Ironwood Picnic Area.

Read Down ↓	Detailed Trail Description	Read Up ↑
0.00	Leave road (elevation 1,780'); head S at sign, crossing 2 small washes.	1.25
0.09	Major wash. Rock-bordered trail parallels wash on its L.	1.16
0.20	Cross wash and ascend gradually.	1.05
0.21	**Junction:** two ends of loop. Go R here and ascend.	1.04
0.26	Turn L (steps lead up). In 100' turn R, then L in 35'.	0.99
0.32	Switchback to R onto short level stretch, then to L and ascend.	0.93
0.40	Areas of "teddy bear" cholla start about here.	0.85
0.44	Turn L and head up crest.	0.81
0.51	**Junction:** level trail turns L here. Spur R leads to summit (2,048', good viewpoint) in 100' (0.53 mi); spur continues back to this trail in another 65'.	0.74

0.54	**Junction:** spur trail back to summit on R. Head gradually down crest, with good walking.	0.71
0.78	Cliff-top (edge of escarpment, 1,920'). Switchback down to L.	0.47
0.82	Switchback to R.	0.43
0.86	Switchback to L at edge of drop-off, then to R.	0.39
0.90	Switchback to L at cliff's edge, descending.	0.35
0.93	Turn L, descending into valley, then making several turns.	0.32
0.98	Parallel small wash.	0.27
1.03	**Junction:** you have now returned to start of loop section.	0.22
1.25	Road and trailhead.	0.00

[B] Pemberton Trail CLOCKWISE

General Description. This is a 15.3-mile *hiker/horse/bike* trail, longest in the park, described here in a clockwise direction in 5 segments. As a hike, this makes a very varied and interesting, but long and strenuous day. There are three stock "tanks" on this trail (often dry), but there is no drinking water for people; carry enough of your own. The total ascent is 800'.

As an old vehicleway, the trail first crosses the Park Drive, then leads across relatively flat terrain and the old Pemberton Ranch area to the Granite Trail [G] at 0.6 mile. It turns west at 2 miles and begins a gradual ascent through a scenic area. At 4.8 miles it leaves the vehicleway and crosses broken terrain past Tonto Tank, unusual rock formations near Rock Knob, then Granite Tank, and the park corner at 9 miles (where there is another walk-in entrance). Here it abruptly turns east, gradually descending an old vehicleway to Cedar Tank at 12.3 miles. Just beyond, it leaves the old vehicleway and crosses the Park Drive at 13.8 miles. The last segment is easy, passing the Scenic Trail [D] junctions at 14.4 miles and 15.2 miles and returning to the Trailhead Group Area *[TGA]* at 15.3 miles.

There are interesting vegetation changes with elevation; these differ somewhat on the two sides of this loop.

Access. There are several access points. The trail description starts at the Trailhead Group Area *[TGA]*, but the trail can also be reached at the end of each segment via other trails or the Park Drive.

NOTE: The description has been divided into segments. This will assist those who are not starting from the centrally-located Trailhead Group Area or who are combining segments of different trails. Total distances to main points of interest from the Trailhead Group Area *[TGA]* are given in *italics* in the tabular descriptions.

Read Down ↓	*Detailed Trail Description*	*Read Up* ↑
	SEGMENT 1 - TGA to Park Drive	
0.00	Trail leaves TGA at its SW side (1,960') on old vehicleway.	0.26
0.26	*McDowell Mountain Park Drive* 2.3 mi from entrance, 0.65 mi from Palisades Way (trail continues across drive). *[15.01 mi ahead back to TGA.]*	0.00

SEGMENT 2 - Park Drive to Park Service Road

0.00	Leave Park Drive (1,985').	1.74
0.09	Cross moderate wash, then go up and down on wide, sandy old vehicleway.	1.65
0.20	Cross wash by going R, then L.	1.54
0.30	Cross moderate wash.	1.44
0.35	**Junction:** on R is Granite Trail [G], 1.23 mi to Wagner Trail [F]. Go straight.	1.39
0.38	Enter wash, turn L to cross it. [There is an intact, unburned area here.]	1.36
0.54	Cross large wash.	1.20
0.61	Cross 5 washes in next 0.31 mi.	1.12
1.08	Old vehicleway angles to R (this is the old Pemberton Ranch area).	0.66
1.09	Ruined water tank and foundation on L.	0.65
1.12	Cross wash, then another.	0.62
1.51	Pass dirt piles and tank on L in eroded area, then go R where vehicleways join. Vehicleway parallels ridge on R briefly.	0.23
1.53	Cross wash.	0.21
1.58	Old vehicleway to R (obscure) [intact, unburned area].	0.16
1.62	Cross major wash and bear R, uphill.	0.12
1.74	**Junction:** to L is Park Service Road, which is not a good access point (3.29 mi to Park Drive near park entrance) (1,860'). Go R to continue *[2.00 mi from start at TGA; 13.26 mi ahead to TGA]*.	0.00

SEGMENT 3 - Service Road to Park Corner and Park Drive

0.00	Go R from **junction**, on old vehicleway. Enter burned-off area.	11.76
0.26	Start gradual ascent away from wash on R. Vehicleway diverges, keep R.	10.50
0.31	Vehicleway branch rejoins. Way becomes rockier, then eroded.	11.45
0.49	Erosion ends on ridge crest in attractive area.	11.27
0.97	Fields of prickly pear, cholla, and staghorn cactus.	10.79
1.11	**Junction:** vehicleway on L; bear slightly R on less obvious vehicleway.	10.65
1.31	Parallel poorer vehicleway that diverges L.	10.45
1.38	Park-like area with fields of prickly pear cactus on both sides.	10.38
1.64	**Junction:** vehicleway enters from L.	10.12
1.80	Vehicleway becomes less well-defined. Park-like area on L.	9.96
2.19	Top of rise. Descend gradually.	9.57
2.31	Bottom of descent. Wash on L.	9.45
2.52	Vehicleway bears R.	9.24
2.55	Bear L, ascend.	9.21
2.84	**Important junction:** leave vehicleway for trail on R, where vehicleway continues straight ahead. Elevation 2,285' *[4.84 mi from start at TGA]*.	8.92
2.98	Cross first of 3 washes.	8.78
3.13	**Junction:** obscure trail of use on R, then another to L in 70'.	8.63
3.21	Cross valley with several washes, turn up one for 25' (old vehicleway follows it), then leave it on R.	8.55
3.30	Cross fence line.	8.46
3.34	Follow fence line on R; trail not well defined here.	8.42
3.38	*Tonto Tank 125' to R (2,300')*. This water-filled depression was for cattle. Use care with several trails of use in area. Head N, toward Rock Knob *[5.38 mi from start at TGA; 9.88 mi ahead to TGA]*.	8.38
3.56	**Junction:** trails of use L & R; descend.	8.20
3.62	Cross moderate wash.	8.14
3.78	Head up branch of small wash, then cross it.	7.98

3.83 **Junction:** trail of use on L.	7.93
4.19 Ascend.	7.57
4.26 Cross moderate wash, ascending to NE.	7.50
4.30 Viewpoint 230' to L toward Superstitions, Four Peaks, Weaver's Needle.	7.46
4.32 Pass large stones on R & L.	7.44
4.46 Top of rise. Descend through very attractive area, crossing several washes, heading NW and W.	7.30
4.83 Go up moderate wash for 50', then leave it on R.	6.93
4.85 Join other wash briefly, then leave it on L.	6.91
4.89 Cross wash. Head N, then NW.	6.87
4.94 Join wash briefly.	6.82
5.22 Cross 2 washes.	6.54
5.33 Trail splits, rejoins in 65'.	6.43
5.59 Bear R.	6.17
5.68 **Junction:** trail of use on L.	6.08
6.00 Huge standing pillar of rock 20' to R; viewpoint (trail splits).	4.68
6.10 Top of rise; drop. Go up & down through rocky area (erosional remnants).	5.66
6.17 Cross broad, flat area, then moderate wash. Ascend.	5.59
6.18 **Junction:** minor trail (alternate route) L leads 100' to viewpoint on top of hump, then descends to rejoin main trail at 6.27 mi.	5.58
6.23 Top of rise.	5.53
6.27 **Junction:** at top of rise, minor trail L is alternate rejoining.	5.49
6.42 Descend into valley; use care with many stock trails, then bear L (E).	5.34
6.46 **Junction:** go L at fork.	5.30
6.53 **Junction:** pass near shed and go R on vehicleway.	5.23
6.58 *Granite Tank on L (2,480') [8.58 mi from start at TGA; 6.69 mi ahead to TGA].*	5.18
6.63 Join fence line and parallel it on L (follow vehicleway) [unburned area].	5.13
6.93 Cross moderate wash.	4.83
7.03 **Junction:** at *Park Corner, new walk-in entrance on L.* Turn R (E). *[9.03 mi from start at TGA; 6.24 mi ahead to TGA.]*	4.73
7.09 **Junction:** vehicleway on L.	4.67
7.25 **Junction:** vehicleway L; keep R here, on old road.	4.51
7.40 Turn R (private home in view, across park boundary).	4.36
8.02 Parallel moderate wash on R, then cross it. [burned area begins]	3.74
8.14 Cross moderate wash.	3.62
8.30 Turn L (N), then cross moderate wash in 100'. Reach top of rise in 300'.	3.46
8.53 Top of rise, descend.	3.23
8.57 Vehicleway bends to L, and again to R in 350'.	3.19
8.66 **Junction:** trail of use on L.	3.10
8.93 Eroded area of vehicleway.	2.83
9.13 **Junction:** trail of use on L.	2.63
10.25 Fence ends at corner.	1.51
10.26 Old rusting water tower on L.	1.50
10.27 *Cedar Tank on L (2,090'). [12.27 mi from start at TGA; 3 mi ahead to TGA.]*	1.49
10.32 Fence corner (barbed-wire).	1.44
10.68 **Junction:** service road continues straight ahead (administrative use only), 1.3 mi to Park Drive (2,025'). To continue, go R on trail *[12.48 mi from start at TGA; 2.78 mi ahead to TGA.]*	1.28
13.30 Turn L into moderate wash for 35.'	0.46
13.64 Enter wash area, then turn R, out of it, in 0.06 mi.	0.12
13.64 *McDowell Mountain Park Drive (1,920'). [13.76 mi from start at TGA; 1.50 mi ahead to TGA.]*	0.00

0.00	Leave Park Drive.	1.50
0.35	Top of rise.	1.15
0.59	**Junction:** Scenic Trail [D] on L up ridge, returns at 1.38 mi (3.43 mi long).	0.91
1.38	**Junction:** Scenic Trail [D] on L.	0.12
1.47	Turn R at barbed-wire fence; ramadas in view.	0.03
1.50	*Trailhead Group Area*, elev. 1,960'. *[15.26 mi from start of circuit.]*	0.00

[C] Hilltop Trail

General Description. From the Trailhead Group Area [TGA], east side, a new trail leads directly up a low ridge, passes a spur trail to the first summit, then runs along a crest to reach a loop that runs around the last summit, with fine views. It is *hiker-only*. Ascent is 100'. The total return trip is only ½ mile.

Access. At the TGA.

Read Down ↓	Detailed Trail Description	Read Up ↑
0.00	Leave TGA. (1,760'). Immediately start ascent.	0.29
0.03	Steps.	0.26
0.05	Ease, views open. Turn R (E).	0.24
0.12	**Junction:** spur 45' to L to summit. Keep R.	0.17
0.13	Reach crest; continue along it.	0.16
0.16	Low point on ridge.	0.13
0.18	**Junction:** trail splits. Continue just below crest.	0.11
0.24	Far end of crest, good views. Trail swings back to W.	0.05
0.26	Swing to L (good viewpoint on R).	0.03
0.29	**Junction:** Back at start of loop (1,860'). It is 0.18 mi back to start.	0.00

[D] Scenic Trail CLOCKWISE

General Description. This is a new 3.4-mile long multi-use trail. It ascends a low, burned-over ridge with good views. At 0.3 mile it reaches the top and from there it continues up and down for 1.3 miles, then makes a steady descent, rounds the ridge and heads west, reaching the valley bottom at 2¼ miles. Heading gradually up the valley, it follows several washes to reach a low pass at 3.2 miles before heading down to the Pemberton Trail [B] not far from the TGA. Total ascent is about 350'.

Access. *From the Trailhead Group Area* at its northern side follow the Pemberton Trail [B] for 0.1 mile (Scenic Trail returning) or (as this description reads) for 0.9 mile to start the clockwise direction. *From the north,* that junction can also be reached from McDowell Mountain Park Drive on the Pemberton Trail, 0.6 mile south of the Drive.

Read Down ↓	Detailed Trail Description	Read Up ↑
0.00	The trail leaves Pemberton Trail [B], heading E toward ridge.	3.43
0.02	Start ascent.	3.41
0.21	Top of rise.	3.22
0.26	Cross ridge crest.	3.17
0.31	Viewpoint on crest. Trail is almost level, heading E.	3.22
0.38	Top of rise. Descend, then go up next hump on ridge.	3.05
0.60	Viewpoint on crest.	2.83
0.67	Head just W of crest.	2.76
0.77	Top of rise on low summit. Descend gradually, slightly R of crest.	2.66
0.84	Bottom of descent.	2.59
0.92	Top of rise.	2.51
1.02	Bottom of descent; trail rises gradually up crest.	2.41
1.18	Top of rise.	2.25
1.34	Bottom of descent.	2.09
1.44	Top of rise. Flat area. Continue along (or just R) of crest.	1.99
1.62	Start descent.	1.81
1.70	Cross over crest, side-hill steadily down L (N) side of ridge.	1.73
2.07	Ease grade of descent. Turn R around end of ridge, heading W.	1.36
2.25	Bottom of descent. Cross moderate wash.	1.18
2.26	Start rising gradually up valley bottom on original trail in this area.	1.17
2.39	Enter wash.	1.04
2.49	Leave wash.	0.94
2.50	Re-enter wash.	0.93
2.54	Bear R along smaller wash.	0.89
2.59	Leave wash to R, then return to it more than once.	0.84
2.70	Out of wash on ascending trail.	0.73
2.81	Re-enter wash.	0.62
2.94	Leave wash.	0.49
2.97	Re-enter wash.	0.46
3.04	Leave wash on L, at arrows.	0.39
3.22	Reach low pass.	0.21
3.23	Cross moderate wash, swing W.	0.20
3.41	Cross moderate wash.	0.02
3.43	**Junction:** Pemberton Trail; turn L on it for only 0.12 mi to TGA (1,___').	0.00

[E] North Trail   COUNTERCLOCKWISE

General Description. This is a *hiker and bike-only* loop trail (with a short "stem") into fine desert terrain. The "stem" of the loop is 140' long, then the loop leads north, crossing many washes, ascending gradually, and then turns west, south, and east again, descending gradually to reach the "stem" again at 2.9 miles. The total round-trip distance from the road is 3.1 miles. Total ascent is 150'. There is very fine vegetation to be seen on this trip, as well as distant views of the Four Peaks, Mazatzal Mountains, and Superstitions.

Access. Take McDowell Mountain Park Drive to Asher Drive South at 5.6 miles from the park entrance and drive 0.4 mile along it to a parking area on the right; the trail is on the left at a sign near some picnic tables.

Read Down ↓	Detailed Trail Description	Read Up ↑
0.00	Trail leaves Asher Drive South at a sign (elev. 1,750'). Trail to R at 40' leads to picnic table.	2.80
0.08	**Junction:** actual loop starts here. Go R here *(counterclockwise)*, as does this description. Trail meanders NE and N.	2.72
0.19	Cross small wash.	2.61
0.22	**Junction:** old trail sharp L is closed. Keep R.	2.58
0.36	Bear L (W), then R in 100'.	2.44
0.43	Bear L. Ascend gradually.	2.37
0.83	Bear L (SW).	1.97
0.96	Bear R (W).	1.84
1.06	**Junction:** old trail continues straight ahead; turn L here.	1.74
1.55	Cross wash. Bear L (SSE) with fine distant views.	1.25
1.60	Huge saguaro on R. Bear L (SE).	1.20
1.79	Hill on R.	1.01
2.21	Cross small wash.	0.59
2.52	Cross small wash.	0.28
2.55	**Junction:** keep R, old trail ahead.	0.25
2.71	Cross wash.	0.09
2.74	**Junction:** old trail sharp L.	0.06
2.80	Back at road and trailhead.	0.00

[F] Wagner Trail - Short Loop COUNTERCLOCKWISE

General Description. The Wagner Trail has two loops, Short, and Long. Both lead through easy terrain and are *hiker-only*. It leaves from the Group Campground parking area, heads north, then northwest, reaching a short spur trail to Palisades Circle North at 0.5 mile. At 0.9 mile it crosses Palisades Drive and at 1.0 mile the Long Loop diverges west; this trail coincides with the Long Loop as it heads south to 1.3 miles, where the trails diverge, the Short Loop turns east at the start of the Granite Trail at 1.4 miles, passes a spur to Palisades Way, and ends at Palisades Circle North. Ascent is 50'.

Access. *For the Short Loop,* leave the Group Campground parking area opposite its entrance off of Palisades Way from Palisades Drive, at a sign. *For the Long Loop,* leave Palisades Circle North between campsites 10 & 13.

Read Down ↓	Detailed Trail Description	Read Up ↑
0.00	Leave Group Campground parking area (1,990').	1.67
0.03	Cross small wash, bear L (N).	1.64
0.17	Swing L (W), ascending gradually.	1.50
0.20	**Junction:** go L on old road that becomes trail, ascending gradually.	1.47
0.37	Go around small hill on L.	1.30
0.45	Turn L; cross moderate wash.	1.22
0.49	**Junction:** spur trail L 415' to Palisades Circle North.	1.18
0.60	Turn R; descend to cross small wash in 25'.	1.07
0.62	Turn L.	1.05
0.64	Turn R, then L.	1.03

0.70	Bear L (S), then to W.	0.97
0.72	Turn R, enter wash for 50', then leave it towards the W.	0.95
0.78	Turn L. In 40', turn R into wash for 20', leaving it on L.	0.89
0.92	**Junction:** Palisades Drive (2,140'). Trail continues across road.	0.75
1.00	**Junction:** Long Loop turns R here. Go sharp L, descending gradually.	0.67
1.12	Edge of valley.	0.55
1.30	**Junction:** Long Loop on R. Go sharp L, descending.	0.37
1.43	**Junction:** where Granite Trail leads straight ahead, this trail turns L (E).	0.24
1.47	Cross small wash.	0.20
1.49	**Junction:** spur trail R leads in 650' to road (Palisades Way, Family CG).	0.18
1.67	This trail ends at Palisades Circle North (2,030'). Sign; map. The road can be followed R to return to the start.	0.00

[F] Wagner Trail - Long Loop   CLOCKWISE

General Description. A self-guided, *hiker-only* trail, 1.2 miles in length, or a total of 1.3 miles as a circuit. Ascent is about 350'. It overlaps the Short Loop, so that description is repeated here.

Access. From three points: (a) from the Group Campground parking area, (b) at campsite #22 on Palisades Circle South; or (c) in the southern Family Campground area from Comfort Station #9 on Palisades Way North at Whitehead Way.

Read Down ↓	Detailed Trail Description	Read Up ↑
0.00	Leave Group Campground parking area (1,990').	4.13
0.03	Cross small wash, bear L (N).	4.10
0.17	Swing L (W), ascending gradually.	3.96
0.20	**Junction:** go L on old road that becomes trail, ascending gradually.	3.93
0.37	Go around small hill on L.	3.76
0.45	Turn L; cross moderate wash.	3.68
0.49	**Junction:** spur trail L 415' to Palisades Circle North.	3.64
0.60	Turn R; descend to cross small wash in 25'.	3.53
0.62	Turn L.	3.51
0.64	Turn R, then L.	3.49
0.70	Bear L (S), then to W.	3.43
0.72	Turn R, enter wash for 50', then leave it towards the W.	3.41
0.78	Turn L. In 40', turn R into wash for 20', leaving it on L.	3.35
0.92	**Junction:** Palisades Drive (2,140'). Trail continues across road.	3.21
1.00	**Junction:** Short Loop turns L here. Keep straight on, with big wash in view, paralleling Maintenance Road on R.	3.13
1.19	Near water tank, bear L. There are fine views of the Four Peaks, Miners Needle in the Superstitions, and the Mazatzals.	2.94
1.57	Bear L (S).	2.56
1.60	Swing R, then L in 70'.	2.53
1.62	Cross major wash to SW.	2.51
1.65	Cross smaller wash, ascend to SW.	2.48
1.71	Swing W.	2.42
1.79	Top of rise (2,170'). Trail rises gradually.	2.34

1.99	**Junction:** trail of use L to viewpoint in 125'. Keep R.	2.14
2.06	Top of rise (2,200'). Turn L, descending steadily S, into valley.	2.07
2.14	Bottom of descent (2,160'). Continue SW.	1.99
2.24	Cross valley floor below rock outcrop on R.	1.89
2.29	Enter wash.	1.84
2.31	Enter wash, another wash joins. In only 15', exit wash to the L (S) - use care here at obscure turn.	1.82
2.34	Turn L. On R 150' is old cement trough. Head E, descending gradually.	1.79
2.77	Cross wash.	1.36
2.83	Re-cross wash.	1.30
3.05	Re-cross wash.	1.08
3.29	Bear L (N).	0.84
3.30	Cross wash.	0.83
3.32	Bear R (NE).	0.81
3.42	Join wash for 25', leave it on L.	0.71
3.48	Swing L & R, cross small wash, ascend gradually E.	0.65
3.59	**Junction:** Short Loop on L (2,120') (Leads 0.3 mi back to start of this trail.)	0.54
3.89	**Junction:** Granite Trail [G] continues straight ahead; this trail turns L (2,080').	0.24
3.93	Cross small wash.	0.20
3.95	**Junction:** spur trail R leads in 650' to road (Palisades Way).	0.18
4.13	**Junction:** This trail ends at Palisades Circle North (2,030'). Sign; map. The road can be followed R to return to the start.	0.00

[G] Granite Trail COUNTERCLOCKWISE

General Description. An old vehicleway is used to descend the bajada from the Wagner Trail [F] for 1¼ miles to the Pemberton Trail [B]. It is *hiker-only*. Descent is 170'.

Access. At its *western end*, from the Wagner Trail, ¼ mile west of Palisades Circle North, or via a shorter spur to the Family Campground. At its *eastern end*, from the Pemberton Trail [B], 1/3 mile west of the Park Drive.

Read Down ↓	Detailed Trail Description	Read Up ↑
0.00	Leave junction with Wagner Trail [F] (2,190').	1.23
0.22	Swing to R (S).	1.01
0.26	Swing to L (good viewpoint on R). Descend gradually.	0.97
1.23	**Junction:** Pemberton Trail [B] L & R (1,930'). To L it is 0.35 mi to Park Drive.	0.00

Verde Valley from Scenic Trail

Pinnacle Peak & Rock Knob from bajada

[H] Scout Trail CLOCKWISE

General Description. An 0.80-mile *hiker and bike-only* trail from the Scout Loop, *for use only by those staying at the Youth Group Area* (available by reservation only). It leads around through typical Sonoran desert. Ascent and descent are 35'.

Access. From the loop in the Youth Group area.

Read Down ↓	Detailed Trail Description	Read Up ↑
0.00	Leave road loop at sign (1,700').	0.80
0.06	Top of rise, descend gradually.	0.74
0.17	Bear L (E).	0.63
0.22	Cross moderate wash. Head S.	0.58
0.29	Turn R.	0.51
0.49	Head W up open area (becomes road); grade gradually increases.	0.31
0.57	Leave road to N; way levels in 120'.	0.23
0.70	Bear L.	0.10
0.80	Road loop just W of water tap.	0.00

[I] Eagle Trail CLOCKWISE

General Description. From Scout Camp Drive this 0.4-mile *hiker-only* trail leads up and over a small knob with good views, then returns to the Loop. Ascent is 85'.

Access. Start on the west side of the Scout Camp Drive loop, 85' from where the stem of the loop enters.

Read Down ↓	Detailed Trail Description	Read Up ↑
0.00	Trail leaves road loop at W side (1,700').	0.40
0.07	Switchback to R.	0.33
0.08	Switchback to L (trail of use descends to R).	0.32
0.13	Top of hill (1,785'). Views of Superstitions, Four Peaks, etc.	0.27
0.15	Turn R (E).	0.25
0.17	Switchback to L, then to W.	0.23
0.23	Cross small wash. In 25' turn R *(use care)*, parallel wash on R.	0.17
0.25	Bear L away from wash at big sag.	0.15
0.26	Enter moderate wash and go down it.	0.14
0.27	Turn R.	0.13
0.30	Edge of wash: veer R, along it.	0.10
0.31	Cross small wash, ascend steps.	0.09
0.32	Top of rise, descend gradually.	0.08
0.40	This trail ends at road loop near N end.	0.00

Maricopa County

Usery Mountain Recreation Area

Goldfield Mountains from Pass Mountain Trail

Introduction. Usery Mountain Recreation Area consists of 3,324 acres, 12 miles northeast of Mesa. The Superstitions are to the east, the Goldfield Mountains on the north and northwest, immediately northwest are the Usery Mountains, and the McDowells are easily visible across the Salt River valley, also to the northwest. Two of the eight dams of the Salt River Project are within 7 miles of Usery Mountain. The lower area of the Recreation Area described here is in Maricopa County, but the main mountain trails are in the adjacent Tonto National Forest.

History. Between what is now the recreation area and the Salt River there was an Indian village and the ruins of the old Hohokam canals. The mountain itself was named for King Usery, a cattleman in the area between 1878 and 1880. It was not an easy way of life in this arid area, and in 1891 he and Bill Blevins (after whom the Blevins Trail was named) held up the Globe-Florence stagecoach and stole two bars of silver bullion. Usery was surrounded at his ranch and was later sentenced to 7 years in the Territorial Prison at Yuma. He was pardoned after only two years, but later was convicted of horse-stealing for which he received a light sentence. Later he disappeared.

The desert plain around the Recreation Area has had some limited grazing use since the 1890s. There were several homesteads in the area, two of which have given names to trails described here. One was Chester McGill's (outside the present recreation area but inside the Tonto National Forest on the old road along the major wash near the Pass Mountain Trail) who held it only from 1932-34; it changed hands many times thereafter. The Coleman homestead existed from 1931-1937, inside the present recreation area, to the east of the junction of the Blevins Trail and the Cat Peaks. Lack of dependable water was the reason the area was not more attractive to settlers. An old wagon road crossed the area near the present Bush Highway, which was constructed early in the century and later improved.

Usery Mountain itself is not mineralized. Eight miles to the east, in the Goldfield Mountains, low-grade gold ores were extensively worked in the 1890s. After World War II open-pit mining was attempted but failed. Many mining claims were filed, but none have become producing mines.

Pass Mountain connects to the Goldfield Mountains to its east and forms the eastern flank of the pass between it and Usery Mountain to the west.

Geology. There are no significant mineral resources. The Recreation Area is part of a granite pediment — a broad, plain-like surface sloping away from the higher mountains with occasional small granite hills and Pass Mountain standing upon it. Most of the nearby washes are shallow and poorly developed. The saddle between the two peaks of Headquarters Hill contains a shear zone marking a fault line (in the wash to the northwest is a prospect pit).

The hills are caused by tilted fault-blocks. Bedrock is thought to be Precambrian granite (1 to $1^1/_2$ billion years old). Volcanic rocks capping Pass Mountain are of Tertiary Age. Pass Mountain has a prominent "tuff" layer[1] that turns greenish after a period of rain. Wind Cave is a hollowed-out portion of this layer that is softer than granite. The region's common northwest trend is evident in parts of this area and its geological faults.

---

[1]A solidified layer of volcanic ash or other ejected material.

Maps. *Our map 21.* The area is shown on the 1:24,000 USGS Apache Junction quadrangle, but the trails are not shown.

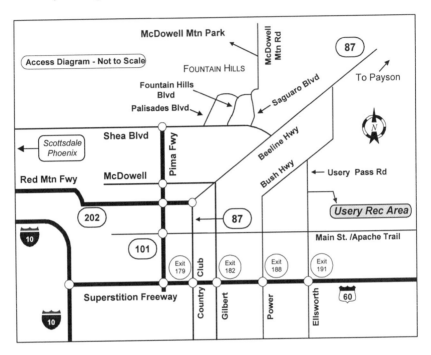

Access. From Phoenix, take the Superstition Freeway (US 60) to exit #191 (Ellsworth) and head north (becoming Usery Pass Road) to turn right on Usery Park Road (the Recreation Area's entrance) at 6.7 miles; the gate is at 7 miles. Blevins Drive is on the right at 7.8 miles, and Wind Cave Drive West is at 8 miles.

From the Recreation Area's entrance, the first road on the right is Buckhorn Camp Drive to the Group Campground. The next road on the left is to the Coleman Trail. From Wind Cave Drive there is access to the Wind Cave, Pass Mountain, and Coleman Trails. The Horse Staging Area is the access point for the Pass Mountain and Blevins Trails, while the Merkle Memorial parking area and picnic area #6 give access to the Merkle Trails. [See access map, this page.]

The other access point is at the north end of Meridian Drive, where there is a trailhead and parking.

Facilities. There are more than 50 picnic sites, a 75-unit Family Campground, a Group Campground (advance reservations required), archery range, Group Picnic Area, and Horse Staging Area (reservations required).

Water is available. Picnic areas and the archery range close at sunset. *Make sure your vehicle is outside the gate by that time if you intend to leave.* No off-road travel or unlicensed vehicles are permitted. Horseback riding is restricted to existing designated trails. There is a $3 daily vehicle fee ($50 for an annual pass). Day use areas close at 6:30 p.m. *(Phone 480-984-0032.)*

Recommended Hikes and Trail Rides. The trail designations used here are those on the official Maricopa County park map and the Tonto National Forest. Of the hiker-only trails, the most popular is the Wind Cave Trail [G] [Forest Service 281] which leads up to a break in the tuff layer below the summit ridge. It has good views to the west. Simplest are the Merkle Memorial Trail [D] and Merkle Vista Trail [E], which circle and climb Headquarters Hill, with good all-around views.

Of the hiker/horse trails, the best wilderness experience is the Pass Mountain Trail [F] [Forest Service 282] which takes the better part of a day for hikers. *Be absolutely sure to carry enough water on this long trip!* The Blevins Trail [I] and Cat Peaks Trail [J] are shorter and have varied terrain, but no significant climbs.

[A] Levee Trail WEST to EAST

General Description. This is an 1.7 mile long *hiker-horse* trail through almost flat desert, crossing several moderate-sized washes and running partly along the top of a dike above the Pass Mountain Diversion of the Buckhorn-Mesa Watershed. Ascent is about 40'.

Access. From the Moon Rock Trail [H] on the west to Spillway Trail [S] on the east.

Read Down ↓	Detailed Trail Description	Read Up ↑
0.00	From the Moon Rock Trail at 1.31 mi, head S, descending gradually (1,820').	1.65
0.46	**Junction:** join old vehicleway from R; go L.	1.19
0.57	**Junction:** on R is gate and road leading out of Recreation Area.	1.08
0.94	**Junction:** where NoSo Trail [N] drops off dike to L, continue on it.	0.71
1.01	Below on L, NoSo Trail [N] can be seen heading N.	0.64
1.65	**Junction:** This trail ends at Spillway Trail [S].	0.00

[B] Coleman Trail

General Description. An easy *hiker only* trail, crossing several washes and displaying a wide variety of flora. Leave the Group Picnic Area and cross 3 washes to reach the Pass Mountain Trail [282] at 0.4 mile, just 350' mile north of the parking area at Wind Cave Drive. Ascent is 50'.

Access. From the east side of the Group Picnic Area parking area, at a sign; or from Wind Cave Drive where the Wind Cave Trail leads north 100' to the Pass Mountain Trail, then left 250' on the latter.

Read Down ↓	Detailed Trail Description	Read Up ↑
0.00	Leave Group Picnic Area (1,990').	0.42
0.02	Cross small wash; bear R.	0.40
0.12	Cross moderate wash.	0.30
0.33	Cross major wash, ascend to NE on other side.	0.09
0.42	**Junction:** Pass Mountain Trail [282], 350' N of Wind Cave Drive trailhead. (Elevation 2,025'.)	0.00

[C] Meridian Trail

General Description. A short, 1-mile, *hiker-horse* trail from Meridian Road to the Blevins Trail [I]. There is no significant ascent.

Access. *On the east,* from Meridian Road (local access only, no parking area); *on the west,* from the Blevins Trail [I].

Read Down ↓	Detailed Trail Description	Read Up ↑
0.00	From Meridian Road (1,830'), just S of Canyon Rd on N, head W.	0.95
0.01	Gate in fence.	0.94
0.08	Cross wash.	0.87
0.11	**Junction:** Palo Verde Trail [L] on L.	0.84
0.21	**Junction:** trail of use on L.	0.74
0.50	Park boundary corner on R.	0.45
0.55	Cross deep wash.	0.40
0.77	**Junction:** Spillway Trail [R] on L.	0.18
0.79	Cross major wash.	0.16
0.80	**Junction:** Cat Peaks Trail [J] on R.	0.15
0.86	Top of rise on side of hill (views).	0.09
0.95	**Junction:** Blevins Trail [I] straight ahead and half-R. This trail ends.	0.00

[D] Merkle Memorial Trail

General Description. The Memorial Trail circles Headquarters Hill and can be reached from the south at the memorial plaque parking and picnic area, or at the northeast picnic area (#6). It is a *hiker-only* trail with moderate ascent and descent along and across minor washes with some views of desert vegetation. It intersects the Merkle Vista Trail [E] at the north and south end, and a side-trail to the Merkle Vista Trail connects on the southeast corner of the circle. Ascent is 100'. It is planned to develop it as barrier-free.

Access. *From the north:* at Area 6 ramada; walk southwest between the comfort station and a ramada to ramada 6C. The spur trail leaves from the far side and crosses a wash. This trail starts at 0.1 mile. *From the south:* park at the memorial area and find the spur trail at a sign directly across the road.

Read Down ↓	Detailed Trail Description	Read Up ↑
0.00	From the Merkle Memorial parking area and plaque at 1,890', find the trail at sign on opposite side of road.	0.94
0.01	Triangular **junction** in only 25': go L for the clockwise direction of the Merkle Memorial Trail (and for S end of Merkle Vista Trail). (Go R for counterclockwise direction.) *This description is for clockwise direction (L).*	0.93
0.04	Turn R and ascend.	0.90
0.05	Turn sharp R.	0.89
0.06	Switchback to L on ascent.	0.88
0.07	**Junction:** Merkle Vista Trail [E] sharp R leads to S Peak in 0.22 mi; to N Peak in 0.40 mi; back to Merkle Memorial Trail in 0.5 mi. Continue straight ahead, ascending gradually.	0.87
0.12	Top of rise. Bear slightly R, descend gradually to N. Cross 3 small washes.	0.82
0.40	**Junction:** trail sharp R at top of rise is Merkle Vista Trail [E] to N Peak in 0.18 mi. Descend.	0.54
0.48	**Junction:** trail R is continuation of this trail. *(Straight ahead, on spur, large wash is crossed in 45', a smaller one in 110', and just beyond is ramada 6C. The road is 460' away.)* Parallel wash, heading S.	0.46
0.51	**Junction:** trail sharp L leads around far side of tree to nature sign "desert hackberry."	0.43
0.52	Trail turns L.	0.42
0.54	Descend; level out in 150'.	0.40
0.61	Bench on R. Continue S, passing picnic tables, then paralleling road.	0.33
0.93	**Junction:** back at triangle just 65' from road and memorial plaque.	0.01
0.94	Trailhead at road opposite memorial picnic area.	0.00

[E] Merkle Vista Trail

General Description. From the Merkle Memorial Trail [D] on the north side of Headquarters Hill, this spur ascends steadily up the ridge with three switchbacks. It reaches a fine viewpoint at North Peak (2,078') at 0.2 mile, then drops to a pass. The main trail skirts the South Peak (2,052') to a junction with the side-trail to that peak at 0.3 mile. The Merkle Memorial Trail is reached again at ½ mile, where this trail ends. Ascent is only 90' to the North Peak.

Access. *From the north (ramada 6C):* take spur to Merkle Memorial Trail [D] for 0.1 mile, go right on it for 0.1 mile to junction; turn sharp left, uphill. *From the south (Merkle Memorial Parking Area):* take the short spur trail to the Merkle Memorial Trail [D], then left on it for 0.1 mile, where the Merkle Vista Trail turns sharp right.

Read Down ↓	Detailed Trail Description	Read Up ↑
0.00	From the Merkle Memorial Trail [D] 0.17 mi from ramada 6C, head sharp L (SE) up the ridge.	0.50
0.03	Trail switchbacks to R, levels briefly, then ascends toward pass.	0.47
0.11	Turn sharp L just before a minor summit.	0.39
0.16	**Junction:** switchback up to R where spur trail L leads to viewpoint in 30'.	0.34
0.18	*Summit of North Peak (2,078').* Descend gradually S.	0.40

0.22	**Junction:** on R 100' is spur to minor summit. Just L of that faint trail is main trail, descending; take it. (Trail straight ahead along main ridge ends in 120'.)	0.36
0.26	Turn L and descend, with minor summit just above on R. Pass rock formations on R just before pass.	0.32
0.30	*Pass* (2,000'). Trail continues straight, mostly level.	0.20
0.33	**Junction:** trail sharp R is spur to South Peak (good view) in 250'. Descend.	0.17
0.47	Switchback to L, then to R in 50'.	0.03
0.50	**Junction:** back at Merkle Memorial Trail (turn L for 345' to road).	0.00

[F] [282] Pass Mountain Trail

General Description. This is a 7.4 mile-long *hiker and horse* trail, long and strenuous, with much up and down. It well repays the effort. Heading east from the Wind Cave Trail [281], it meanders along the flat slopes of Pass Mountain and skirts private property. After about 2 miles it heads north (passing the ¼-mile spur to Meridian Trailhead at 2.1 miles), ascends the west side of the valley, then swings around and switchbacks up just below a rocky pinnacle, entering the pass at 3.9 miles where there are dramatic views, an ascent of 600'. There is then a gradual descent (with many washes to be crossed) along the eastern slopes, swinging around to the west side at about 5.7 miles. Much of this trail is in the Tonto National Forest. The section heading south along the fence line back to the start is inside the Recreation Area. *[For hikers, the counter-clockwise direction is strongly recommended, whereas for equestrians the reverse is recommended.]*

Note: In using the mileages below, if you start from the Horse Staging Area, *subtract* 0.61 mile for counterclockwise travel; *add* the same for clockwise travel.

Access. (1) From the south picnic loop at the Horse Staging Area (east end); (2) at the start of the Wind Cave Trail [281], from Wind Cave Drive West (north picnic loop at Area #8), off the park road near a washroom; or (3) from Meridian Trailhead. The start is marked with a prominent sign. *Distances here are from access point (2).* (It may also be reached via the Coleman [B] or Blevins [I] Trails.)

Read Down ↓	Detailed Trail Description	Read Up ↑
0.00	From **junction** on Wind Cave Trail [281] 100' beyond trailhead (elev. 2,030'), turn R (S) and cross a wash in 180'.	7.41
0.05	Cross fence. Descend gradually S.	7.36
0.23	**Junction:** trail R leads to ramada. Continue straight ahead.	7.18
0.26	Cross wash, bear R and parallel it.	7.15
0.61	**Junction:** trail to Horse Staging Area and ramada on R. Turn L here.	6.80
0.66	Cross major wash. Head straight toward the Superstition Mountains.	6.75
0.71	Cross moderate wash; switchback to L out of it.	6.70
0.73	Cross wash, switchback out of it, then ascend toward pass.	6.68
0.82	Cross wash.	6.59
0.89	Cross wash, then head into low pass.	6.52
1.01	Cross large wash, switchback out of it.	6.40

1.11	**Important junction:** spur trail R 190' thru fence leads to Cat Peaks Trail [J].	6.30
1.26	Cross small wash and descend toward private homes in view ahead.	6.15
1.42	Fence alongside on R. Switchback to L and cross wash.	5.99
1.44	Cross wash.	5.97
1.46	**Junction:** trail of use on L. Descend to R to join fence line and parallel it.	5.95
1.56	Leave fence line.	5.85
1.62	Cross major wash; ascend briefly on rocky trail.	5.79
1.73	Cross major wash.	5.68
1.75	Bear R, toward Superstitions, ascending gradually. Road below on R.	5.66
1.93	Top of rise; descend.	5.48
1.99	Cross small wash; major wash is some distance away on R; parallel it.	5.42
2.11	**Important junction:** on R is trail to N Meridian Rd Trailhead *[Details: in 60', keep L at junction, then at 140' descend into steep-walled canyon, crossing major wash at 235' and following it for 90', then ascend out of it. At 515' reach a 4-way junction with a trail along the wash bank. At another junction, at 0.23 mi, go straight, not R. Keep L at 0.25 mi, then reach gate at 0.26 mi.]*	5.30
2.24	**Junction:** side-trail to R (not very obvious) crosses wash to side-trail.	5.17
2.47	Top of rise.	4.94
2.51	Major wash; follow it for 50', then ascend to L.	4.90
2.75	**Junction:** where old trail continued ahead, new and much-improved trail turns L and ascends steadily [GPS location 0445650/3704035]	4.66
2.82	Turn R on easier grade. From here the trail route and footway are excellent.	4.59
2.89	Cross small wash (2,200').	4.52
3.40	Cross moderate wash (2,390').	4.01
3.43	Landmark: pass between huge boulders.	3.98
3.45	Ascend steadily.	3.96
3.48	Begin long traverse to R across face of mountain (2,420').	3.93
3.62	Excellent viewpoint where trail swings L around shoulder.	3.79
3.67	**Junction:** where old trail descends to R, go L and up on it.	3.74
3.70	Switchback to L. Use caution up steep rocks.	3.71
3.76	Switchback to R, then to L in 75'.	3.65
3.80	Ease grade of ascent; pass below cliff on R.	3.61
3.86	*PASS (Elevation 2,588')*; excellent viewpoint with grassy areas. Trail of use on R leads to crest and better view in 340'. From pass the terrain changes. Descend gradually.	3.55
3.93	Cross small wash.	3.48
4.00	Cross draw and wash.	3.41
4.22	Cross small wash.	3.19
4.28	Landmark: pass between 2 conglomerate boulders.	3.13
4.38	Cross wash.	3.03
4.40	Switchback to L.	3.01
4.48	Cross major wash.	2.93
4.68	**Junction:** trail of use on R; descend steadily.	2.73
4.70	Top of rise, viewpoint.	2.71
4.73	Cross wash, ascend.	2.68
4.95	Top of rise.	2.36
5.09	Cross wash; new trailway begins.	2.32
5.40	**Junction:** in pass, spur R to viewpoint in 235' (2,470').	2.01
5.50	**Junction:** side-trail R 30' to viewpoint.	1.91
5.65	**Junction:** cross dirt road (2,310'). Cross small wash in 280'.	1.76
5.83	Cross large wash.	1.58
5.86	Pass through fence (from Tonto National Forest into Recreation Area).	1.55
6.20	Cross deep wash.	1.21

6.40	Cross wash.	1.01
6.45	Cross major wash.	0.96
7.05	Descend into wide wash.	0.36
7.26	Cross major wash and turn R in it, then ascend out of it to L in 120'.	0.15
7.35	**Junction:** Coleman Trail [B] on R (0.70 mi to road). Go L, into wash.	0.06
7.41	**Junction:** *back at starting point* — Wind Cave Trail [281] on L (1.29 mi to Wind Cave on side of Pass Mountain). Road is 100' to R on this trail.	0.00

[G] [281] Wind Cave Trail

General Description. This 1.6-mile *hiker-only* trail involves a steady ascent of the flank of Pass Mountain almost to its south peak. From the trailhead you quickly cross the Pass Mountain Trail [282], enter the Tonto National Forest, and ascend gradually along a wash. The grade increases beyond 0.6 mile, with many switchbacks. Past the last rest stop (at 0.9 mile) the way meanders along the base of the prominent geological layer ("tuff") to reach Wind Cave at 1.6 miles. There are some good views, both distant and close-up, of the unusual geological formations on the mountain.

Access. From Wind Cave Drive West (north picnic loop at Area #8), off the park road, near a washroom. The start is marked with a prominent sign.

Read Down ↓	Detailed Trail Description	Read Up ↑
0.00	From parking area at sign and washrooms (2,020'), trail ascends gradually.	1.61
0.02	**Junction (4-way):** cross Pass Mountain Trail [282].	1.59
0.08	Cross fence thru gate (Tonto National Forest boundary) from Recreation Area.	1.53
0.17	Cross wash; parallel it on R from 0.25 mi.	1.44
0.19	Cross wash, switchback to L.	1.42
0.21	Switchback to R, ascend beside wash, paralleling brink.	1.40
0.29	Turn L, ascending steadily, then turn R.	1.32
0.33	Switchback to R, then to L in 225'.	1.28
0.38	**Junction:** old trail straight ahead; keep L here. Turn R in 50'.	1.23
0.46	**Junction:** R in 35' to stone wall and boulders.	1.15
0.64	Switchback to L. at wash, ascend.	0.97
0.71	Switchback to R.	0.90
0.73	Bear L on level; swing L & R.	0.88
0.77	Landmark: around boulders; start steady ascent.	0.84
0.81	Switchback to L.	0.80
0.85	Steps.	0.76
0.87	"Rest area."	0.74
0.88	Switchback to R, level.	0.73
0.91	Switchbacks start.	0.70
0.95	Switchback to L, then to R in 125'. Go back and forth among boulders.	0.66
1.01	Switchback to R and make a long traverse.	0.60
1.05	Switchback to L at edge of wash, then to R in 40'.	0.56
1.09	Switchback to L, up some steps, then make a long traverse.	0.52
1.15	Switchback to R, then to L in 40' and to R in 70'.	0.46
1.22	Switchback to L (N).	0.39
1.24	Rest area on L. Turn R (E) here.	0.37
1.30	Cross wash area. Climb below tuff cliffs, making a long traverse.	0.31

1.36	Holes in tuff on L.	0.25
1.41	Base of tuff cliff at wash. Ascend gradually.	0.20
1.48	Top of rise; descend gradually.	0.13
1.49	Ascend steadily.	0.12
1.52	Switchback to L, then to R in 50'.	0.09
1.55	Switchback to L, then to R in 25'.	0.06
1.59	Switchback to L at cliff face. Sign prohibiting further ascent.	0.02
1.61	*Wind Cave (elevation 2,840').* There may be bee hives here, above among the rocks.	0.00

[H] Moon Rock Trail

General Description. From the Blevins Trail [I] as it gradually descends the bajada, Moon Rock Trail makes a circuitous way west, south, then north to meet the Levee Trail [A] and then ends at the Blevins Trail [I] at 1½ miles. This is an easy *hiker/horse* trail. Ascent is about 30', descent about 75'.

Access. *From the north,* at the Blevins Trail [I] (heading counterclockwise) at 0.6 mile; *from the south,* at the Blevins Trail at 1 mile.

Read Down ↓	Detailed Trail Description	Read Up ↑
0.00	Leave Blevins Trail [I] at 0.62 mi. (1,870'). Head W, descending gradually.	1.45
0.59	Turn L (S).	0.86
0.99	Turn sharp L (NE). Ascend gradually.	0.46
1.28	Turn R (E).	0.17
1.31	**Junction:** on R is start of Levee Trail [A]. Continue straight ahead.	0.14
1.45	**Junction:** Blevins Trail [I] L and straight (1,820'). This trail ends. Crismon Wash Trail [P] is 190' ahead.	0.00

[I] Blevins Trail COUNTERCLOCKWISE

General Description. This *hiker/horse* trail has been re-routed as part of the new trail development in this portion of the Recreation Area. There are many washes to cross and several sections along dirt roads in its 3 miles. Total ascent is about 220'. *The description here is in a counterclockwise direction.*

Access. From the south picnic loop (southwest end of Horse Staging Area).

Read Down ↓	Detailed Trail Description	Read Up ↑
0.00	Leave Horse Staging Area parking area near its SW end (elevation 1,910').	3.05
0.06	Road is close on R, along broad wash.	2.99
0.14	Cross minor wash.	2.91
0.18	Cross flat wash; head R in it, past picnic table and playground.	2.87
0.20	**Junction:** where this trail heads L out of wash, short spur trail R passes ramada into Merkle Memorial Trail parking lot (200' to road).	2.85
0.32	**Junction:** cross old vehicleway.	2.73
0.34	Descend and cross major wash. Crismon Wash Trail [P] **junction.**	2.71
0.36	**Junction:** spur trail R 0.1 mi to road and parking area.	2.69

0.38	**Junction:** old vehicleway on R.	2.67
0.44	Cross shallow wash.	2.61
0.46	**Junction:** old vehicleway sharp R.	2.59
0.47	**Important junction (4-way):** turn L onto dirt Crismon Road (quarter section boundary, also of Recreation Area and Tonto National Forest).	2.58
0.62	**Junction:** Moon Rock Trail [H] goes R on trail, off Crismon Road, heading W. Go straight on, descending very gradually.	2.43
0.98	**Junction:** Moon Rock Trail [H] R (to Levee Trail in 0.14 mi (1,820'). Turn sharp L here. Head E, descending gradually.	2.07
1.02	Cross major wash. **Junction** here with Crismon Wash Trail [P].	2.03
1.29	Cross wash, then another in 150'.	1.76
1.42	**Junction:** No-So Trail [N] crosses (L to Horse Staging Area in 0.5 mi). Continue on wide, straight trail.	1.63
1.49	**Junction:** Amigos Wash Trail [M] at major wash crossing.	1.56
1.72	Cross small wash ("Night Hawk Trail" for equestrians).	1.33
1.74	**Junction (4-way):** old vehicleway crosses.	1.31
1.79	Cross wash.	1.26
1.88	Cross wash.	1.17
2.05	**Junction:** where Meridian trail [C] continues ahead past southernmost of Cat Peaks, go sharp L on wide trail.	1.00
2.15	**Junction:** Cat Peaks Pass Trail [K] on R.	0.90
2.28	**Junction:** Cat Peaks Trail [J] on R. Ascend gradually.	0.77
2.51	Cross wash.	0.54
2.75	**Junction:** Amigos Wash Trail [M] sharp L, then cross wash.	0.30
2.84	Cross wash.	0.21
3.05	**Junction:** Horse Staging Area; this trail ends.	0.00

[J] Cat Peaks Trail CLOCKWISE

General Description. An easy loop is made from the Blevins Trail [I] around the northern Cat Peak, meeting a spur to the Pass Mountain Trail [282] at 0.9 mile, then dropping south to intersect the Cat Peaks Pass Trail [K] at 1.4 miles and end at the junction of the Levee [A] and Palo Verde [L] Trails at 1.7 miles. Ascent is about 130'.

Access. From the Blevins Trail [I] (heading counterclockwise) at 2 ½ miles.

Read Down ↓	Detailed Trail Description	Read Up ↑
0.00	Leave Blevins Trail [I] at 2.28 mi (1,820'). Head N ascending along wash on L.	1.56
0.94	**Junction:** on L is short connector (190') to Pass Mountain Trail [282] (1,925'). Turn R, descend to SE.	0.60
1.39	**Junction:** On R is Cat Peaks Pass trail [K] to Pass in 0.17 mi. Continue S.	0.17
1.56	**Junction (4-way):** on L & R is Meridian Trail [C] (1,795').	0.00

Pass Mountain and its prominent tuff layer

At the end of the Wind Cave Trail

Maricopa County

White Tank Mountain Regional Park

Introduction. The rugged 26,337-acre White Tank Mountain Regional Park is located on the eastern slope of the White Tank Mountains (which separate the Phoenix Basin from the Hassayampa Plains) 15 miles west of Glendale. Wilderness and archeological interest are here combined, with excellent hiking and riding opportunities. The story goes that the mountains were named after either the light-colored eroded stony depressions that collected water ("tinajas" in Spanish), or possibly for a Mr. White who had dug a well near the north end of the mountain for use by the Prescott-to-Phoenix stage. Elevations in the park range from 1,400' to 4,083'. Reached by jeep roads, several microwave relay stations now perch on the main peaks of the range.

History. Early Indian hunting parties frequented the area and harvested the fruit of the prickly pear and saguaro. There are petroglyphs, pictographs, and eleven Hohokam archeological sites (500-1100 A.D.) in the park, mostly where large canyons lead out of the mountains on the east and north. Prospecting yielded nothing of value. The lower slopes were seasonally grazed by small herds as is obvious from the remains of dams and corrals. Homesteading was limited by the quick water run-off and the lack of permanent watercourses.

Geology. The geomorphology of the area is that of a tilted fault block, characteristic of the Basin and Range Province, oriented north-northwest, tilted upward on the northeast side. Internal structure is complex. Topography is steep-sloped and rugged, due to rapid up-lifting above surrounding older rocks and subsequent erosion. There are thought to have been at least two intrusions of granite. In places eroded fault zones have had dikes of resistant igneous rock injected. The rocks are mostly of Precambrian age (1 billion to 500 million years ago), the oldest dominant types being granite and gneiss, with many variations and mixtures.

The "tanks" are a series of huge steps in the bottom of steep-walled gorges. Progressive erosion caused sharp vertical drops adjacent to fault zones. Occasional torrents of water carried rock debris, dropping off each step and scouring out "tanks" at the base.

Maps. *Our map 22.* The USGS White Tank Mountains Quadrangle (1:62,500, 1957) is useful only for general topography. Better are the maps in the 1:24,000 series, Waddell and White Tank Mountains (1957, photorevised 1971). None shows the trails, though some old vehicleways are indicated.

Access. There is only one access point: from Olive (extension of Dunlap west of 43rd Avenue) to the park entrance at White Tank Mountain Road.

Facilities. There are comfort stations, many covered picnic sites, cooking grills, 4 large group picnic areas with ramadas (reservations required, fee charged), a group campground (advance reservations and fee), 40 family campsites and a tent camping area. There is a $3 entrance fee for vehicles ($50 annual park pass).

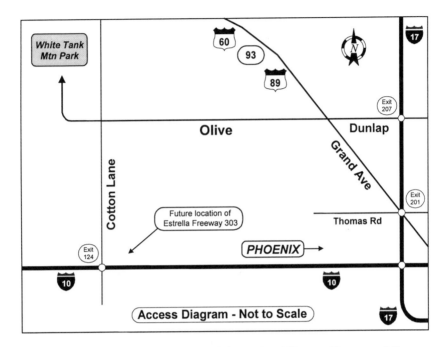

Picnic areas are closed at sunset and the gate at 7 p.m. No ground fires are allowed and the park is closed to all off-road travel and all unlicensed motor vehicles. Horseback and mountain bike riding are restricted to designated trails.

Recommended Hikes. Only official trails are described here. The best trail (for hikers only) for an easy taste of the park is the popular Waterfall Trail [D]. The Goat Camp Trail [A] and the Ford Canyon Trail [F] are moderately difficult and have excellent views; the latter has now been extended around to meet the former, providing a superb set of circuit trips. The Mesquite Springs Trail [E] is more difficult but has fine views into rugged country. The Black Rock Trail [C] is an easy walk in a less well known area.

Cautions. *The terrain in this park is very rugged, with many steep canyons. Be absolutely certain to carry sufficient water for your own needs and allow enough time. Leave word of your plans and remember: it is especially hazardous to travel off trails on your own.* Rattlesnakes are common in the area.

[A] Goat Camp Trail

General Description. This is a pleasant *hiker/horse* trail into wild canyon country. For the first mile and one-half it keeps to the north side of a flat area, just beneath the mountain, then leads into Goat Canyon and becomes increasingly rocky with some steady ascents. The next mile is a spectacular route through the canyon with cliffs and rock spires above. The trail reaches an old corral with some stone work ("Goat Camp") on the valley floor at 3 miles, then rises steadily to a ridge crest with fine views at 3.2 miles. Descending to cross a valley and rise to another pass at 3.7 miles, the trail makes a long, switchbacking descent to the last valley before ascending to a major ridge at 4.7 miles. Here it meets the Ford Canyon Trail [F] at 5.2 miles, and then descends to reach the Mesquite Springs Trail [E] at 7.1 miles. Total ascent is about 1,600'.

Access. For the *southern end,* park at the northwest end of picnic loop #1, just off Black Canyon Drive North, 0.2 mile beyond the park entrance. There is a sign at the start. At the *northern end,* at 1 mile on the Mesquite Springs Trail [E].

Read Down ↓	Detailed Trail Description	Read Up ↑
0.00	Leave parking area (1,500') ascending gradually.	7.13
0.39	Parallel wash on R.	6.74
0.66	Level out at 1,640'. In 135' start brief ascent again.	6.47
0.77	**Junction:** South Loop Trail [J] on L back to road in 1.04 mi. Ascend gradually, in and among rocks.	6.36
1.02	Parallel major wash.	6.11
1.03	Cross wash (1,700') and ascend more steadily to NW.	6.10
1.06	Edge of wash, ease grade of ascent.	6.07
1.20	Footway roughens.	5.93
1.44	Top of rise (1,880'). Wash on L.	5.69
1.51	Ascend more steadily on rocky, rougher trail.	5.62
1.57	Level out (1,970').	5.56
1.62	Turn L to cross bouldery moderate-sized wash. Switchback to L & R out of it.	5.51
1.68	Switchback to L, then to R in 110'. Steady climb.	5.45
1.75	Bear R after crossing very small wash. Good views here.	5.38
1.82	Trail follows along ledge (2,160').	5.31
1.87	Pass below rocky knob on L. From here, trail ascends the valley side with pinnacles above, a spectacular route.	5.26
2.06	Level out very briefly, then ascend again.	5.07
2.10	With cliff ahead, canyon narrows (2,450').	5.03
2.18	Climb above dry waterfall, switchbacking L & R. [Ascent is easier from here.]	4.95
2.20	Level out. Looking back, there are several rock "faces" on the cliff.	4.93
2.22	Switchback to L, then to R.	4.91
2.23	Lovely view of upper valley and towers ahead. Trail passes through a fine stand of prickly pear cactus.	4.90
2.85	Cross rocks of side-canyon (2,970'). Yuccas and agaves beyond here.	4.28
2.89	Rock walls below on R.	4.24
2.93	Descend briefly.	4.20
2.96	Cross brushy wash (3,000'). Down this wash is an old rock corral ("Goat Camp"). On far side of wash, trail continues N, ascending steadily.	4.17
3.02	View on R to valley. Continue steeply up, heading NW and N.	4.11
3.11	Ease grade of ascent, then rise steadily in another 75'.	4.02
3.18	Top of ridge. Fine views (3,180'). Side-hill down to W at an easy grade, with canyon on R.	3.95
3.36	Go above rocks on R, descending gradually into valley.	3.77

3.41	Bottom of descent in valley. Ascend gradually (3,100').	3.72
3.47	Cross wash.	3.66
3.51	Switchback to R.	3.62
3.52	Turn L, ascending to SW.	3.61
3.55	Bear R. Towers can be seen high above on L. Head NW at easy grade.	3.58
3.65	Turn L, ascend steadily (3,250').	3.48
3.66	Switchback to R.	3.47
3.69	Pass on crest with good views. Keep R here, along crest.	3.44
3.74	Switchback to L off top, to WNW, down side-ridge.	3.39
3.84	Switchback to R, steep (use care).	3.29
3.88	Switchback to L.	3.25
3.91	The way is confusing here. USE CARE.	3.22
3.94	Drop off crest of ridge toward S, making long side-hill traverse.	3.19
4.03	Switchback to R.	3.10
4.04	Stock tank below on L.	3.09
4.16	Ease grade of descent. Red rocks on L.	2.97
4.31	Descend into valley.	2.82
4.33	Turn L, drop into side-wash. In 30', follow wash bottom or just N of it.	2.80
4.35	Leave wash at cairn, turn L and head N.	2.78
4.38	Trail post on L.	2.75
4.39	Switchback to R, ascend steadily.	2.74
4.41	Switchback to R.	2.72
4.46	Top of rise (2,820'). Head NW into valley.	2.67
4.57	Swing W.	2.56
4.95	Almost at top, head NE, then descend to N.	2.18
5.07	Bottom of descent (3,030'). Go up & down along crest.	2.06
5.16	**Junction:** in open area (3,000'). Ford Canyon Trail [F] leads L, downhill toward Willow Springs and Ford Canyon [to TH at Horse Staging Area in 7.81 mi.]. Head R, keeping E of crest	1.97
5.20	Top of rise. Descend rocky trail to SE.	1.93
5.34	Sag between humps on ridge, go L of next one (2,920').	1.79
5.38	Bottom of descent. Side-hill (almost level).	1.75
5.50	Start descent near crest.	1.63
5.54	Switchback down steeply to L.	1.59
5.57	Turn L (NW), then N, descend steeply.	1.56
5.61	Turn R (E).	1.52
5.69	Pass peak on R. Steep pitch down.	1.44
5.80	Level area.	1.33
5.82	Ascend rocky trail.	1.31
5.88	Top of rise (2,620'). Begin steady descent.	1.25
5.90	**Junction:** keep R.	1.23
5.94	**Junction:** trail of use ahead. Switchback to L.	1.19
5.96	Bad, steep descent. Use care.	1.17
6.07	Bottom of descent.	1.06
6.17	Top of rise.	0.96
6.26	Bottom of descent.	0.87
6.54	**Junction:** where well-worn trail goes L (level), go R, ascending rocky hillside.	0.59
6.68	Top of rise.	0.45
6.80	Descend steep pitch.	0.33
6.92	Bottom of descent.	0.21
7.02	Top of rise.	0.11
7.13	**Junction:** Mesquite Canyon Trail [E] on L. This trail ends (2,970')	0.00

[B] South Trail

General Description. This is a short alternate to the start of the Goat Camp Trail [A]. It follows an old road for part of its 1 mile. Ascent is 160'.

Access. Leave picnic loop #1 (Black Canyon Drive South) at southwest end at a sign ("South Trail"). This trailhead is 0.2 mile south of the Goat Camp Trailhead on the same road.

Read Down ↓	Detailed Trail Description	Read Up ↑
0.00	From picnic loop #1 head S, then W on trail.	1.04
0.05	Cross small wash.	0.99
1.04	**Junction:** Go R 0.77 mi to return to road. To L, trail [A] leads to "Goat Camp" in 1.92 mi.	0.00

[C] Black Rock Trail - Long Loop

General Description. This is a short barrier-free *hiker-only* loop trail (1.25 miles) with a short side-trail (0.15 mile) to the Waterfall Trail [B]. Ascent is 90'.

Access. From road junction directly across from Group Picnic Area access road on White Tank Mountain Road.

Read Down ↓	Detailed Trail Description	Read Up ↑
0.00	Leave White Tank Mountain Road opposite Group Picnic Area road (1,470'). Only 15' from road, reach **junction:** Short Loop goes R (one-way), keep R.	1.24
0.18	**Junction:** Long Loop R (Keep R on narrower trail, to W). To L is Short Loop.	1.16
0.24	Approach edge of wash on R.	1.00
0.61	**Junction:** Waterfall Connector R (sign). Keep L. [For *Connector:* head W, ascending gradually, then at 290' drop to NW. Cross main wash at 0.08 mi, head R in it, then L out of it to flat area at 0.11 mi. Here, head W and uphill to Waterfall Trail [D] at 0.15 mi.]	0.63
1.01	Turn L (NE).	0.23
1.16	**Junction:** Short Loop. To L, Short Loop/Long Loop junction is 0.18 mi. Keep R here.	0.08
1.24	**Junction:** Short Loop re-enters from L. Road is 15' ahead; back at start.	0.00

[C] Black Rock Trail - Short Loop

General Description. This short barrier-free *hiker-only* loop trail is only 0.4 mile long, with interpretive signs. Description is for counter-clockwise direction of travel only. At 0.18 mile and 0.27 mile it intersects the Long Loop. Ascent is 90'.

Access. From road junction directly across from group picnic area access road on White Tank Mountain Road. Alternatively, there is a 200'-long trail paralleling the Group Picnic Area access road to the highway at the start of this trail.

Read Down ↓	Detailed Trail Description	Read Up ↑
0.00	Leave White Tank Mountain Road opposite Group Picnic Area (1,470'). Only 15' from road, reach **junction:** Long Loop goes L. Short Loop goes R (one-way). Keep R.	0.44
0.12	Bench. Old petroglyphs on rocks above.	0.32
0.18	**Junction:** Long Loop goes R here. Head L (S), circling small, rocky peak. Then head E.	0.26
0.36	**Junction:** Long Loop (other branch) goes R (S).	0.08
0.44	**Junction:** loop entering L (start of this trail) Keep R; reach White Tank Mountain Road in 15', back at start.	0.00

[D] Waterfall Trail

General Description. This is a short, easy *hiker-only* trail to the most popular area in the park. The first half is barrier-free. Ascent is only 180'.

Access. Leave White Tank Mountain Road at 1.65 miles from the entrance, taking Waterfall Canyon Road to the left, then a very short spur road. The trail leaves this branch road at a sign 2 miles from the park entrance near the picnic ramadas and comfort station #6.

Read Down ↓	Detailed Trail Description	Read Up ↑
0.00	From road at 1,520' elevation, head W on trail.	0.88
0.38	**Junction:** on L is connector trail across wash to Black Rock Long Loop in 0.15 mi (0.75 mi to road). End of barrier-free section.	0.50
0.39	**Junction:** on L 70' is meadow-like area. In 310' turn R, then R again.	0.49
0.46	Turn sharp R, then keep to L.	0.42
0.49	**Junction:** trail R rejoins. Keep L, then swing around to R, paralleling wash.	0.39
0.58	Ascend rocky area beside wash on L.	0.30
0.61	**Junction:** alternate route goes sharp R here (passes Burke K. Bird Memorial Bench in 60', rejoining main trail at an obscure point in 175').	0.27
0.72	Edge of wash on L.	0.16
0.79	Old steel water tank on R (rancher's attempt to provide water for his cattle here). Many petroglyphs near here. Ascend gradually.	0.09
0.81	Petroglyphs on L.	0.07
0.88	Bottom (1,700'). Trail ends at rock jumble about 375' downstream from "waterfall," which only runs after a significant rainfall. *NOTE:* The rocks above are used by rock-climbers, but this is extremely dangerous — there have been fatalities here.	0.00

[E] Mesquite Canyon Trail

General Description. The lower section of this *hiker/horse* trail is an eroded steep "cat" road. It is known locally as the "Cat Scratch," built by a bulldozer driven by a rancher coming out of the park interior where he was making water catchment stock ponds. Above 1 mile, the way improves and leads over a ridge into the very attractive Mesquite Valley at 1½ miles. It then climbs 240' out of that valley in another third of a mile to a pass, where it starts around the ridge into the valley of Willow Springs. There is considerable up and down before an old shack and the Springs area is reached at 1.8 miles (2.9 miles total). Total ascent is 1,230' (first segment 630', second 600'). It continues up to meet the Ford Canyon Trail [F] at 3.1 miles.

Access. Leave road at Ramada Way off Waterfall Canyon Road at picnic area #7. This is one-third of a mile north of start of the Waterfall Trail [B].

Read Down ↓	Detailed Trail Description	Read Up ↑
0.00	From road at picnic area #7 (1,650'), follow wide trail.	1.04
0.28	Start ascent.	0.77
0.85	Steep pitch on badly eroded road.	0.20
0.93	Steady climb again.	0.11
0.99	Ease briefly, then start final ascent.	0.05
1.04	**Junction:** to L is Goat Camp Trail [A], to Ford Canyon [F] Trail in 1.90 mi.	0.00

Read Down ↓	Detailed Trail Description	Read Up ↑
0.00	Leave **junction** (2,280'), ascending on rocky trail.	2.10
0.07	Ascend with upper part of Waterfall Canyon in view on L.	2.03
0.11	Top of rise (2,430'), excellent viewpoint. Descend.	1.99
0.19	Turn L, reach top of rise (ridge crest) (2,410') with good views over valley. Descend slightly to W on good trail.	1.91
0.26	Level off; trail narrows, descends.	1.84
0.34	Go over rocks, turn L, descend briefly. Note rock wall across valley.	1.76
0.41	Parallel wash, then turn L (S).	1.69
0.42	Bear R, descending to SW, level off, then descend again.	1.68
0.46	Reach and enter moderate wash below "Mesquite Springs" (2,270').	1.64
0.48	Leave wash on R, ascending parallel to it.	1.62
0.58	Reach end of rocky side-ridge; use care here (elev. 2,450'). Way is easy and gradual beyond here.	1.52
0.80	Pass (2,510'). Descend gradually, then steadily, into Willow Springs valley.	1.30
0.99	Above cliffs: side-hill along ridge beyond, ascending gradually.	1.11
1.06	Top of rise (2,490'). Descend.	1.04
1.10	End of side-ridge (2,460'); old barbed wire here. Descend steadily.	1.00
1.33	Reach wash, follow it to L (2,340'). Use care.	0.77
1.41	Leave wash on R, ascend slope.	0.69
1.57	Top of rise (2,480'). Side-hill down.	0.53
1.63	Reach wash again and turn R in it.	0.47
1.70	Ascend out of wash on L; parallel it, cross it in 300'.	0.40
1.84	Willow Springs area (2,460'). Tank on L, wrecked corral; springs area is further along wash at base of rock "fall". Up path 60' is ruined shack. Trail continues up.	0.26
1.91	Start steady ascent.	0.19
2.08	Swing L.	0.02
2.10	**Junction:** Ford Canyon Trail [F] (2,620'). L to Goat Camp Trail [A] in 0.91 mi. R to White Tank Mountain Road in 6.9 mi.	0.00

[F] Ford Canyon Trail

General Description. This is a good multi-use trail with fine views, though some sections are not suitable for horses or mountain bikes. There are several access points. The main trail leaves from the Horse Staging Area. Hikers and mountain-bikers may prefer to access the trail from Area 9 on Ford Canyon Road. The first 3 miles consists of new sections of trail and old vehicleway, crossing several low hills to reach the mouth of Ford Canyon. From there the trail climbs into the canyon with some very scenic rocky areas to 4.6 miles. Ascent is 700'. From here, the new trail heads up a wash, then south up a ridge with fine views to reach the Mesquite Springs Trail [E] at 6.9 miles. It then continues south to meet the Goat Camp Trail [A] on top of the ridge at 7.8 miles, making a long, scenic circuit from Goat Camp to Ford Canyon Trail, including a mile of road walking.

Access. *From White Tank Mountain Road*, turn right at the Horse Staging Area (just before Waterfall Canyon Road on the left). For Area 9, take either Ford Canyon Road (past Willow Canyon Road), or Waterfall Canyon Road past Willow Canyon Road junction, to the trailhead opposite area 9 at a sign. Another approach is the Waddell Trail [H] for 0.6-mile trail from Ford Canyon Road near Willow Canyon Road, rejoining the main trail ½ mile west of the Area 9 Trailhead.

Read Down ↓	Detailed Trail Description	Read Up ↑
0.00	Leave Horse Staging Area trailhead on the N. Head N, mostly level.	7.81
0.25	Cross small wash.	7.56
0.67	Cross White Tank Mountain Road.	7.14
0.85	Cross main wash.	6.96
1.09	**Junction:** Ironwood Trail on R.	6.72
1.39	**Junction:** Area 9 Trailhead Spur on L. *[Details: descend steadily, at 150' switchbacking to R, crossing major wash at 255'. Climb steadily out of it to 380', then reach Ford Canyon Road at 0.10 mi, elevation 1,510'.]* Continue along brink of major wash.	6.42
1.43	Keep R on newer location, away from edge.	6.39
1.47	Old location rejoins on L.	6.34
1.68	Head slightly R, away from wash.	6.13
1.72	Trail on L is closed.	6.09
1.73	**Junction:** on R is Ironwood Trail to several trailheads (1,600').	6.08
1.92	**Junction:** Waddell Trail [H] sharp L, 0.59 mi to Ford Canyon Road just N of Willow Canyon Road. Main trail bends to R here.	5.89
2.12	Bottom of descent; start ascent.	5.69
2.17	Reach pass between hills (1,640').	5.64
2.20	Cross old trail, now fading into disuse.	5.61
2.22	Bottom of descent.	5.59
2.26	Ascend steadily to W.	5.55
2.33	Cross wash.	5.48
2.35	Start ascent over hillside.	5.46
2.55	Bottom of descent.	5.26
2.57	Cross small wash. Ascend gradually along valley floor.	5.24
2.81	**Junction:** old trail, go L on it.	5.00

3.02	Bottom of descent.	4.79
3.05	Ascend steadily SW.	4.76
3.13	Road loops and ends, excellent trail starts.	4.68
3.18	Cross side wash.	4.63
3.40	Above wash on R.	4.41
3.42	Cross moderate-sized wash. Ascend.	4.39
3.52	Landmark: boulders, views, top of rise (1,960').	4.29
3.56	Enter canyon. **Caution:** *not recommended for horses or bikes beyond here.*	4.25
3.58	Steep pitch up rocks. Head toward rock wall and into a spectacular side-canyon, ascending steadily.	4.23
3.67	Steep section, turn L.	4.14
3.68	Switchback to R and up.	4.13
3.71	Top of rise.	4.10
3.73	Dry waterfall below; reach top of rise.	4.08
3.76	Steep pitch up rocks.	4.05
3.78	Top of rise. Very picturesque area.	4.03
3.82	Cross side-wash.	3.99
3.89	Switchback to L and continue scenic route with care. Rock spires above.	3.92
3.92	Top of rise. Viewpoint; turn L.	3.89
3.95	Switchback to L, steeply up rocks.	3.86
3.97	Switchback to R, still ascending steadily. Use care; spectacular route.	3.84
4.02	Top of rise. Upper canyon ahead, rock bowl.	3.9
4.05	Cross main wash, go up rocks on opposite side. Cairned route leads up wash bed, over occasional rocks.	3.76
4.19	Go up rocks.	3.62
4.20	Tinaja on R.	3.61
4.41	Leave wash on L.	3.40
4.50	Shelter rock on L.	3.31
4.54	Enter defile for 130', huge boulders above on L.	3.27
4.57	Go up steep rocks with care, then down.	3.24
4.61	"Tanks" in Ford Canyon Wash; note silted-in stone masonry dam built by ranchers for their cattle. (Area is likely to be dry except after a rain.) (2,260'.)	3.20
4.72	Swing to S, following wash.	3.09
5.11	Go up rock shelf with care; keep L at its top.	2.70
5.46	**Junction:** leave wash at sign, ascending ridge on new trail (1998).	2.35
5.54	Switchback to L.	2.27
5.71	Switchback to R.	2.10
5.75	Turn L at end of ridge.	2.06
5.92	Switchback to R, and to L in 350'.	1.89
6.14	Ascend steadily.	1.67
6.22	Top of rise; pass (2,860').	1.59
6.30	Switchback to L and down.	1.51
6.44	Turn L, level.	1.37
6.66	Round end of ridge.	1.15
6.71	Bottom of descent. Cross small wash.	1.10
6.90	**Important junction:** Mesquite Canyon Trail [E] on L (2,620'). Leads 0.26 mi to Willow Springs area, 3.14 mi to trailhead.	0.91
6.99	Cross wash, head S.	0.82
7.01	Cross main wash.	0.80
7.03	Start ascending out of valley.	0.78
7.10	Cross small wash. Side-hill up, making a series of long traverses.	0.71
7.25	Switchback sharp L.	0.56
7.32	Switchback to R (S).	0.49

7.64	Switchback to L (N).	0.17
7.74	Switchback to R, starting final traverse.	0.07
7.81	**Junction:** Goat Camp Trail [A] L & R.	0.00

[G] Ironwood Trail   NORTH to SOUTH

General Description.   Several access points can make this new trail confusing. Starting from a junction with the Ford Canyon Trail at 1¾ mile, it heads across the bajada for 0.9 mile, with several branches, back to Ford Canyon Trail.

Access. From several points off the park drive, plus Ford Canyon Trail [F].

Read Down ↓	Detailed Trail Description	Read Up ↑
0.00	From Ford Canyon Trail [F] at 1.73 mi, descend gradually N, then NE.	0.92
0.10	Bear R (E), then L.	0.82
0.25	Turn L (N).	0.67
0.29	Swing R (E), parallel small wash.	0.63
0.51	**Junction:** on R (S) is continuation of Ironwood Trail. Spur continues NE 0.19 mi to Group CG, ramadas, road, parking area.	0.41
0.66	Bench on L.	0.26
0.68	**Junction:** on L, spur reaches road at Family CG in 385'. Keep R, thru nice stand of teddy-bear cholla and saguaros.	0.24
0.92	**Junction:** Ford Canyon Trail [F] L & R. To L, 0.33 mi to Youth Group Area via spur trial off Ford Canyon Trail. this point is at 1.09 mi on Ford Canyon Trail.	0.00

[H] Waddell Trail

General Description. This short trail (0.6 mile) was built in 1997 to provide an alternative access from Ford Canyon Road near Willow Canyon Road to Ford Canyon Trail [F]. Ascent is 50'.

Access. From Ford Canyon Road near Willow Canyon Road and Waterfall Canyon Road, 0.9 mile west of White Tank Mountain Road.

Read Down ↓	Detailed Trail Description	Read Up ↑
0.00	Leave road, heading NW.	0.59
0.05	Bear R.	0.54
0.11	Turn R.	0.48
0.20	Leave old route; keep R, to NW, ascending gradually.	0.39
0.39	Above wash on R. Descend.	0.20
0.43	Cross Willow Canyon wash. Ascend N.	0.16
0.47	Top of rise.	0.12
0.50	Cross small wash.	0.09
0.59	**Junction:** Ford Canyon Trail [F] L & R. To R, 0.19 mi, is Ironwood Trail [G].	0.00

Sonoran Loop Trail

There is a 5.6 mile long Sonoran Loop Competitive Track for racing bikes, horses, and runners. The track is completely separated from the hiking and riding trails. It is located at the very north end of the park drive, just 0.2 mile past the side-road to the park headquarters and Group Campground.

Petroglyphs near Waterfall Trail

Arizona State Parks

An Introduction

"Managing and conserving Arizona's natural, cultural, and recreational resources for the benefit of the people, both in our Parks and through our Partners."

As we enter the 21st Century, the future of Arizona State Parks is one of growth and challenges to meet the demands of an expanding population and increased interest in what Arizona's recreational, historic, and cultural resources have to offer. Arizona has the distinction of being one of the youngest states in the nation, and Arizona's State Parks System is also among the nation's youngest.

The creation of the Arizona State Parks Board in 1957 was a major victory for conservationists, outdoor interests and civic leaders from around the state, the result of years of dedicated effort. Since its creation, Arizona State Parks has grown from three employees and an appropriation of $30,000 to an agency with wide-ranging responsibilities. These include managing 24 historic, recreation, and conservation parks, statewide planning for Arizona's recreational and natural resources, developing and expanding partnerships, administering grants for acquisition and development of recreation areas, and coordinating programs to preserve and protect cultural and historic properties.

The Arizona State Committee on Trails, established by the Arizona State Parks Board, advises the Board on trails of special interest and significance to be included in the State Trails System and assists the Board in the preparation of a State Trails Plan which guides trail development and programs throughout the state. The overall mission of the Arizona State Trails Program, in partnership with the Arizona State Committee on Trails, is to promote, develop, and preserve non-motorized trail opportunities throughout the state. An Arizona Trails Heritage Fund Grants Program and a National Recreational Trails Fund program assist in the development of trail opportunities throughout Arizona.

The State Trails System now has over 600 trails in it, which provide over 4,000 miles of trail opportunities for Arizona's residents and visitors. When complete, the cross-state nonmotorized Arizona Trail will stretch from Utah to the Mexican border. The Trail is two-thirds complete and the vision is to complete it by the end of 2000. Trails throughout the state offer an opportunity to enjoy, experience, and imagine the sights and sounds of Arizona's vast beauty and history. The benefits of trails are many: they provide opportunities for education, social interaction, solitude, and re-creation. In addition trail use increases health and fitness, protects resources by keeping people on trails, provides transportation alternatives, and enhances a community's quality of life. Trails also increase property values, create jobs, attract new or relocating businesses, and generate a sense of "community" where one can get to know one's neighbor.

Arizona State Parks invites you to take a trip to one of the many recreational park sites and experience Arizona's outdoor adventure. Or visit a conservation park and learn about Arizona's landscapes. Spend a day on one of the many trails throughout the state with family or friends, or enjoy quiet solitude as you softly walk through a ponderosa pine or saguaro forest.

Jeff Hrycko, State Trails Coordinator

Arizona State Parks

Lost Dutchman State Park

Prospector's View Trail

Introduction. Lost Dutchman State Park is a 320-acre area located below the precipitous western flank of the Superstition Mountains, 5 miles northeast of Apache Junction, with dramatic views. Except for the Siphon Draw Trail, the trails described here were recently constructed. Most are within the adjacent Tonto National Forest, but outside the Superstition Wilderness.

History. The park name derives from the discredited legend of the fabulous Lost Dutchman Gold Mine. It is said that Jacob Walz (a German immigrant and miner known as "the Dutchman") had re-discovered the mine originally developed by the Peralta family of Sonora, Mexico. Most of the family were reputed to have been killed by Apaches at the Massacre Grounds, but one of them helped Walz to the site. Over the next 20 years he supposedly cached gold dust in various places in the Superstitions and killed several partners. That he died of pneumonia before imparting any details (other than that Weaver's Needle pointed in the right direction) made it somewhat understandable that fortunes were spent on the futile search (and the search still goes on!). The geological evidence was that the Superstitions themselves had no significant mineralization (short periods of production were, however, successful in the Goldfield Mountains to the west).

The Apache Trail [highway] was built in 1905 as a supply route for the construction of Roosevelt Dam (1905-1911), the first Bureau of Reclamation project in the west and the world's highest masonry dam.

Geology. Very active volcanic lava flows and explosions occurred during the Tertiary period around 29 million years ago, forming the Superstitions by deposition of dacite tuff and agglomerate on deeply eroded Pre-Cambrian granite. It is thought that about 20 million years ago there was a resurgent dome formed from a "collapse caldera," followed by further explosions and ash deposition up to 15 million years ago. This gave the Superstitions their dramatic form.[1] Mineral exploration was at its peak in the 1870s and 1880s, but no mines in the Superstitions have ever resulted in production.

Access. (a) From Phoenix/Tempe, the Superstition Freeway (US 60) has an exit (#196) at Idaho Road. From there head north on SR 88, cross Old West Highway at 2 miles, turn right on Apache Trail at $2^1/_4$ miles, reaching the entrance at 5 miles. (b) For the Broadway Trailhead, take the Superstition Freeway to its end at Old West Highway, then take the first left turn onto Mountain View Road. Drive north for $1^3/_4$ miles to Broadway Avenue, then right 1 mile to the trailhead.

Maps. *Our map 22.* The USGS Goldfield 1:24,000 quadrangle (1956, photorevised 1981), the Earth Tracks "Superstition Wilderness West Recreation Map" (1985), and the Forest Service's 1994 "Superstition Wilderness, Tonto National Forest" map all show the area but not the recently constructed trails. There is a trail map available from the ranger station and the park brochure shows the roads and trailheads.

---

[1]M. & J. Sheridan (1984). *Recreational Guide to the Superstition Mountains and the Salt River Lakes*, pp. 21-29 (published by authors); and Nations & Stump (1983), pp. 166-8 and 173-4.

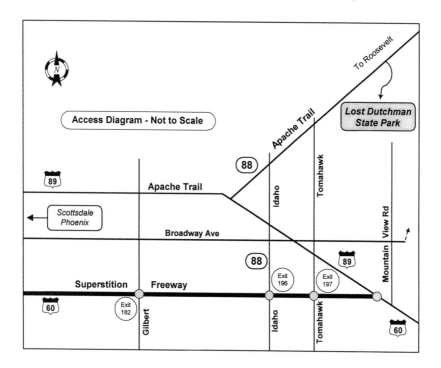

Facilities. There are 35 developed campsites, rest-rooms, showers, drinking fountains, and picnic facilities including tables, 2 group ramadas and 13 single ramadas. The park's address is 6109 N. Apache Trail, Apache Junction 85219 (Phone: 520-982-4485).

Recommended Hikes. With the exception of the un-numbered Discovery Trail, the descriptions that follow are referred to by the official numbers of the Tonto National Forest. Hikes with significant but not difficult ascents are [53], [56], and [57]. Jacob's Crosscut [58] has many brief up-and-down stretches. (The Siphon Draw Trail [53] has a much rougher footway than the other trails.) There is also a short self-guiding Native Plant Trail near the park entrance, not described here.

Cautions. Beware the temptation to rock-climb on spires and cliffs without adequate equipment and training. Stay out of old mine shafts. Summer heat here can exceed 115° and there is little shade; be absolutely sure to bring enough water and appropriate clothing for prolonged exposure to the sun.

Park Regulations. Except for Jacob's Crosscut, these trails are *hiker-only*. Keep pets under control and pack out all garbage. Shooting is forbidden.

[53] Siphon Draw Trail

General Description. From the Campground trailhead, an old vehicleway crosses into the Tonto National Forest and ascends gradually, reaching the Wilderness Boundary. Beyond, the trail is undesignated and steeper, entering a very scenic area at the western end of the mountains at about 1.1 miles. It then follows a wash and reaches the end of trail at a box canyon at 1.6 miles with views among the cliffs and spires. Ascent is 1,030'. *NOTE:* if there is any possibility of a rain-storm in the vicinity, stay out of washes to avoid the danger of a flash flood.

Access. Park at the Siphon Draw Trailhead in the Campground area.

Read Down ↓	Detailed Trail Description	Read Up ↑
0.00	Leave trailhead at sign (elevation 2,080').	1.61
0.05	**Junction:** to L is Discovery Trail to Saguaro Picnic Area.	1.56
0.20	**Junction:** dirt road to R at Park and National Forest boundary. Continue straight, on dirt road.	1.42
0.21	Pass through gate in fence, ascending gradually on old vehicleway.	1.40
0.38	**Junction:** Prospector's View Trail [58] on L (0.59 mi to junction with Treasure Loop [56]; 310' to junction with Jacob's Crosscut [58]).	1.23
0.43	**Junction (4-way):** Jacob's Crosscut Trail [57] on L & R (225' L to Prospector's View Trail [58]; 4.38 mi R to Broadway Avenue).	1.18
0.63	**Junction:** trail of use sharp R leads back to Jacob's Crosscut in 0.21 mi.	0.98
0.72	Pass foundation of building on L; way steepens.	0.89
0.77	Vehicleway narrows to trail at Wilderness boundary; this trail is undesignated beyond here.	0.84
0.87	**Junction:** trail of use R, to rock.	0.75
0.95	**Junction:** trail braids, keep L.	0.67
0.99	This trail leads along edge of wash on R.	0.63
1.01	Cross wash.	0.61
1.02	Way braids again; go L around boulder.	0.59
1.04	Trails rejoin (they braid again ahead).	0.57
1.12	Level out.	0.49
1.13	Cross small wash; enter scenic area with cliffs above on L.	0.48
1.22	**Junction:** short spur trail descends to R to giant boulders. Ascend steadily.	0.39
1.35	Flat area with good views; canyon in view ahead. Bear L.	0.26
1.42	Go along base of sloping rocks, then cross more rocks.	0.19
1.53	Cross below cliff on L.	0.08
1.55	Cross small wash under trees and ascend.	0.06
1.56	Cross wash into very scenic area.	0.05
1.58	Sloping rocks ahead.	0.04
1.61	*Siphon Draw.* Trail ends in box canyon at elevation 3,110'. Trailless route into western Superstitions can commence here, but is definitely not for ordinary hikers.	0.00

Superstition Mountain from Jacob's Crosscut

Siphon Draw

[56] Treasure Loop Trail WEST to EAST

General Description. This fine trail is actually a partial loop. The northern half ascends gradually from the Cholla Picnic Area, crossing Jacob's Crosscut Trail [58] at 0.4 mile. It then steepens, leading around the Green Boulder, an area of rocky spires just below the cliffs of the Superstitions, to a junction with the Prospector's View Trail [57] at 1.3 miles. Total ascent is 460'. Beyond, the loop descends 0.7 mile to intersect the Jacob's Crosscut Trail and reaches the Saguaro Picnic Area at 1.1 miles, for a total distance of 2.4 miles. Most of the trail is in the Tonto National Forest. (Two descriptions are given: both are for the *ascent* via either branch of the Loop.)

Access. From Cholla Picnic Area near restrooms, head east through picnic area D. Or if starting on the southern half, leave from the Saguaro Picnic Area through area E.

Read Down ↓	Detailed Trail Description	Read Up ↑
0.00	Leave road at Cholla Picnic Area (elevation here is 2,080').	1.32
0.03	Signpost.	1.29
0.05	Gate and fence line (Tonto National Forest). Beyond, ascend gradually up excellent trail with wash on L.	1.27
0.24	Drop off bench into wash on R.	1.08
0.26	**Junction:** go R (trail straight ahead ends).	1.06
0.36	**Junction (4-way):** trail L is Jacob's Crosscut [58] to First Water Trailhead in 1.12 mi. On R, Jacob's Crosscut [58] leads 0.09 mi to other branch of [56] and another 0.76 mi to Prospector's View Trail [57], then another 0.11 mi to Siphon Draw Trail [53].	0.96
0.38	Bear R. Grade of ascent gradually increases through very attractive area.	0.94
0.91	Trail bears R, then L, and steepens.	0.41
1.00	Ascend among rock pinnacles with Green Boulder ahead.	0.32
1.05	Bear R and ease ascent.	0.27
1.13	Trail swings L, then around to R, ascending.	0.19
1.16	**Junction:** trail straight ahead is closed; keep R.	0.16
1.19	Level out.	0.13
1.23	Cross rocky wash.	0.09
1.26	**Junction:** trail L closed, keep R.	0.06
1.27	Cross wash.	0.05
1.32	**Junction:** Prospector's View Trail [57] ahead; (straight ahead 0.59 mi to Jacob's Crosscut Trail [58]). Turn R, descend 1.10 mi to continue on this trail to Saguaro Picnic Area [use reverse of description in following section].	0.00

0.00	Leave Saguaro Picnic Area at sign near water fountain (2,100').	1.10
0.02	**Junction:** L is cross trail thru picnic area to other branch of this trail near Cholla Picnic Area in 250'.	1.08
0.09	Cross through fence line into Tonto National Forest at signboard with map.	1.01
0.11	Turn L along top of hogback.	0.99
0.20	**Junction:** trail L to gate in 475'; cross trail at 0.14 mi (Cholla Picnic Area in another 295' to R; 310' L to Saguaro Picnic Area parking), road in 0.15 mi; turn R.	0.90
0.38	**Junction (4-way):** Jacob's Crosscut Trail [58] crosses. (To L it is 0.09 mi to northern half of this trail; to R it is 0.76 mi to Prospector's View Trail [57]).	0.72

0.60	Start ascent, then follow edge of wash on R.	0.50
0.97	Switchback to R, then to L, ascending with Green Boulder on L.	0.13
1.02	**Junction:** short-cut trail re-enters from R; trail of use on L; cairn. Ascend 4 switchbacks.	0.08
1.10	**Junction:** Prospector's View Trail [57] on R (0.59 mi to Jacob's Crosscut Trail [56]). This trail continues to L, passing around Green Boulder, descending back to Cholla Picnic Area in 1.32 mi [see description above]. (2,540'.)	0.00

[57] Prospector's View Trail SOUTH to NORTH

General Description. This trail ascends from a start at the Siphon Draw Trail [53], near Jacob's Crosscut Trail [58], for 0.7 mile to end at the Treasure Loop [56] above the Green Boulder. The trail is in good condition and has fine views. It can be combined with [56] for a circuit trip. Ascent is 360'.

Access. To start at the bottom, take the Siphon Draw Trail [53] for 0.4 mile to the junction. To start at the top, take either branch of the Treasure Loop [56] from the Cholla or Saguaro Picnic Areas.

Read Down ↓	Detailed Trail Description	Read Up ↑
0.00	Leave Siphon Draw Trail [53], 0.38 mi from Campground trailhead (2,180').	0.70
0.06	**Junction:** on R is Jacob's Crosscut Trail [58]. Bear L.	0.64
0.11	**Junction:** Jacob's Crosscut Trail [58] to L (0.76 mi to Treasure Loop [56]). Ascend E with wash on R.	0.59
0.34	Bear L, away from wash.	0.36
0.36	Switchback to R.	0.34
0.38	Edge of wash, bear L; pass trail of use on R.	0.32
0.43	Switchback to R.	0.27
0.46	Switchback to L.	0.24
0.49	Switchback to R, parallel wash on R.	0.21
0.51	**Junction:** trail of use on R. Ascend beside valley, then grade eases.	0.18
0.70	**Junction:** Treasure Loop Trail [56] on L (sharp L descends 1.10 mi to Saguaro Picnic Area; straight ahead leads to Cholla Picnic Area in 1.32 mi).	0.00

[58] Jacob's Crosscut Trail NORTH to SOUTH

General Description. This moderately long *hiker/horse* trail leads along the base of the mountain. From First Water Trailhead (FR 78) it crosses the northern half of Treasure Loop [56] at 1.1 miles, the second segment of the Loop at 1.2 miles, and the Prospector's View Trail [57] at 1.9 miles. Siphon Draw Trail is crossed at 2 miles; finally the end of Broadway Avenue at 6.4 miles. The trail offers fine views of the Superstitions. It can be combined with the Discovery Trail or [56] or [57] for circuit trips. Elevation change is 400'.

Access. *At the northern end:* from FR 78, 0.7 mile from SR 88 where there is an open area on the right. It can also be reached from the Treasure Loop from the Cholla Picnic Area at 0.4 mile; or from the Siphon Draw Trail [53] at 0.4 mile. *At the southern end:* at the eastern end of Broadway Avenue.

Read Down ↓	Detailed Trail Description	Read Up ↑
0.00	Leave FR 78 from parking area on R; walk W 125' to turn L to wash (2,100').	6.35
0.06	Cross major wash and ascend far bank.	6.29
0.23	**Junction (4-way):** cross dirt road, gate on W.	6.12
0.50	**Junction (4-way):** cross faint road.	5.85
0.88	Cross moderate wash, then old mine road in 0.06 mi.	5.47
1.12	**Junction (4-way):** Treasure Loop [56] at 0.36 mi from Cholla Picnic Area trailhead. (Elevation 2,120'.) Head S on a level grade.	5.23
1.21	**Junction (4-way):** cross southern half of Treasure Loop [56] (0.47 mi to R is Saguaro Picnic Area; 0.71 mi to L is junction with [57] above Green Boulder).	5.14
1.28	Turn L, ascend (note parallel trail [56] on next bench to N). This trail zigzags.	5.07
1.42	Head R and level off.	4.89
1.54	Switchback to L, then to R.	4.81
1.55	Turn sharp L, then R.	4.80
1.56	Cross moderate wash and ascend out of it.	4.79
1.77	Reach edge of major wash. Turn L, then cross it.	4.58
1.84	**Junction:** Prospector's View Trail [57] on L (2,200').	4.47
1.89	**Junction:** Prospector's View Trail departs R, to Siphon Draw Trail in 310'.	4.42
1.97	**Junction (4-way):** Siphon Draw Trail [53] L & R.	4.38
2.15	**Junction (4-way):** L 0.21 mi to Siphon Draw Trail; R to private land.	4.20
3.42	**Junction:** on R trail of use descends.	2.93
3.49	Cross large wash. Excellent views open.	2.86
3.84	**Junction (4-way):** cross old track.	2.51
4.28	Bottom of major wash.	2.07
5.15	Turn W and descend steadily.	1.20
6.35	Gate at end of Broadway Avenue (1,830').	0.00

Discovery Trail SOUTH to NORTH

General Description. This level, un-numbered trail is entirely within the State Park. It connects the Siphon Draw Trail [53] and Campground Area with the Saguaro Picnic Area and is useful for circuit trips.

Access. *At the southern end:* from 270' east of the Siphon Draw Trailhead. *At the northern end:* at the south side of the Saguaro Picnic Area road loop just west of the restrooms.

Read Down ↓	Detailed Trail Description	Read Up ↑
0.00	Leave Siphon Draw Trail [53] 260' E of its trailhead.	0.56
0.02	Swing around to cross small wash, paralleling campground road.	0.54
0.23	**Junction:** spur trail L leads to campground road loop in 120'. Continue N.	0.33
0.27	Cross major wash.	0.28
0.41	Cross moderate wash; ascend gradually.	0.15
0.42	**Junction:** go R (straight ahead to road in 320').	0.14
0.53	**Junction:** trail goes R, toward restrooms (L is spur to road).	0.03
0.56	Trail ends at road beside washrooms on R. (Treasure Loop [56] trailhead is just beyond, at other end of parking area.)	0.00

Bureau of Land Management

An Introduction

The Bureau of Land Management administers more than 14 million acres of public lands in Arizona that provide a wide range of recreation opportunities to visitors and residents alike. Whether you look for solitude found in one of the 47 wilderness areas or enjoy the popular areas along the Colorado River, public lands are there for you. For those who travel by motor home, 4-wheel drive, car, tourist train, boat, mountain bike, horseback, or on foot, we manage many unique places for your enjoyment. And if you like the grasslands in the southeast, the desert mountains and valleys in the west, or the canyon lands in the north, we have some suggestions for you.

Our developed trail system is improving each year. The public can thank the partnerships that are being built on behalf of the recreating public. With the help of Heritage Funds administered by Arizona State Parks and Arizona Game and Fish Department, BLM has been able to improve trails, trailheads, and visitor facilities throughout the state. We would not have been able to accomplish this with federal funds alone. By joining funds and staff skills, your public agencies have been able to provide better trails, better facilities at trailheads, better trail information, and in some cases interpretive information to foster a greater appreciation of our public lands.

But more important than the trail improvements are the volunteers who give us more and more assistance in maintaining these important travelways. Individuals, organized groups, and clubs are helping the BLM on National Trails Day and throughout the year to maintain and improve these trails. We invite you to help us take care of your trails. We can use your help, whether as an official volunteer, or just acting as our "eyes and ears" in the field. You can help us pack out some of what those ahead of you forgot to take with them. You can report any trail maintenance or vandalism problems to any of our field offices. Any help is most appreciated. Make your trail experience a little bit better by making the trail a little bit better before you leave. The next travelers will appreciate it.

Let's become trail partners.

Denise Meridith, State Director, Arizona

USDI Bureau of Land Management

(in collaboration with Maricopa County)

Black Canyon Trail

Emery Henderson Trailhead

Black Canyon Trail

New River Road to Table Mesa Road SOUTH to NORTH

Introduction. The Black Canyon Trail was officially opened on October 23, 1992. This is the first detailed description. The first section is almost 10 miles. It provides access for equestrians and hikers to a surprisingly wild country, including several high points with excellent vistas of the surrounding mountains and buttes. For much of the way, no signs of civilization are visible except for the trail and its markers.

A section further north to the Maricopa-Yavapai County Line at the Agua Fria River still has a contested route, so at the time of this publication is not recommended. The section from near the Gillette Ruins north to near SR 69 southeast of Prescott has been located, and a brochure is available from the Phoenix Field Office. Check with them if you are interested in it. Eventually the trail will extend about 62 miles to near the Dugas Interchange of Interstate 17, passing rugged terrain just east of the Bradshaw Mountains, including the Castle Creek Wilderness (Prescott National Forest).

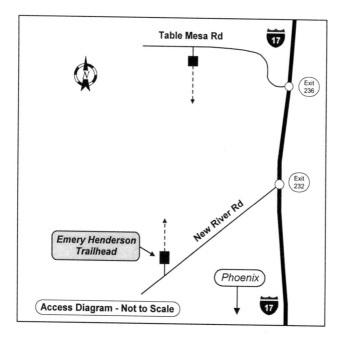

The Trail is managed by a joint agreement between Maricopa County, Yavapai County, and the USDI Bureau of Land Management. The trailhead facilities, managed by Maricopa County, are unusual and have won several prizes.

History. In 1919 the Department of the Interior laid out the route as a livestock driveway, used mostly by valley wool growers to herd sheep from their summer range in the mountains. The last sheep were herded in 1974. On May 14, 1987 the trail was formally dedicated by the Bureau of Land Management and Maricopa and Yavapai Counties, the Arizona State Horsemen's Association, Verde Valley Horseman's Council, Spring Valley Horsemen's Association, and the Prescott Saddle Club. At the ceremonies the three land management agencies signed a management agreement for the support and enhancement of the trail for hiking and equestrian use (it is now being used by mountain-bikers as well).

Many trail segments roughly parallel the old Black Canyon stagecoach road between Phoenix and Prescott. Stage stations were at New River, Gillette, Black Canyon City, Bumble Bee, and Cordes. Bandits used several blind turns as favorite ambush sites. When the Sante Fe, Prescott & Phoenix Railway extended its tracks from Prescott to Phoenix, the days of the stagecoach were numbered. The final blow was the increasing use of automobiles after 1910.

The second segment of this trail, when finally completed, will cross the Agua Fria River near Gillette (named after the superintendent of the Tip Top Mine), where only a stone foundation remains of the community built on the west side to process the ore. The mine produced more than $2 million in gold and silver, and was located $4^1/_2$ miles west of the trail.

General Description. Leaving the Emery Henderson Trailhead, the trail crosses a fairly flat plain, dissected by several washes, gradually ascending. At 3.9 miles the trail splits, with a Western and Eastern Loop rejoining at 4.9 miles. (The Eastern Loop, 1.3 miles, is all new trail construction, the Western Loop mostly old vehicleway.) A pass with fine views is reached at 5.5 miles. A vehicleway is joined from 5.8 to 7.2 miles, with another good view from the heights on a constructed trail section. A vehicleway is then taken from 8.1 miles to Table Mesa Road at 9.5 miles. Total elevation gain is 800'.

Access. *Southern end:* from exit 232 of Interstate 17, head southwest for 3.1 miles to a paved side road on the right to Emery Henderson Trailhead at 3.3 miles. *Northern end:* from exit 236 of I-17, head northwest on Table Mesa Road (gravel) for 2.1 miles.

Maps. *Our Map 24.* The USGS 1:24,000 New River quadrangle (1964, photorevised 1981) covers the approaches but shows only some sections of the trail that follow old roads. The route on our map is based on Global Positioning System locations provided by the BLM, and our observations.

Marking is by special Black Canyon Trail signs and more general hiker-horse signs, as well as occasional cairns.

Cautions. Please note that until usage better defines the trailway, care must be exercised to take the correct route because of many junctions with other stock trails and vehicleways. Much of the trail follows old vehicleways, but portions consist of new trail construction. Trail posts with distinctive markers have been installed, but may not be visible at every junction. *We advise that you check for marking frequently.* Because of extreme temperatures, summer usage is not recommended.

Read Down ↓	Detailed Trail Description, Including West Loop	Read Up ↑

0.00   From the kiosk 0.19 mi (1,000') N of Emery Henderson Trailhead, the trail
heads N, initially descending, and is rocky. Cross a wash in 755'. 9.46
0.22   **Junction:** cross gas pipeline road. 9.24
0.53   **Junction:** ignore vehicleway on L. 8.93
0.74   Top of rise. 8.72
0.95   **Junction:** vehicleway on L. Keep R, paralleling wash. 8.51
0.98   **Junction:** vehicleway on L. Keep R on a level, heading E. 8.48
1.06   Cross major wash, head NE. 8.40
1.10   **Junction:** with road ahead, go L, swing around to W, paralleling wash. 8.36
1.60   **Junction:** obscure track goes L; stay R (1,940'). 7.86
1.66   **Junction:** keep R where vehicleway goes L. 7.80
1.70   **Junction:** cross power line and road. 7.76
1.75   **Junction:** vehicleway sharp R back to power line road. 7.71
1.79   **Junction:** vehicleway sharp L; ascend to R. 7.67
1.82   Cross wash, ascend to NE, then E. 7.64
2.12   **Junction:** vehicleway on L. 7.34
2.13   Top of rise (1,960'). 7.33
2.23   Cross wash, head SE. 7.23
2.25   **Junction:** turn L (to NNE), leaving road (1,970'). 7.21
2.55   **Junction:** go L where vehicleway continues straight on. 6.91
2.62   **Junction:** vehicleway on R rejoins this one; head N. 6.84
2.89   **Junction (4-way):** vehicleway on R; on L is stock tank. 6.57
2.96   **Junction:** vehicleway sharp L back to stock tank. Ascend gradually. 6.50
3.27   **Important junction:** with road continuing R and ascending, bear L onto
trail (2,030'). 6.19
3.45   Cross very small wash at angle (narrow trail joins, sharp L). 6.01
3.55   **Junction (4-way):** cross wide gravel road (2,090'). Descend. 5.91
3.61   **Junction:** vehicleway sharp L; turn R, descend. 5.85
3.63   **Junction:** turn R where vehicleway continues. 5.83
3.71   **Junction:** ignore vehicleway on L. 5.68
3.78   Cross major wash. Ascend rocky stretch. Head NW. 5.68
3.93   **Important junction:** West and East Loops diverge here (sign).
Take West Loop here. *For East Loop, see separate description below.* 5.41
3.99   **Junction:** road on L; keep R. 5.47
4.07   **Junction:** keep L (W) where road diverges R. 5.39
4.27   Mine pit on R (2,140'). 5.19
4.40   Top of rise (2,170'). Descend N into pleasant, high valley. 5.06
4.52   Gate in barbed-wire fence. 4.94
4.55   Top of rise. 4.91
4.59   **Important junction:** at bottom of descent, keep straight where road goes L. 4.87
4.61   Deep, dangerous mine pit on L. *Stay away from edge.* 4.85
4.62   **Junction:** road sharp L; keep slightly R (N). 4.84
4.67   Top of rise in open area (2,220'). 4.79
4.73   Top of rise. 4.73
4.88   **Junction:** road on L; descend steadily straight ahead. In 50' cross steep
wash. 4.58
4.89   **Important junction:** *East Loop on R, just before steep wash.* 4.57
4.96   Top of rise (2,280'). 4.50

5.01	Road becomes trail (2,290'). In 210' pass mine pit across wash on R.	4.45
5.08	Top of rise; descend for 35', then ascend.	4.38
5.18	Top of rise (2,340').	4.28
5.24	Cross main wash	4.22
5.54	Major pass on ridge (2,450'). Fine views N & S. Summits to E & W may be easily ascended without trail for more extensive views. Descend steadily to N on trail. Use care with stock trails in area.	3.92
5.76	Trail ends; vehicleway starts.	3.70
5.78	Descend very steadily almost into wash, then *at bottom do NOT continue ahead along wash, but switchback up to R.*	3.68
5.84	Water tank off to L in bottom of wash (spring). There are a few deciduous trees nearby. Descend steadily down rocky vehicleway, paralleling wash.	3.62
5.92	Cross major wash where two branches come together; ascend.	3.54
5.98	Top of rise.	3.48
6.07	Cross major wash.	3.39
6.23	Top of rise with view to SE.	3.23
6.30	**Junction of roads:** keep R where jeep road diverges L.	3.16
6.41	Top of rise in pass with views (2,370').	3.05
6.74	Top of rise. (Below is projected future wilderness campground area.)	3.28
7.20	**Important junction:** turn L from road onto trail. It meanders slowly up the hillside at an easy grade.	2.26
7.63	Switchback to R.	1.83
7.71	Top of rise (2,450') with good view to S. Descend narrow trail.	1.75
7.82	Switchback to L on descent.	1.64
7.97	Switchback to R, then to L in 70', and L again in 105'; then descend steeply.	1.49
8.11	Trail ends, vehicleway begins.	1.35
8.14	**Junction of roads:** keep L where road R leads to corral and windmill. In 200' reach open area (projected future rest area).	1.32
8.28	**Junction:** go straight where vehicleway goes R. Descend, then top a rise.	1.18
8.51	Cross small wash, then top a low rise.	0.95
8.60	**Junction of roads:** keep R where road goes L (power line service road). Ascend a long, rocky stretch of road.	0.86
9.00	Top of rise near power lines (2,200'). Good views N & W. Wild Burro Mesa (2,997') is prominent to the W. Descend road.	0.46
9.10	Pass under double power line.	0.36
9.38	**Junction:** avoid road to L; continue ahead with Table Mesa Road in sight.	0.08
9.46	Table Mesa Road (1,980').	0.00

Read Down ↓	Detailed East Loop Trail Description	Read Up ↑
0.00	From junction, angle toward wash.	1.27
0.07	Descend.	1.20
0.08	Cross wash.	1.19
0.09	Switchback to L, out of it.	1.18
0.15	Switchback to R, descend for 100' to flat near main wash. Use care with route.	1.12
0.18	Reach main wash, then leave it on L in 35'.	1.09
0.31	Cross very small wash.	0.96
0.36	Small quartz summit on R.	0.91
0.48	Trail side-hills wash on R.	0.69
0.51	Cross side-wash.	0.72
0.57	Turn R at barbed-wire fence.	0.80
0.58	Gate in barbed-wire fence.	0.79

0.63	Cross side-wash.	0.64
0.73	Cross side-wash.	0.54
0.75	Top of rise.	0.52
0.80	Top of rise.	0.47
0.88	Ascend steadily up rocky trail.	0.39
0.89	Top of rise.	0.38
0.90	Cross small side-wash.	0.37
1.04	Top of rise.	0.23
1.11	Cross side-wash.	0.16
1.14	Up & down above wash.	0.13
1.27	**Junction:** West Loop on L, 4.89 mi N of Emery Henderson TH, 4.57 mi S of Table Mesa Road.	0.00

Note: The total distance is from the kiosk; adding the short trail section to New River Road makes the total 9.65 miles, or a 19.3-mile return trip. We recommend that hikers use a car shuttle, because of the long distance for the round trip, and that they travel north to south if the weather is warm (because of the multiple ascents in the northern portion, which would be done in the heat of the afternoon).

Tonto National Forest

An Introduction

From the desert to the tall pines, the Tonto National Forest contains nearly 2,900,000 acres of cactus, chaparral, pine, lakes, rivers and reservoirs just a few miles north and east of Phoenix and the Valley of the Sun.

A wide variety of multiple uses occur within this vast area. Of special importance are the many and varied recreation opportunities and experiences that are available. This National Forest (established by President Theodore Roosevelt in 1908) is among the most-visited in the entire country, and it is easy to see why.

One of the types of recreation facilities provided by the Forest Service, USDA, is a system of trails found throughout the Tonto National Forest. At the present time over 900 miles of trails are available within that system. These trails vary from easy loop hikes near town to trails only an experienced backcountry hiker or equestrian can follow through the rugged Mazatzal Wilderness.

Such trails, however, are of little value if they cannot be located or followed by the public; this is where trail guidebooks become invaluable. A good guidebook must not only be user-friendly, it must also be accurate when written and revised regularly to be kept accurate. In the years I have worked with Roger and Ethel Freeman, they have shown that their standards are high and that they can both produce and update an excellent trail guidebook. I know that many people will benefit from their efforts and will make good use of their guidebook.

We invite each of you to come and use our trails, recognizing that the Forest Service is unable to maintain them as well as we would like. If you encounter a particular problem on the trail or need additional information, you are welcome to contact our office in Phoenix, or any of the six Ranger Stations located nearby. (See Appendix B for addresses and phone numbers.)

Pete Weinel
Assistant Group Leader for Public Service

USDA Tonto National Forest

Seven Springs Area

Skull Mesa

Introduction. Cave Creek is a perennial stream with fine riparian areas and steep mountain slopes. This route between Seven Springs and the area north of Cave Creek village was used as a stage route. There are also prehistoric aboriginal sites. The improvements in trail condition and marking has been dramatic in the past 10 years, so that we can now highly recommend this area. In the fall, the changing colors of deciduous trees in the creek valley makes for excellent photo opportunities.

Maps (for All Trails). *Our Maps 26-27.* The USGS 1:24,000 New River Mesa and Humboldt Mountain quadrangles (1964, photoinspected 1978) cover the approaches, and part of the trails on the south.

> *Note: gates on maps ("dumbbell" symbol) are for location purposes only and do not indicate that the trail is blocked, except to motorized traffic.*

[4] Cave Creek Trail NORTHEAST to SOUTHWEST

General Description. This trail leads along the hillside above the camp-grounds to a crossing of FR 24B at 0.6 mile. It then parallels Cave Creek, with access to the Cottonwood Trail [247] at 0.8 mile. It leads through a beautiful riparian area along Cave Creek, crossing it at 1.9 miles. At 2.6 miles it climbs to a fine viewpoint, then descends to parallel the creek to two more crossings The Skunk Tank Trail [246] is at 4.2 miles. The final crossing of Cave Creek is at 4.9 miles. After crossing the flats, the trail starts a long and sometimes rocky 300' ascent to a pass, where there are good views. Winding along the flank of Skull Mesa, it crosses a number of small canyons, the most impressive of which is Chalk Canyon at 8½ miles. At 9½ miles there is another pass and the trail then side-hills down a ridge to a junction with FR 1533 at 9.9 miles. Continued descent leads to the junction with the Cottonwood Trail [247] at 10.3 miles and Spur Cross Trailhead at Cave Creek at 10.4 miles. Ascent is 500' from east to west, 1,200' west to east.

Access. *At the northeastern end:* take Carefree Highway east from Cave Creek Road, turn left at 2.1 miles onto Scottsdale Road (Tom Darlington Road), then right onto Cave Creek Road at 4 miles. At 10.3 miles the Bartlett Dam Road diverges right; keep left, passing the Forest boundary marker 2 miles further, and the pavement ends at 12.8 miles. (This road is FR 24.) Pass through Camp Creek residential area (road briefly paved here) at about 15.8 miles. At 18 miles the Bronco Trail diverges sharp left. At 19.9 there is a paved one-lane road on the right (FR 562) leading to the Humboldt Mountain tower. Cross Seven Springs Wash (may be flooded) at 20 miles. At 21.7 miles the road switchbacks right, past the Cartwright Ranch, and 0.2 mile further crosses the creek again, next to the Seven Springs Campground. The road left to the Campground is at 22.1 miles. At 22.2 miles a branch left (FR 24B) crosses Cave Creek and leads to the Ashdale Administrative Site (closed to public use). Keep right, up Cave Creek, passing the CCC Camp-ground road on the left at 22.5 miles and then crossing Cave Creek. At 22.6 miles the parking area for the Cave Creek Trailhead is on the left. *Park here.* (Motor vehicles are prohibited on the trails.)

At the southwestern end: leave Carefree Highway, going north on Cave Creek Road. Turn left on Spur Cross Road after the bend of the highway to the right. The road briefly goes right, then left again. At 6.8 miles it is "posted" as it crosses private land (access may be denied at any time; a new housing and resort complex is proposed that would further change access). From here the road deteriorates and is often passable only by high clearance or 4WD vehicles. At 7.7 miles there is a wide horse trail on the right (crosses private property). Cross Cave Creek (when the water is low) at 7.9 miles, passing the National Forest boundary marker at 8.0 miles. Cave Creek is crossed again at 8.5, 8.7, and finally at 8.9 miles. On the far bank is Spur Cross Trailhead. Take Forest Road 1533 sharp right, uphill. (Motor vehicles are prohibited.)

Cautions. Cave Creek drains a major basin. In times of high water it may be impossible to ford it, especially on foot. At such times, access to the higher-level trails can be made via the undesignated trail along the Cartwright Ranch fence off FR 24, at the top of the hill above Seven Springs Campground. This connects to trails [246] and [247]. The new Bronco Trail also gives access to the Cottonwood Trail. Livestock frequent much of the area; leave fence gates as you found them. The area outside of the Cave Creek valley itself is little traveled, providing the pleasures and hazards of solitude. *Note that the use of motorized vehicles on the trail is prohibited.*

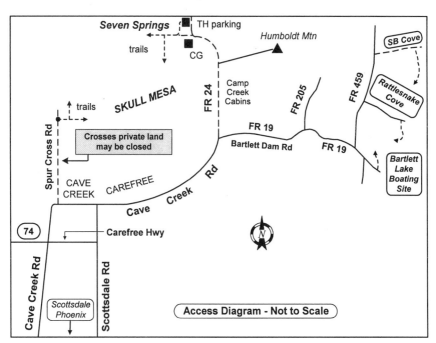

Read Down ↓	Detailed Trail Description	Read Up ↑

0.00   From CCC Recreation Site parking area, ascend to W (3,280'). 10.40

0.07   Top of rise above CCC Recreation Site. Continue S. 10.33

0.41   **Junction:** trail of use descends on L toward Seven Springs Campground. 9.98

0.64   **Junction:** cross FR 24B, back to FR 24 on L. Descend. 9.76

0.69   **Junction:** horse route diverges on L. 9.71

0.71   Steps over barbed-wire fence. 9.68

0.74   **Junction:** alternate horse route rejoins on L. 9.66

0.81   **Important junction:** Cottonwood Trail [247] diverges L at signpost (crosses
        Cave Creek). Ascend. 9.59

0.89   Top of rise. 9.50

0.93   On flats beside Cave Creek. 9.46

1.30   Locked gate on R in fence. 9.10

1.40   Gate on R in barbed-wire fence. 9.00

1.51   Cross side-creek. 8.89

1.81   Beside Cave Creek. 8.58

1.86   Gate. Follow bank of Cave Creek. 8.54

1.90   Cross Cave Creek. 8.50

2.18   Leave creek bank, ascend. 8.22

2.32   Top of rise (3,190'), views. Follow high level, with continuing views. 8.08

2.66   Switchback down to R, then to L in 100'. 7.74

2.76   Reach bench beside Cave Creek, then ascend. 7.64

2.89   Turn L at bend in creek (views). Descend steadily to Cave Creek. 7.50

2.96   Cross Cave Creek with care (3,040'). 7.44

3.08   Level off. 7.32

3.17   Top of rise. 7.23

3.22   **Junction:** trail descends L to Cave Creek. 7.17

3.32   Top of rise (3,060'). 7.07

3.44   Bottom of descent (2,960'). 6.95

3.68   Good viewpoint. 6.71

3.77   **Junction:** trail of use on L. 6.63

4.00   Cross Cave Creek. 6.40

4.18   **Important junction:** on L is Skunk Tank Trail [246] (2,960'). Trail narrows. 6.21

4.22   Switchback up to L. 6.17

4.24   Cross side-creek. 6.16

4.44   Cross Cave Creek, side-hill, then pass through riparian area with lots of cacti. 5.96

4.91   Cross Cave Creek again, then cross flat area. 5.49

5.06   Trail of use on R to Cave Creek. 5.34

5.10   Trail of use on R to Cave Creek. 5.30

5.25   Cross side-creek. 5.14

5.27   Switchback up to L. 5.12

5.30   Cross open gate in barbed-wire fence; corral is on R (this was once a stop
        on the stagecoach route). 5.10

5.61   Cross side-creek. 4.79

5.99   Cross very small, steep-sided creek. Ascend. 4.41

6.22   Gate in barbed-wire fence in pass (3,190'). Viewpoint. Go up and down. 4.18

6.65   Top of rise (3,140'). 3.74

6.86   Bottom of descent. 3.54

7.01   On flat crest (3,160'). 3.39

7.17   **Junction:** trail R at cairn leads down to 6L Ranch (private). 3.23

7.27   On crest. 3.13

7.35   Top of edge of canyon (3,050'). Bear L, descend. 3.05

7.41	Main creek crossing. Ascend.	2.99
7.46	Edge of valley. Bear L.	2.94
7.50	Swing to R.	2.90
7.65	Brink of canyon (3,020').	2.75
7.78	Come around head of small valley. Ascend.	2.62
7.88	Top of rise.	2.52
7.95	**Junction:** trail of use ascends on L.	2.45
7.97	**Junction:** apparent trail of use goes R toward viewpoint.	2.43
8.30	Top of rise (2,900'). Descend steadily.	2.09
8.51	**Junction:** faint trail to R descends to grassy camping area. Descend.	1.89
8.54	Cross creek at bottom of Chalk Canyon (2,780').	1.86
8.60	Switchback to R, past rock retaining wall.	1.80
8.62	Turn L.	1.78
8.68	Top of rise along brink of Chalk Canyon.	1.72
9.00	Leave brink of Chalk Canyon.	1.39
9.19	Start around head of small ravine.	1.22
9.48	Top of rise in pass (2,810'), with views. Descend vehicleway.	0.92
9.51	**Junction:** vehicleway on R leads to viewpoint in 180' in pass (2,780') (continues downhill). Bear L here, downhill.	0.88
9.92	**Junction (4-way):** on R is steep, eroded short-cut to Spur Cross Trailhead (not recommended); sharp R is jeep road to private land in Cave Creek valley. Continue ahead on FR 1533.	0.48
9.93	Closed gate in barbed-wire fence (2,600').	0.47
10.31	**Important junction:** on L is Cottonwood Trail [247] descending.	0.09
10.33	Top of rise. Descend.	0.07
10.40	*Spur Cross Trailhead* (2,410'). Spur Cross Road (4WD only) leads S to town of Cave Creek, crossing private land.	0.00

[246] Skunk Tank Trail (Western Segment) WEST to EAST

Cave Creek Trail [4] to Quien Sabe Trail [250]

General Description. This trail makes a steady, switchbacking, 800' ascent up the ridge with fine views to Skunk Tank at 1½ miles. Another 500' of ascent up a private ranch road leads to a junction with the Quien Sabe Trail [250] to the Skull Mesa Trail [248] at 2.4 miles. Total elevation gain is 1,300'.

Access. *At the northwestern end:* take the Cave Creek Trail [4] for 4.2 miles from Cave Creek Trailhead, or take the same trail from Spur Cross Trailhead for 6.2 miles. *At the southeastern end:* from Seven Springs Trailhead, take the Cave Creek Trail [4] for 0.8 mile to a junction, then the Cottonwood trail [247] for 0.4 mile, and the Skunk Tank Trail (Eastern Segment) for 2.8 miles. Motorized vehicles are prohibited.

Read Down ↓	Detailed Trail Description	Read Up ↑
0.00	From the Cave Creek Trail [4] this trail starts by ascending at sign (2,960'), saying "2 mi" to Quien Sabe Trail.	2.38
0.08	Switchback to L, toward N.	2.30
0.11	Crest (3,060'). Bear R, up it.	2.27

0.13	Go off crest to L, side-hilling.	2.25
0.17	Switchbacks start, to L.	2.21
0.25	Switchback to R, crossing over crest. Fine views open.	2.13
0.30	Switchback to L, then to R in 200'.	2.08
0.43	Switchback to L, then to R in 40'.	1.95
0.46	Switchback to L (3,320') on S side of crest, then to R in 70'.	1.92
0.48	Switchback to L and cross over crest.	1.90
0.50	Switchback to R, over crest, then switchback to L in 115'.	1.88
0.52	Switchback to R just at crest.	1.86
0.59	Sag on crest (3,400').	1.79
0.61	Switchback to R, then switchback to L in 70'.	1.77
0.64	Switchback to R, then ease grade with fine views. Side-hill ridge on S side.	1.74
0.72	Continue side-hilling with steep canyon on R with drop-off; *use care*.	1.66
0.89	Ascend steadily (3,530').	1.49
0.90	Switchback to L, then to R in 25'. Trail is very rocky.	1.48
0.93	Viewpoint on level trail (3,580'). Continue side-hilling.	1.45
0.98	Ascend steeply, side-hilling.	1.40
1.04	Above bend in canyon (3,640'). In 250' cross small wash, swing S, ascending.	1.34
1.15	Top of rise above side-canyon.	1.23
1.19	Cross small wash; ascend to SW.	1.19
1.21	**Junction:** avoid trail of use on L; descend to R.	1.17
1.40	Cross creek (3,640').	0.98
1.41	Switchback to L, toward SE.	0.97
1.46	Skunk Tank (3,660'). Trail goes sharp L here, without cairns. *Use care.*	0.92
1.47	Gate in barbed-wire fence. Follow cairns to E, ascending gradually and paralleling fence line. Trail is not very well defined through here.	0.91
1.58	**Junction:** stay R (unmarked trail on L crosses pass and descends to Cave Creek. Bottom connection with Trail [4] is not obvious).	0.80
1.60	Ascend steadily.	0.78
1.64	Top of rise (3,750').	0.74
1.66	Easy, level walking on jeep road. Side-hill into small valley.	0.72
1.83	Ascend steeply.	0.55
2.03	**Junction:** go R on jeep road where trail continues ahead (3,920').	0.35
2.08	**Junction:** swing R and ascend steeply (straight ahead ends quickly).	0.30
2.18	Top of rise. Flat road S is visible ahead, along crest (4,020').	0.20
2.26	Ascend steeply.	0.12
2.38	**Junction:** Quien Sabe Trail [250] (road) to R; this trail descends L (4,100').	0.00

Note: By the Quien Sabe Trail it is 2.6 miles to the Skull Mesa Trail [248]. To the left, the next section of this trail leads to the Cottonwood Trail at 2.8 miles, and to the Cave Creek Trailhead in another mile (3.8 miles total).

[246] Skunk Tank Trail (Eastern Segment) EAST to WEST

Cottonwood Trail [247] to Quien Sabe Trail [250]

General Description. This is a hiker/horse/bicycle trail. Motorized vehicles are prohibited. Marking is by occasional cairns and signposts at junctions. From the Cottonwood Trail [247], a private ranch road ascends out of a draw, heading generally west with good views to the north, to 2.8 miles where it reaches the Quien Sabe Trail [250] There is some up and down. Total elevation gain is 900'. Motorized vehicles are prohibited.

Access. *At the western end:* take Cave Creek Trail [4] for 4.2 miles, or take the same trail from Spur Cross Trailhead for 6.2 miles. Then ascend the ridge for 2.4 miles on the Western Segment of this trail [preceding section]. *At the eastern end:* take the Cave Creek Trail for 0.8 mile to the Cottonwood Trail [247], cross Cave Creek and proceed uphill for 0.4 mile further.

Read Down ↓	Detailed Trail Description	Read Up ↑
0.00	From Cottonwood Trail [247] (3,460') this trail heads S, level.	2.77
0.11	Bottom of descent; ascend gradually.	2.66
0.29	Top of rise.	2.48
0.31	Bottom of descent. Ascend.	2.46
0.61	Bottom of descent.	2.16
0.70	**Junction:** trail of use sharp R. Bear L on road.	2.07
0.80	Bottom of descent.	1.97
0.96	Top of rise (4,000'). Views over Seven Springs area. Descend rocky stretch.	1.81
1.07	Start rocky descent.	1.70
1.17	Bottom of descent.	1.60
1.27	Top of rise (3,940').	1.50
1.38	Cross wash.	1.30
1.39	**Junction:** rough road ascends steeply L to Quien Sabe Spring (3,840'). Keep R, ascend steep, rocky road.	1.29
1.61	Top of rise (4,000').	1.16
1.63	Cross small wash.	1.14
1.68	Top of rise (4,080'). Descend.	1.09
1.70	Level.	1.07
1.73	Top of rise (4,070').	1.04
1.88	Bottom of descent.	0.89
1.89	Top of rise.	0.88
2.30	Bottom of descent. Level.	0.47
2.36	Switchback to R (3,850'). Ascend.	0.41
2.77	**Junction:** Quien Sabe Trail [250] to L (4,080'); this trail descends R.	0.00

Note: By the Quien Sabe Trail it is 2.6 miles to the Skull Mesa Trail [248]. To the left, the next section of this trail leads to the Cottonwood Trail at 2.8 miles, and to the Cave Creek Trailhead in another 1.2 miles (4 miles total).

[247] Cottonwood Trail (Western Segment) WEST to EAST

Spur Cross Trailhead to Skull Mesa Trail [248]

General Description. Because few people will come this far from Seven Springs if access to this trailhead is blocked, this section is described in reverse direction from the others that follow. The trail actually starts just above the Spur Cross Trailhead. It drops to the creek, then ascends high above with fine views for almost a mile, crossing a creek at 1.1 miles, then climbing again above a canyon to 1.9 miles, and again ascending at 2.3 miles to reach a small crest and the trail junction at 2½ miles. Total elevation gain is 900'. Motorized vehicles are prohibited.

Access. *At the western end:* from Spur Cross Trailhead, 0.1 mile east (north) on the Cave Creek Trail [4]. *At the eastern end:* 8½ miles from Ashdale Road near Seven Springs via the Cottonwood Trail [247] or 7¾ miles via the Skull Mesa [248], Quien Sabe [250] and Skunk Tank [246] Trails.

Read Down ↓	Detailed Trail Description	Read Up ↑
0.00	From Trail [4] just 450' above Spur Cross Trailhead, descend sharp R at dip in road. Switchback to L in 175'.	2.48
0.04	Cross creek, ascend NE over hill, descend slightly to creek level, parallel it.	2.44
0.13	Cross creek, follow it.	2.35
0.14	Bear R, out of creek, ascending steadily, then steeply.	2.34
0.27	View of Skull Mesa ahead. Continue ascending NE at slightly easier grade.	2.21
0.36	Top of rise (2,750'). Level off, then ascend gradually.	2.12
0.42	Flat top (2,740').	2.06
0.65	Cross very small creek, ascend, then bear R.	1.83
0.72	Top of rise (2,690').	1.76
0.77	Reach crest (2,700'). Descend minor ridge, with views.	1.71
0.82	Descend slightly left, down hogback.	1.66
0.91	Cross small creek.	1.57
0.98	Start descent; trail of use sharp R.	1.50
1.07	Cross creek. Stock tank on R (2,690'). Ascend.	1.41
1.12	Switchback to L, ascend.	1.36
1.30	Top of rise (2,920').	1.18
1.40	Top of rise (2,960'). Ascend crest to N, with views.	1.08
1.79	Start ascent beside canyon on L.	0.69
1.83	**Junction:** trail of use continues straight; keep L.	0.65
1.84	Switchback to R, ascending rocky trail.	0.64
1.90	Switchback to R above head of canyon (3,160').	0.58
1.91	Top of rise, descend S.	0.57
2.11	Turn L, level off (3,060'), then ascend NE.	0.37
2.14	Descend steadily R.	0.34
2.15	Bottom of descent. Ascend.	0.33
2.16	Top of rise.	0.32
2.18	Start descent.	0.30
2.21	Cross small creek (3,050'). Ascend.	0.27
2.23	Switchback to L, ascend, turn L and ease in 55'.	0.25
2.27	Descend loose rock.	0.21
2.30	Cross creek, then ascend with loose rock.	0.18
2.37	Ease, still ascending (3,110').	0.11
2.39	Ascend steadily, then steeply.	0.09
2.43	Switchback to L, ascend.	0.05
2.48	**Junction:** beyond gate in barbed-wire fence, the next trail section heads E, then S. Skull Mesa Trail [248] ascends L, paralleling fence. (Elev. 3,150').	0.00

[247] Cottonwood Trail (Middle Segment) WEST to EAST

West End to East End of Skull Mesa Trail [248]

General Description. A complex, twisting route along and above the wash characterizes this trail. In wet weather the footway can be difficult. The first section descends to Cottonwood Creek at 0.8 mile and follows it, then at 2½ miles leaves the valley by switchbacking up a scenic route above a steep canyon to the Skull Mesa Trail [248] at 3.1 miles. Total ascent is 700'.

Access. *At the western end:* from this trail, 2.6 miles east of Spur Cross Trailhead. *At the eastern end:* 5.6 miles east of Spur Cross Trailhead or 5½ miles south of FR 24B near Seven Springs. Motor vehicles are prohibited.

Read Down ↓	Detailed Trail Description	Read Up ↑
0.00	From **junction** (3,150'), head E, then descend to NE.	3.06
0.13	Level off. Ascend past cliffs on L (good views).	2.93
0.17	Start descent to SE and S, beside canyon on L.	2.89
0.31	Turn L, descend to creek (3,040').	2.75
0.33	Cross creek, ascend.	2.73
0.39	Gate in barbed-wire fence. Descend rocky trail.	2.67
0.43	**Junction:** keep R (level), where cattle trail goes L. In 80' descend.	2.63
0.47	Cross creek (2,950'). Barbed-wire fence above.	2.59
0.48	Parallel fence to SE, level out, then ascend.	2.58
0.52	**Junction:** On R is gate and trail back to Cave Creek (town) via private land. Go L here, descending loose rock.	2.54
0.62	Switchback down to R along creek. In 20' cross small side-creek.	2.44
0.65	Cross main creek (pipe on far side, tank 200' farther on).	2.41
0.69	Open gate in barbed-wire fence. Parallel it.	2.37
0.74	Corral on R. Go thru gate. Descend, heading NE.	2.32
0.80	Reach Cottonwood Creek (2,760').	2.26
0.83	**Junction:** keep L (trail of use goes R).	2.23
0.85	Beside Cottonwood Creek again.	2.21
0.88	**Junction:** avoid cattle path ascending L. Keep straight on (may be briefly overgrown).	2.18
0.89	Bear R, cross creek in 15'. Go uphill.	2.17
0.94	Rejoin creek; cross it in 55', then ascend.	2.12
0.99	Pass waterfall on R in picturesque area.	2.07
1.01	Top of rise. Descend gradually.	2.05
1.03	Cross Cottonwood Creek to R, to L in 150', then to R in another 200'.	2.03
1.13	Cross Cottonwood Creek to L. *Do not follow main branch;* head NE into valley of subsidiary creek.	1.93
1.15	Cross creek to R, ascending briefly. Re-cross to L in 115'.	1.91
1.18	Switchback to R, then L, ascending steadily.	1.88
1.20	Follow minor creek bed.	1.86
1.21	Leave it on R, ascending steadily up hillside.	1.85
1.35	Ease grade of ascent, with views.	1.71
1.59	Top of rise, pass (3,160'). Descend steadily.	1.47
1.64	On flats of Cottonwood Creek.	1.42
1.68	Corral on R. In 40' go thru open gate in barbed-wire fence, ascending gradually.	1.38

1.78	Cross Cottonwood Creek to R.	1.28
1.85	Cross Cottonwood Creek to L.	1.21
1.93	Cross Cottonwood Creek to R.	1.13
2.00	**Junction:** cattle path goes sharp L. Keep R into main creek valley.	1.06
2.04	Cross Cottonwood Creek to L, to R in 90', to L in 80'.	1.02
2.12	Cross Cottonwood Creek to R; parallel it, either in creek bed or beside it (use care — way is not always distinct; may be impassable in rainy weather).	0.94
2.18	Leave creek bed, ascending R.	0.88
2.23	Cross Cottonwood Creek to L, in 150' to R. Go alongside creek.	0.83
2.34	*Creek forks: follow branch to R (3,160').*	0.72
2.38	Cross creek.	0.68
2.39	Switchback to L, ascending steeply. Use care.	0.67
2.41	Ease grade of ascent. Turn R up crest.	0.65
2.44	Turn R, ascending steeply. In 60', turn L, side-hilling.	0.62
2.50	Switchback to R, making easy traverse.	0.56
2.53	Switchback to L onto crest, ascending steadily, very high above Cottonwood Canyon on R. Fine views. (Use care at edge.)	0.53
2.56	Trails of use on R.	0.50
2.59	Switchback to R, then to L in 85', rising steeply.	0.47
2.66	Turn L on crest . Spectacular views of canyon below, with waterfalls in season. Follow N side of crest, descending gradually.	0.40
2.78	Bottom of descent. Ascend steadily up loose, eroded rocky trail.	0.28
2.82	Regain crest; leave it on L in 100'.	0.24
2.88	Regain crest.	0.18
2.89	Top of rise. Descend gradually.	0.17
2.92	Bottom of descent. Ascend.	0.14
2.97	Top of rise (3,600').	0.09
3.04	Go thru open gate in barbed-wire fence.	0.02
3.06	**Junction:** Skull Mesa Trail [248] goes straight ahead on crest (first part is obscure — follow cairns). This trail turns slightly R, descending off crest.	0.00

[247] Cottonwood Trail (Eastern Segment) SOUTH to NORTH

Skull Mesa Trail [248] to Cave Creek Trail [4]

Introduction. A varied terrain of ridges and valleys makes this section worthwhile. The section in the Bronco Creek drainage has been largely re-routed recently to get out of the creek bed, and as a consequence offers good views. The Forest Service is to be congratulated for a good improvement.

General Description. The route leads along the Cottonwood drainage to near its head, then crosses over to the top of the Bronco Creek drainage where there is a new trail (Bronco) to FR 24 at 2¼ miles. It then descends the Bronco Creek valley, at 3 miles leaving the valley on new trail, side-hilling with good views, then re-crossing the wash and ascending to reach the Skunk Tank Trail [246] at 4.9 miles, with a steady descent to Cave Creek Trail [4] at 5.3 miles. Total elevation gain is 500'. Motorized vehicles are prohibited.

Access. *At the western end:* from this trail, 5.6 miles east of Spur Cross Trailhead. *At the eastern end:* from 5.4 miles south of Cave Creek Trail [4].

Read Down ↓	Detailed Trail Description	Read Up ↑

0.00 From Skull Mesa Trail [248], descend (3,590'). 5.30
0.15 Join creek bed. Ascend along it or in it, thru riparian vegetation. 5.15
0.59 Landmark: sandstone conglomerate boulder on L. Continue in or along wash. 4.93
1.56 **Junction:** non-system trail on R. Ascend switchback to L. 3.74
1.65 Gate in fence. Ascend. 3.65
1.91 Top of rise (3,900'). 3.39
2.24 Cross wash. 3.06
2.27 **Important junction:** sharp R, uphill, is unmarked **Bronco Trail** to FR 24 in 3.72 mi (elevation 3,720'). Turn L here and descend gradually in wide valley, narrowing soon to a canyon. 3.03
2.44 Cross main wash. 2.86
2.70 Cross side-wash (from L). 2.60
2.80 Cross main wash. 2.50
3.00 **Junction:** original trail continues ahead (3,670'), new trail angles off to R. 2.30
3.68 **Junction:** rejoin original trail in wash. Cross wash. 1.62
3.83 **Junction:** where vehicleway continues ahead, trail ascends hillside on L. 1.47
4.45 Switchback to R, then to L in 120'. 0.85
4.53 Switchbacks start. 0.77
4.63 **Junction:** sharp R, in pass (3,550'), is old trail descending in 0.23 mi to original location, and to non-system side-trail to FR 24 at ranch fence line at 0.56 mi (total). 0.67
4.72 Switchback to L. 0.58
4.76 Bottom of descent. Start slight ascent. 0.54
4.91 **Junction:** turn L (where vehicleway continues to ranch on R); descend. 0.39
4.94 **Junction:** Skunk Tank Trail [246] joins from L (multi-use vehicleway, motorcycles permitted). Turn R, descending. 0.36
5.14 Turn L, then R, starting descent. 0.16
5.20 Switchback to L, descending steeply. Two more follow, then turn L along bank of Cave Creek. 0.10
5.25 Turn R from bank of Cave Creek; cross it. 0.05
5.30 **Junction:** Cave Creek Trail [4] (3,320'). Turn R here for Seven Springs. 0.00

[248] Skull Mesa Trail WEST to EAST OVER SKULL MESA

Cottonwood Trail [247] to Quien Sabe Trail [250]

Introduction. Skull Mesa is prominent from the Cave Creek area, though only about 2 miles long (New River Mesa is much larger). Its southern and eastern flanks are quite steep and offer commanding views. The trail is very steep in places, with many switchbacks, but the trickiest part is actually crossing the rather flat mesa, where footway is often overgrown and cairns must be followed carefully. The trip over the mesa is not advised in poor weather with limited visibility. In good weather this is a high-quality trip to be long remembered.

General Description. From the Cottonwood Trail junction, the climb starts immediately, with many switchbacks but compensatory views. At 1.1 miles the top is in view, reached at 1.2 miles, an ascent of 1,150'. A summit is accessible without trail just to the west. The trail continues eastward over the mesa, with mostly gradual ascent to a high point very close to the actual summit at 4,595'. From here there are wonderful views to the east. A short but steep descent of 0.9 mile leads to the junction at the Quien Sabe Trail, a total of 3.1 miles. Total ascent is 1,400'. Motorized vehicles are prohibited.

Access. *At the western end:* from the Cottonwood Trail, 2.6 miles east of Spur Cross Trailhead. *At the eastern end:* from the Quien Sabe Trail [250], 2.6 miles from the Skunk Tank Trail [246].

Read Down ↓	Detailed Trail Description	Read Up ↑
0.00	From the Cottonwood Trail [247] 2.57 mi E of Spur Cross Trailhead (3,150') at gate in barbed-wire fence, head up broad ridge, generally following fence line.	3.07
0.10	Bear R, away from crest of ridge.	2.97
0.29	Top of minor ridge (3,380'). Keep to R of it.	2.78
0.44	Make almost level traverse.	2.63
0.47	Switchback to R. Parallel fence line, then zigzag about 100' E of fence.	2.60
0.60	Switchback to L (3,660'). Make 9 more switchbacks.	2.47
0.70	Switchback to L; start steep ascent up rocky trail (3,780'). Use care.	2.37
0.71	Turn R, up crest. In 35; turn L, level briefly. In another 50' ascend over exposed rock with good views. This is a relatively long traverse.	2.36
0.79	Switchback to L. Make 6 more switchbacks.	2.28
0.91	Switchback to R (3,990'). Make long traverse to pass beneath cliffs.	2.16
0.96	Start steep ascent.	2.11
0.99	Switchback to L, then 5 more, passing cliffs.	2.08
1.10	Switchback to L. Top of mesa is in view.	1.97
1.13	Level off (4,220').	1.94
1.16	*Top of Skull Mesa.* To L is low summit (4,285') with cliffs and excellent views, reachable in 470' without trail. To continue, head N & NE across mesa, following cairns with great care — footway is poorly defined.	1.91
1.24	Start gradual ascent.	1.83
1.33	Ascend, switchback to R.	1.73
1.36	Top of rise at higher level of mesa.	1.71
1.63	Bottom of descent.	1.44
2.00	Top of rise at huge cairn.	1.07
2.07	Head E.	1.00
2.10	Head SE. Ascend gradually.	0.97
2.46	Top of rise.	0.61
2.48	E end of Skull Mesa (4,590'), views. Trail descends steeply from here.	0.59
2.52	Switchback to L, then to R in 20', making long traverse.	0.55
2.61	Switchback to L, then to R in 65'	0.46
2.65	Switchback to L, then 16 more. There are fine views.	0.42
2.82	Switchback to R; grade eases; trail is very rocky and makes zigzags.	0.25
2.92	Switchback to R. Use care with route.	0.15
3.05	Turn L (N).	0.02
3.07	**Junction:** Quien Sabe Trail [250] on L, 2.56 mi to Skunk Tank Trail [246]. For continuation of this trail to Cottonwood Trail [247], 1.89 mi, continue ahead (about 250' of ascent, 800' of descent). Elevation 4,080'.	0.00

[248] Skull Mesa Trail EAST to WEST

Cottonwood Trail [247] to Quien Sabe Trail [250]

Introduction. This is the description for those ascending from the Cottonwood Trail [247] to reach the southern end of the Quien Sabe Trail or to access Skull Mesa from the north or east. There are good views.

General Description. This trail leaves the Cottonwood Trail, follows a crest a few times, and starts climbing steeply at 0.4 mile. There is some up and down, and several broad summits are crossed before meeting the Quien Sabe Trail (to Cave Creek Trail [4] and Seven Springs) at 1.9 miles. Total ascent is about 800'.

Access. *At the eastern end,* from the Cottonwood Trail, 5.6 miles east of Spur Cross Trailhead, and 5.8 miles southwest of Ashdale Road near Seven Springs. *At the western end,* from the Quien Sabe Trail [250] or the western section of this trail, 3.1 miles from the Cottonwood Trail, 2.6 miles from Spur Cross Trailhead (5.6 miles total). Motorized use is prohibited.

Read Down ↓	Detailed Trail Description	Read Up ↑
0.00	From the Cottonwood Trail [247] go straight, along crest, where [247] descends R off crest. (Elevation 3,590'.)	1.89
0.14	Pass sandstone eroded cliffs on L. In 65' start steep ascent to WNW.	1.75
0.29	Top of rise. Keep just L of crest.	1.60
0.38	Cross over crest, ascend to R of it.	1.51
0.42	Turn L, ascend steeply, then L again in 85'.	1.47
0.46	Back on crest. Ascend to R of it.	1.43
0.48	Steep, loose rock, use care.	1.41
0.54	Small, level area, then turn R and rise very steeply for 100'.	1.35
0.62	Descend for 100', then rise again.	1.27
0.71	Switchback to R, then to L in 70', then R & L. Use care with steep ascent.	1.18
0.78	Top of rise; descend (4,110').	1.11
0.84	Gate in barbed-wire fence (closed). In 25' turn L (W), follow cairns with care, ascending gradually.	1.05
0.98	Switchback steeply up to L, then to R in 30'.	0.91
1.00	Switchback to L on loose rock, then ease grade (4,190').	0.89
1.01	Switchback to R. In 65' bear L, then R.	0.88
1.11	Top of rise (4,260'). Drop to NW.	0.78
1.15	Bear L (W). Descend steadily.	0.74
1.24	Descend to NW, then W. In 0.2 mi start ascent.	0.65
1.48	Big cairn; avoid false trail to L. Ascend to R.	0.41
1.52	Top of rise (4,140'). The Quien Sabe Trail is in view ahead.	0.37
1.55	Bottom of descent. Ascend.	0.34
1.60	Top of rise (4,140'). Head W, descending gradually.	0.29
1.72	Bottom of descent; level.	0.17
1.79	Top of rise.	0.10
1.86	Bottom of descent (4,020'). Ascend gradually.	0.03
1.89	**Junction:** Quien Sabe Trail [250] on R (4,080'). To continue up Skull Mesa, ascend to SSW up steep, switchbacking trail for 0.59 mi to E end of Mesa, W end is a further 1.32 gradually descending miles.	0.00

[250] Quien Sabe Trail NORTH to SOUTH

Skunk Tank Trail [246] to Skull Mesa Trail [248]

Introduction. This is the only connection between the northern and southern trails. Distances are long. Watch the weather! **General Description.** A ranch road ascends over Quien Sabe Pass to 1.1 miles, then drops to pass a stock tank at 2.1 miles, becoming trail. A steady ascent leads to the junction with the Skull Mesa Trail at 2.6 miles. There are good views. Total elevation gain is about 520'.

Access. *At the northern end:* via the Skunk Tank Trail [246] 2.4 miles from Cave Creek Trail [4] at a point 3.7 miles from FR 24B near Seven Springs. *At the southern end:* from Skull Mesa Trail [248] 5.6 miles from Spur Cross Trailhead, or 1.9 miles from Cottonwood Trail 5.7 miles from its end at Cave Creek Trail [4], 0.2 mile from FR 24B. Motorized vehicles are prohibited.

Read Down ↓	Detailed Trail Description	Read Up ↑
0.00	From the Skunk Tank Trail [246], 2.38 mi from Cave Creek Trail [4], head S (uphill) on ranch road (elevation 4,100').	2.56
0.08	Reach crest of ridge.	2.48
0.19	Top of rise (4,220'). Level off.	2.37
0.38	Cross top of small ridge; ascend SE.	2.18
0.70	Ascend steeply.	1.86
0.88	Ease and almost level off.	1.68
1.04	Cross wash, ascend (4,460').	1.52
1.08	Quien Sabe Pass (4,460'); views. Descend into valley.	1.48
1.79	Bottom of descent in valley; ascend gradually, then descend.	0.77
2.05	Bottom of descent, cross creek (3,990'). Turn L, ascend steadily.	0.51
2.09	Old stock tank on R. Continue ascent on narrower trail.	
	Important: in 35' turn R (W) in level area.	0.47
2.12	Ascend again.	0.44
2.16	Switchback to L.	0.40
2.26	Start steady ascent.	0.30
2.35	Start steady ascent again.	0.21
2.53	Cross very small wash, turn L (E).	0.03
2.56	**Junction:** Skull Mesa Trail [248] L & R (4,080').	0.00

Note: To the left, Skull Mesa Trail leads 1.9 miles to the Cottonwood Trail. To the right, it climbs steeply over Skull Mesa (0.6 mile) and descends at 1.9 miles to the Cottonwood Trail 2.6 miles east of Spur Cross Trailhead.

Bronco Trail EAST to WEST

General Description. New routes into the back country are always welcome. This one has very good views as it traverses ridges and passes. It was built in 1999 to connect sections of vehicleways and some new trail. It begins on FR 2048, which starts climbing a steep, eroded hill at ¼ mile (not recommended for vehicles), reaching the crest at 0.4 mile. The rough vehicleway follows the ridge crest (with expanding views) to the high point at 1.1 miles and ends at 1.4 miles. From there, the trail side-hills up a creek valley, reaching a pass (4,260') at 2.4 miles. It then drops about 180' to Upper Bronco Tank at 2.7 miles, joins an overgrown old jeep road, climbs over another pass at 2.9 miles, and descends 300', following the route of the old road to the valley floor, where it ends at the Cottonwood Trail [247] at 3.7 miles. Total ascent is 800'.

Access. *At the eastern end,* from FR 24, 7.7 miles north of the junction of FR 24 and FR 19 (Bartlett Dam Road). The road to the trail leaves at a sharp left turn and is not readily visible when traveling north; the exact spot is 1.7 miles north of where paving ends beyond Camp Creek. *At the western end,* from Trail [247] 3.8 miles south of the trailhead for Cave Creek trail [4] north of Seven Springs.

Maps. *Our Map 27.* The USGS 1:24,000 Humboldt Mountain quadrangle (1964, photoinspected 1978) covers the approach on FR 24, but does not show FR 2048. The trail from Upper Bronco Tank to Trail [247] is shown as a "jeep trail."

Read Down ↓	Detailed Trail Description	Read Up ↑
0.00	From FR 24, FR 2048 leads S (3,700').	3.72
0.10	Road bends to R.	3.62
0.17	Sag. Ascend L.	3.55
0.23	At turnaround on road, turn L, ascend steeply up eroded road.	3.49
0.37	Ease grade of ascent on crest, road bends to R.	3.35
0.53	Top of rise on crest.	3.19
1.06	High point on crest (4,034'). Follow it W.	2.66
1.35	Vehicleway ends at loop on crest. Trail starts off to W, side-hilling.	2.37
1.42	Turn R, descend for 80'.	2.30
1.49	Top of rise above valley.	2.23
1.69	Top of rise.	2.03
1.73	Descend.	1.99
1.75	Cross small wash, ascend to R thru nice grassy area. Views open.	1.97
2.13	Bottom of descent.	1.59
2.34	Top of rise.	1.38
2.41	Pass (4,260'). Start rocky descent.	1.31
2.67	Upper Bronco Tank on R.	1.05
2.68	At Upper Bronco Tank, trail heads N, then turns L (SSW), uphill on old vehicleway.	1.04
2.84	Pass (4,240'). Follow cairns SW; use care finding first part of route.	0.88
2.87	Turn R (use care with route). Vehicleway becomes clearer, rockier.	0.85
3.02	Bottom of descent.	0.70
3.04	Viewpoint (4,120'), level area. Steep descent starts in 0.2 mi.	0.68
3.27	**Important junction:** old vehicleway L & R, go R, descending narrow, rocky trail.	0.45
3.32	Turn L, head N (brushy).	0.40
3.41	Start ascending.	0.31
3.42	Gain crest, descend it, steadily to W.	0.30
3.61	Gate in barbed-wire fence.	0.11
3.72	**Junction:** Cottonwood Trail [247] L & R, elevation 3,710'.	0.00

Sears-Kay Ruin from FR 24

Introduction. The Sears-Kay Ruin (listed in the National Register of Historic Places) is one of a chain of desert hilltop forts built by the Hohokam people about 1,000 years ago north of Phoenix and gives a glimpse of their lifestyle. There are remains of about 40 rooms in 5 "compounds." It was discovered by soldiers patrolling from nearby Camp McDowell in 1867. The Hohokam and other prehistoric people vanished in the mid-14th Century for reasons still debated.[1] They developed many miles of irrigation canals in the Valley of the Sun. Nearby to the southeast is the Sears-Kay Ranch established in 1887.

General Description. This trail consists of two loops. It ascends steadily up the slopes south of the ruin, then attacks the summit itself, reaching the other branch of the loop at 0.4 mile, heading up to the second loop over the summit and the ruins. It loops around the north side of the crest back to the main trail at 0.6 mile, then heads down the vehicleway, descending on trail to the trailhead at 0.9 mile. Elevation gain is about 340'. Please do not disturb the site.

Access. *At the southern end:* off of FR 24, 2.7 miles east of the junction with the Bartlett Dam Road, east of Carefree. Turn right at a sign onto paved road for 0.3 mile and park. Facilities consist of ramadas, parking for 10 vehicles, and a toilet, as well as interpretive signs at the ruin.

Maps. *Our Map 27 [inset].* The USGS 1:24,000 New River Mesa quadrangle (1964, photoinspected 1978) shows the terrain but not the trail.

Read Down ↓	Detailed Trail Description	Read Up ↑
0.00	Leave parking area at trailhead sign.	0.92
0.01	**Junction:** go R on trail where returning route goes straight ahead.	0.91
0.04	Bottom of descent.	0.88
0.06	Bear L, ascend to N.	0.86
0.09	**Junction:** ignore trail to L. Keep R, uphill.	0.83
0.11	Bear L and up.	0.81
0.14	**Junction:** join vehicleway, go L on it, ascending.	0.78
0.23	**Junction:** steep vehicleways on R. Keep L on trail, side-hilling.	0.69
0.26	Bear L, ease ascent. Old vehicleway parallels trail, on R. Ascend NW toward large rocks.	0.66
0.31	Switchback to R, steeply up. Views open.	0.61
0.32	Boulder pile on R.	0.60
0.35	Switchback to R.	0.57
0.38	**Junction:** old vehicleway on crest; sign across way. Go R on it, uphill.	0.54
0.40	**Junction:** old parking area. Loop 2 returns on L. Go uphill.	0.52
0.44	Top of ruin with interpretive signs, fine views (3,583').	0.48
0.49	End of ridge crest. Descend to L, side-hill to S.	0.43
0.60	Return to Loop at 0.40 mi. Descend vehicleway.	0.32
0.76	**Junction:** keep L where vehicleway descends steeply sharp R.	0.16
0.80	**Junction:** in level area, this trail descends to L, off crest, side-hilling.	0.12
0.91	**Junction:** first loop on L.	0.01
0.92	Trailhead.	0.00

---

[1]A brochure "Sears-Kay Ruin" is available from the Forest Service.

USDA Tonto National Forest

Lower Salt River/Saguaro Lake Area

"Red Mountain" across the Salt River

Introduction. The Lower Salt River area has varied trails (both short and moderately long) with excellent water (river and lake) and mountain views. Most of these are very popular on weekends, especially in summer, when the heat makes a trip to a lake or to float down a river in a tube quite attractive.

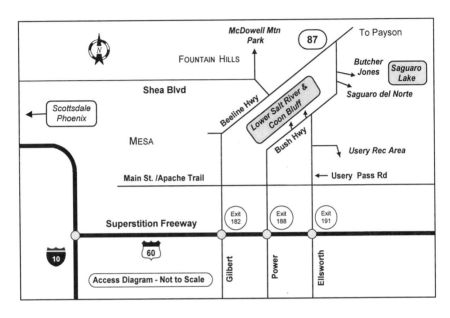

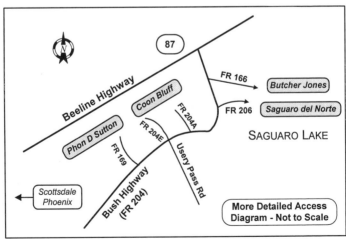

[6] Lower Salt River Interpretive Trail

Introduction. This short loop trail was built by the Student Chapter of the Arizona Wildlife Society in 1985. Its main attraction is the transition between the river-bottom (flood-plain or "riparian") environment and the Lower Sonoran desert, made more meaningful by many in-depth interpretive signs. The trail is designed for sequential, one-way use.

General Description. Near the start and for the first half mile there is a good view of "Red Mountain" across the river; beyond this point the trail moves inland but there are good views of the Goldfield Mountains. There is no significant ascent as the trail runs for a short way along the river bank, then through the flood-plain with its varied forest and desert. After a little more than a mile the trail turns south and east to rejoin itself at the river bank at just under 2½ miles. The elevation is approximately 1,340'.

Access. Turn left from Bush Highway (FR 204) onto FR 169 to the intersection to the Phon D. Sutton Recreation Site in 1.3 miles. The trail leaves from the northwestern corner of the parking lot behind the toilets. *Note:* It is closed to motorized vehicles and to bicycles.

Maps. *Our map 27.* The USGS 1:24,000 Stewart Mountain quadrangle (1964) does not show the trail.

Cautions. Although this is an excellent short hike during the mild winter months, it can be very hot in summer. Note that there are many minor washes and vehicle travelways (now closed to traffic) which can be confusing away from the river. Be sure to follow the metal or carsonite trail posts.

Read Down ↓	Detailed Trail Description	Read Up ↑
0.00	From toilets at S end of parking area trail descends.	2.46
0.02	**Junction:** on R is old route along river. Go L here.	2.44
0.09	Cross wash. Swing R.	2.37
0.11	Re-cross wash.	2.35
0.17	**Junction:** join old trail from R; keep L along river bank.	2.29
0.20	**Junction:** old vehicleway bears L.	2.26
0.21	Sign: "The River," at edge of river bank. Across the river is a filtration plant near junction of Verde and Salt Rivers.	2.25
0.22	**Junction:** undesignated trail angles L.	2.24
0.26	Sign: "Fishes." *(NOTE: Near here trail returns, on L, forming a loop; junction is not marked).*	2.20
0.30	Sign: "Bald Eagle."	2.16
0.41	**Junction:** go straight where vehicle travelway bears L. From here trail heads inland away from river.	2.05
0.50	**Junction:** trail turns R onto vehicle travelway.	1.96
0.57	**Junction:** turn sharp R (SW), leaving vehicle travelway at post with arrow.	1.89
0.59	Sign: "Mistletoe."	1.87
0.61	**Junction:** vehicle travelway on L; bear R, heading generally SW, then S.	1.85
0.78	Sign: "Salt Cedar."	1.68
0.84	Trail briefly narrows through a rocky, treed area.	1.62
0.89	Sign: "Cottonwood and Willow Forest."	1.57
0.91	Sign: "The Old Giants."	1.55

0.93	Turn L; vehicle travelway (now closed) on R.	1.53
1.08	Sign: "Mesquite Woodland."	1.38
1.13	Sign: "Mesquite: Food for Wildlife."	1.33
1.15	Sign: "Food for Riparian Plants."	1.31
1.23	Trail turns toward E (half-way point).	1.23
1.28	Sign: "The Transition."	1.18
1.63	Cross vehicle travelway.	0.63
1.68	Sign: "Desert Plant Adaptations."	0.71
1.74	Cross vehicle travelway.	0.72
1.91	Sign: "Seedlings and Nurse Plants."	0.55
2.06	Cross vehicle travelway.	0.40
2.15	Turn L on vehicle travelway.	0.31
2.20	**Junction:** trail rejoins original section near "Fishes" sign (0.17 mi). Turn R here to return to parking lot.	0.26
2.46	Parking lot.	0.00

[100] Salt River Trail

Introduction. Easy walking with distant views characterizes this trip, which can be varied by taking different segments from Coon Bluff or Goldfield Recreation Sites, or the side-trip up Coon Bluff.

General Description. From Phon D. Sutton Recreation Site Road [FR 169] near its junction with Bush Highway, the Salt River Trail heads east along the base of Coon Bluff. At 0.4 mile there is a connection to the main road, and a spur leads 0.1 mile up Coon Bluff, where it then leads 0.3 mile further to the end of the ridge, with fine views. From the junction, the main trail continues northeast to the Coon Bluff Recreation Site Road [FR 204-E] at 1.1 miles. An old vehicleway continues northeast to the Goldfield Recreation Site Road [FR 204A] at 2.1 miles. There another section then leads another 0.8 mi to the Salt River Recreation parking area at 3 miles.

Access. *At the western end:* leave Bush Highway on FR 169 at the junction for Phon D. Sutton Recreation Site; drive only 215' where a dirt road on the right leads 100' to a parking loop. The trail leaves on the right just before the end of the loop. *At the southern end of the middle of the section,* take the Coon Bluff Recreation Site Road [FR 204-E] for ½ mile, where the trail crosses (both directions signed). *At the northern end of the middle section,* 1¼ miles further along Bush Highway take the Goldfield Recreation Site Road [FR 204-A] for 1¼ miles to its end; the trailhead is at the southwest corner of the parking area. For the new section there is no good public parking; the Salt River Recreation lot is open on weekends and crowded with tubers, and closed on weekdays at least part of the year. (The trailhead is mid-way along the western edge of the huge parking area.)

Maps. *Our map 27.* The USGS 1:24,000 Stewart Mountain quadrangle (1964) does not show the trail.

Read Down ↓	Detailed Trail Description	Read Up ↑

0.00 Leave parking area (1,450'), go thru fence in 60', turning right 25' beyond at trail sign. 2.07
0.09 Cross main wash. 1.98
0.30 Top of rise; parallel highway on R. 1.77
0.31 **Junction:** avoid trail of use heading slightly L. 1.76
0.37 **Important junction (4-way):** trail R is somewhat obscure; follow wash 0.20 mi to spur road off Bush Highway [*NOTE:* near road, you have to divert to R to pass thru fence (use care), then turn L to road loop]. *For trail L up Coon Bluff, see below.* 1.70
0.43 Cross wash. 1.64
0.57 Descend more steadily. 1.50
0.73 Cross small wash. 1.34
0.77 Cross small wash. Cross bottom of bluff. 1.30
0.94 Cross small wash, then another in 300'. 1.13
1.05 Sign, fence. 1.02
1.06 Parking loop. 1.01
1.10 **Junction:** FR 204-E (1,410'). Trail continues across the road. 0.97
1.12 Go thru gate. Trail sign 25' beyond. [*NOTE:* there are many trails of use on this section.] 0.95
1.36 Cross small wash. 0.71
1.47 Cross small wash. 0.60
1.56 Cross small wash. 0.51
1.85 **Junction:** keep R where trail of use heads L [ends]. 0.22
1.93 Cross major wash in valley. 0.14
1.97 **Junction:** avoid trail of use sharp R. 0.10
2.06 Trail sign; gate 25' beyond. 0.01
2.07 Parking area (1,390') of Goldfield Recreation Site [FR 204A]. Trail continuation is 575' (0.11 mi) to R along edge of parking area. 0.00

0.00 Leave eastern end of parking area on S at sign. 0.84
0.23 **Junction (4-way):** cross old vehicleway. 0.61
0.29 **Junction:** turn R on vehicleway. 0.55
0.34 **Junction:** vehicleway again. Parallel wash on R, ascending gradually. 0.50
0.84 Trail ends at parking area and fence, gate, and sign near parking lot of Salt River Recreation (total of 3.02 mi from start at Phon D. Sutton Recreation Site Road). 0.00

Spur up Coon Bluff

Access. At 0.37 mile heading east on the Salt River Trail [100], or at 1.7 miles heading west from the Goldfield Recreation Site.

Read Down ↓	Detailed Trail Description	Read Up ↑

0.00 Leave main Trail [100] (1,480') and ascend NW on old vehicleway. 0.65
0.14 **Junction:** reach open plateau on end of bluff with views. To L, trails of use lead up summits to W and to old mine site in valley. Go R, following cairns. 0.51
0.23 **Junction:** join old mine road, turn L (1,560'), side-hilling up Coon Bluff. 0.42
0.24 Keep L on better footway. Steady ascent. 0.41

0.33   **Junction:** join trail (old vehicleway) on crest (1,580'). Views. Keep L (N).
[Sharp R, trail leads 0.15 mi to a summit, then descends to bottom at 0.49
mi, where one must follow the barbed wire fence L for 175' to 0.52 mi.] 0.32

0.41   **Junction:** on summit, trail (old vehicleway) descends steeply R, straight
down 0.27 mi to Coon Bluff Recreation Site [see below]. Excellent viewpoint
here of Goldfield Mountains, 4 Peaks, "Red Mountain," Bradshaws.
To continue, descend NW on old vehicleway along crest 0.24

0.42   **Junction:** trail L descends to valley. 0.23

0.48   **Junction:** poor (re-vegetated) track descends on R. 0.17

0.51   **Junction:** vehicle travelway on R. Ascend gradually. 0.14

0.53   **Junction:** on crest, poor trail descends on R. Go up and down along crest. 0.12

0.65   Trail ends at last peak (1,593'). Good viewpoint over junction of Salt &
Verde Rivers. 0.00

Coon Bluff

General Description. The first part of this unofficial trail from Coon Bluff
Recreation Site requires crossing a barbed-wire fence. It then ascends
steadily up the side of the Bluff for 0.3 mile, ascent 260', giving good views
over the valley and toward distant mountains. At the top is a branch of trail
[100] which can be followed down to the main trail and back toward the
Recreation Site.

Access. On Bush Highway, pass FR 169 and take the next road left (FR
204E, about 1.6 miles) to Coon Bluff Recreation Site. There are two paved
parking areas, one after the other. Park near the far end of the first area.
The trail leaves near the "reserved" parking sign and is not very obvious at its
start, but it can be seen ascending the side of a small ridge. Cross the
barbed-wire fence with care to pick up this route.

Maps. *Our map 27.* The USGS 1:24,000 Stewart Mountain quadrangle
(1964) does not show the trail.

Read Down ↓	Detailed Trail Description	Read Up ↑
0.00	Leave first parking area (1,340') Cross small wash, head up slope, cross barbed wire fence (no gate) in 100'.	0.27
0.04	Old concrete foundations on L. Ascend.	0.23
0.21	**Junction:** track descends sharp R. Ascend more steadily.	0.06
0.27	**Junction:** on flat area on summit (1,600') is branch of Salt River Trail [100]. Excellent viewpoint here. Turn R for 0.24 mi to end of Bluff, or 0.41 mi to L to main branch of [100].	0.00

[462] Saguaro Lake Vista Trail

General Description. From the road, the trail immediately starts to climb
past a ramada to a spur to another ramada on the right at 0.1 mile and yet
another ramada at 0.3 mile. A four-way junction (with good views) is reached

at a ridge crest at 0.4 mile, where there is another ramada on the left. From here the main trail drops briefly to reach the exit road from the Recreation Area at 0.6 mile. (From the 4-way junction a well-worn non-system trail, much used by equestrians, ascends northward near the crest with ever-widening views to Summit 1938 at 0.8 mile. From here the views toward Saguaro Lake, the Four Peaks, and the Goldfield Mountains are superb. The trail then drops a further 0.4 mile to Bush Highway, which is the easiest approach to the viewpoint.) Ascent is 60' to the 4-way junction. There is a 20' drop on the main trail to the road. The side-trail to Summit 1938 has 360' of ascent from the lake; there is then a 380' descent to its end at Bush Highway.

Access. *From Saguaro Lake,* find the trail at the far end of the road loop along the lake at Saguaro del Norte Recreation Area, past the boat launching areas and just before a toilet on the bank on the left (sign). *From FR 206B* [Saguaro del Norte exit road], the trail starts at a sign only 100' from Bush Highway. *From Bush Highway,* the non-designated side-trail (unsigned) leaves opposite a dirt road [FR 3566] that enters Bush Highway at a sharp angle. This is 0.3 mile south of Butcher Jones Road and 0.4 mile north of Saguaro del Norte exit road.

Maps. *Our Map 28.* The USGS 1:24,000 Stewart Mountain and Mormon Flat Dam quadrangles (1964, photoinspected 1978) cover the approach but do not show the trail.

Read Down ↓	Detailed Trail Description	Read Up ↑
0.00	At trail sign (1,560'), just W of toilet, go uphill and pass trail to toilet in 80'. Head W.	0.58
0.04	Switchback to R.	0.54
0.05	Ramada on L. Continue N on steady ascent, then head W.	0.53
0.14	**Junction:** sign points to ramada on R (215'), and to "West Ramadas" on continuation of this trail.	0.44
0.21	Cross wash, head S on level.	0.37
0.29	**Junction:** ramada on L (1,620'). Head R (W).	0.29
0.33	Bear L (SW).	0.24
0.35	Bear W, ascend.	0.22
0.42	**Junction (4-way):** ramada straight ahead 120' (viewpoint); half-right is main trail, descending. *[Details: sharp R is non-system trail, ascending minor ridge and leveling off on crest at 0.23 mi. Switchback to L up trenched section of trail to reach crest, then go up and down it, reaching the summit at 0.39 mi (1,938') with excellent views. Continue down ridge, switchbacking several times, then going over a rise to reach Bush Highway at 0.78 mi.]*	0.16
0.58	Trail ends at Saguaro del Norte exit road. Bush Highway is 100' to R.	0.00

[463] Butcher Jones Trail WEST to EAST

Introduction. Excellent water and mountain views are almost constant from this trail, which is closed to motor vehicles. The only potential disadvantage for some users is the lack of solitude due to the large number of people and the noise of power boats on the lake.

General Description. This trail starts from a popular picnic and beach site, leading along the lake shore first as a paved 0.3-mile barrier-free interpretive nature trail. From 0.6 mile it ascends onto a crest, with side-trails to the lake shore at 0.9, 1.7, 1.9 (Camper Cove), and 2.5 miles. The trail then descends to parallel the lake shore, finally ascending onto a spur and ending at 3.3 miles. Total elevation gain is 400'. Allow extra time for exploring side-trails.

Access. *At the western end:* from Bush Highway 0.8 mile north of the Saguaro del Norte Recreation Site turn-off, follow FR 166 east for 1.7 miles to the parking loop (one-way road) within the Butcher Jones Recreation Site. The trailhead, with sign indicating Saguaro Lake Nature Trail, is at 1.9 miles.

Maps. *Our Map 28.* The USGS 1:24,000 Stewart Mountain and Mormon Flat Dam quadrangles (1964, photoinspected 1978) show roads but not the trail.

Read Down ↓	Detailed Trail Description	Read Up ↑
0.00	Leave road at beach (paved trail, elev. 1,570'). In 100' turn L.	3.25
0.04	Turn R (winds along cove).	3.21
0.14	Interpretive sign: "What is a Riparian Area"?	3.11
0.25	Sign: "Wild Anglers."	3.00
0.27	**Junction:** on R is view of marina. Paving ends; keep straight on.	2.98
0.29	Gate at Peregrine Point.	2.96
0.53	Trail winds up and down about 20' above the water.	2.72
0.55	Peregrine Cove. Start ascent to W.	2.70
0.85	**Junction:** "Shoreline Access - 1/4" on R. [This side-trail crosses minor gullies at 0.09 and 0.16 mi, then along the shoreline from 0.19 mi. Beach access is at 0.20 mi. At 0.23 mi the trail ascends away from the shore, crosses a small gully at 0.27 mi, and reaches its end at 0.32 mi.]	2.40
0.95	Cross small gully.	2.30
1.05	**Junction:** at top of rise, trail of use along minor crest R. Viewpoint on crest. Head into valley.	2.20
1.13	Switchback to R at gully.	2.12
1.21	Top of rise. Descend gradually, side-hilling.	2.04
1.24	End of crest.	2.01
1.29	Trail bends to R.	1.96
1.35	Top of rise (high point). Switchback to L. Superb viewpoint. Head E.	1.90
1.43	Descend with trail in view ahead.	1.82
1.50	Cross ravine, switchback to R. . Descend steadily.	1.75
1.60	Trail of use on R. to point. Turn L, on level, then descend.	1.65
1.67	Turn R at ravine and cross it.	1.58
1.69	**Junction:** Camper's Cove Access Trail to the R (says 1/4 mi). [On this trail, head S, reaching the beach at only 0.10 mi.] (1,630'). Head E & NE.	1.56
1.79	Top of rise. Head E.	1.46
1.83	Switchback to R (S).	1.42
1.89	**Junction:** "Shoreline Access 1/2" [Details: descend, reaching a wash bottom at 240', turning L at 275', then ascending to R. Cross small gullies at 0.12, 0.15, and 0.18 mi. Turn L (E) and ascend at 0.18 mi; cross a moderate gully at 0.25 mi, pass a huge rock above on the L at 0.36 mi, then reach beach in a pleasant area at 0.40 mi. *NOTE:* at this point, you can ascend N up a small ridge for 180' beside a rock pinnacle, then L to a top with excellent views in 325'.] On main trail, descend into deep ravine.	1.36
1.93	Top of rise.	1.32

2.20	Ease grade of ascent.	1.05
2.34	Keep L.	0.91
2.42	Viewpoint at top of rise.	0.83
2.44	**Junction:** trail of use R 70' to viewpoint on knob. Descend to N.	0.81
2.53	Trail sign "Burro Cove Shore Access 1/2". [Details: head E on level trail. At 300' trail side-hills, with viewpoint over lake and Four Peaks. Cross over crest at 0.11 mi, descend; head E at 0.23 mi, reaching excellent viewpoint at 0.27 mi. Bear R along edge, descend to water at 0.34 mi.] For main trail, continue NE.	0.72
2.60	Cross wash.	0.65
2.66	**Junction:** trail of use R 120' to beach.	0.59
2.79	Dump on R (mess from boaters).	0.46
3.06	**Junction:** obscure trail R to beach in 100'.	0.19
3.14	Enter rocky area; trail is less distinct.	0.11
3.23	Trail becomes rocky and ascends.	0.02
3.25	Trail ends on hillside.	0.00

Butcher Jones Trail at Saguaro Lake

USDA Tonto National Forest

Bartlett Reservoir

Introduction. Bartlett Reservoir is formed by Bartlett Dam, constructed in 1936-39 on the Verde River. The dam is 800 feet long and 283 feet high, forming a lake 12 miles long with a 33-mile shore-line. Maximum depth is 174 feet. The reservoir's normal elevation is 1,798' above sea level. It is one of 6 dams on the Salt and Verde Rivers to provide irrigation water (and in some cases, but not this one) hydroelectric power. It is managed jointly by the Salt River Project, Tonto National Forest, and Arizona Game & Fish Department.

Two of the trails described here were built by partnership with the Federal Bureau of Prisons in 1993.

Access. From Phoenix, take Cave Creek Road (or Scottsdale Road from Scottsdale) to Carefree Highway. Continue north to Cave Creek Road (which becomes FR 24). Take it east to a signed junction (FR 19) to Bartlett Reservoir and Horseshoe Dam (see access map). Head east across several ranges and valleys, with views becoming more impressive, to a road junction at 6.4 miles. Horseshoe Dam Road (FR 205) goes left. Continue straight ahead on FR 19, to the junction with FR 459 at 13.3 miles. Here you head down the hill to the Jojoba Trail [511] or turn left for the Palo Verde Trail [512]. See details with each trail description.

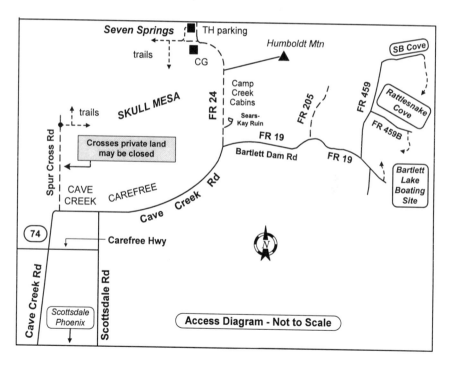

- 245 -

Map (for all trails). *Our Map 29.* The USGS 1:24,000 Maverick Mountain and Bartlett Dam quadrangles (1964) cover the terrain, but do not show the trails or the complete location of the approach roads.

[511] Jojoba Trail SOUTH to NORTH

Introduction. Good views of the Lower Sonoran desert, Bartlett Reservoir, and surrounding high mountains (the Mazatzals on the east) are the features of this trail, which parallels the shoreline north of the Jojoba Boating Site. A quick return via road (although slightly longer in measured distance) can also be made. The entire trip can take as little as 2 hours or else a half day.

General Description. The trail heads north, with many ups and downs, in and out of coves, with periodic views of the lake and surrounding mountains. At 0.3 and 0.7 mile there are two side-trails to the beach. Then at 0.8 mile there is a nice side-trail for 0.4 mile to a promontory jutting into the lake. The main trail continues up and down, ending at 1.3 miles at FR 459A. Total elevation gain is 320' (if the side-trail is taken, add 80' for a total of 400').

Access. *At the southern end:* from FR 194 at the north side of the parking area at Jojoba Boating Site, 0.6 mile east of the junction with FR 19 (Bartlett Dam Road). *At the northern end,* from FR 459A[1] on the west side of Rattlesnake Cove Recreation Site, 0.4 mile downhill from FR 459.

Read Down ↓	Detailed Trail Description	Read Up ↑
0.00	From FR 194 (1,840') parking area, cross paved road, start trail, turn L, then R in 120'. Head N.	1.32
0.04	Switchback to R, then turn L.	1.28
0.06	Top of rise.	1.26
0.09	Turn L (winds among boulders).	1.23
0.13	Top of rise.	1.19
0.15	Switchback to R, descend.	1.17
0.18	Bottom of descent.	1.14
0.19	Cross wash, ascend NE out of it.	1.13
0.20	Take steps up steady stretch. Head E, paralleling wash.	1.12
0.23	Ascend steadily to NE.	1.09
0.24	Top of rise (1,850').	1.08
0.26	Switchback to R, head SE, then level off.	1.06
0.28	Descend to S, then to SE.	1.04
0.29	Switchback to L.	1.03
0.30	Turn R.	1.02
0.32	**Junction:** trail-of-use on R onto beach in 250'. Ascend NE.	1.00
0.34	Top of rise (1,860').	0.98
0.37	Bottom of descent.	0.95
0.40	Top of rise, descend gradually to E, then to SE along promontory.	0.92
0.43	Turn L, off of it, to N.	0.89
0.47	Bottom of descent, ascend steadily.	0.85
0.54	Turn L onto ridge.	0.78

---

[1]May be signed 459A, but officially it is 459B. There has been some confusion on this.

0.56	Top of rise (1,910'). Descend to N just W of crest.	0.76
0.65	Turn R on crest, off of it.	0.67
0.66	**Junction:** trail of use on R to cove. Switchback to L (W). *[Exactly half-way.]*	0.66
0.68	Cross wash.	0.64
0.71	Cross wash.	0.61
0.73	On minor crest, ascend to NW, then to W.	0.59
0.81	Switchback to L, ascend.	0.51
0.83	**Important junction:** side-trail R leads to promontory with good views of Bartlett Reservoir. *[Details: Head NE, reaching the top of a rise on a hump in 300'. Go down then up again, switchbacking down at 0.23 mi, then off the crest at 0.28 mi, crossing a rocky, narrow crest again at 0.36. Switchback down to the L at 0.38 mi, reaching end of point of land at 0.41 mi.]*	0.49
0.88	Top of rise, level off for 200', head W.	0.44
0.94	Switchback to R, descend steadily.	0.38
0.96	Switchback to L, then to R.	0.36
1.01	Forest Service trail sign.	0.31
1.02	Bottom, at cove. Barriers for 4WDs. Go up sandy vehicleway.	0.30
1.30	Gate (closed).	0.02
1.32	**Junction:** FR 459A. This trail ends.	0.00

From the end on FR 459A, you can retrace your steps, or walk back the roads (1.6 miles). To do so, go up the road thru a gate to reach FR 459 at 0.4 mile. Go left on it for 0.7 mile to a junction with FR 19, then downhill toward Jojoba Boating Site another 0.6 mile to return to the trailhead parking.

[512] Palo Verde Trail SOUTH to NORTH

Rattlesnake Cove to SB Cove Recreation Site

Introduction. This is a much longer trail than the Jojoba Trail (almost 3 times as long), with similar scenery. For those with more time, it offers a longer hike. It has much exposure and can be very hot in the summer months.

General Description. This new trail leads up and down, in and out of boulders, washes, and over high hilltops with excellent views of the lake and surrounding mountains. At 2.9 miles there is a junction (the loop to the right leads around the lake side for 1.2 miles to rejoin the main trail). The main trail continues north for 0.3 mile, then meets the loop trail returning, and continues for another half mile to SB Cove. Total elevation gain is several hundred feet, but due to the innumerable short pitches we have not attempted to sum these up. Be aware that this trail can be very hot, there is little shade, and more ascent and descent than you might expect. It is best taken in the cooler months. *Carry enough water.*

Access. *At the southern end:* from the junction of FR 24 and FR 19, east of Carefree (Bartlett Dam Road), head east across several ranges and valleys, with views becoming more impressive, to a road junction at 6.4 miles. Horseshoe Dam Road (FR 205) goes left. Continue straight ahead on FR 19, to the junction with FR 459 at 13.3 miles, turn left on it, then turn right at FR 459A at 14 miles. Descend this road to the lower parking area at 14.8 miles.

Find the trail northeast of the bottom of two sets of steps at the northern end of the parking area. *At the northern end:* from SB Cove Recreation Site. From the junction of FR 459 and FR 459A at Rattlesnake Cove turn-off (at 14 miles), continue north to SB Cove at 16.2 miles.

Read Down ↓	Detailed Trail Description	Read Up ↑
0.00	From Rattlesnake Cove Picnic Area, walk to N end, descend both sets of steps, find trail heading NE. Cross two small washes; side-hill above Bartlett Reservoir.	3.69
0.05	Round end of promontory, enter valley.	3.64
0.11	Switchback to R at end of cove.	3.58
0.15	Switchback to L, ascending.	3.54
0.17	Descend to cove.	3.52
0.23	**Junction:** with trail of use ahead to beach, turn L.	3.46
0.26	**Junction:** keep R where trail of use goes straight.	3.43
0.28	End of cove.	3.41
0.40	Reach shoreline; ascend.	3.29
0.42	Top of rise.	3.27
0.45	Switchback to L, then to R in 30'.	3.24
0.46	Top of rise.	3.23
0.56	Cross major wash and ascend steadily.	3.13
0.62	Viewpoint at end of crest. High route continues with very fine views.	3.07
0.66	Round end of small indentation on lake shore.	3.03
0.70	Cross small rocky wash; ascend to.	2.99
0.79	**Junction:** Top of rise with fine viewpoint to R. Descend and side-hill.	2.90
0.98	Switchback to R, then L on descent.	2.71
1.13	**Junction:** on R is short spur to viewpoint. Descend to NW, then to SW.	2.56
1.19	Cross wash, Switchback to L and to R.	2.50
1.22	Shoreline at cove.	2.47
1.23	Switchback to R. 35' beyond is landmark: switchback to L under rock face.	2.46
1.25	Switchback to R.	2.44
1.27	Switchback to L and to R.	2.42
1.30	Switchback to R and to L.	2.39
1.37	Wind around near lake shore.	2.32
1.39	Cross wash.	2.30
1.42	Cross broad wash and ascend.	2.27
1.50	Top of rise, again in 100' and in 200'.	2.19
1.60	End of minor crest.	2.09
1.69	Cross rock-bottomed small wash.	2.00
1.75	Viewpoint just off trail on R. Then circle this hump on ridge.	1.94
1.85	Descend crest above double cove.	1.84
1.87	Switchback to L.	1.82
1.92	Cross wash area above cove.	1.77
1.99	Switchback to L, then to R.	1.70
2.06	Top of crest with good views. Switchback to L, ascending to R of crest.	1.63
2.12	On crest again with fine views; drop off it in 125', then regain crest.	1.57
2.26	Turn L (W) onto subsidiary crest for 100'.	1.43
2.41	Top of crest. Descend SE.	1.28
2.50	Switchback to R.	1.19
2.61	Cross dirt road above major cove.	1.08
2.66	Cross wash, ascend L.	1.03

2.71	Top of rise.	0.98
2.82	Turn L, then to R (N).	0.87
2.90	**Junction:** main trail ascends wash to L. Loop trail continues straight ahead, 1.22 mi to next junction, or 0.91 mi longer than the main trail. *[See separate description below.]*	0.79
3.00	Switchback to R.	0.69
3.07	Turn L (use care).	0.62
3.21	**Junction:** trail R is loop returning. Descend.	0.48
3.28	Top of rise.	0.41
3.31	Switchback to L.	0.38
3.34	Cross wash. In 35' pass cove.	0.35
3.36	Switchback to L, then to L again in 100'.	0.33
3.50	**Junction:** trail of use on R.	0.19
3.64	Eroding section above beach.	0.05
3.68	Enter small ravine, then turn R in a branch of it after 20' (Use care here). *Note for the opposite direction:* the start of the trail is just E of the latrine.	0.01
3.69	SB Cove area (1,820') and dirt road. No trail sign here.	0.00

Loop Trail (Side-Trail)

Read Down ↓	Detailed Trail Description	Read Up ↑
0.00	From **junction** at 2.90 mi from wash above Rattlesnake Cove (0.79 mi from SB Cove), head N (1,820').	1.22
0.21	Cross wash	1.01
0.34	Top of rise	0.88
0.39	Cross wash.	0.77
0.40	Switchback to R.	0.76
0.46	Round end of cove	0.70
0.53	At beach.	0.63
0.60	Cross wash.	0.58
0.72	Just above beach.	0.50
0.78	Switchback to L. In 85' switchback to R, then to L. Trail continues with many turns, up and down.	0.44
1.05	On crest.	0.17
1.22	**Junction:** in wash, just above beach in cove, are trail signs for main trail. The main trail continues N for 0.48 mi to SB Cove. (1,810').	0.00

Appendix A. Glossary

AGGLOMERATE – A volcanic rock consisting of rounded and angular fragments.

ARROYO – A dry, steep-walled canyon [Spanish].

BAJADA – A gradually sloping alluvial fan below steep mountains.

BERM – A narrow ledge or shelf along a slope.

CAIRN – A pile of stones used to mark a trail or trail junction.

CALDERA– A large crater formed by a volcanic explosion or the collapse of a volcanic cone.

COL – A pass between two peaks or a gap in a ridge.

DRAW – A small valley that narrows as it rises.

ESCARPMENT – A steep slope or long cliff resulting from erosion or faulting and separating two relatively level areas of differing elevations.

GORGE – A deep narrow passage with precipitous rock sides, enclosed between mountains.

JOG – To "jog" left or right on a trail or road means to join it briefly and then diverge from it.

NON-DESIGNATED TRAIL [NDT] – In Phoenix, a trail of use that should not be used by the public.

RAMADA – A man-made shelter from sun and rain, usually for picnicking.

SAG – A minor depression, less dramatic than a pass or canyon.

SIDE-HILL – As a verb, means to angle along a hillside without going straight up.

SPUR – The lateral ridge projecting from a mountain or or mountain range.

SWITCHBACK – A sudden reversal of direction, like a "hairpin bend" on a road.

TANK – A depression (natural or artificial) that holds water for stock.

TINAJA – Another word [Spanish] for tank.

TRACK – A broad way, not as narrow as an ordinary trail. It may previously have been a constructed or unofficial road.

TRAILHEAD – Where the trail starts, usually at a road or ramada.

TRAIL OF USE – A minor or obscure trail developed by irregular usage, not constructed or designated. It often peters out or serves as a short-cut. In parts of the desert minimal use can create such a trail.

TRAVERSE – A long segment of switchbacking trail that leads across a hillside.

TUFF – Solidified layer of volcanic ash or other ejected material.

VEHICLE TRAVELWAY or **VEHICLEWAY** – A term used by some agencies for a way created by unplanned vehicular use (i.e., not a constructed road).

WASH – An eroded channel that is ordinarily dry except after prolonged or intense rain.

Appendix B. Resources

Arizona State Parks
1300 West Washington Street, Phoenix 85007
(Phone: 602-542-4174 general; 800-285-3703 from [520] area code)
(State Trails Coordinator 602-542-7116)

Lost Dutchman State Park
6109 North Apache Trail, Apache Junction 85219
(Phone: 520-982-4485)

Bureau of Land Management, Phoenix Field Office
2015 West Deer Valley Rd., Phoenix, AZ 85027
(Phone: 623-580-5500)

Forest Service, USDA, Tonto National Forest
2324 East McDowell Road, Phoenix 85006
(Phone: 602-225-5230)

Mesa Ranger District
26 N. MacDonald, Mesa 85211-5800; P.O. Box 5800
(Phone: 480-610-3300)

Cave Creek Ranger District
40202 N. Cave Creek Rd.
Scottsdale 85262
(Phone: 480-488-3441)

Glendale, City of, Leisure Services
5850 West Glendale Avenue, Glendale 85301
(Phone: 623-930-2830)

Maricopa County Parks and Recreation Department
3475 West Durango Street, Phoenix 85009
(General phone: 602-506-2930)
Cave Creek 623-465-0431
Estrella 623-932-3811
McDowell 480-471-0173
Usery 480-984-0032
White Tank 623-935-2505

Phoenix Parks, Recreation & Library Department
200 West Washington Street, 16th Floor, Phoenix 85003
(Phone: 602-262-6862)

Central/East District Office [Camelback, Papago]
1001 North 52nd Street, Phoenix 85008
(Phone: 602-262-4599)

Northeast District Office [Lookout, Shadow, North Mountain/Shaw Butte, Stony, Squaw]
17642 North 40th Street, Phoenix 85032
(Phone: 602-262-7901, Ranger Station)

Northwest District Office [Deem Hills]
3901 West Glendale Avenue, Phoenix 85051
(Phone: 602-262-6575)

South District Office [South Mountain]
10919 South Central Avenue, Phoenix 85040
(Phone: 602-534-6324 Environmental Education Center; 602-261-8457 gatehouse)

Scottsdale, City of, Parks & Recreation
3939 Civic Center Blvd
Scottsdale, AZ 85251
(Phone: 480-312-2722)

Appendix C. Bibliography

Barnes WC & Granger B. 1988. *Arizona Place Names.* Tucson: University of Arizona Press.

Bowers JE. 1993. *Shrubs and Trees of the Southwestern Deserts.* Tucson: Southwest Parks and Monuments Association.

Chronic H. 1986. *Roadside Geology of Arizona.* Missoula, Montana: Mountain Press Publishing Company.

Desert Botanical Gardens. 1988. *Desert Wildflowers.* Phoenix: Arizona Highways Magazine.

Dodge NN. 1985. *Flowers of the Southwestern Deserts.* Tucson: Southwest Parks and Monuments Association.

Farrand J., Jr. & Udvardy MDF. 1994. *National Audubon Society Field Guide to North American Birds: Western Region, 2nd ed.* New York: Alfred A. Knopf.

Holbert H. 1979. *South Mountain Park: The Time and the Man.* Privately published by Harry Holbert, printed by Hearne's Bookcrafts of Riverside, 3669 Sixth St., Riverside, CA 92501.

Little, EL. 1980. *National Audubon Society Field Guide to North American Trees: Western Region.* New York: Alfred A. Knopf.

Luckingham B. 1995. *Phoenix: The History of a Southwestern Metropolis.* Tucson: University of Arizona Press.

McMahon JA. 1985. *Deserts (Audubon Society Nature Guides).* New York: Alfred A. Knopf.

Nations D & Stump E. 1997. *Geology of Arizona, 2nd Edition.* Dubuque, IA: Kendall/Hunt Publishing Company.

Spellenberg, R. 1979. *National Audubon Society Field Guide to North American Wildflowers: Western Region.* New York: Alfred A. Knopf.

Stoops ED & Wright A. 1993. *Snakes and Other Reptiles of the Southwest.* Phoenix: Golden West Publishers.

Van Cleve PW. 1973. *An Open Space Plan for the Phoenix Mountains.* Phoenix: City Government.

Weir B. 1999. *Arizona Traveler's Handbook, 7th Edition.* Chico, CA: Moon Publishers.

How This Book Was Prepared

For those interested in details, here's how we did it:

Field data collection. USGS topograpgic maps, US Forest Service Geometronics revisions of some of those maps, special maps and some airphotos provided by the City of Phoenix and Maricopa County all were used. The City of Phoenix, City of Glendale, and Maricopa County also supplied site maps for new facilities. We had many meetings with knowledgeable personnel during this time. We utilized these maps and airphotos, a Thommen® Swiss altimeter, a compass, a trail measuring wheel (Rolatape®), and in recent years, a Magellan Trailblazer® and then a Garmin® GPS 45XL handheld Global Positioning System. These systems are accurate to within about 100 feet[1] but cannot always obtain a satellite fix when surrounded by trees or rocks. Accuracy was determined by measuring some trails twice, or in both directions.

Review. In all cases, drafts were sent to agencies for review, then re-edited.

---

[1]These devices acquire data from 3 or 4 satellites simultaneously, then calculate one's position. The satellite system is operated by the US Department of Defense, which has been concerned over the negative side of accuracy, namely usage for terrorist or enemy attacks. It has therefore introduced a random error ("Selective Access") so that the ideal resolution of the system is never reached. Federal agencies or others with special permission can gain full accuracy (of about 2-3 feet) by use of an approved decryption device or the use of an additional base station. It was recently announced that this limitation will be gradually eliminated over the next 10 years, so that very fine accuracy will be available to everyone.

Map Legend

Note:
(1) All local streets are not shown
(2) On some maps City of Phoenix where there is a high density of many trails, rough vehicleways and trails may not be clearly distinguished from each other and are then both shown as trails.

	Described	Not Described	
Paved road	————	————●	cul-de-sac
		━┓■	parking area
Unpaved, driveable	– – – – –	– – – – –	
Unpaved, 4-wheel drive only	=====	=====	
Main or major trail (with designation)	– – – – – Ⓒ	– – – – –	
— Charles M. Christiansen Trail*	·–·–·–·		
— Perl Charles Trail*	┝─┥─+─+─+─┥		
— Both coinciding*	●┼●┼●┼●┼●┼		
Minor or secondary trail			

Boundaries	– – — – —			
Water features (wash; canal; river; lake)	——·——	▬▬▬	～	⬭
Water tank	●			
Building	▬			
Gate	——┃——			
Ramada (where shown)	▱			
Spot elevation	· 2429			
Summit of importance	△ 2429			
Contour lines	—2000—			

*Phoenix Mountains Preserve

Map 1

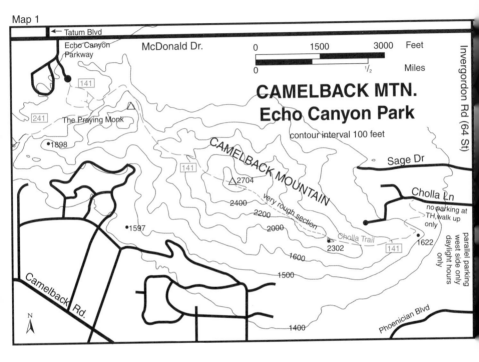

← Tatum Blvd

Echo Canyon
Parkway

McDonald Dr.

0   1500   3000   Feet

0   ½   Miles

CAMELBACK MTN.
Echo Canyon Park

contour interval 100 feet

141

241

The Praying Monk

•1898

CAMELBACK MOUNTAIN

141

△2704

2400

very rough section

2200

2000

•1597

Cholla Trail

2302

1600

1500

Invergordon Rd (64 St)

Sage Dr

Cholla Ln

no parking at
TH, walk up
only

1622

141

parallel parking
west side only
daylight hours
only

Camelback Rd.

N

Phoenician Blvd

1400

Map 2

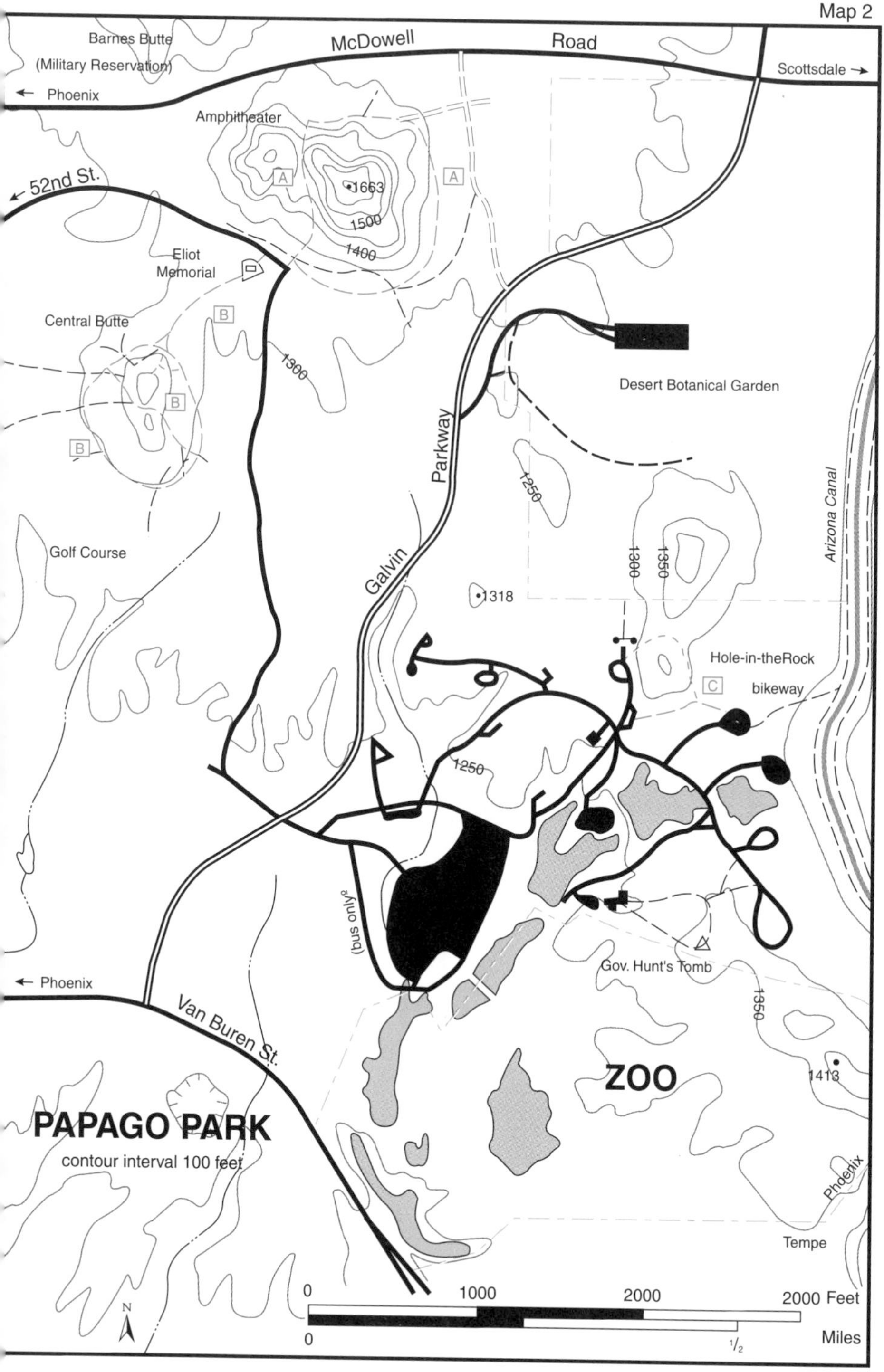

Barnes Butte
(Military Reservation)

McDowell Road

← Phoenix

Scottsdale →

Amphitheater

← 52nd St.

A

●1663

1500

1400

A

Eliot
Memorial

Central Butte

B

B

B

1300

Desert Botanical Garden

Parkway

1250

Golf Course

Galvin

1350

1300

Arizona Canal

●1318

Hole-in-the Rock

C

bikeway

1250

(bus only)

1250

Gov. Hunt's Tomb

← Phoenix

Van Buren St.

1350

PAPAGO PARK

contour interval 100 feet

ZOO

●1413

Phoenix

Tempe

N

| 0 | 1000 | 2000 | 2000 Feet |

| 0 | | 1/2 | Miles |

Map 3

LOOKOUT MOUNTAIN

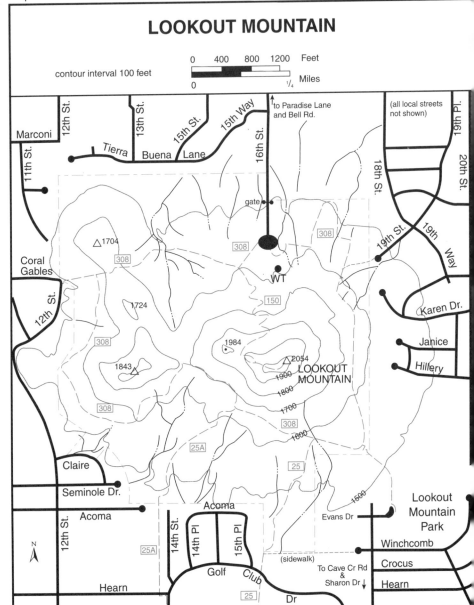

0   400   800   1200   Feet

contour interval 100 feet

0   ¹/₄   Miles

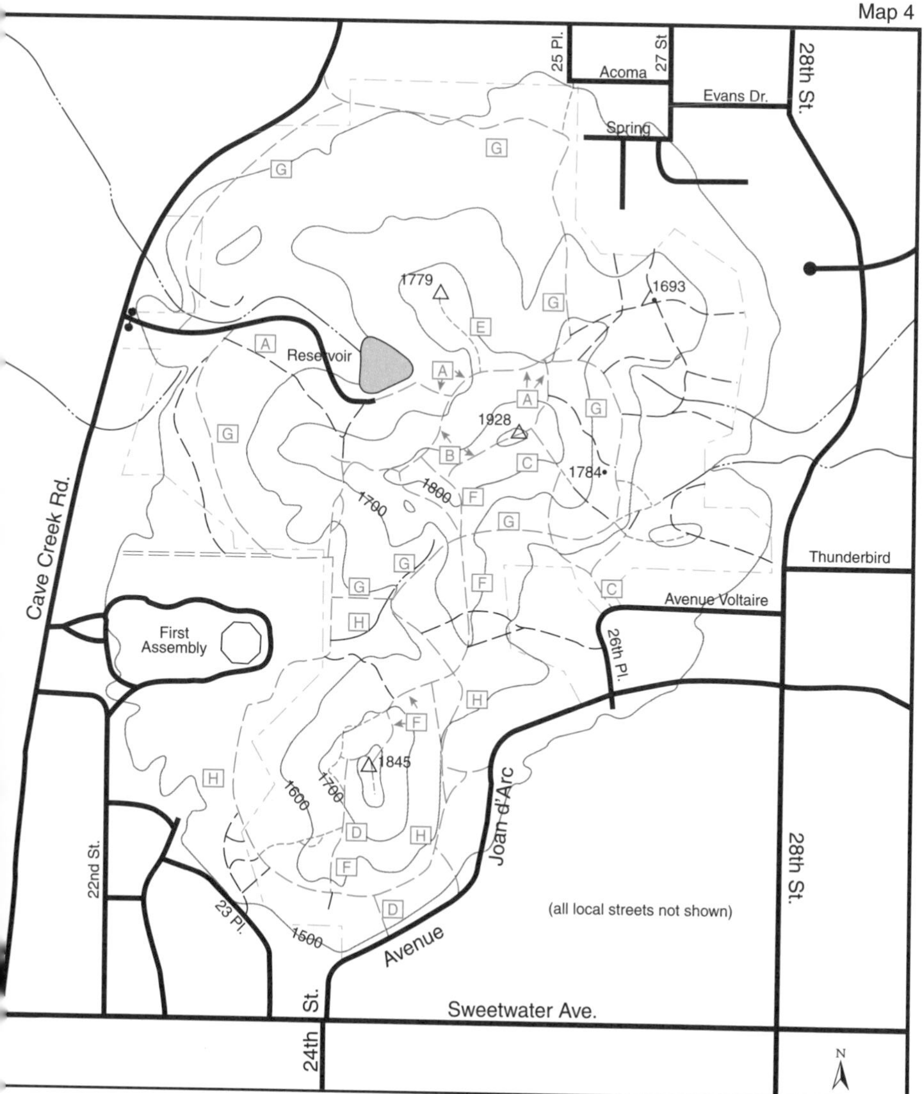

Map 4

25 Pl.

27 St

Acoma

28th St.

Evans Dr.

Spring

G

G

G

1779
△

E

1693

A

Reservoir

A

A

1928
△

G

G

B

C

1784

1700

1800

F

G

Thunderbird

G

F

C

Avenue Voltaire

G

H

First
Assembly

26th Pl.

H

F

H

1845
△

Joan-d'Arc

28th St.

H

1600

1700

D

H

22nd St.

F

(all local streets not shown)

23 Pl.

D

1500

Avenue

24th St.

Sweetwater Ave.

N

SHADOW MOUNTAIN

contour interval 100 feet

| 0 | 1000 | 2000 | 3000 Feet |

| 0 | | ¹/₂ | Miles |

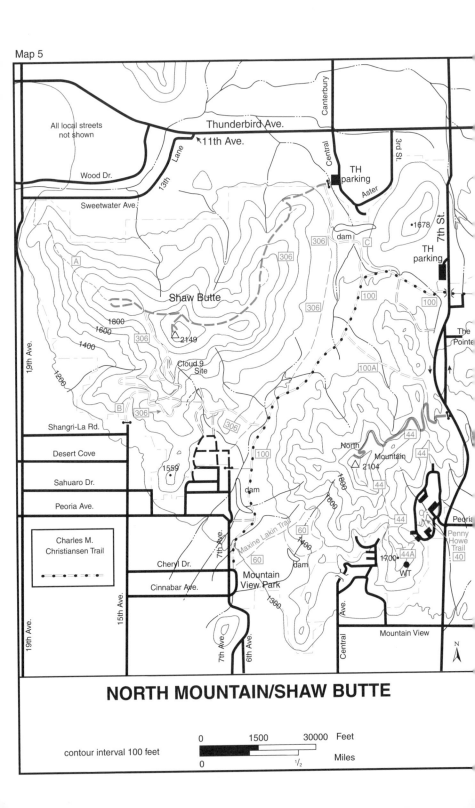

Map 5

NORTH MOUNTAIN/SHAW BUTTE

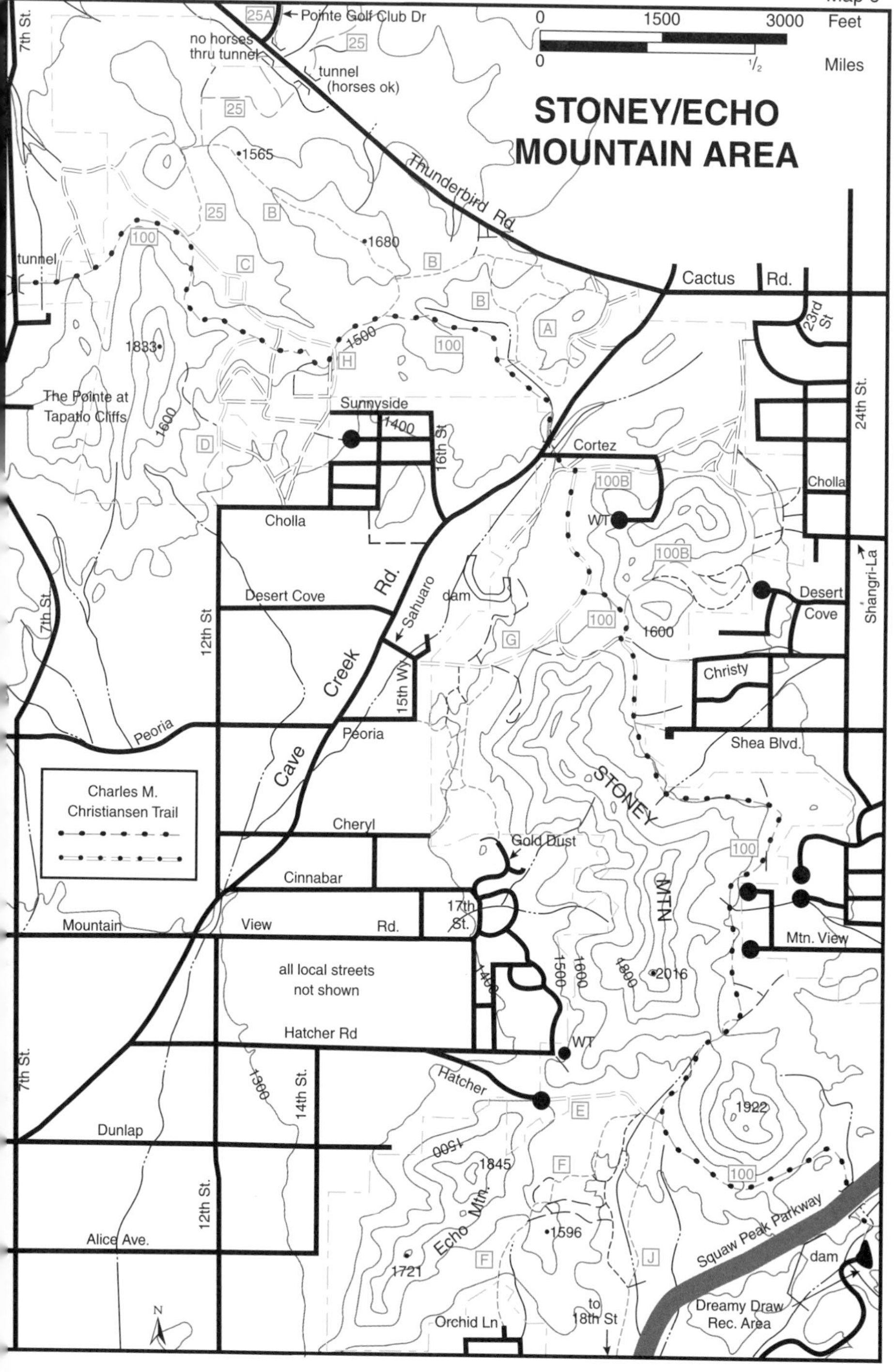

Map 6

STONEY/ECHO MOUNTAIN AREA

7th St.

25A ← Pointe Golf Club Dr
no horses
thru tunnel
25
tunnel
(horses ok)

0   1500   3000   Feet
0   ½   Miles

•1565

25   B

100   C   B

•1680   B

B

A   Cactus   Rd.

23rd St.

1500   100

1833•   H

24th St.

The Pointe at
Tapatio Cliffs   1600   Sunnyside   1400

16th St.   Cortez   Cholla

D   100B   Christy

Cholla   100B   WT

12th St.   Desert Cove   dam   100   1600   Desert Cove

Shangri-La

Sahuaro   G   Christy

7th St.   Peoria   15th W.   100

Cave   Peoria   Shea Blvd.

Creek   Rd.

Charles M.
Christiansen Trail   Cheryl   STONEY   100

•———•———•
•———•———•

Cinnabar   Gold Dust

Mountain   View   Rd.   17th
St.   MTN   Mtn. View

all local streets
not shown   •2016

1400   1500   1600   1800

Hatcher Rd   WT

14th St.   Hatcher   E   1922

1300   F

Dunlap   1500   1845   100

12th St.   •1596   Squaw Peak Parkway   dam

Alice Ave.   J   to
18th St   Dreamy Draw
Rec. Area

1721   F

N   Orchid Ln

Map 7

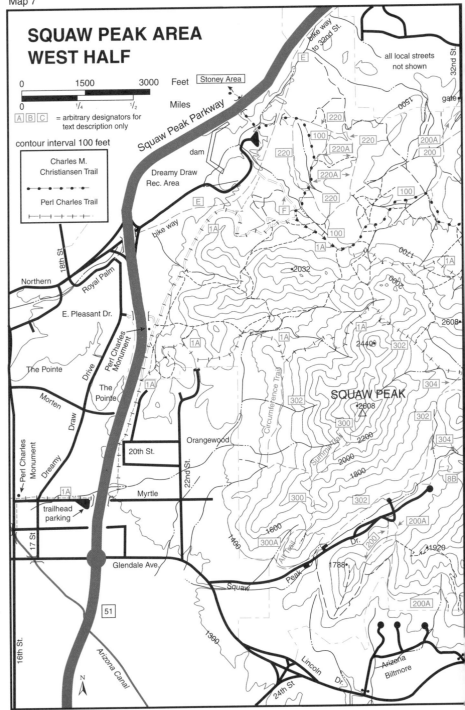

SQUAW PEAK AREA
WEST HALF

Feet | Miles

Stoney Area

A B C = arbitrary designators for text description only

contour interval 100 feet

Charles M. Christiansen Trail

Perl Charles Trail

all local streets not shown

gate

Squaw Peak Parkway

dam

Dreamy Draw Rec. Area

bike way to 32nd St.

32nd St.

1500

bike way

Northern

18th St.

Royal Palm

E. Pleasant Dr.

The Pointe

Perl Charles Monument

Drive

The Pointe

Morten

Draw

Dreamy

Perl Charles Monument

17 St

trailhead parking

20th St.

22nd St.

Orangewood

Myrtle

Glendale Ave.

Squaw

Circumference Trail

SQUAW PEAK

Summit Trail

Peak

Dr.

AH Trail

1788

1920

16th St.

51

Arizona Canal

N

24th St.

Lincoln

Dr.

Arizona Biltmore

2032

2608

2440

2608

1700

2000

2200

2200

2000

1800

1600

1400

1600

1300

2608

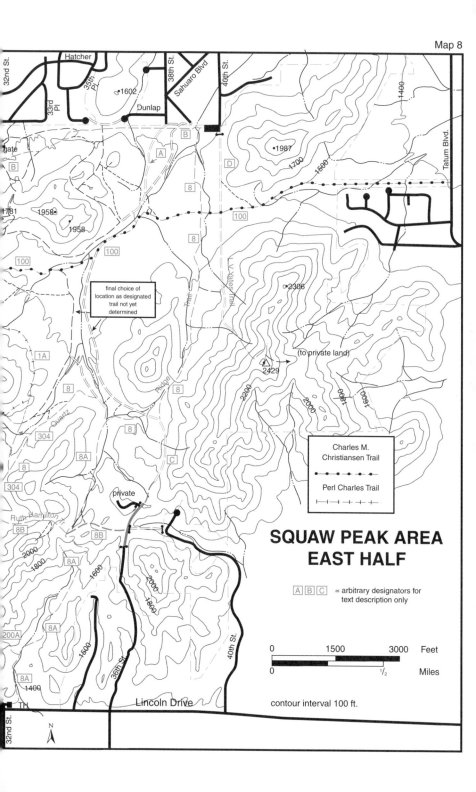

Map 8

Hatcher
32nd St.
35th Pl
38th St.
Sahuaro Blvd
40th St.
33rd Pl
•1602
Dunlap
1400
Tatum Blvd.
B
A
•1987
D
B
1700
1500
8
1781
1958•
100
100
1958
100
100

final choice of
location as designated
trail not yet
determined

•2306
Ridge Trail
L.V. Yates Trail

1A

(to private land)

8
2429
8

304

8
2200
2000

8A

1800
1600
1600

8
C

private

Charles M.
Christiansen Trail

Perl Charles Trail

304
8

Ruth Hamilton
8B
8B

2000
1800
8A
1600

SQUAW PEAK AREA
EAST HALF

A B C = arbitrary designators for
text description only

200A
8A
2000
1800
36th St.
40th St.

8A
1400
TH

0   1500   3000   Feet
0   ½   Miles

32nd St.

Lincoln Drive

contour interval 100 ft.

N

Map 9

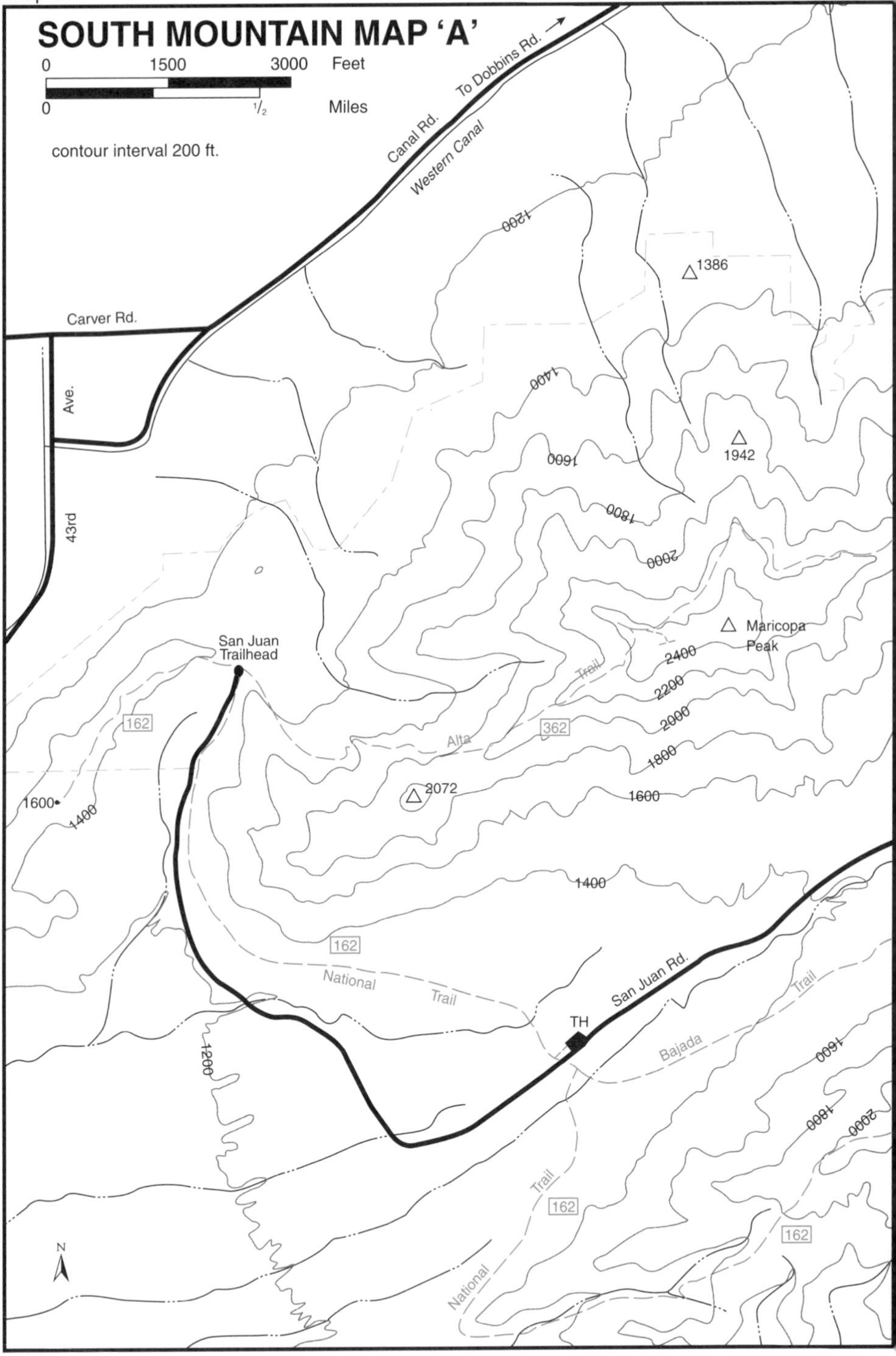

SOUTH MOUNTAIN MAP 'A'

0   1500   3000   Feet

0   1/2   Miles

contour interval 200 ft.

Canal Rd. To Dobbins Rd.

Western Canal

Carver Rd.

Ave.

43rd

1200

△ 1386

1400

1600

△ 1942

1800

2000

San Juan
Trailhead

△ Maricopa
Peak

Trail

2400

2200

2000

162

Alta

362

1800

1600

1400

△ 2072

1600•

1400

162

National   Trail

San Juan Rd.

Trail

TH

Bajada

1600

1800

2000

1200

162

National

Trail

162

N

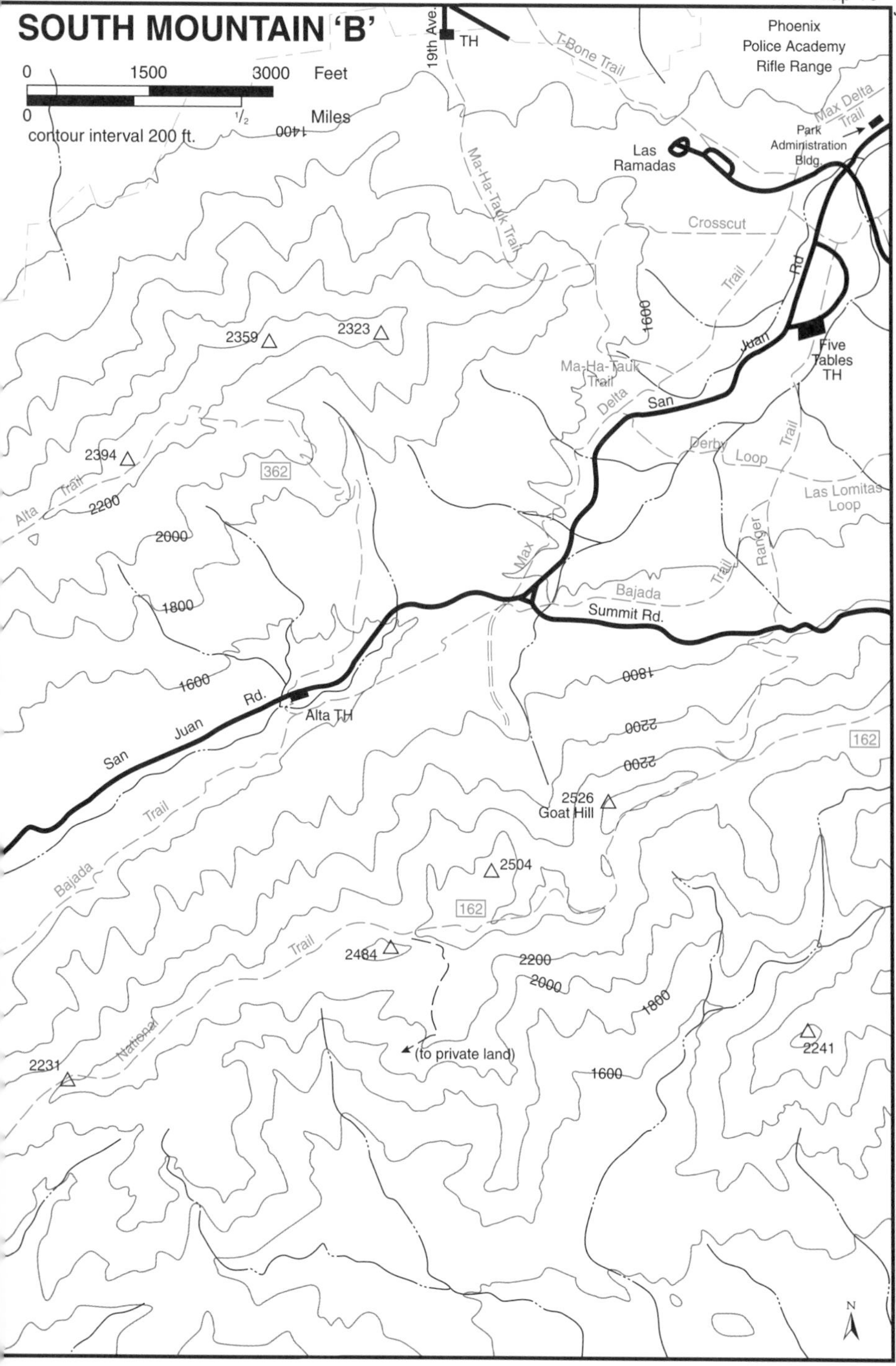

Map 10

SOUTH MOUNTAIN 'B'

0   1500   3000   Feet

0   ½   Miles

contour interval 200 ft.

Joins 'C'

19th Ave.

TH

T-Bone Trail

Phoenix
Police Academy
Rifle Range

Max Delta Trail

1400

Las
Ramadas

Park
Administration
Bldg

Crosscut

Ma-Ha-Tauk Trail

Trail

Rd.

2359 △

2323 △

1600

Juan

Five
Tables
TH

Ma-Ha-Tauk
Trail

Delta

San

2394 △

362

Derby

Loop

Las Lomitas
Loop

Alta

Trail

2200

2000

Max

Ranger

Trail

1800

Bajada

Summit Rd.

△

1600

San

Juan

Rd.

Alta TH

1800

2200

2200

162

2526
Goat Hill △

△ 2504

162

2484 △

2200

2000

1800

△
2241

(to private land)

1600

Bajada

Trail

National

2231 △

N

Map 11

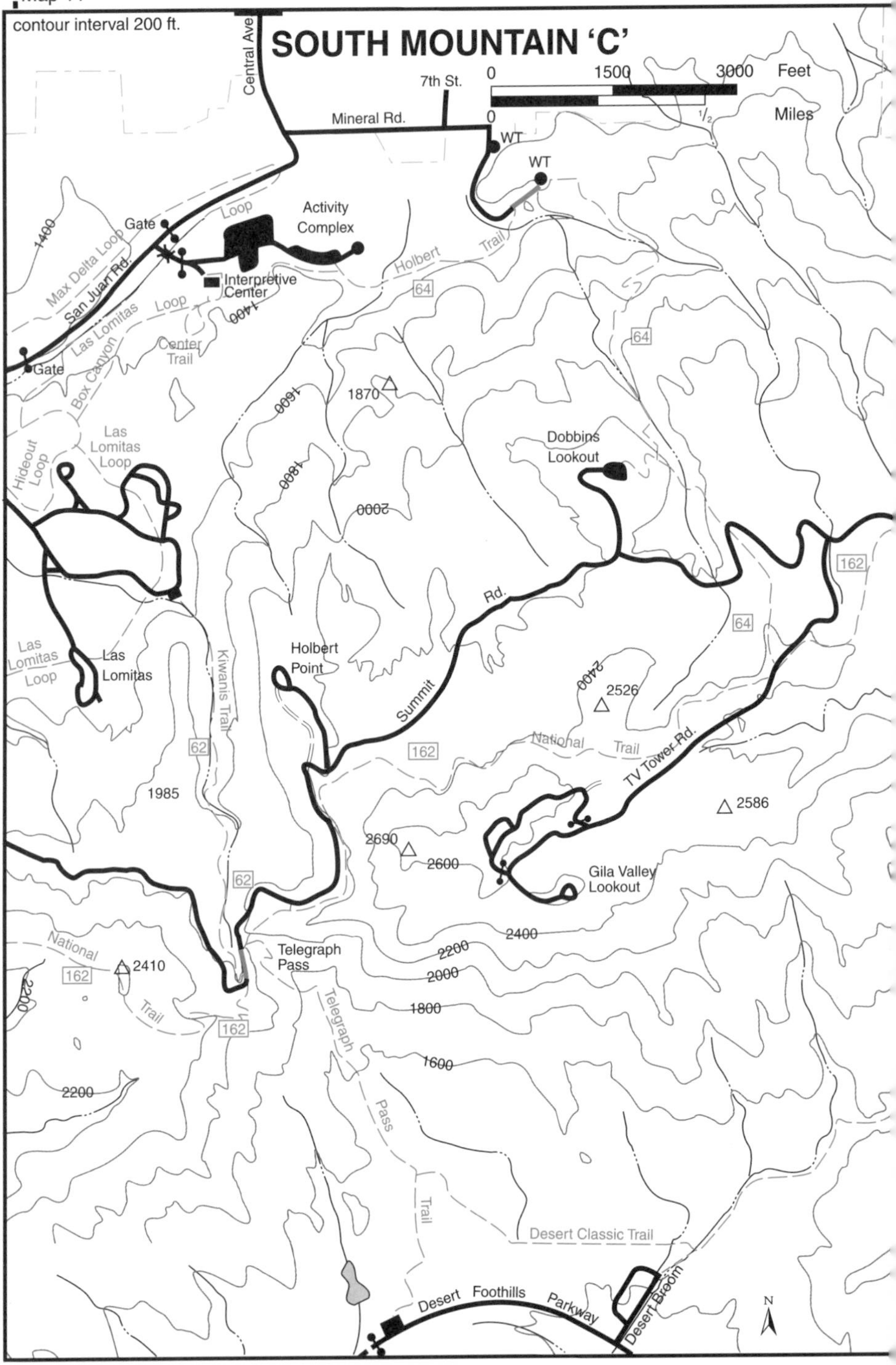
joins C
contour interval 200 ft.
SOUTH MOUNTAIN 'C'
0
1500
3000
Feet
0
1/2
Miles
Central Ave
7th St.
Mineral Rd.
WT
WT
Activity Complex
Interpretive Center
Gate
Gate
San Juan Rd.
Max Delta Loop
Loop
Holbert Trail
64
64
64
1400
1400
Las Lomitas Loop
Box Canyon
Center Trail
Hideout Loop
Las Lomitas Loop
1870
1600
1800
2000
Dobbins Lookout
Summit Rd.
162
162
Holbert Point
Las Lomitas
Las Lomitas Loop
Kiwanis Trail
62
62
1985
2400
2526
National Trail
TV Tower Rd.
2586
2690
2600
Gila Valley Lookout
2400
2200
2000
1800
1600
Telegraph Pass
National Trail
162
162
2410
2200
2200
Telegraph Pass Trail
Desert Classic Trail
Desert Foothills Parkway
Desert Broom
N

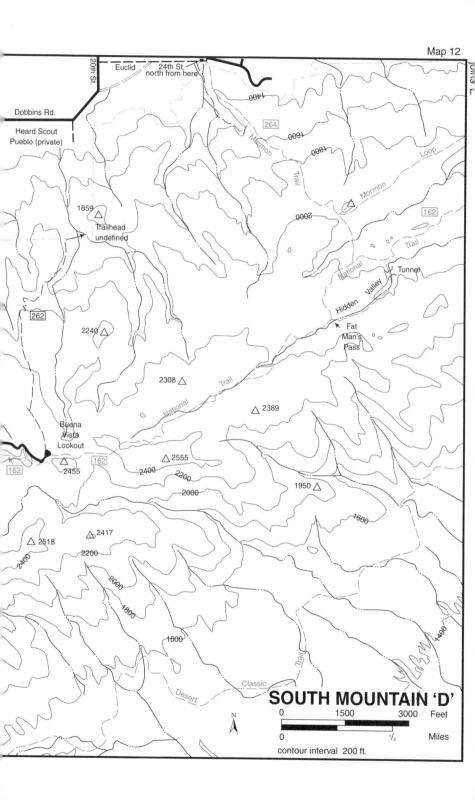

Map 12

20th St.

Euclid

24th St.
north from here

Dobbins Rd.

Heard Scout
Pueblo (private)

1400

264

1600

1800

Mormon

Trail

Mormon

Loop

1859 △
Trailhead
undefined

2000

162

Trail

National

Tunnel

Hidden

Valley

262

2240 △

Fat
Man's
Pass

2308 △

National

Trail

2389 △

Buena
Vista
Lookout

162

△
2455

162

2555 △

2400

2200

2000

1950 △

1600

2417 △△

2518 △

2200

2000

1800

1600

1400

Trail

Classic

Desert

SOUTH MOUNTAIN 'D'

0   1500   3000   Feet

0   ½   Miles

contour interval 200 ft.

N

Map 13

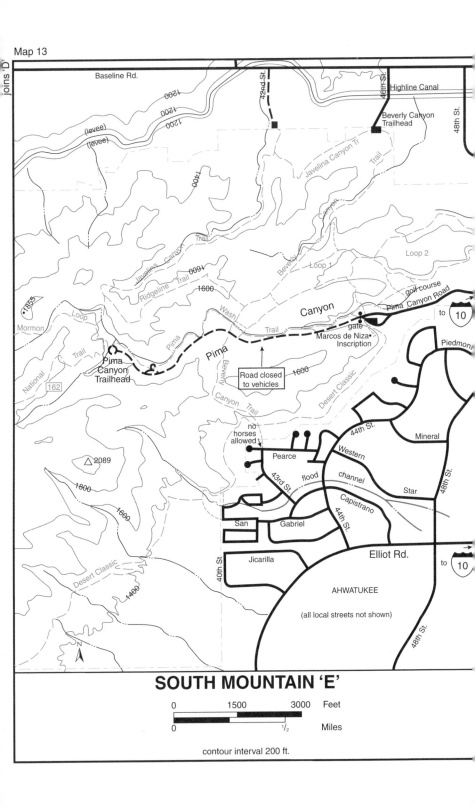

Baseline Rd.

Highline Canal

Beverly Canyon
Trailhead

joins 'D'

(levee)
(levee)

1200
1200
1200

1400

42nd St.

46th St.

48th St.

Javelina Canyon Tr

Beverly Canyon Trail

Loop 2

Loop 1

golf course

Pima Canyon Road

to 10

Javelina Canyon Trail

Ridgeline Trail

1600

1600

Wash

Canyon

Pima Trail

Pima

Trail

Canyon

gate
Marcos de Niza
Inscription

Piedmont

•1855

Loop

Mormon

National Trail

162

Pima
Canyon
Trailhead

Beverly Canyon Trail

Road closed
to vehicles

1600

Desert Classic

44th St.

Mineral

48th St.

no
horses
allowed

Pearce

Western

43rd St.

flood

channel

Star

△ 2089

Capistrano

1800

1600

San

Gabriel

44th St.

40th St.

Jicarilla

Elliot Rd.

to 10

Desert Classic

1400

AHWATUKEE

(all local streets not shown)

48th St.

N

SOUTH MOUNTAIN 'E'

0   1500   3000   Feet

0   ½   Miles

contour interval 200 ft.

Map 14

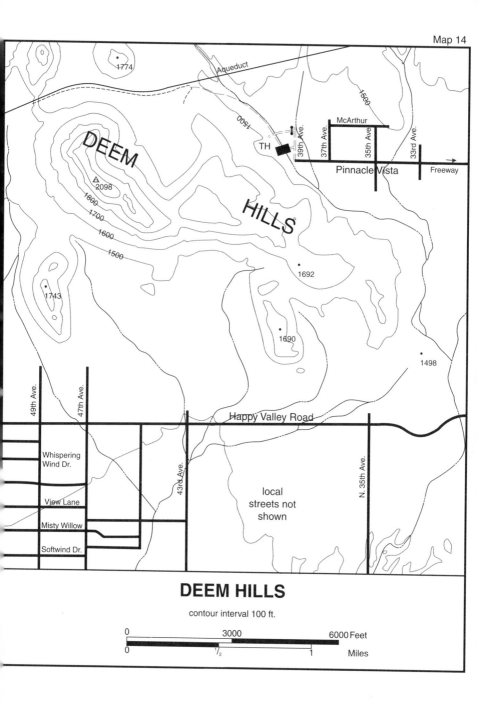

· 1774

Aqueduct

1580

DEEM

McArthur

TH

39th Ave.

37th Ave.

35th Ave.

33rd Ave.

1500

1500

HILLS

Pinnacle Vista

Freeway

△ 2098

1800

1700

1600

1500

1692 ·

· 1743

1690 ·

1498 ·

49th Ave.

47th Ave.

Happy Valley Road

43rd Ave.

N. 35th Ave.

Whispering
Wind Dr.

local
streets not
shown

View Lane

Misty Willow

Softwind Dr.

DEEM HILLS

contour interval 100 ft.

| 0 | 3000 | 6000 Feet |

| 0 | ½ | 1 | Miles |

Map 15

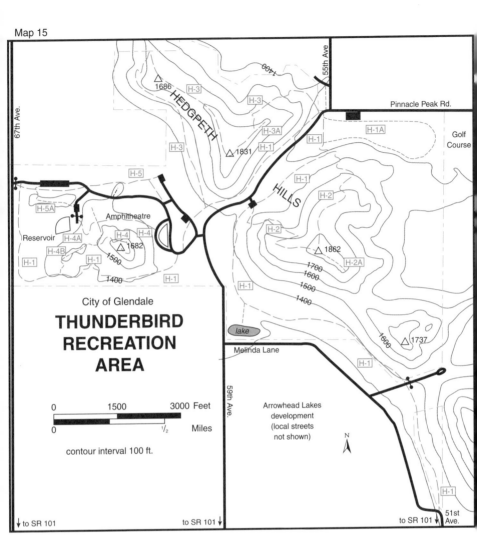

67th Ave.

1686

H-3

H-3

55th Ave.

1400

HEDGPETH

Pinnacle Peak Rd.

H-3A

H-3

H-1A

Golf
Course

1831

H-1

H-1

H-5

HILLS

H-1

H-5A

H-2

Amphitheatre

H-4   H-4

Reservoir

H-4A

1682

H-2

H-1

H-4B

1500

1862

H-2A

H-1

H-1

1700

1400

1600

H-1

1500

1400

City of Glendale

**THUNDERBIRD
RECREATION
AREA**

lake

Melinda Lane

1600

1737

H-1

| 0 | 1500 | 3000 Feet |

| 0 | | ½ | Miles |

contour interval 100 ft.

59th Ave.

Arrowhead Lakes
development
(local streets
not shown)

N

H-1

51st
Ave.

to SR 101

to SR 101

to SR 101

Map 16

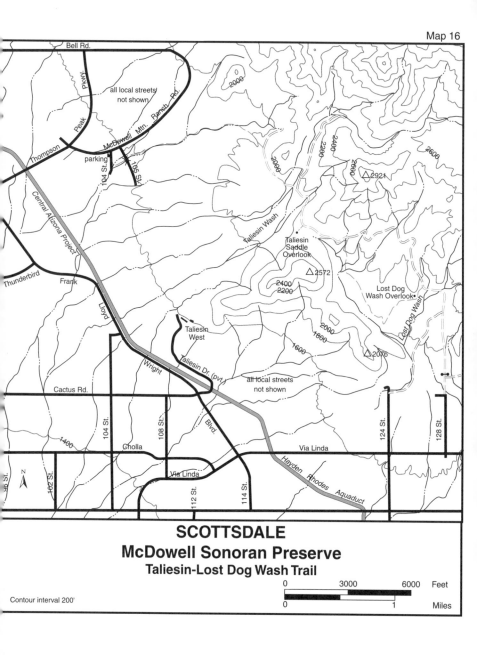

SCOTTSDALE
McDowell Sonoran Preserve
Taliesin-Lost Dog Wash Trail

Contour interval 200'

| 0 | 3000 | 6000 | Feet |

| 0 | | 1 | Miles |

Map 17

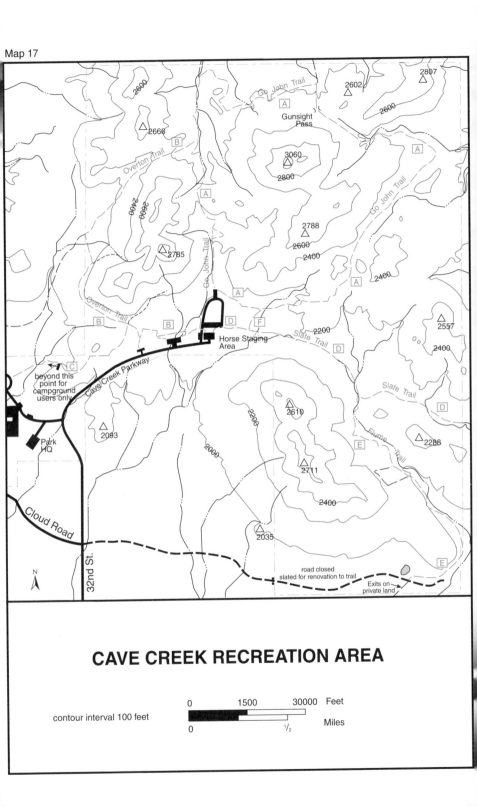

CAVE CREEK RECREATION AREA

contour interval 100 feet

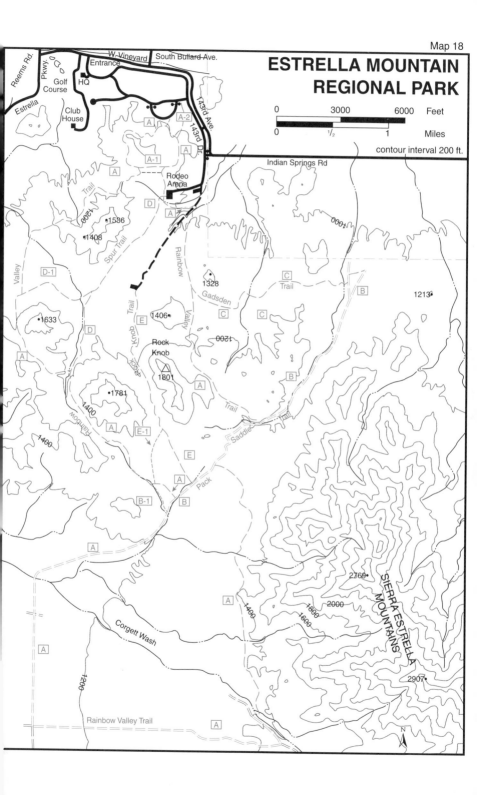

Map 18

ESTRELLA MOUNTAIN
REGIONAL PARK

0   3000   6000   Feet

0   ½   1   Miles

contour interval 200 ft.

Reems Rd.

Estrella Pkwy.

W. Vineyard   South Bullard Ave.

Entrance

Golf Course

HQ

Club House

143rd Ave.

143rd Dr.

Indian Springs Rd

A

A-2

A-1

A

A

Trail

Rodeo Arena

1586

1408

Spur Trail

Rainbow

D-1

Valley

1200

D

A

Knob Trail

1633

D

E

1406

Rock Knob

1801

1781

Rainbow

1400

A

E-1

E

A

B-1

B

A

1328

Gadsden

Valley

C

C

1200

A

A

Trail

Saddle

Pack

C

Trail

B

1213

C

B

A

Trail

2760

2000

Corgett Wash

A

A

1400

1600

1200

SIERRA ESTRELLA MOUNTAINS

2907

Rainbow Valley Trail

A

N

Map 19

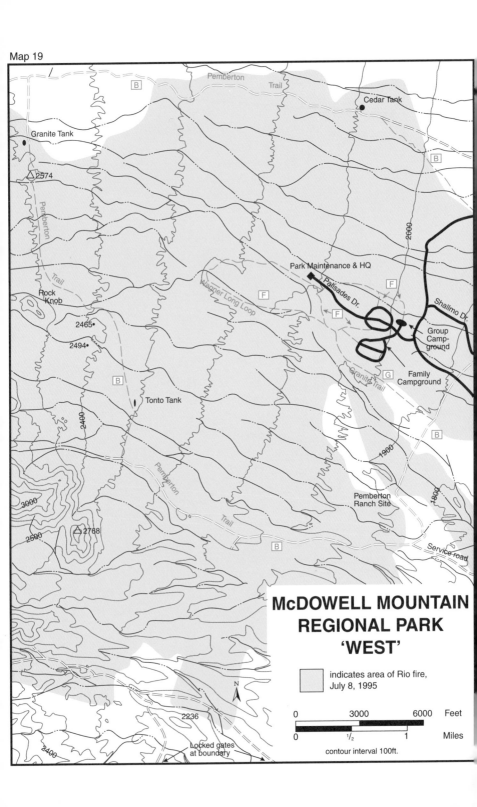

Pemberton Trail

Cedar Tank

Granite Tank

△2574

Pemberton Trail

Rock Knob

2465•

2494•

Wagner Long Loop

F

F

F

Park Maintenance & HQ

Palisades Dr.

Shallmo Dr.

Group Camp-ground

B

Tonto Tank

2400

Granite Trail

G

Family Campground

Pemberton

Trail

B

1900

B

1800

3000

2500

△2768

Pemberton Ranch Site

Service Road

2600

McDOWELL MOUNTAIN REGIONAL PARK 'WEST'

indicates area of Rio fire, July 8, 1995

N

2236

2400

Locked gates at boundary

0	3000	6000	Feet
0	1/2	1	Miles

contour interval 100ft.

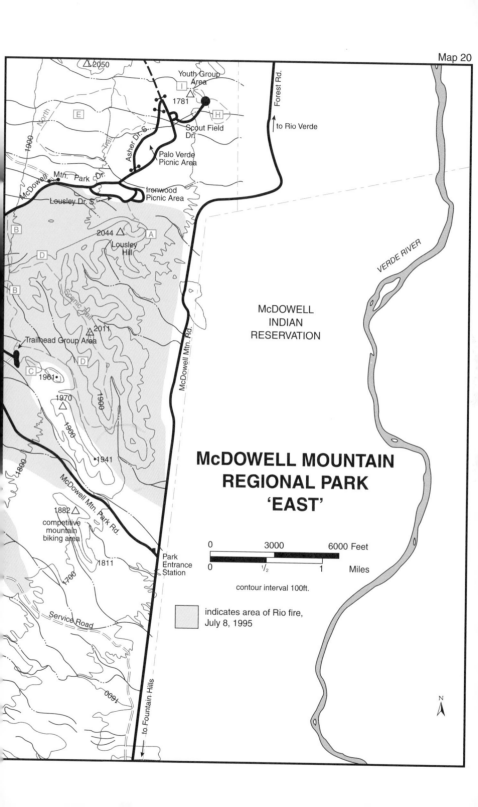

Map 20

△2050

Youth Group Area
I △
1781

Forest Rd.

to Rio Verde

E

North ... Trail

1900

Asher Dr. S.

Scout Field Dr.

H

Palo Verde Picnic Area

McDowell Mtn. Park Dr.

Lousley Dr. S.

Ironwood Picnic Area

B

D

△2044
Lousley Hill

A

Scenic Trail

B

VERDE RIVER

△2011

Trailhead Group Area

D

McDowell Mtn. Rd.

McDOWELL INDIAN RESERVATION

C 1961•

1970 △

1900

1900

•1941

1800

McDowell Mtn. Park Rd.

1882 △
competitive mountain biking area

1811

1700

Park Entrance Station

McDOWELL MOUNTAIN REGIONAL PARK 'EAST'

0   3000   6000 Feet

0   ½   1   Miles

contour interval 100ft.

indicates area of Rio fire, July 8, 1995

Service Road

1600

to Fountain Hills

N

Map 21

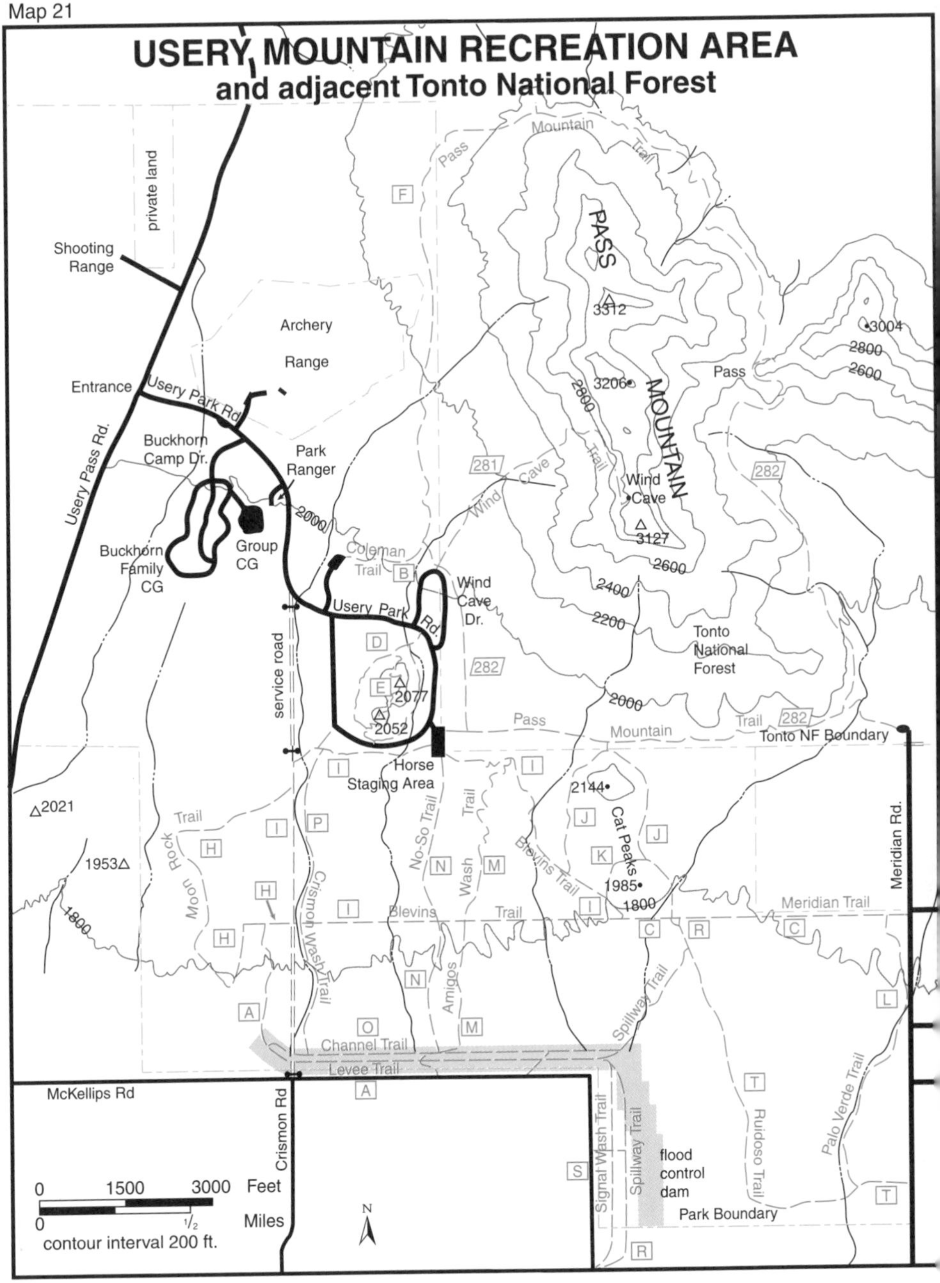

USERY MOUNTAIN RECREATION AREA
and adjacent Tonto National Forest

private land

Shooting Range

Entrance

Usery Park Rd

Usery Pass Rd.

Buckhorn Camp Dr.

Buckhorn Family CG

Group CG

Archery Range

Park Ranger

Coleman Trail

B

Usery Park Rd

D

E

△2077

△2052

Horse Staging Area

F

PASS MOUNTAIN

3312

•3004

2800

2600

3206•

2800

Pass

3127

Wind Cave

△3127

Wind Cave Dr.

281

282

2600

2400

2200

2000

Tonto National Forest

Pass   Mountain   Trail   282

Tonto NF Boundary

△2021

1953△

1800

Moon Rock Trail

Crismon Wash Trail

H

I

P

H

H

A

No-So Trail

N

Wash

M

Blevins   Trail

N

O

M

Channel Trail

Levee Trail

A

McKellips Rd

Crismon Rd

I

I

I

I

I

Meridian   Trail

2144•

J

K

1985•

1800

C

R

C

Meridian Rd.

L

Cat Peaks

J

Blevins Trail

Spillway Trail

S

Signal Trail

Spillway Trail

T

flood control dam

Park Boundary

Ruidoso Trail

Palo Verde Trail

T

R

0   1500   3000 Feet

0   ¹⁄₂   Miles

contour interval 200 ft.

N

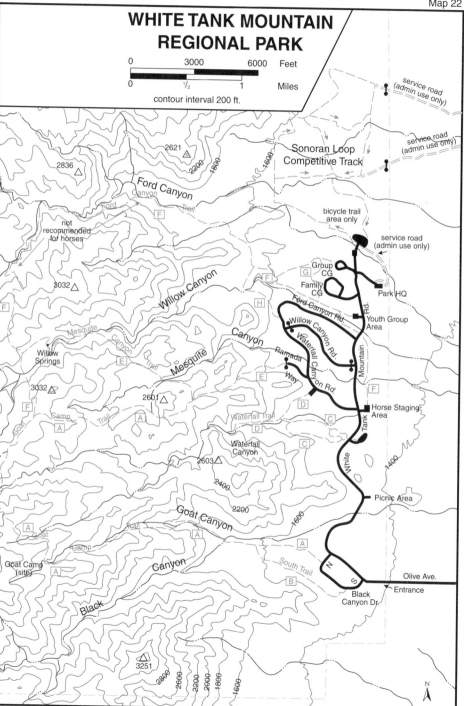

Map 22

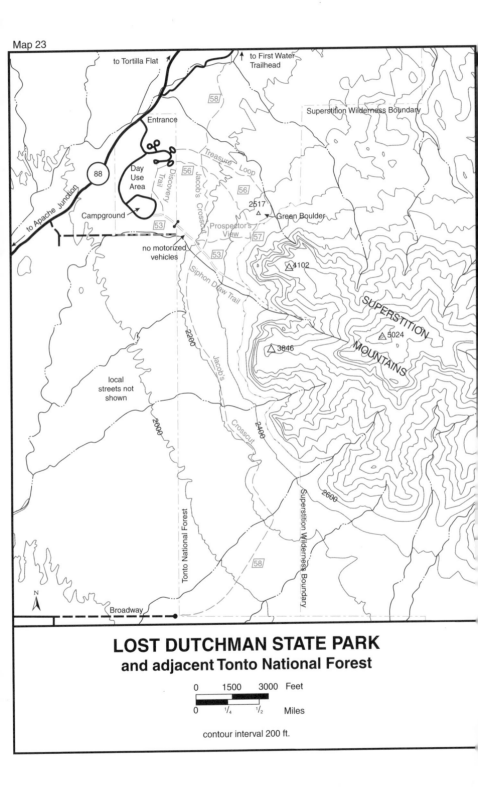

Map 23

to Tortilla Flat

to First Water Trailhead

58

Superstition Wilderness Boundary

Entrance

88

Day Use Area

Treasure Loop

56

Discovery Trail

Jacob's Crosscut

56

2517

Green Boulder

Campground

53

Prospector's View

57

4102

no motorized vehicles

53

Siphon Draw Trail

SUPERSTITION

2200

3846

5024

MOUNTAINS

local streets not shown

Jacob's

2000

Crosscut

2400

Tonto National Forest

2600

Superstition Wilderness Boundary

58

N

Broadway

LOST DUTCHMAN STATE PARK
and adjacent Tonto National Forest

0   1500   3000   Feet

0   ¼   ½   Miles

contour interval 200 ft.

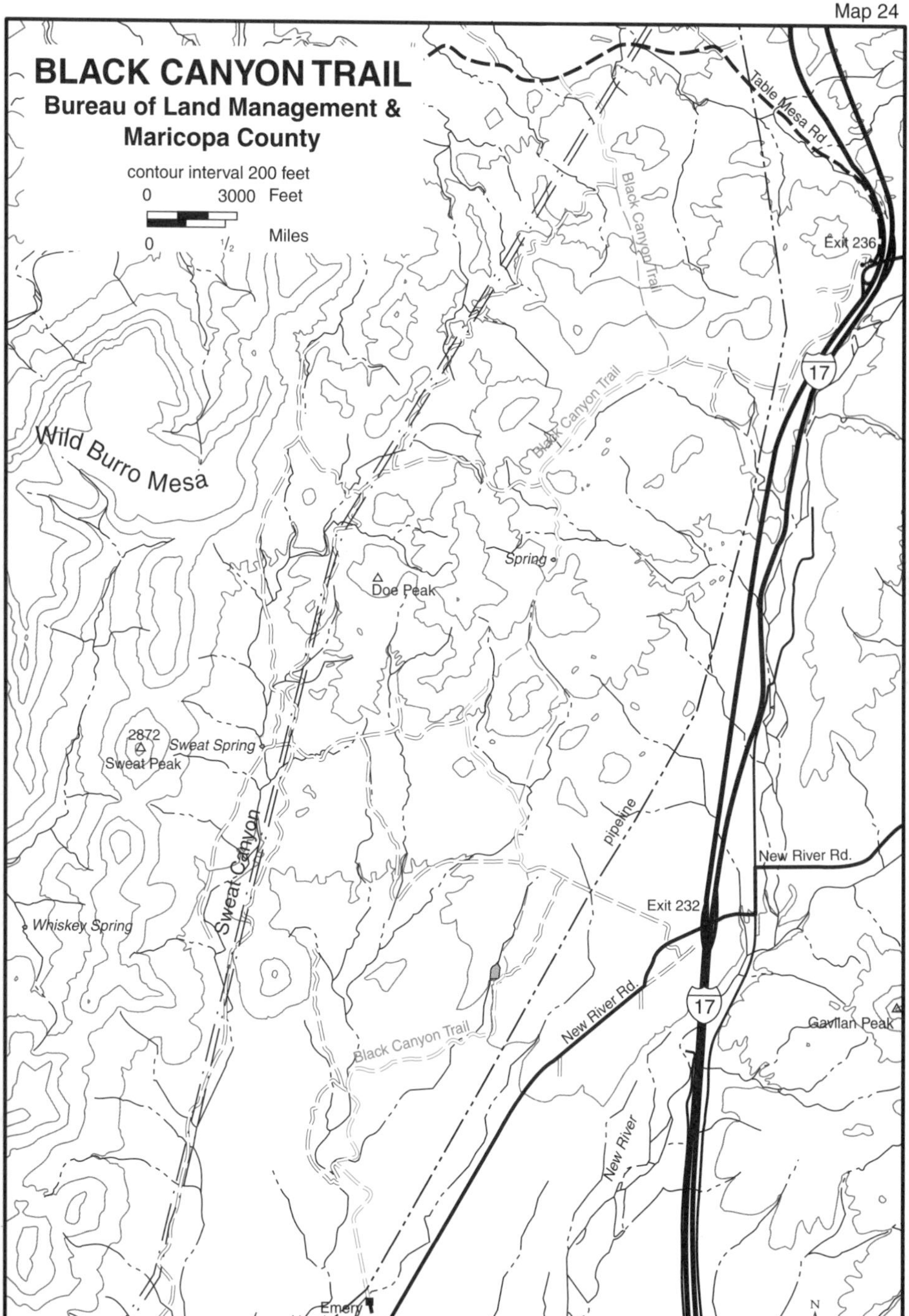

Map 24

BLACK CANYON TRAIL
Bureau of Land Management &
Maricopa County

contour interval 200 feet

0   3000   Feet

0   ½   Miles

Table Mesa Rd.

Exit 236

Black Canyon Trail

17

Black Canyon Trail

Wild Burro Mesa

Spring

Doe Peak

2872
Sweat Spring
Sweat Peak

Sweat Canyon

pipeline

New River Rd.

Whiskey Spring

Exit 232

New River Rd.

17

Gavilan Peak

Black Canyon Trail

New River

Emery
Henderson
TH

N

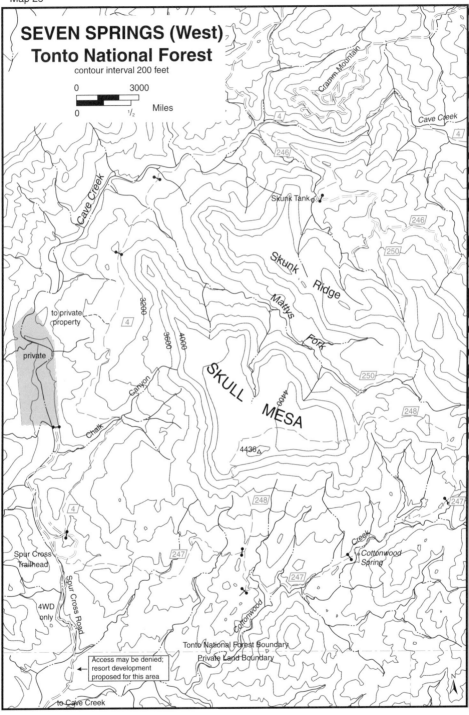

Map 25

SEVEN SPRINGS (West)
Tonto National Forest
contour interval 200 feet

0   3000

0   ½   Miles

Cradm Mountain

Cave Creek

4

Cave Creek

246

Skunk Tank

246

250

Skunk Ridge

Mattys Fork

to private property

4

3200

3600

4000

private

250

SKULL MESA

4400

248

Canyon

Chalk

4436 △

248

247

4

Creek

Cottonwood Spring

247

Spur Cross Trailhead

247

Spur Cross Road

4WD only

Cottonwood

Tonto National Forest Boundary

Private Land Boundary

Access may be denied; resort development proposed for this area

to Cave Creek

N

Map 26

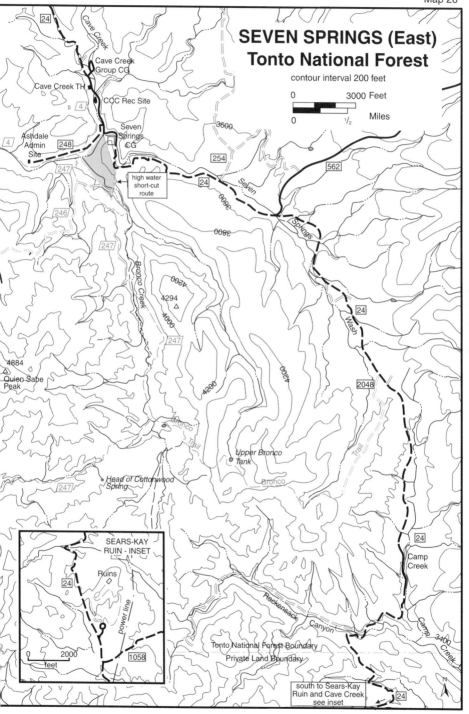

SEVEN SPRINGS (East)
Tonto National Forest
contour interval 200 feet

0   3000 Feet

0   ½   Miles

24

Cave Creek

Cave Creek
Group CG

Cave Creek TH

4

CCC Rec Site

Ashdale
Admin
Site

4

248

Seven
Springs
CG

3600

254

562

247

high water
short-cut
route

24

Seven

246

3800

Springs

3600

247

Bronco Creek

4200

4294
△

4000

247

24

Wash

4884
△
Quien Sabe
Peak

4200

4200

2048

Bronco

Trail

Upper Bronco
Tank

Bronco

Head of Cottonwood
Spring

247

24

Camp
Creek

SEARS-KAY
RUIN - INSET

24

Ruins

Power line

0   2000
feet

1058

Rackensack

Canyon

Tonto National Forest Boundary
Private Land Boundary

Camp

Creek

3400

south to Sears-Kay
Ruin and Cave Creek
see inset

24

Map 27

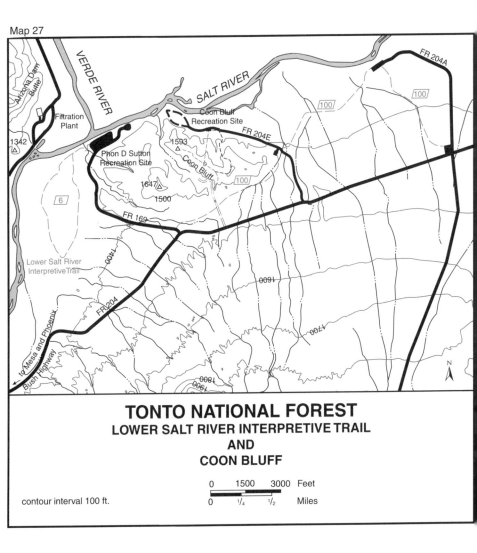

TONTO NATIONAL FOREST
LOWER SALT RIVER INTERPRETIVE TRAIL
AND
COON BLUFF

contour interval 100 ft.

0   1500   3000   Feet

0   1/4   1/2   Miles

Map 28

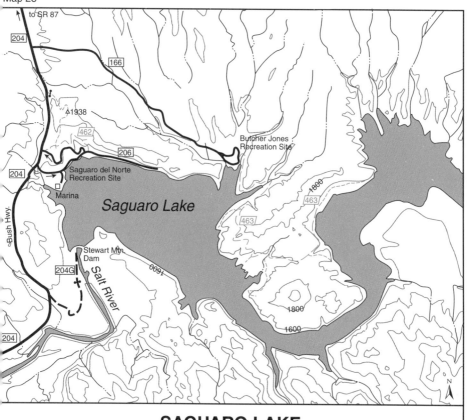

204

166

A1938

462

206

204

Saguaro del Norte
Recreation Site

Marina

Saguaro Lake

Butcher Jones
Recreation Site

1800

463

463

Stewart Mtn.
Dam

1600

204G

1600

Salt River

1800

1600

204

Bush Hwy.

N

SAGUARO LAKE
Tonto National Forest

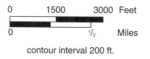

0   1500   3000 Feet

0   ¹/₂   Miles

contour interval 200 ft.

Map 29

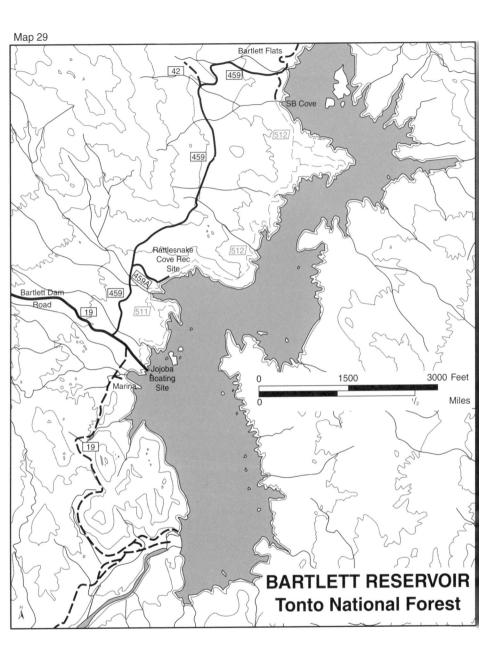

Bartlett Flats

42
459

SB Cove

512

459

512

Rattlesnake
Cove Rec
Site

459A

Bartlett Dam
Road

459

19

511

Jojoba
Boating
Site

Marina

0   1500   3000 Feet

0   ¹/₂   Miles

19

BARTLETT RESERVOIR
Tonto National Forest

N

Notes

Trip/Correction Reports

Please help us make this a better book in its next printing or edition by informing us of any errors or changes that you find, using these forms

- -

I have found the following error or change in the area covered by *Day Hikes and Trail Rides In and Around Phoenix*:

Area name:_____   Pages: _____   Map No. _____

Details: _____
_____
_____
_____
_____
_____
_____
_____
_____

Send these comments to:

Roger D. Freeman, M.D., Box 2033, Point Roberts, WA 98281
  e-mail: roger_freeman@usa.net
  Phone: (604) 263-3900

- -

I have found the following error or change in the area covered by *Day Hikes and Trail Rides In and Around Phoenix*:

Area name:_____   Pages: _____   Map No. _____

Details: _____
_____
_____
_____
_____
_____
_____
_____
_____

Send these comments to:

Roger D. Freeman, Box 2033, Point Roberts, WA 98281
  e-mail: roger_freeman@usa.net
  Phone: (604) 263-3900